Middle-Class Providence, 1820-1940

MIDDLE-CLASS PROVIDENCE, 1820-1940

John S. Gilkeson, Jr.

PRINCETON UNIVERSITY PRESS

PRINCETON, NEW JERSEY

Publication of this book has been aided by a grant from
The Andrew W. Mellon Foundation

This book has been composed in Linotron Baskerville

Clothbound editions of Princeton University Press books
are printed on acid-free paper, and binding materials
are chosen for strength and durability
Printed in the United States of America
by Princeton University Press
Princeton, New Jersey

For my parents

CONTENTS

ACKNOWLEDGMENTS

OVER the past few years I have incurred a number of debts that I am pleased to acknowledge. I should like to thank the Brown University Library and the Rhode Island Historical Society for the use of their holdings. At the latter, Paul Campbell, Harold Kemble, and Denise J. Bastien were especially helpful. R. Burr Litchfield and the Brown University History Department generously made computer time available to me. Grants from the Faculty Development Committee at DePauw University supported my summer research. While in Providence I enjoyed the hospitality of the Douglas and Krawczyk families.

For their assistance in preparing this manuscript for publication, I should like to thank Andrew and Mary Cayton, John Dittmer, Robert A. Gross, Daniel Horowitz, Lary May, Sharon H. Nolte, and my editor, Gail Ullman. I am also grateful to Elizabeth Gretz for her meticulous copyediting.

Above all, I am indebted to James T. Patterson and John L. Thomas, two master craftsmen who have taught me most of what I know about the historian's craft.

Middle-Class Providence, 1820-1940

Introduction

AMERICANS have long believed that theirs is a middle-class society. In February 1940, with nearly 15 percent of the work force unemployed, a Roper poll commissioned by *Fortune* magazine reported that 79 percent of the respondents considered themselves middle-class. Few of those polled, even among factory workers, assigned themselves to the "working" or "laboring" class; even fewer still assigned themselves to the "upper" class. As the magazine's editors concluded, the United States was "a middle class country," one in which the average American "regards himself as 'middle class.'" This book traces the development of middle-class consciousness from its origins in the antebellum temperance and antislavery crusades through the consumer movement of the 1920s and 1930s. In particular, it emphasizes the middle-class search for social and cultural homogeneity—a middle-class America—in a mobile, heterogeneous, and stratified society.[1]

Until recently, historians simply assumed that the United States had always been a middle-class society. In the 1950s Louis Hartz, Robert E. Brown, and other "consensus" historians attributed the homogeneity of the postwar United States to the relatively undifferentiated social structure, with neither hereditary nobility nor degraded peasantry, that had presumably prevailed on this side of the Atlantic since the first English settlements.[2] But recent studies by Paul E. Johnson and Mary P. Ryan date the formation of the American middle classes in the years from 1820 to 1860. Far from reflecting a homogeneous society, as the "consensus" historians presumed, middle-class consciousness was a product of the social and economic

---

[1] "The Fortune Survey," *Fortune* 21 (February 1940): 14.

[2] Louis Hartz, *The Liberal Tradition in America: An Interpretation of American Political Thought since the Revolution* (New York: Harcourt, Brace & Co., 1955); Robert E. Brown, *Middle-Class Democracy and the Revolution in Massachusetts, 1691-1780* (Ithaca: Cornell University Press, 1955). See also John Higham, "The Cult of the 'American Consensus,'" *Commentary* 27 (February 1959): 93-100.

differentiation wrought by the rise of domestic manufacturing, rapid urbanization, and the Second Great Awakening.[3]

This book builds a bridge between these studies of the antebellum North and accounts of the progressive era, 1890-1920, a critical period in the history of the American middle classes. Robert H. Wiebe, Samuel P. Hays, and other "organizational" historians posit a shift, sometime around the turn of the century, from an entrepreneurial "old middle class" of the self-employed to a bureaucratic "new middle class" of professionals and salaried office workers.[4] But as Clyde Griffen and Richard L. McCormick have shown, the drive for efficiency and expertise associated with this new middle class never completely displaced the moral fervor that had fired middle-class reformers since the antebellum temperance and antislavery crusades.[5] In fact, nostalgia for the neighborliness and participatory democracy of small-town America inspired Jane Addams, Robert A. Woods, and others in their attempts to organize urban neighborhoods around social settlements.[6] Still other middle-class Americans, as Richard Hofstadter and David P. Thelen have pointed out, broke during the progressive period with their heritage as producers to redefine themselves as consumers.[7] Efficiency and expertise,

[3] Paul E. Johnson, *A Shopkeeper's Millennium: Society and Revivals in Rochester, New York, 1815-1837* (New York: Hill and Wang, 1978); Mary P. Ryan, *Cradle of the Middle Class: The Family in Oneida County, New York, 1790-1865* (Cambridge: Cambridge University Press, 1981). On social and economic differentiation in the antebellum North, see Edward Pessen, *Riches, Class and Power before the Civil War* (Lexington, Mass.: D. C. Health & Co., 1973).

[4] Robert H. Wiebe, *The Search for Order, 1877-1920* (New York: Hill and Wang, 1967); Samuel P. Hays, "The New Organizational Society," in *Building the Organizational Society: Essays on Associational Activities in Modern America*, ed. Jerry Israel (New York: Free Press, 1972), 1-15; Louis Galambos, "The Emerging Organizational Synthesis in Modern American History," *Business History Review* 44 (Autumn 1970): 279-90.

[5] Clyde Griffen, "The Progressive Ethos," in *The Development of an American Culture*, ed. Stanley Coben and Lorman Ratner, 2nd ed. (New York: St. Martin's Press, 1983), 144-80; Richard L. McCormick, "The Discovery that 'Business Corrupts Politics': A Reappraisal of the Origins of Progressivism," *American Historical Review* 86 (April 1981): 247-74; ibid., *From Realignment to Reform: Political Change in New York State, 1893-1910* (Ithaca: Cornell University Press, 1981).

[6] Allen F. Davis, *American Heroine: The Life and Legend of Jane Addams* (New York: Oxford University Press, 1975); Jean B. Quandt, *From the Small Town to the Great Community: The Social Thought of Progressive Intellectuals* (New Brunswick, N.J.: Rutgers University Press, 1970).

[7] Richard Hofstadter, *The Age of Reform: From Bryan to F.D.R.* (New York: Vintage

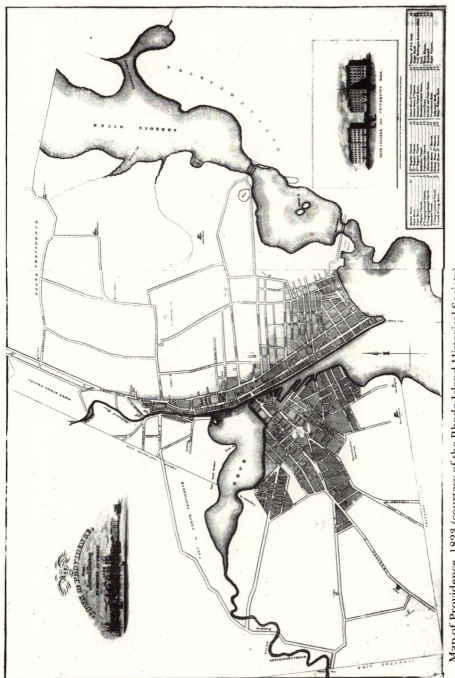

Map of Providence, 1823 (courtesy of the Rhode Island Historical Society)

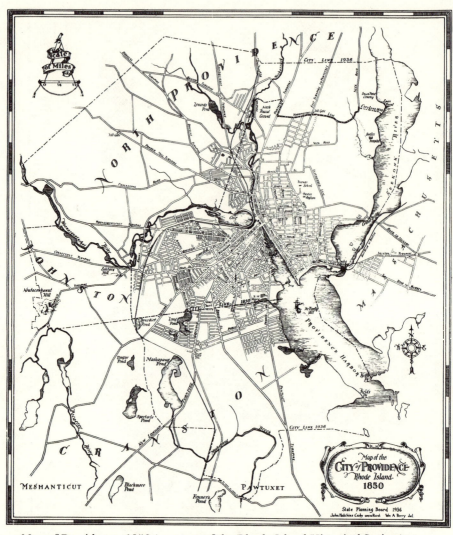

Map of Providence, 1850 (courtesy of the Rhode Island Historical Society)

morality, neighborhood, and the consumer interest—all were key words for middle-class Americans after 1880.[8]

Focusing on a single community, the medium-sized industrial city of Providence, Rhode Island, illuminates how social and economic differentiation, which gave rise to middle-class consciousness in the antebellum period, forced later generations of middle-class Americans to revise their notions of a classless, homogeneous society. Today the quaint gateway to the attractions of Newport and Narragansett Bay, Providence was once a "bee hive of industry." Following the establishment of the nation's first factory in nearby Pawtucket in 1790, industrialization transformed Providence and its environs into a premier manufacturing center. Over the course of the nineteenth century, cotton and woolen plants sprouted on the banks of nearby streams and rivers, while precision machine, metal, and jewelry firms clustered in Providence. Thousands of migrants left the state's farms for its cities, making Rhode Island the most urbanized state in the Union. Providence, still a small town in 1790 with fewer than 6,400 inhabitants, grew to more than 17,000 by the time of its incorporation in 1832. On the eve of the Civil War, the city's population stood at 51,000, then soared to 224,000 in 1910 before reaching an all-time high of 268,000 in 1925. Also fueling this substantial population growth were immigrants from Ireland, Quebec, eastern Europe, Italy, and Portugal. By 1905, when seven out of every ten Rhode Islanders were either first- or second-generation Americans, Rhode Island had become the first state in the Union with a Roman Catholic majority.

Books, 1955), esp. 168-73; David P. Thelen, *The New Citizenship: Origins of Progressivism in Wisconsin, 1885-1900* (Columbia: University of Missouri Press, 1972); ibid., "Patterns of Consumer Consciousness in the Progressive Movement: Robert M. La Follette, the Antitrust Persuasion, and Labor Legislation," in *The Quest for Social Justice*, ed. Ralph M. Aderman (Madison: University of Wisconsin Press, 1983), 19-47.

[8] In a recent historiographical essay, Daniel T. Rodgers suggests that what united progressive reformers was their "ability to draw on three distinct clusters of ideas—three distinct social languages—to articulate their discontents and social visions." To the three clusters of ideas that Rodgers enumerates—antimonopolism, an emphasis on social bonds, and the worship of efficiency and expertise—I have added a fourth: the consumer interest. See "In Search of Progressivism," *Reviews in American History* 10 (December 1982): 113-32 (quotation from p. 127). My approach also reflects the influence of Quentin Skinner, who has made historians more sensitive to the historicity of language. For an introduction to Skinner's work, see "The Idea of a Cultural Lexicon," *Essays in Criticism* 29 (July 1979): 205-24.

As the middle-class residents of Providence grappled with industrialization, urbanization, immigration, and other changes that profoundly affected their lives, they turned to collective organization. Ever since Alexis de Tocqueville visited the United States in the early 1830s, observers have invariably remarked on the American penchant for joining voluntary associations. "Americans of all ages, all conditions, and all dispositions constantly form associations," Tocqueville observed. Similarly, the American "habit of association" impressed the British traveler, James Bryce, in the 1880s. Asserting that "associations are created, extended, and worked in the United States more quickly and effectively than in any other country," Bryce marveled at the "executive talent" they fostered in their members. "In the past and up to the very present," wrote Max Weber shortly after the turn of the twentieth century, "it has been a characteristic precisely of the specifically American democracy that it did *not* constitute a formless sand heap of individuals, but rather a buzzing complex of strictly exclusive, yet voluntary associations."[9]

Relatively few in number until the 1770s, voluntary associations multiplied rapidly after the American Revolution for four reasons.[10] Tocqueville suggested two: hostility to the state, which the Revolution only intensified, and the "equality of conditions" that characterized the young republic. "Wherever at the head of some new undertaking you see the government in France, or a man of rank in England," Tocqueville observed, "in the United States you

[9] Alexis de Tocqueville, *Democracy in America*, trans. Henry Reeve, ed. Phillips Bradley, 2 vols. (New York: Vintage Books, 1945), 2:114; James Bryce, *The American Commonwealth*, 2nd ed., 2 vols. (London: Macmillan Co., 1891), 2:269; Max Weber, "The Protestant Sects and the Spirit of Capitalism," in *From Max Weber: Essays in Sociology*, trans., ed., and with an introduction by H. H. Gerth and C. Wright Mills (New York: Oxford University Press, 1946), 310. All emphasis in quotations here and below appears in the original unless otherwise noted. There is an enormous literature on voluntary associations. A good place to start is Constance Smith and Anne Freedman, *Voluntary Associations: Perspectives on the Literature* (Cambridge: Harvard University Press, 1972). See also Stephen Yeo's emphasis on the "ecology," or the common organizational context, of voluntary associations at particular stages in the development of a capitalist economy in *Religion and Voluntary Organisations in Crisis* (London: Croom Helm, 1976).

[10] Richard D. Brown, "The Emergence of Voluntary Associations in Massachusetts, 1760-1830," *Journal of Voluntary Action Research* 2 (April 1973): 64-73; ibid., "The Emergence of Urban Society in Rural Massachusetts, 1760-1820," *Journal of American History* 61 (June 1974): 29-51; Arthur M. Schlesinger, "Biography of a Nation of Joiners," *American Historical Review* 50 (October 1944): 1-25.

will be sure to find an association." Forming voluntary associations for collective action was soon considered essential among a democratic people where "all the citizens are independent and feeble," and thus "can hardly do anything by themselves."[11] Urbanization was yet a third reason for voluntarism. Dislodged from the moorings of stable family and community life by the rapid growth of antebellum towns and cities, migrants joined associations for new forms of social solidarity to take the place of attenuated kinship bonds.[12] Finally, voluntarism also stemmed from the Second Great Awakening, the revivals that flashed intermittently after 1800 until the annus mirabilis of 1858, when they blazed across the North. Not only did the typical Protestant church itself virtually become, in the words of Sidney Mead, "a voluntary association of explicitly convinced Christians," but the Benevolent Empire, a loose national network of interdenominational moral reform societies, endeavored to remake the North along more Christian lines.[13]

In mobilizing hundreds of thousands of shopkeepers and artisans, what might be called the antebellum organizational revolution crystallized middle-class consciousness.[14] Voluntary associations composed of peers whom common interest united took the place of local notables in molding public opinion. In addition to propagating such new values as total abstinence from alcohol and immediate emancipation of slaves, these associations promoted the social and cultural organization of rapidly growing communities, defined new occupational identities, organized sociability, and provided insurance against sickness and death. For much of the nineteenth cen-

---

[11] Tocqueville, *Democracy in America*, 1:3, 2:114-15.

[12] Jeffrey G. Williamson, "Antebellum Urbanization in the American Northeast," *Journal of Economic History* 25 (December 1965): 592-608. In modern West Africa, voluntary associations have proliferated as the continent has urbanized and new forms of economic activity have arisen. Kenneth Little, *West African Urbanization: A Study of Voluntary Associations in Social Change* (Cambridge: Cambridge University Press, 1965).

[13] Sidney E. Mead, "The Rise of the Evangelical Conception of the Ministry in America, 1607-1850," in *The Ministry in Historical Perspectives*, ed. H. Richard Niebuhr and Daniel D. Williams (New York: Harper & Brothers, 1956), 224.

[14] Donald G. Mathews, "The Second Great Awakening as an Organizing Process, 1780-1830: An Hypothesis," *American Quarterly* 21 (Spring 1969): 23-43; ibid., *Religion in the Old South* (Chicago: University of Chicago Press, 1977); Paul Boyer, *Urban Masses and Moral Order in America, 1820-1920* (Cambridge: Harvard University Press, 1978), 54-64; Gordon S. Wood, "Evangelical America and Early Mormonism," *New York History* 61 (October 1980): 359-86.

tury, voluntary associations also served as surrogates for government. As the United States became more corporate and bureaucratic, these groups evolved into lobbies that framed policy, trained bureaucrats, and mediated between their members and an ever more powerful state. Voluntary associations were thus the agencies by which middle-class Americans disseminated their values and defended their class interests whenever those appeared to be threatened by the special interests of seemingly better organized, more powerful classes at the social margins. Yet throughout, middle-class Americans persisted in viewing themselves not as advocates of divisive special interests but as representatives of the broader public interest.

Key episodes in the history of the middle classes in Providence highlight the development of middle-class organization and consciousness. A distinctive version of middle-class consciousness, which set the stable, industrious, sober middle classes of society conspicuously apart from the presumed vices of the rich and the poor and defined for them a superior middle ground, crystallized in moments of cultural conflict when advocates of abolition and prohibition challenged the traditional values defended by gentlemen, on the one hand, and by workingmen, on the other. Elaborate organizational networks, discussed in chapters 1 and 2, enabled middle-class reformers to redefine old values like sobriety, propagate new values like immediate emancipation, and regard themselves as members of a national moral community. As values like domesticity, total abstinence, strict Sabbath observance, and self-improvement began to shape the ways in which people used their spare time, middle-class campaigns to remodel traditional patterns of leisure generated the characteristic cultural institutions of industrial cities like Providence—public schools, lyceums, libraries, museums, and parks.

But the hegemony of this ascetic culture was short-lived. The antebellum organizational revolution soon led to the segmentation of work and leisure, described in chapters 3 and 4. What had once been a broad producers' community fragmented as first professionals, then businessmen and manufacturers, and finally workingmen began to define themselves as members of more specialized, and all too often antagonistic, occupational groups. The inclusive civic culture also fragmented as clubs and lodges proliferated. Recreational activities, which had previously brought urban dwellers together, began to sort them out along lines of neighborhood, ethnicity, sex, and social status.

Four middle-class responses to the perceived fragmentation of their society and their once unitary culture are identified in chapters 5–8. Single Taxers, Christian socialists, prohibitionists, and other moralists waged campaigns of righteousness against the collusion between machine politicians and monopolists in a futile attempt to re-create the antebellum moral community. Recreational reformers attempted to perpetuate the ideal of a classless, homogeneous society in urban neighborhoods organized around parks, playgrounds, settlement houses, institutional churches, socialized schools, and other social centers. Systematizers—businessmen, social workers, clubwomen, Protestant clergymen, city planners, and other middle-class Americans who worshiped efficiency and expertise—looked to federation as a solution to the problem of reconciling voluntarism with the public interest. Finally, housewives, academics, and white-collar workers envisioned a middle-class America that consisted not of independent producers, but of voluntary associations of consumers. On the eve of the Second World War, though much more diffuse than they had been a hundred years earlier, the American middle classes remained the broad and inclusive basis for a stable social order.

1 THE STABLE, INDUSTRIOUS, SOBER
MIDDLE CLASSES OF SOCIETY

IN the late summer and fall of 1835, townspeople in Providence and four other communities in Rhode Island heeded the summons of local notables to assemble at public meetings at which they frowned "into silence and utter contempt, the unholy efforts and projects of those reckless fanatics," the abolitionists, whose vitriolic denunciations of slavery had riled southerners and threatened to "let slip the dogs of civil war." Braving the contempt of their social betters were shopkeepers, artisans, and itinerant agents bent on organizing a network of antislavery societies. In their attempts to turn public opinion against slavery, these intrepid abolitionists painted the peculiar institution as the most heinous of sins, asserted their constitutional right to raise the issue of immediate emancipation for public discussion, and denounced the collusion between self-interested "gentlemen of property and standing" and the disorderly rabble employed to break up antislavery meetings. "In *every* instance," they charged, alluding to the recent mobbings of their colleagues in Boston and Utica, New York, "the mobs have been *excited* by the incipient *nobility* of the country, who have called to their aid the *lowest dregs* of society, the intemperate—the desperate—the unthinking. The stable, industrious, sober, middle classes of society have always been the *victims* of their attacks; and freedom of speech, and of the Press, have been the *objects* at which their blows have been levelled."[1]

The middle-class consciousness expounded by the abolitionists in their clash with defenders of traditional values presumed a har-

---

[1] *Rhode Island Republican*, 16 September 1835; *Proceedings of the Rhode-Island Anti-Slavery Convention, Held in Providence, on the 2d, 3d and 4th of February, 1836* (Providence: H. H. Brown, 1836), 32. The term "gentlemen of property and standing" is from Leonard L. Richards, *"Gentlemen of Property and Standing": Anti-Abolition Mobs in Jacksonian America* (New York: Oxford University Press, 1970).

mony of interests among producers (whether self-employed or wage earners), celebrated the dignity of labor, regarded great wealth as a threat to virtue, and expressed a commitment to an open, meritocratic society. In particular, it emphasized the distinction between the industry, frugality, and sobriety of middle-class northerners and the presumed idleness, extravagance, and dissipation of the rich and the poor. In their attacks on the liquor trade and slavery, antebellum moral reform societies defined and disseminated the values around which the middle classes coalesced, pioneered new means of molding public opinion, and propagated a new social order resting on self-discipline rather than on deference to external authority.[2]

Until 1750 or so, Providence had consisted of "but a long straggling street by the water front, where on summer evenings the inhabitants sat in the doorways, smoked their clay pipes, and fought the swarms of mosquitoes that rose from the marsh opposite." The town stood in the shadow of Newport, some thirty miles nearer the Atlantic Ocean. Blessed with a deeper harbor, more fertile hinterland, and easier access to overseas trading routes, Newport was a bustling seaport and the home of such renowned merchants as Abraham Redwood and Aaron Lopez. In the two decades preceding the American Revolution, however, Providence merchants began to challenge Newport's dominance. Led by the four Brown brothers—Nicholas, Moses, John, and Joseph—they started small candle and iron factories, attempted to establish direct trade with Europe, and backed Stephen Hopkins in his gubernatorial contests

[2] On the antebellum free-labor ideology, see Eric Foner, *Free Soil, Free Labor, Free Men: The Ideology of the Republican Party before the Civil War* (New York: Oxford University Press, 1970), esp. 11-39; and John L. Thomas, *Alternative America: Henry George, Edward Bellamy, Henry Demarest Lloyd and the Adversary Tradition* (Cambridge: Harvard University Press, 1983). On the role of group conflict in class formation, E. P. Thompson has written that "classes do not exist as separate entities, look around, find an enemy class, and then start to struggle. On the contrary, people find themselves in a society structured in determined ways (crucially, but not exclusively, in productive relations), they experience exploitation (or the need to maintain power over those whom they exploit), they identify points of antagonistic interest, they commence to struggle around these issues and in the process of struggling they discover themselves as classes, they come to know this discovery as class consciousness. Class and class-consciousness are always the last, not the first, stage in the real historical process." "Eighteenth-Century English Society: Class Struggle without Class?" *Social History* 3 (May 1978): 149.

against Samuel Ward, leader of the Newport faction. In 1770 they even managed to attract Rhode Island College (later Brown University), which had outgrown its former site in Warren. On the eve of the American Revolution, Providence, whose population was still less than half that of Newport, had almost pulled even in the race for commercial and political supremacy in Rhode Island.[3]

The Revolution ensured Providence's future as New England's "southern gateway." The very remoteness that earlier had penalized the town in its commercial rivalry with Newport now protected it from British marauders. Colonial import duties were removed and Newport's custom-house monopoly broken. Privateering flourished. When the British navy occupied Newport, Providence merchants quickly captured their rivals' trade with Europe; after the Treaty of Paris, they established lucrative trade routes with China and the East Indies. As conspicuous ornaments of their newfound wealth, they built stylish brick houses on College Hill, near Brown University. John Quincy Adams pronounced one of these, John Brown's mansion, "the most magnificent and elegant private mansion that I have ever seen on this continent."[4]

While the town's merchants flourished, its artisans fell on hard times. Exposed to conscription during the war, they faced a flood of British imports "dumped" on the American market after peace was concluded. Rhode Island's highly inflated currency and the state's reluctance to ratify the Constitution also hurt interstate trade.[5] Beginning to define themselves as members of a mechanics' community whose interest was distant from that of either farmers or merchants, artisans organized to nurture infant American manufactures and to promote the development of a nascent domestic economy. In February 1789 fourteen master craftsmen, follow-

[3] James G. Hedges, *The Browns of Providence Plantations: The Colonial Years* (Cambridge: Harvard University Press, 1952), xvii; Lynne Withey, *Urban Growth in Colonial Rhode Island: Newport and Providence in the Eighteenth Century* (Albany: State University of New York Press, 1984), 39-50.

[4] Withey, *Urban Growth in Colonial Rhode Island*, 84-89, 96-97; Nancy Fisher Chudacoff, "The Revolution and the Town: Providence 1775-1783," *Rhode Island History* 35 (August 1976): 71-89; Adams quoted in *College Hill: A Demonstration Study of Historic Area Renewal* (Providence: City Plan Commission, 1967), 26. On the state's maritime economy, see Peter J. Coleman, *The Transformation of Rhode Island, 1790-1860* (Providence: Brown University Press, 1963), chap. 2.

[5] Chudacoff, "The Revolution and the Town," 82-83.

View of Market Square, Providence, c. 1844-1849 (courtesy of the Rhode Island Historical Society)

ing the example of their peers in Boston, New York, and Philadelphia, founded the Providence Association of Mechanics and Manufacturers. Dedicated to "the Promotion of Home Manufactures, the cementing the Mechanic Interest," and "raising a Fund to Support the Distressed," the new association sent letters and copies of its charter to artisans all over the country, exhorting them "to join as one Man" to make their voices heard because "the mechanic Interest is but weakly represented in all Legislative Bodies." After Rhode Island became the last of the thirteen colonies to join the Union in May 1790, the association turned its attention to protecting its members from foreign competition and lobbied for the more stringent inspection of imported manufactures and the adoption of a protective tariff.[6]

Until the War of 1812, the Mechanics' Association saw itself as standing "almost alone in advocating" domestic manufacturing. Traditional mercantilist theory focused almost exclusively on overseas commerce, and popular prejudice held that agriculture "constitutes the first rank of useful employment" and "that the good old-fashioned phrase, WE THE PEOPLE . . . means nothing more or less than *we the farmers*."[7] To make a case for the role of mechanic arts and crafts and the men who plied these trades, spokesmen for the association advanced a new conception of society. They suggested that society consisted of "three great classes," or functional economic groupings—"the Agricultural, the Commercial, and the Mechanic and Manufacturing." Artisans thus mediated between farmers on the one side and merchants on the other. In this triad of mutually dependent classes, "the true Interest of one cannot be opposed to the real Interest of either of the others." Both the artisan and the merchant depended on the farmer to raise their food, and

[6] Records of the Providence Association of Mechanics and Manufacturers, vol. 1, 27 February 1789, 21 July 1790, 7 November 1791, Rhode Island Historical Society Library, Providence (hereafter cited as RIHS); Gary John Kornblith, "From Artisans to Businessmen: Master Mechanics in New England, 1789-1850" (Ph.D. diss., Princeton University, 1983), esp. chap. 1; Withey, *Urban Growth in Colonial Rhode Island*, 102-106. On the emergence of a "mechanic consciousness" that cut across craft lines in Philadelphia, see Eric Foner, *Tom Paine and Revolutionary America* (New York: Oxford University Press, 1976).

[7] Records of the Mechanics' Association, vol. 3, 10 April 1820, RIHS; John Howland, *An Address delivered before the Providence Association of Mechanics and Manufacturers, April 9, 1810* (Providence: Jones & Wheeler, 1810), 8.

the farmer, in turn, depended on the artisan to provide his implements and on the merchant to export his surplus. "It is plainly dis-
cernible," as Isaac Greenwood, a charter member of the association,
told his fellow master craftsmen in 1798, "that a nation peopled only
by farmers, must be a region of indolence and misery."[8]

Greenwood's call for the development of the domestic economy
did not fall on deaf ears. Providence merchants, who recognized
that a major reason for Newport's stagnation was its lack of a hinterland, hoped to tap the rich interior of southern New England.
From the 1790s on they deepened the harbor, chartered banks, and
established insurance companies. Over the opposition of the state's
farmers, they built turnpikes that channeled the trade of eastern
Connecticut and southeastern Massachusetts through Providence.
The Mechanics' Association did its part by purchasing shares in
these turnpike ventures and investing its surplus funds in bank
stock.[9]

At the same time some of the town's merchants, well aware of the
risks of ocean-borne commerce, explored investment opportunities
that would enable them to lessen their risks. In 1789 Moses Brown
and his son-in-law, William Almy, recruited an enterprising English
craftsman, Samuel Slater, to build an Arkwright spinning mill in
nearby Pawtucket. As early as 1804 commercial capital began to
shift into manufacturing ventures, and the Embargo of 1807, the
War of 1812, and the Tariff of 1816 all accelerated this shift. Cotton
and woolen factories soon sprouted on the banks of nearby rivers,
where they harnessed the region's abundant water resources. By
1815 there were an estimated 165 mills within a thirty-mile radius
of Providence, most of them small, unincorporated, and operated
personally by their owners. Within another decade, Rhode Island-

---

[8] Records of the Mechanics' Association, vol. 2, 27 January 1800, RIHS; Isaac
Greenwood lecture to the Mechanics' Association, 9 July 1798, reprinted in Edwin
M. Stone, *Mechanics' Festival: An Account of the Seventy-First Anniversary of the Providence
Association of Mechanics and Manufacturers* (Providence: Knowles, Anthony & Co.,
1860), 6; Kornblith, "From Artisans to Businessmen," chap. 3.

[9] Timothy Dwight, *Travels in New England and New York*, ed. Barbara Miller Solomon, 4 vols. (Cambridge: Harvard University Press, 1969), 2:20-21; Withey, *Urban
Growth in Colonial Rhode Island*, 97-98. In July 1806, for example, the association instructed its treasurer to buy stock in the Smithfield Turnpike, which would benefit
not only the community but especially the mechanics. Records of the Mechanics' Association, vol. 2, 14 July 1806, RIHS; *Charter, By-Laws, Rules and Regulations of the Providence Association of Mechanics and Manufacturers* (Providence: J. Carter, 1808), 29.

ers of all persuasions sang the praises of domestic manufacturing in bringing prosperity to the remotest corners of the state. "American Manufactures and the proper estimation of improvements and perfection in the mechanick [sic] arts," observed John Howland, president of the Mechanics' Association, in 1825, "are now the theme of every public journal."[10]

The rise of manufacturing along the Pawtuxet, Woonasquatucket, and Blackstone rivers acted as a powerful magnet, drawing thousands of newcomers from rural New England and from overseas to Providence and neighboring mill towns. Providence's population, which had nearly doubled from 6,380 in 1790 to 11,767 in 1820, soared another 43 percent to 16,836 in 1830. Rapid urban growth, however, came at the expense of social order. The influx of thousands of strangers into what had been a relatively homogeneous community disrupted traditional face-to-face relationships and eroded consensual values. Although Providence was still a small town compared to cities like New York, Philadelphia, and Boston, it too had to cope with the problems of racial and ethnic animosity, juvenile delinquency, and what appeared to be an alarming increase in intemperance.

During the 1820s, a number of signs pointed to serious inadequacies in the town's institutional arrangements. One was racial conflict, kindled by the decline of co-residence by servants. Since the War of 1812, the town's blacks, who numbered perhaps a thousand thanks to a steady stream of migration from rural South County, had been moving out of the homes of their white employers into several straggling neighborhoods. There they fashioned a spare but autonomous community life centered on their own churches, schools, and voluntary associations. Though excluded because of their race from

---

[10] *Charter, By-Laws, Rules and Regulations of the Providence Association of Mechanics and Manufacturers. With a List of Members, and the Address of John Howland, Esq., delivered before the Association, January 10th, 1825* (Providence: A. C. Greene, 1850), 9; Peter J. Coleman, "The Entrepreneurial Spirit in Rhode Island History," *Business History Review* 37 (Winter 1963): 327-32; Caroline Ware, *The Early New England Cotton Manufacture: A Study in Industrial Beginnings* (1931; reprint, New York: Russell & Russell, 1966), 56, 138, 148. On early industrialization in Rhode Island, see Kurt B. Mayer, *Economic Development and Population Growth in Rhode Island* (Providence: Brown University Press, 1953), 26-36; Coleman, *Transformation of Rhode Island*. B. Michael Zuckerman discusses the rise of a "pro-manufacturing consensus" following the War of 1812 in "The Political Economy of Industrial Rhode Island, 1790-1860" (Ph.D. diss., Brown University, 1981), chap. 2.

employment as textile operatives and from apprenticeship to white mechanics, they seized opportunities in drayage, catering, and other service occupations. Some even managed to acquire fairly substantial amounts of property.[11]

These same neighborhoods, where brothels, dance halls, and other places of ill repute sprang up, attracted sailors out for a good time. After blacks routed one such expedition in October 1824, a white mob returned to lay waste to the black neighborhood of Hard Scrabble, while the town watch prudently refrained from interfering. When several of the rioters were later arraigned for inciting to riot, their defense attorney convinced the jury that his clients had simply struck a blow for "the morals of the community." Invoking an American version of the "moral economy of the crowd," he pointed out that the defendants had not indiscriminately attacked private property, but had rather demolished a "notorious nuisance" that had long been "the resort of the most corrupt part of the black population." In vain did the prosecutor argue that "the recognition of a doctrine of this kind would tend to the subversion of all order in society."[12]

The Hard Scrabble Riot illustrates how rapid in-migration undermined a hierarchical social order resting on racial homogeneity and consensual values. But blacks were not the only "foreign" element whose presence in Providence raised fears about the breakdown of traditional institutions like the town watch. Irish immigrants were also finding their way to the area, attracted by such construction projects as the Blackstone Canal, which linked Providence to Worcester, Massachusetts. By 1827 there were enough of them for a priest to celebrate mass in the Old Town House. Over the next three decades their presence reversed Rhode Islanders' tolerance of Roman Catholicism. Protestant clergymen, particularly, feared that obedience to papal decrees would subvert the self-discipline that the young republic so imperatively required.[13]

---

[11] Julian Rammelkamp, "The Providence Negro Community, 1820-1842," *Rhode Island History* 7 (January 1948): 20-33; William J. Brown, *The Life of William J. Brown, of Providence, R.I.* (Providence: Angell & Co., 1883); *Liberator*, 18 October 1839; Robert J. Cottrol, *The Afro-Yankees: Providence's Black Community in the Antebellum Era* (Westport, Conn.: Greenwood Press, 1982).

[12] *Hard-Scrabble Calendar* (Providence: privately printed, 1824), 16, 18, 21. See also E. P. Thompson, "The Moral Economy of the British Crowd in the Eighteenth Century," *Past and Present* 50 (February 1971): 76-136.

[13] Rev. A. Dowling, "The Diocese of Providence," in the Very Rev. Wm. Byrne et

In addition to racial and ethnic antagonisms, Providence experienced an epidemic of juvenile delinquency, Sabbath-breaking, and intemperance. By the mid-1820s local newspapers were filled with complaints about rowdy gangs of boys who loitered on street corners, set upon black pedestrians, and even disrupted Sabbath evening services. There were also numerous complaints that gambling and the sale of liquor on Sundays desecrated the Sabbath. By 1826 some citizens had concluded that the town needed a central police agency where "the suppression of disorder and the protection of personal and proprietary rights may be promptly and effectively obtained." Still others believed that Providence was experiencing a moral decline from the more sober and upright ways of the past. In a memorial to the town council in September of that year they deplored "the alarming increase of the vice of Intemperance," "the multiplication of common dram shops," and "the introduction of new places of resort [and] amusement of different grades furnished with every variety of refreshments including strong liquors."[14]

Townspeople considered several solutions to this apparent breakdown of social order. One was to remodel the town's institutional arrangements. In the aftermath of the Hard Scrabble Riot the town council sent the town watch out two hours earlier than usual and doubled its size from twelve to twenty-four men. When a larger watch failed to stem the epidemic of crime, a number of prominent citizens proposed that Providence emulate Boston in exchanging an antiquated town meeting for a "modern" city government. Even though favored by most of the town's elite, municipal incorporation fell short of the necessary three-fifths majority when it appeared on the ballot in 1830. Too many townspeople, it seemed, shared the opinion of a group of citizens calling themselves the "Middling Interest" who protested that the proposed city government would substantially raise their taxes. A majority of the town's freemen did not swing behind incorporation until bloody riots in September 1831 dramatized the fragility of the town's institutions.[15]

---

al., *History of the Catholic Church in the New England States*, 2 vols. (Boston: Hurd & Everts, 1899), 1:355-63. See also Patrick T. Conley and Matthew J. Smith, *Catholicism in Rhode Island: The Formative Era* (Providence: Diocese of Providence, 1976).

[14] Petition dated 25 September 1826, Providence Town Papers, vol. 127, RIHS; *Rhode Island American and Providence Gazette*, 26 September 1826; Welcome Arnold Greene, *The Providence Plantations for Two Hundred and Fifty Years* (Providence: J. A. & R. A. Reid, 1886), 114.

[15] "In all the contentions between the aristocracy of this town, and the middling

On the night of 21 September 1831, a row between sailors "on a frolic to some houses of ill fame" and the black residents of Olney's Lane erupted into four nights of rioting, destruction, and death. In vigilante action that recalled the Hard Scrabble Riot of 1824, white rioters again struck at what they claimed was the source of "midnight revels, the succession of severe and bloody affrays and the frequent, bold and open riots" about which neighboring property owners had complained to the town council for years. There the parallel ended. This time the civil authorities did not look the other way, and community sentiment condemned the rioters' actions. When "the utmost exertions" of the sheriff and town watch failed to halt the mob's "systematic attacks," the civil authorities summoned the assistance of the state militia. On the last night of the riots, the militiamen, surrounded by rioters who pelted them with stones, fired into the crowd, killing four and mortally wounding a fifth. Though regretting the lives lost, the town meeting that investigated the Olney's Lane Riots praised the "prompt and energetic exercise of military aid." Attributing the bloody affray to "the want of an *efficient execution* of present laws," a majority of Providence's freemen apparently agreed. In November 1831 they voted to exchange their town meeting for a city council and "a vigorous and efficient Executive Magistrate," empowered to detain "any dissolute person," search any building suspected of harboring vice, and in place of the sheriff, enforce the riot act. Providence, as the city's new mayor explained at his inauguration in June 1832, had simply grown "too heterogeneous and unmanageable" for the town meeting to govern any longer.[16]

---

interest, where the latter have been contending for their pecuniary rights, they have invariably carried their point," declared the *Providence Patriot* in 1830. "When the men of gold, in the pride of their hearts, said, 'Let us have a City Charter,' the men of business, in the firm honesty of their hearts, said, 'We will have no such thing,' and as the men of business said, so it came to pass." "The Middling Interest *versus* the Big Bugs," *Providence Patriot*, 23 October 1830. On events leading to municipal incorporation, see Howard P. Chudacoff and Theodore C. Hirt, "Social Turmoil and Governmental Reform in Providence, 1820-1832," *Rhode Island History* 31 (February 1972): 21-31. Before Boston incorporated in 1822, the "Middling Interest," a faction composed of shopkeepers, mechanics, and other small property owners, had insisted that municipal officers be elected by ward rather than at large. See Robert A. Mc-Caughey, "From Town to City: Boston in the 1820s," *Political Science Quarterly* 88 (June 1973): 191-213; and Andrew R. L. Cayton, "The Fragmentation of a 'Great Family': The Panic of 1819 and the Rise of the Middling Interest in Boston," *Journal of the Early Republic* 2 (Summer 1982): 143-67.

[16] *Providence Journal*, 26 September 1831; "Resolutions presented by John Whipple

Against this backdrop of heightened community concern over social disorder, the temperance movement promised to revitalize paternalism and restore the close supervision that social superiors—whether gentlemen or master craftsmen—had once exercised over their inferiors when Providence had been a smaller and more close-knit community. But temperance also embodied a program for respectability for mechanics and other members of the town's middling interest. Whereas earlier appeals for temperance had been directed at "parents, magistrates, [and] men of influence" who "form the manners of a people and give a stamp to public opinion," the rapid spread of the movement after 1827 mobilized men and women drawn from the emergent middle classes who envisioned a new society, one in which self-discipline would take the place of the external restraints that social and economic differentiation undermined.[17]

Providence's temperance movement traced its origins to a republican jeremiad delivered by the Reverend David Pickering, pastor of the First Universalist Church, in January 1827. Intemperance, Pickering observed, had converted "many useful and industrious members of the community . . . into contemptible drones." A rapidly growing population and increasing wealth, "for which this favoured clime stands unrivalled in the annals of nations," had spawned luxury "as a necessary consequence," and "plenty drew along her accustomed retinue of idleness, extravagance and dissipation." Pickering pointed to members of the town's elite as the unwitting agents of this decline from what "was once the sanctuary of temperance and sobriety." From the "side-boards" of the wealthy and fashiona-

---

respecting the late Riots and passed September 25, 1831," Records of the Town Meeting, Office of the City Clerk, Providence; John A. C. Randall to Mowry Randall, 25 September 1831, Randall MSS, Brown University Library; *History of the Providence Riots, From Sept. 21 to Sept. 24, 1831* (Providence: H. H. Brown, 1831), 19; *Charter of the City of Providence . . . Also, the Mayor's Address to the City Council, delivered at the Organization of the City Government, June 4th, 1832* (Providence: William Marshall & Co., 1832), 3, 19.

[17] Joseph Snow et al., "A Friendly Address to the Inhabitants of the Town of Providence," 19 December 1794, quoted in William R. Staples, *Annals of the Town of Providence, from Its First Settlement, to the Organization of the City Government, in June, 1832* (Providence: Knowles & Vose, 1843), 361. The earliest temperance societies, like the Massachusetts Society for the Suppression of Intemperance and the Connecticut Society for the Reformation of Morals, both founded in 1813, urged local notables to curb the alcoholic consumption of their dependents. Ronald G. Walters, *American Reformers, 1815-1860* (New York: Hill and Wang, 1978), 126.

ble, who "give a tone to the morals and practices of society," intemperance was spreading at an alarming rate through the ranks of their social inferiors "who are always emulous to ape their examples." To Pickering, the solution appeared simple. If only the town's leading citizens set the right example by moderating their own consumption, townspeople could return to the republican simplicity and morality of an earlier generation.[18]

Pickering's sermon galvanized a large and influential segment of the Providence community. Spurred no doubt by Lyman Beecher's seminal *Six Sermons on Intemperance* and the formation of the American Society for the Promotion of Temperance the preceding year, several hundred townspeople assembled in April 1827 to frame a set of temperance resolves. The subscribers agreed "to abstain from the habitual and unnecessary use of ardent spirits," "to discountenance the practice of drinking intoxicating liquors in public places of resort," and to "persuade labourers and all other persons in our employ, or under our control, to refrain from the habitual and unnecessary use of ardent spirits," and "to accept of an equivalent in money for the customary perquisite allowed them in intoxicating liquors." Some employers went even further, vowing to give preference in hiring to those who abstained from ardent spirits. Others promised to dismiss the habitually intemperate among their employees. Most of the audience, however, preferred to inculcate new industrial work habits through moral suasion and personal example. Fearing that coercion might array one portion of the commu-

[18] David Pickering, *Effects of Intemperance, a Discourse delivered on Sabbath Evening, January 14, 1827* (Providence: Miller & Grattan, 1827), 7, 6, 19. For the history of the antebellum temperance movement in Providence, see Sidney S. Rider, "The Rise and Progress of the Temperance Reformation During the First Quarter Century of Its Existence in Providence, 1828-1853," MS, Rider Collection, Brown University Library; and Dow A. Wieman, "The Reformer's Looking Glass: The Antebellum Temperance Movement in Providence" (seminar paper, Brown University, 1974), RIHS. The best account of the national temperance movement is Ian R. Tyrrell, *Sobering Up: From Temperance to Prohibition in Antebellum America, 1800-1860* (Westport, Conn.: Greenwood Press, 1979). See also Norman H. Clark, *Deliver Us from Evil: An Interpretation of American Prohibition* (New York: W. W. Norton & Co., 1976); Joseph R. Gusfield, *Symbolic Crusade: Status Politics and the American Temperance Movement* (Urbana: University of Illinois Press, 1963); John Allen Krout, *The Origins of Prohibition* (New York: Alfred A. Knopf, 1925); W. J. Rorabaugh, *The Alcoholic Republic: An American Tradition* (New York: Oxford University Press, 1979); and Robert L. Hampel, *Temperance and Prohibition in Massachusetts, 1813-1852* (Ann Arbor: UMI Research Press, 1982).

nity against another, they disclaimed any intent "to impose the slightest restraint or dictation upon any individual." Rather, they placed their faith in "the concentration of public opinion."[19]

Over the next two decades thousands of Rhode Islanders took the temperance pledge. Among the most enthusiastic recruits were the 275 members of the Mechanics' Association, who endorsed the temperance resolves in May 1827. These master craftsmen had two good reasons for resolving "to abstain from the habitual and unnecessary use of spirits" and to "prevail" on their journeymen and apprentices to give up the customary "grog ration." First, they obviously considered intemperance a threat to their hard-earned but still rather precarious respectability. By this time most of them were modest property owners: approximately two-thirds owned property valued between two hundred and five thousand dollars. Another quarter did not own enough property to pay taxes.[20] "You may be assured," the association's Select Committee admonished a habitually intemperate member, "that the habit of intemperance when it becomes fixed on a man will most certainly lead its victim to his ruin."[21]

Second, to the members of the Mechanics' Association, intemperance seemed a relic of pre-industrial patterns of work and leisure. Long interested in rationalizing business practices, they believed that an industrializing economy demanded revision of customary patterns of work, leisure, and consumption. In their eyes, the "monster" of intemperance embodied unproductive expenditure, idleness, and self-indulgence. A sober artisan, they believed, was not only more industrious and punctual than an intemperate one, he also spent his money on more productive expenditures and thus stimulated the growth of the domestic economy. Francis Wayland,

[19] *Report of a Committee at a Meeting of the Citizens of Providence, Friendly to the Promotion of Temperance* (Providence: F. Y. Carlile, 1828), 3-5; *Manufacturers and Farmers Journal*, 19 April 1827.

[20] Records of the Mechanics' Association, vol. 3, 29 May 1827, RIHS. I traced members listed in the *Charter, By-Laws, Rules and Regulations of the Providence Association of Mechanics and Manufacturers* (Providence: Walter R. Danforth, 1827) to the city directory and tax list for 1828. See also William Gerald Shade, "The Rise of the Providence Association of Mechanics and Manufacturers: A Workingman's Organization, 1789-1850" (M.A.T. thesis, Brown University, 1962).

[21] Select Committee to Samuel C. Bodge, 13 November 1828, Records of the Mechanics' Association, RIHS.

president of Brown University and perhaps Providence's foremost advocate of temperance, set forth the mechanics' case in a lecture in 1831: "Whatever therefore enables the buyer to *labor more*, or to *labor to better advantage*, will enable him to *buy more* and to *pay better*; whatever, on the contrary, *disenables* him from labor, or renders that labor *less valuable*, forces him to *buy less*, and to *pay less punctually*." But the master craftsmen did not have to glean this argument for temperance from Wayland's writings or attend temperance meetings to hear Wayland himself. They well knew from experience the desultory work patterns and the drinking that made their workshops "scenes of disorder and ruin." In promoting the rationalization of the American economy, the temperance movement at once expanded the domestic market and enhanced these craftsmen's claim to respectability.[22]

The temperance movement also appealed to the town's Protestants, particularly its evangelicals. Since a wave of revivals had swept their churches between 1816 and 1820, local Baptists and Congregationalists had disciplined fellow church members who were overly fond of drink. Intemperance, these evangelicals believed, was doubly wrong. It not only undermined the self-discipline so carefully nurtured in their churches, it was also an abhorrent evil. "To look at an evil, to mourn over it, to ask whether it can be corrected, is not enough," Wayland announced. "It becomes us to ask, has not the time come to strike one effectual blow, and banish this vice from among us altogether?" In May 1827, the same month that the Mechanics' Association endorsed the temperance resolves, the Richmond Street Congregational Church added a clause to its covenant that made abstinence from the use of ardent spirits a condition of membership. One by one, the other Congregational and Baptist churches in Providence followed suit. The Pine Street Baptist Church proudly reported to the Warren Association in 1832, "eleven of our members, some of whom were doing an extensive and lucrative trade in the sale of ardent spirits, have abandoned the

[22] Francis Wayland, *An Address, delivered before the Providence Association for the Promotion of Temperance, October 20, 1831* (Providence: Weeden & Knowles, 1831), 14; Records of the Mechanics' Association, vol. 4, 12 April 1847, RIHS. On the connection between self-discipline and respectability, see Gusfield, *Symbolic Crusade*, 44-51; and Brian Harrison, *Drink and the Victorians: The Temperance Question in England, 1815-1872* (Pittsburgh: University of Pittsburgh Press, 1971), esp. 107-178.

trade in the article altogether." As a result, the church had "become virtually a Temperance Society."[23]

Though never adding the pledge to their covenants, the city's other Protestant churches did join the crusade against alcohol. Pickering's own First Universalist Church suspended members for their "intemperate use of ardent spirits." In 1829 two men resigned their membership rather than account for their intemperance. By 1832 the Methodists had organized their own temperance society. Episcopalian and Unitarian clergymen lectured on the evils of intemperance and even exchanged pulpits with ministers from other denominations to promote the cold-water cause. At a time when evangelicals and liberals were skirmishing in pamphlet warfare over their conflicting interpretations of the Scriptures and practical Christianity, temperance appeared to be an issue that would heal the rift in the Protestant community. As one measure of how far temperance reform had proceeded within the city's churches, temperance spokesmen in July 1833 claimed that only three members of all the religious societies in Providence still sold alcohol.[24]

[23] Wayland, *Address before the Providence Association for the Promotion of Temperance*, 3; *The Doctrinal Articles and Covenant of the Richmond-St. Congregational Church, Providence, R.I.* (Providence: Philanthropic Press, 1833), 21; *A Sketch of the Pine-Street (2D) Baptist Church, in Providence* (Providence: H. H. Brown, 1837), 15.

[24] First Universalist Church, Records of the Church, 16 November 1827, 29 June, 28 October 1829, RIHS; *Providence Journal*, 29 July 1833. Unlike in Rochester, New York, where revivals conducted by Charles Grandison Finney reconciled a badly divided middle class, religious enthusiasm in Providence fired sectarian controversy. During the 1820s five new churches were organized in Providence: the Baptists established two; the Episcopalians, Unitarians, and Universalists, one each. But the founding of the First Universalist Church in 1821 prompted evangelicals to take the offensive. In 1825 they established the Providence Religious Tract Society to circulate tracts aimed at confounding the "dangerous error" of universal salvation. In 1832 Unitarians, who had also received their share of criticism from evangelicals, countered by organizing the Providence Auxiliary Unitarian Association. "So great is the majority which is opposed to us in the christian church in this immediate region," they explained, that organization was necessary "to diffuse the knowledge, and promote the interests of pure christianity." *Fourth Annual Report of the Providence Religious Tract Society* (Providence: H. H. Brown, 1829), 11; *First Semi-Annual Report of the Providence Auxiliary Unitarian Association* (Providence: Thomas Doyle, 1832), 3, 15; A. J. Carlson, "Evangelical Dispute: Universalists and Limitarians in Providence, Rhode Island, 1821-1832" (seminar paper, Brown University, 1980). On the revivals in Rochester, see Paul E. Johnson, *A Shopkeeper's Millennium: Society and Revivals in Rochester, New York, 1815-1837* (New York: Hill and Wang, 1978). Timothy L. Smith points out Rochester's uniqueness in *Revivalism and Social Reform: American Protestantism on the Eve of the Civil War* (1957; reprint, Baltimore: Johns Hopkins University Press, 1980), 256.

The temperance movement originated as a paternalistic reform that relied on community deference to an ad hoc group of local notables. As temperance societies proliferated and more categorical definitions of alcohol were adopted, the movement evolved from the revision of the work and leisure of employees, servants, and dependents into a program for middle-class respectability and a sharp critique of fashionable taste. By preaching "intelligent self-control" temperance spokesmen helped propagate a new social order, one resting more on self-discipline than on external sanction. Intemperance, as they never tired of pointing out, was neither "an involuntary evil" nor "a sort of fatality, inseparable from human existence" but rather "a *self-affliction*, a misery which men bring upon themselves by an idle indulgence, and as easy to be avoided as it is for a man to avoid setting fire to his own dwelling."[25]

The multiplication of temperance societies in neighboring towns after 1827 put pressure on adherents in Providence, who had simply gone on record in favor of moderation, also to organize formally. In March 1830 some one hundred men formed the Providence Association for the Promotion of Temperance. Soon afterwards, over heated opposition, the members agreed to admit women. A number of other temperance organizations were eventually organized, which enrolled blacks, sailors, youth, and "reclaimed drunkards." Most of these societies framed constitutions, elected officers, and sent delegates to the annual conventions of the state temperance society established in 1831. Some aggressively promoted the temperance cause: borrowing techniques pioneered by the tract societies, they employed agents to distribute temperance literature. By 1838 the state temperance society was publishing its own newspaper. Voluntary associations composed of peers thus took the place of local notables in molding public opinion.[26]

[25] Providence Association for the Promotion of Temperance, *Quarterly Report of the Committee, for July, 1830* (Providence: Hutchens & Weeden, 1830), 16.

[26] "An Early Wave of Temperance," clipping, 1908, Rhode Island Scrapbook, vol. 16, RIHS. For a discussion of the differences between ad hoc and more permanent organizations, see Brian Harrison, "Religion and Recreation in Nineteenth-Century England," *Past and Present* 38 (December 1967): 100-101; Tyrrell, *Sobering Up*, 54-86; Lois W. Banner, "Religious Benevolence as Social Control: A Critique of an Interpretation," *Journal of American History* 60 (June 1973): 39-41; and Mary P. Ryan, "The Power of Women's Networks: A Case Study of Female Moral Reform in Antebellum America," *Feminist Studies* 5 (Spring 1979): 68-70. Although by the late 1830s women

The proliferation of temperance societies created new leadership opportunities for ambitious middle-class men and women. Of the fifty-two officers of local temperance societies from the 1830s who can be identified, twenty-four were shopkeepers, clerks, and small manufacturers. Another five were skilled craftsmen, and one drove a stagecoach. Only seven were merchants or gentlemen, the men who had led previous community reforms. Moreover, of the fifty-two men, only thirteen ranked in the top fifth of the city's taxpayers, those who owned more than six thousand dollars in property. Fourteen did not possess enough property—two hundred dollars—even to pay taxes. Thus many of the officers were elected to their posts without having first acquired the personal wealth or social status on which community leadership had formerly depended.[27] Shopkeepers and artisans, who clustered in the middle ranks of the city's property owners, made up the bulk of the membership in both the Providence Young Men's Temperance Society (1833) and the Union Temperance Society (1835), the two antebellum temperance societies whose membership lists have survived.[28]

---

outnumbered men by a margin of two to one in the city's temperance societies, they do not appear to have organized their own society until the 1850s. *Seventh Annual Report of the Rhode-Island State Temperance Society* (Providence: H. H. Brown, 1838), 14-16; *Constitution of the Ladies City Temperance Society* (n.p., 1855). See also Ian R. Tyrrell, "Women and Temperance in Antebellum America, 1836-1860," *Civil War History* 28 (June 1982): 128-52.

[27] I have traced the men to city directories and tax lists from the 1830s. In an analysis of the pro- and anti-prohibition camps in Worcester, Massachusetts, Ian Tyrrell finds strong support for prohibition among upwardly mobile manufacturers and mechanics who identified with new industrial patterns of work and leisure. He also suggests that "evangelical religion and temperance tended to occur together as part of the same response to the social and economic changes which were transforming Worcester in the 1830s." *Sobering Up*, chap. 4 (quotation from p. 110). See also W. J. Rorabaugh, "Prohibition as Progress: New York State's License Elections, 1846," *Journal of Social History* 14 (Spring 1981): 425-43. Rorabaugh concludes that "the temperance men were the era's 'go-ahead' men" (p. 435).

[28] Of the 225 members of the Young Men's Temperance Society whose occupations can be determined, 110 were mechanics. Another 45 were shopkeepers or small proprietors. Clerks, manufacturers, and large dealers comprised another third. The figures are comparable for the Union Temperance Society. Of the 328 members whose occupations are known, 131 were craftsmen, another 63 small proprietors. In both associations, fewer than a tenth of the members were merchants and professionals. Substantially underrepresented were men who pursued either semiskilled or unskilled occupations; they comprised less than 5 percent of either society. As small proprietors and skilled craftsmen, these advocates of temperance clustered in the middle ranks of the city's property owners. Only 119 members of the Young Men's

As it became better organized, the temperance movement confirmed the fears of its more conservative supporters that organization would set one portion of the community against another. As
early as 1830, some "ultra-temperance men" began to call for municipal regulation of the liquor trade. Their call alienated grocers
who continued to traffic in hard liquor. Licensing, the grocers
charged, was class legislation. Having "made their fortunes by im-
porting ardent spirits, [and] retired from business," the proponents
of licensing "wish to avoid playing the customary taxes" by shifting
the tax burden to those who sold liquor. The gorcers' pointed protest,
however, did not deter the ultras, who first urged that license fees
be raised and the number of licenses be reduced, and then that no
licenses be granted at all. Ironically, liquor licenses became an important source of municipal revenue after the town council raised
the fee for a retail license in 1830 from sixteen to twenty-eight dollars a year. In the future, this revenue would be a powerful argument in favor of high licenses instead of outright prohibition.[29]

As the temperance movement shifted from moral suasion toward
legal compulsion, it adopted a more categorical definition of alcohol. Only three years after the resolves of 1827 urged moderation,
temperance spokesmen demanded abstinence from all ardent spirits. Annulling the distinction formerly made between temperate
and intemperate drinking, they argued that the use of alcohol was
addictive. "Every sot reeling about our streets, or who has been cast
into yonder poor-house," Dr. Usher Parsons pointed out in 1831,
"might once have said that the [temperance] address was inapplica-
ble to him; for he too was once only a temperate drinker, and
loathed the sight of a drunkard as much as we do; but his temperate
drinking insensibly led to intemperate drinking, to loss of property,

---

Temperance Society owned property, most of them less than twenty-five hundred
dollars. The members of the Union Temperance Society were slightly wealthier because they were generally older. Yet only 198 were property owners, and more than
half possessed less than twenty-five hundred dollars in property. *Constitution and List
of Members of the Providence Young Men's Temperance Society* (n.p., 1833), 4-12; Providence Union Temperance Society, Minutes, 1835-37, RIHS.
    [29] *Providence Patriot*, 16, 23 October 1830; *Providence Journal*, 31 July 1833, 22 Au-
gust 1834; John Pitman, *An Address, delivered before the Providence Union Temperance
Society, February 24, 1835* (Providence: Knowles & Burroughs, 1835), 16-17; Howard
Kemble Stokes, *The Finances and Administration of Providence* (Baltimore: Johns Hopkins University Press, 1903), 141, 162-63.

of friends, of character."[30] When cholera threatened Providence in 1832, allopaths like Dr. Parsons warned their patients to "*shun*" the temperate use of brandy, traditionally thought a preventive, "*as you would the pestilence itself.*" "It is undeniable," they asserted, "that intemperance is a powerful predisposing cause" to the disease. One temperance spokesman declared that "drunkenness is a disease, far more contagious, far more pestilential and far more fatal in its effects, than the so much dreaded Cholera."[31]

After the temperance movement embraced teetotalism, or abstinence from all wine, cider, and fermented beverages, some of its original leaders became the objects of its rebuke for setting the wrong example. Hardly a year passed after 1836, when the American Temperance Union adopted the teetotal pledge, without temperance spokesmen condemning the refusal of the wealthy and fashionable to abide by the conventions of the abstemious majority. Thus in 1838 the Providence County Temperance Society condemned "wine drunkenness," or the consumption of champagne, which "has the sanction of fashionable life more than drunkenness from ardent spirits; and inasmuch as it generally costs more money, it is considered a more *genteel* mode of intoxication." In 1844, three years after the state temperance society officially adopted the "comprehensive pledge," which enjoined abstinence from all fermented as well as distilled beverages, exasperated temperance men expressed their frustation over how "the Temperance Reformation" had been "greatly *retarded* by the course of those individuals in the fashionable walks of life who *refuse to co-operate.*"[32]

By 1844, temperance spokesmen had arrived at a new understanding of public opinion. As late as 1830 they had been content to appeal to gentlemen to set the right tone for the rest of society and

[30] Usher Parsons, *An Address, delivered before the Providence Association for the Promotion of Temperance, May 27, 1831* (Providence: Weeden & Knowles, 1831), 15.

[31] *Remarks on the Cholera, Embracing Facts and Observations collected at New-York, During a Visit to the City Expressly for that Purpose* (Providence: W. Marshall & Co., 1832), 29; Sylvester G. Shearman, *An Address delivered before the North Kingstown Temperance Society, on the 4th Day of November, 1832, at the Baptist Meeting House in Wickford, R.I.* (Providence: William Simons, Jr., 1832), 7; Tyrrell, *Sobering Up*, 89-90.

[32] *Constitution of the Providence County Temperance Society, together with an Address of the Board of Officers, to All the Local Societies within the County* (Providence: H. H. Brown, 1838), 8; *Providence Journal*, 6 December 1844. For debates over extending the pledge to prohibit wine and other fermented beverages, see Providence Union Temperance Society, Minutes, December 1835-37, RIHS.

had looked forward to the community's consensual conversion to total abstinence. Since then, temperance societies had divided the community into two warring camps, the righteous and the sinful. In urging the abstemious majority to resist the blandishments of fashion, wealth, and rank, teetotalers identified morality with the conscience and sense of duty of the middle classes. As sobriety became a measure of respectability, the temperate gradually began to view themselves as members of the stable, industrious, sober middle classes, defined less by occupation or wealth (though most teetotalers were shopkeepers, artisans, clerks, or their wives), than by the values they cultivated. Moreover, in their eyes, the rich appeared to be just as intemperate, idle, and self-indulgent as the vice-ridden poor.

By the late 1830s a temperance network, linking societies in all the towns of Rhode Island, made it possible to mobilize adherents into a powerful lobby. In 1838 advocates of prohibition persuaded the General Assembly to pass a local option law, which allowed voters to instruct their town governments not to grant licenses for the sale of intoxicating drinks. To mobilize dry sentiment, the state temperance society hired a permanent agent, began to publish its own newspaper, and even attempted to organize juvenile temperance societies in every school district in Rhode Island. In the view of these advocates of prohibition, the existing licensing system taxed productive Rhode Islanders for the benefit of a small number of self-interested men. Licensing, they charged, "gives to a few men the privilege, for their own pecuniary profit, of *legally* converting good citizens into paupers, maniacs and criminals, and then imposes upon the whole community the cost of supporting them when they have become such." Marshaling statistics to demonstrate the link between intemperance and other social problems, they contended "that *nearly nine tenths of the crime*, and *at least four fifths of the pauperism*" in Providence "are caused by the use of intoxicating liquor."[33]

Bitterly dissenting from this opinion, grocers who sold alcohol condemned prohibition as "an infringement of individual liberty not consistent with a free government." Local option, they con-

---

[33] *Seventh Annual Report of the Rhode-Island State Temperance Society*, 3-4; *Extracts from the Proceedings and Reports of the Rhode-Island State Total Abstinence Society* (Providence: B. T. Albro, 1846), 18; City Temperance Society, "Crime, Pauperism, Intemperance," broadside, 23 February 1841, Rider Collection, Brown University Library.

tended, would leave "the whole law, relative to the sale and use, or regulation of the sale, of distilled liquors and wines, to be administered by a strongly organized, self-constituted and irresponsible [temperance] society." They obviously feared the power of an increasingly well organized temperance movement to shape public opinion and turn it against even such an entrenched custom as social drinking. Though Tocqueville might praise "the liberty of association" as "a necessary guarantee against the tyranny of the majority," the grocers had learned from painful experience that the selfsame organizations could direct the majority's will against a beleaguered minority like their own. Indeed, from their perspective, temperance societies engineered just this oppressive social conformity.[34]

Once heralded as a reform that would unite the respectable citizens of the community, the temperance movement now provoked bitter controversy. In August 1838, the first of a series of referenda on prohibition triggered violent clashes between the opposing sides in Providence. Opponents cut down the trees of one prohibitionist, blew up another's house, and shot at a third—all to no avail. By a slim margin the city's freemen voted not to grant any liquor licenses. When two months later the General Assembly reversed itself and ordered the attorney general to refrain from any further prosecutions of rum sellers, an outraged Providence County Temperance Society declared its intention "to withhold our suffrages from political men of *all parties*, who openly or secretly give their influence to sustain *intemperance* in our community." After a string of petitions quickly forced the General Assembly to reinstate local option, Providence freemen again voted against licensing.[35]

During the 1840s the temperance movement enlisted recruits from two previously neglected groups. Roman Catholics, put off by the movement's manifest Protestantism, had kept their distance un-

[34] *Providence Journal*, 28 August 1838, 21 February 1839; Alexis de Tocqueville, *Democracy in America*, trans. Henry Reeve, ed. Phillips Bradley, 2 vols. (New York: Vintage Books, 1945), 1:201-202.

[35] *"None but Suitable Persons." A Rhode-Island Temperance Tale, By a Rum-Seller* (Providence: B. T. Albro, 1839), 64; *Providence Journal*, 5 October 1838. See also John H. Stiness, *A Sketch of Rhode Island Legislation against Strong Drink* (Providence: Sidney S. Rider, 1882). For one temperance man's anger over the "flagrant acts" of the General Assembly, see Stephen S. Wardwell, Diary, 1818-39, vol. 17, 6 November 1838, Vestry of the Beneficent Congregational Church, Providence.

til 1840, when local priests established the first parish temperance societies. Their members pledged not to consume alcohol in public places. Though never embracing either teetotalism or prohibition, these Catholics did help to propagate sobriety, by this time a middle-class convention, among the city's immigrants.[36] The temperance movement cast its net even further in the summer of 1841 with the founding of the Providence Washington Total Abstinence Society. Modeled on a society that had been established in Baltimore the preceding year, the new organization endeavored to reclaim inebriates from the ranks of the semiskilled, the unskilled, and mariners. Volunteers scoured the streets, befriending drunks, whom they clothed and even lodged. At "experience meetings" individuals like Deacon Thomas G. Northup, a tailor who had been excommunicated from the First Baptist Church for drunkenness, recalled the glorious moment when they had thrown off the shackles of enslavement to Demon Rum.[37]

In the meantime the Rhode Island State Total Abstinence Society mobilized the state's drys. Between 1841 and 1846 its agent, Thomas Tew, traveled the state, delivering an estimated fifteen hundred addresses and collecting more than twenty thousand signatures on petitions to the General Assembly in favor of statewide prohibition. Temperance men also mounted challenges to unfriendly officeholders. In 1847, for example, they backed stove manufacturer Amos C. Barstow in his unsuccessful attempt to unseat incumbent Providence mayor Thomas Burgess, a wealthy merchant of "rank, style and station," who seemed "notoriously in favor of the illegal rum traffic." In a letter to the *Providence Journal*, several of Barstow's supporters described him as "a plain, but highly intelligent, thrifty and respectable young mechanic—a carpenter's son—who belongs to the great, safe, middling interest class of the community." Undeterred by Barstow's defeat, the prohibitionists persisted. Their lobbying paid off in 1852 when the General Assembly

[36] Conley and Smith, *Catholicism in Rhode Island*, 32-33, 67; Robert W. Hayman, *Catholicism in Rhode Island and the Diocese of Providence, 1780-1886* (Providence: Diocese of Providence, 1982), 83-84.

[37] *First Quarterly Report of the Providence Washington Total Abstinence Society* (Providence: S. M. Millard, 1841), 4-5; Providence Washington Total Abstinence Society, MS Records, 1841-42, RIHS; Krout, *Origins of Prohibition*, 182-208; Tyrrell, *Sobering Up*, 203-18; Sean Wilentz, *Chants Democratic: New York City and the Rise of the American Working Class, 1788-1850* (New York: Oxford University Press, 1984), 306-314.

enacted a version of the Maine Law, which mandated statewide prohibition. Steering the act through the assembly was Amos Barstow, state representative from Providence. Later that year, the city's voters chose him as their first "businessman" mayor. According to his biographer, Barstow stood for mayor "not as a politician, but as an earnest advocate of moral principles."[38]

Rhode Island's adoption of statewide prohibition in 1852 capped a revolution in manners within less than a quarter of a century. Until the 1820s drink had figured prominently in the work and leisure of respectable townspeople of all social classes. Workingmen had customarily laid down their work in the morning and then again in the afternoon for their grog ration, and alcohol had lubricated practically all social occasions—from the ordination of a minister to the celebration of a national holiday. By the 1850s, however, the city's middle-class residents not only abstained from drinking, but basked in their reputations as "cold water" men and women. At the same time the temperance movement shed its paternalistic aspects to become a perfectionist reform aimed at nothing less than suppressing the use of alcohol. The changing meaning of the word "temperance" encapsulated the radicalization of the movement. Although once it had meant moderation, in 1852 it designated abstinence from all intoxicating beverages, whether distilled or fermented. The creation of a network of voluntary associations, the shift from reliance on moral suasion to legal compulsion, and the rise of a middle-class lay leadership had gradually transformed the temperance movement into a reform crusade crucial to the self-definition of the city's emergent middle classes.

The history of the local abolitionist movement telescoped these same developments into a much briefer and more dramatic episode. Abolitionism, unlike temperance, began with a much more radical program—immediate emancipation—that imperiled the self-interest of a number of substantial Providence merchants and textile manufacturers. Indeed, these "gentlemen of property and standing" felt sufficiently threatened to call a town meeting in November

---

[38] *Address of the Committee of the State Temperance Convention, Holden in the City of Providence, January 6, 1847* (Providence: Amsbury & Lincoln, 1847), 3; letter from "All True Law and Order Men," *Providence Journal*, 11 May 1847; *Biographical Cyclopedia of Representative Men of Rhode Island* (Providence: National Biographical Publishing Co., 1881), 310.

1835 at which they censured, amid great fanfare, the abolitionists' "fanatical" behavior. Openly defying this public condemnation, state abolitionists strove to dispel their image as fanatics bent on tearing apart the Union. In defense of their constitutional right to debate the merits of immediate emancipation, they formulated a class-based language of moral reform in which middle-class northerners, distinguished from both the rich above and the poor below by their adherence to industry, frugality, and sobriety, asserted their claim to a superior morality and identified their class interests with the public interest.

Rhode Island abolitionism dated from July 1832, when the Quaker Arnold Buffum, a hatter by trade and past president of the New England Anti-Slavery Society, lectured in eight towns around the state. Three months later, William Lloyd Garrison, the editor of the Boston antislavery newspaper the *Liberator*, came to Providence to speak before a recently organized black temperance society. While in Providence, where he met his future wife, Helen Benson, he gave two lectures on immediate emancipation at the Beneficent Congregational Church. His visit spurred the formation of the Providence Anti-Slavery Society in June 1833. The city's first advocates of immediate emancipation were shopkeepers and artisans active in the temperance movement, moral reform societies, and their respective churches. Four were also members of the Mechanics' Association. Apart from the blessings of the aging Quaker patriarch Moses Brown, there was little to provide continuity between the Providence Anti-Slavery Society and the earlier Providence Society for Abolishing the Slave Trade, founded in 1789, which had exerted moral force and even, in some cases, brought legal action against slave traders like John Brown. Only two members of the original Society for Abolishing the Slave Trade, George Benson, former partner of Moses Brown and father-in-law of William Lloyd Garrison, and Thomas Truesdell, a grocer, appear to have been active in the later antislavery movement.[39]

[39] "Abolition Society Book," 1789-1827, MS, Archives of the Yearly Meeting of Friends for New England, RIHS; *The Report and Proceedings of the First Annual Meeting of the Providence Anti-Slavery Society* (Providence: H. H. Brown, 1833), 12. My account of the antislavery movement in Rhode Island draws on John L. Myers, "Antislavery Agencies in Rhode Island, 1832-1835," *Rhode Island History* 29 (Summer and Fall 1970): 82-93; ibid., "Antislavery Agents in Rhode Island, 1835-1837," ibid. 30 (Winter 1971): 20-31; and Arline Ruth Kiven, *Then Why the Negroes: The Nature and Course*

The city's abolitionists quickly acknowledged their debt to the temperance movement. When asked how they would achieve abolition, they answered, "by means precisely like those which have been employed with so much effect towards the subversion of Intemperance." Confident that they wielded a marvelous *"moral power—the power of the truth,"* they proposed "to circulate Tracts urging upon the consciences of our fellow-citizens the heinous wickedness of Slavery." To rally public support, they scheduled antislavery rallies on the Fourth of July. After the formation of the American Anti-Slavery Society in December 1833, a number of well-known lecturers—including Unitarian minister Samuel J. May, former slaveholder James Birney, and the controversial Englishmen Charles Stuart and George Thompson—stopped off in Rhode Island on their way from New York to Boston. In 1834 the national society appointed two local agents, Elder Ray Potter, a controversial Free Will Baptist from Pawtucket, and Reverend Thomas Williams, a Congregational minister, whom it could only afford to pay eight dollars a week plus traveling expenses.[40]

The efforts of peripatetic national figures and part-time, ill-paid agents, however, did not carry the doctrines of immediate emancipation very far beyond the bounds of Providence and Pawtucket. Broadcasting the message to the rest of the state awaited the appointment by the American Anti-Slavery Society of Henry B. Stanton as agent for Rhode Island in June 1835. A gifted public speaker and an experienced antislavery agent, Stanton employed the same methods his mentor Theodore Dwight Weld had perfected.[41] Beginning "at the outskirts" and working his "way as quietly as possible to the centre," Stanton thoroughly canvassed the state in a model organizational campaign. From mid-June 1835 to February 1836, he visited twenty-four Rhode Island towns, lecturing at least five or six times and distributing antislavery tracts in each. His activities, as an-

of the Anti-Slavery Movement in Rhode Island, 1637-1861 (Providence: Urban League of Rhode Island, 1973), 28-65.

[40] *First Annual Meeting of the Providence Anti-Slavery Society,* 8-9.

[41] Arthur Harry Rice, "Henry B. Stanton as a Political Abolitionist" (Ed.D. diss., Columbia University, 1968); Henry B. Stanton, *Random Recollections,* 3rd ed. (New York: Harper & Brothers, 1887), 43-55. On Weld, see Gilbert Hobbs Barnes, *The Antislavery Impulse, 1830-1844* (1933; reprint, Gloucester, Mass.: Peter Smith, 1957), 79-87; and Robert H. Abzug, *Passionate Liberator: Theodore Dwight Weld and the Dilemma of Reform* (New York: Oxford University Press, 1980).

other antislavery agent described them, "were not so much directed to the organization of societies, as to the communication of that information which is requisite, in order that the people may think for themselves, and do their duty in the light presented to their consciences." At each of his stops Stanton impressed upon his audiences their moral duty as Christians. Since slavery was a sin, he told his listeners, it was incumbent on each of them to make use of all available means to bring about its abolition. Stanton suggested that they could begin to dismantle slavery by banning the slave trade from the District of Columbia.[42]

Their interest whetted by Stanton's oratory, Rhode Islanders organized a host of antislavery societies. By the fall of 1835 auxiliaries of the American Anti-Slavery Society were springing up everywhere. Nor were these for men only. Women, for whom joining an antislavery society frequently marked their first extensive public involvement outside the church, formed their own societies, which held teas and bazaars to raise money for the abolitionist cause. A lecture by George Thompson in April 1835 at the Pine Street Baptist Church prompted 106 women to form the Providence Ladies' Anti-Slavery Society. An antislavery society for young girls had already been organized. Another antislavery cell consisted of Paulina Wright Davis, the noted feminist who later edited the *Una*, one of the first women's rights newspapers in the country; Sarah Helen Whitman, the Providence widow who captured Edgar Allen Poe's heart; the daughter of Arnold Buffum, Elizabeth Buffum Chace, who was to become one of the state's most energetic reformers; and Susan R. Harris, who along with her husband, Dunbar, published the *Rhode Island Freeman*, dedicated to "Free Soil, Free Speech, Free Labor, and Free Men." All four women were to be among the charter members of the Rhode Island Woman Suffrage Association in 1868. At the center of this burgeoning network of antislavery societies was a reading room in Providence that distributed penny literature graphically depicting the evils of slavery.[43]

[42] W.G. to *Emancipator*, April 1836; Stanton's address at an antislavery meeting in Warwick, Rhode Island, reported in the *Liberator*, 30 May 1835.

[43] *Liberator*, 18 April, 26 December 1835; Eliza J. Chace to Emily A. Winsor, 27 July 1837, Rhode Island MSS, Brown University Library; Nancy Kathleen Cassidy, "A History of the Rhode Island Woman Suffrage Association" (history honors thesis, Brown University, 1973), chap. 1; Amy L. Nathan, "Paulina Wright Davis" (history honors thesis, Brown University, 1977), RIHS; and Charles R. Crowe, "Transcendentalism and the Providence Literati," *Rhode Island History* 14 (July 1955): 65-78.

The conjunction of Stanton's thorough organizational work and the southern outcry over the "postal campaign," as abolitionists flooded the mail with thousands of antislavery tracts, aroused the opposition of some of the state's wealthiest and most influential citizens. In the late summer and fall of 1835 Providence and four other Rhode Island communities held anti-abolitionist town meetings. As the organizers of these meetings explained, the abolitionists' "exaggerated statements and inflammatory appeals" had frightened southerners into burning antislavery tracts and apprehending alleged agents. There was even talk of secession, a specter raised three years earlier when South Carolina attempted to nullify the Tariff of Abominations. The town meetings thus took place in an atmosphere of intense public concern, in what Providence anti-abolitionists termed a "crisis" that was "big with peril to the Union of the States and to the supremacy of the laws." Townspeople assembled to discuss how such a dangerous threat to the peace of their communities and to the survival of the young republic should be met.[44]

Local notables dominated each of these meetings, drafting resolves designed both to allay southern fears and to intimidate the abolitionists. The thirty-six men who called the town meeting in Providence on 2 November 1835 included representatives from some of the city's most illustrious families.[45] Nicholas Brown and his kinsman Moses Brown Ives represented the firm of Brown & Ives, which had became extensively involved in cotton manufacturing after making a fortune in maritime commerce. Ives's brother-in-law, Professor William G. Goddard of Brown University, also attended the meeting. Joining the Brown clan were a number of other prominent men: Edward Carrington, scion of an old merchant family; Wilbur Kelley, Carrington's partner in a cotton mill; Samuel Dexter, who ran a large bleachery; John Slater, son of the pioneer manufacturer and manager of the family's office in Providence; and Benjamin Cozzens, proprietor of a Warwick mill employing more

[44] *Providence Journal*, 4 November 1835. Anti-abolitionist meetings were held in Woonsocket on 22 August, Pawtucket on 9 September, Newport on 14 September, Lime Rock (Smithfield) on 16 October, and Providence on 2 November 1835. For accounts of these meetings, see the *Woonsocket Patriot*, 29 August 1835; *Pawtucket Chronicle*, 11 September 1835; *Newport Mercury*, 19 September 1835; and the *Providence Journal*, 27 October, 4 November 1835, respectively.

[45] Providence anti-abolitionists were those men whose names appeared as signers of the resolutions printed in the *Providence Journal*, 4 November 1835.

than four hundred operatives. Flanking them on the platform were former governor James Fenner and future U.S. Senator John H. Clarke. Of the twelve men for whom detailed biographical information is available, nine were born into families that gave them wealth, business connections, higher education, and a tradition of family prominence, or some combination of these advantages. Those without inherited family wealth or connections—like Smith Bosworth, an agent for a bleaching company—had fared well enough to join forces with members of the Providence elite at a critical moment in the city's history.[46]

More than kinship and business ties, however, bound the anti-abolitionists. Their ad hoc organization reflected a corporate identity based on occupational status, property holding, residential propinquity, and religious affiliation. Half of the thirty-six men were merchants. Five were wealthy gentlemen whose occupations were not given in the city directory. Seven were manufacturers or agents. Two more were cashiers, another two city officials, and still another a wholesale grocer. Goddard was the sole professor among them. Unlike anti-abolitionists in Utica, New York, and Cincinnati, Ohio, most of these men had successfully made the transition from a mercantile to a manufacturing economy.[47] Certainly the textile manufacturers among them had a vested interest in preserving comity—and trade—with the South. Thirty-three of the men ranked among the top two-fifths of the city's property owners (owning property valued at more than twenty-seven hundred dollars); twenty were among the top 10 percent with property worth more than fourteen thousand dollars. Six boasted more than one hundred thousand dollars in property. Though residential segregation was not yet pronounced in Providence by 1835, most of these men lived within a few blocks of each other in the wealthiest neighborhoods of the city: either on College Hill, or just across the Providence River along Westminster Street in what was soon to become the central business district. At least fourteen were Episcopalians, another ten Unitari-

<hr>

[46] James B. Hedges, *The Browns of Providence Plantations: The Nineteenth Century* (Cambridge: Harvard University Press, 1968), 184-85, 248-53; *Biographical Cyclopedia of Rhode Island*, 49-50, 209, 223-26; Zuckerman, "The Political Economy of Industrial Rhode Island," 28, 49, 75.

[47] Richards, *"Gentlemen of Property and Standing,"* 134-50. Cf. Mary P. Ryan, *Cradle of the Middle Class: The Family in Oneida County, New York, 1790-1865* (Cambridge: Cambridge University Press, 1981), 113-15, which qualifies Richards's interpretation.

ans. Two more were trinitarian Congregationalists. Nicholas Brown was the sole Baptist among them.

If they were joiners, the anti-abolitionists favored meliorist associations like the short-lived Society for the Encouragement of Faithful Domestic Servants, organized in January 1831. Dismayed by the casual work habits of black servants who took "service by the day," the society attempted to establish a registry of reliable servants. Many of its charter members, who included sixteen anti-abolitionists, also led the drive for municipal incorporation. Heading the society was merchant Samuel W. Bridgham, the city's first mayor. Eleven anti-abolitionists belonged to the Rhode Island Bible Society, which had distributed New Testaments around the state since its founding in 1813; another was active in its auxiliary, the Young Men's Bible Society. Singularly few of the anti-abolitionists, however, took an active part in the temperance movement. Only four appear to have been officers in any of the city's antebellum temperance organizations; the names of four others appear on the two membership lists extant from the 1830s. In addition, the elderly Nicholas Brown signed a memorial in 1840 against the navy's practice of giving rum to its seamen.[48]

These notables called the public meeting in Providence as a sign to anxious southerners that the "large majority" of the city's inhabitants, particularly its merchant elite, did not condone abolitionist agitation. Although conceding the evils of slavery, they feared that immediate emancipation would produce far greater evils. "All coercive measures for the abolition of slavery," they declared, "are in violation of the sacred rights of property, and of the fundamental provisions of the national compact." Since the Constitution sanc-

---

[48] *First Annual Report of the Providence Society for the Encouragement of Faithful Domestic Servants* (Providence: H. H. Brown, 1832), 6; "Memorial on the Spirit Ration in the Navy," 20 December 1840, Miscellaneous Uncatalogued MSS, RIHS. For a discussion of meliorist voluntary associations like the Society for the Encouragement of Faithful Domestic Servants, see Carroll Smith Rosenberg, *Religion and the Rise of the American City: The New York City Mission Movement, 1812-1870* (Ithaca: Cornell University Press, 1971). See also Susan Porter Benson's analysis of the activities of the elite women who belonged to the Providence Employment Society, three of whom were married to anti-abolitionists (only one to an abolitionist, Henry Cushing). Like their male counterparts, these women preferred meliorist reforms to the temperance or antislavery movement. "Business Heads and Sympathizing Hearts: The Women of the Providence Employment Society, 1837-1858," *Journal of Social History* 12 (Winter 1978): 306-307.

tioned the peculiar institution, slave states should "be left to act, in this the most important of their municipal concerns, equally free from dictation, interference or control." Attempts to ban the slave trade from the District of Columbia were especially "inexpedient" considering "the present irritable state of public sentiment." Their great respect for local rule reflected the anti-abolitionists' particularistic view of the Union. Federalism, as they interpreted it, reserved a large measure of autonomy for states and communities. Local control, in turn, tended to mean rule by elites who normally controlled the organs of public opinion and, through personal influence, set the tone for the rest of society.[49]

The public meetings gave the anti-abolitionists the opportunity to reassert their customary prerogatives of leadership and play the same paternalistic role they had played in years past. On this occasion they sought to calm "public sentiment" while at the same time meeting a dire threat to community stability. For this reason, they were careful in their condemnation of the abolitionists to distinguish antislavery agents, particularly Charles Stuart and George Thompson, "foreign emissaries, with large appointed salaries," from the rank and file of the movement, men, women, and even children who did not suspect "the criminal designs of those leaders." In making this distinction, the anti-abolitionists reaffirmed an older view of society consistent with their paternalism. According to this perspective, society consisted of two well-defined groups: an elite, distinguished by badges of wealth, birth, and culture, who customarily debated the options open to the community and recommended a course of action for the people to follow; and the people, who, deferring to the "superior capacity" of their leaders, ratified the elite's recommendation and, in this way, gave it the appearance and force of community consensus.[50]

This is precisely what occurred at the Providence anti-abolitionist

[49] *Providence Journal*, 4 November 1835. On the particularistic views that federalism enshrined, see Thomas Bender, *Community and Social Change in America* (New Brunswick, N.J.: Rutgers University Press, 1978), 78-108. And on the heightened concern with order (and disorder) among anti-abolitionists in Boston, see Theodore M. Hammett, "Two Mobs of Jacksonian Boston: Ideology and Interest," *Journal of American History* 62 (March 1976): 845-68.

[50] *Newport Mercury*, 19 September 1835. My discussion of deference draws on J.G.A. Pocock, "The Classical Theory of Deference," *American Historical Review* 81 (June 1976): 516-23.

meeting. A committee reported ten resolutions condemning the abolitionists. After these had been "unanimously adopted," several "gentlemen" spoke "in a very spirited manner, on the constitutionality of the subject, and the danger of interfering with the vested rights of other States, as guaranteed by the Constitution." Remembering all too well the "exasperated passions and the terrific despotism of the mob," the speakers invoked "the supremacy of the laws," and maintained that "it is the duty of Legislatures, of Courts, and of Juries, by all constitutional and legal means, to take care of the public safety and happiness." A mob might put abolitionists to flight in Utica, but anti-abolitionists in Providence preferred gag laws and the judicious use of vagrancy statutes. In short, the community's traditional leaders would themselves see to it that the abolitionist menace was quelled.[51]

Neither the public outcry over the postal campaign nor the formidable stature of their critics, however, kept Stanton and other abolitionist agents from their appointed rounds. Early in 1836 more than 850 Rhode Islanders signed a call for the formation of a state antislavery society. For three days in February, about 375 state delegates, joined by seventy-five delegates from out of state, assembled at Providence's High Street Congregational Church. From their meeting emerged the Rhode Island Anti-Slavery Society.

One hundred and two men from Providence either signed the call for a state convention or represented the city at this convention; of these ninety-six can be identified.[52] Whether compared in terms of occupation, property holding, religious affiliation, or associational membership, local abolitionists stood in striking contrast to the gentlemen of property and standing who opposed them. None of them belonged to the city's elite. To be sure, a few by 1836 had accumulated significant amounts of property. Joseph Bogman, a

[51] *Providence Journal*, 4 November 1835; Richards, *"Gentlemen of Property and Standing,"* 85-92. In October 1835 Newport anti-abolitionist Benjamin Hazard introduced a gag law in the General Assembly. This bill was still pending when the state antislavery convention met in February 1836. By means of strenuous lobbying antislavery forces defeated the bill the following summer. William Goodell, *Slavery and Antislavery: A History of the Great Struggle in Both Hemispheres* (New York: W. Harned, 1852), 415-20.

[52] These men were traced to the city directory and the tax list for 1836. For their names, see *Proceedings of the Anti-Slavery Convention,* 4; and the *Providence Journal,* 2 February 1836.

forty-seven-year-old carpenter, with fifteen thousand dollars in real estate, was the richest man among the abolitionists. James Eames, who dealt in stoves, possessed property valued at nine thousand dollars. Henry Cushing, who had come to Providence in 1800 to work as an apprentice for his brother, had accumulated four thousand dollars' worth of property as the proprietor of a paperhanging shop. Stephen S. Wardwell, thirty-five years old, was a cashier worth approximately two thousand dollars.[53]

More typical, however, were the young men who were just launching their careers. Amos C. Barstow, only twenty-two, still clerked for his father-in-law, James Eames; before the year was out, he had established his own stove company. Its success made him a near-millionaire by the time of his death in 1894. Twenty-nine-year-old Nicholas A. Fenner had completed a three-year stint as a carpenter's apprentice, spent another year in the employ of his former master, and then worked a year as a journeyman. At the time of the antislavery convention he and a partner built machinery for cotton mills. In 1842 Fenner was among the founders of the New England Butt Company, one of the first manufacturers of braiders and wire machinery in the country. Irish-born Thomas Davis, also twenty-nine years old, had immigrated to Providence while still a child. Entering the jewelry business at an early age, he prospered as a manufacturing jeweler. Elected state representative from North Providence in 1845, Davis then represented Rhode Island in Congress from 1853 to 1855 as an antislavery Democrat. There he won fame throughout the North for opposing the Kansas-Nebraska Act and reputedly leading three thousand Democratic voters into the new Republican party.[54]

These men were some of the more successful, or at least less anonymous, abolitionists. But the features of their lives—common school educations followed by apprenticeships or clerkships, occupations as skilled craftsmen or shopkeepers, and comfortable if, in most cases, unspectacular prosperity or expectations of upward mo-

[53] Information for these sketches came from Richard M. Bayles, ed., *History of Providence County, Rhode Island*, 2 vols. (New York: W. W. Preston Co., 1891), 2:604-605; and Arthur E. Wilson, *Paddy Wilson's Meeting-House in Providence Plantations, 1791-1839: Being an Account of a Genial Irish Parson Who Shaped a Community's Culture and Life* (Boston: Pilgrim Press, 1950), 156-74.

[54] *Biographical Cyclopedia of Rhode Island*, 309-311, 345; *Providence Journal*, 27 July 1895.

bility—typified those of the other abolitionists. Twenty-four of the men whose occupations can be determined were shopkeepers or small proprietors, twelve more worked as clerks, cashiers, and teachers, and twenty-nine were artisans. Indeed, fully a quarter of the abolitionists (as opposed to only two of the anti-abolitionists) belonged to the Mechanics' Association; Henry Cushing was its long-time treasurer and Amos Barstow later served as its president. The abolitionists also numbered five clergymen, three attorneys, and a dentist. Only six of the abolitionists, including the two blacks in the sample, pursued semiskilled or unskilled occupations. A few, like Wyllys Ames, a Sabbath school agent, and editor William Goodell, were among the first Americans to make a profession out of moral and social reform.[55] Not a single one, however, was a merchant or a gentleman. The abolitionists, then, represented not a rival elite but the city's "bone and muscle," artisans and shopkeepers drawn from the city's middle classes.

Not surprisingly, the abolitionists were far less wealthy than their opponents. As a group, they were only slightly better off than the city's taxpayers as a whole. Forty-five (44 percent) of them did not pay taxes because they owned property worth less than two hundred dollars. (Approximately three-fifths of the city's adult white males were not assessed.) About a third were among the lower half of all taxpayers in Providence, with less than nineteen hundred dollars in taxable wealth. Only fourteen ranked among the top two-fifths of the city's property holders. But the wealth of even the richest, Joseph Bogman, paled in comparison to the six anti-abolitionists worth more than one hundred thousand dollars each.

Those abolitionists who remained in Providence, however, had reasonable expectations of bettering their condition. Of the sixty men from this sample still in the city in 1850, half had risen in occupational status—generally from skilled craftsmen to shopkeepers—or had acquired substantially more property. None of the others slipped. Few abolitionists, however, ever became as wealthy or as prominent as an Amos Barstow, Nicholas Fenner, or Thomas Davis. John Prentice appears to have been one of the more successful. The federal census of 1850 reported that Prentice, a merchant

[55] Ronald G. Walters, *The Antislavery Appeal: American Abolitionism after 1830* (1978; reprint, New York: W. W. Norton & Co., 1984), 22-23.

tailor who possessed less than two hundred dollars in property at the time of the antislavery convention, was the proprietor of a small shop employing four men and ten women, capitalized at ten thousand dollars. Most of the abolitionists achieved more modest success. Typical was Horace Reed. Born in the small town of Coventry, Rhode Island, he had migrated while still a young man to Providence, where he worked as a paperhanger. After saving enough money to open a grocery store in 1853, Reed eventually retired to a farm in Coventry in 1867.[56]

The Second Great Awakening helps explain why many of these men joined the antislavery crusade.[57] Fully two-fifths of the sample were members of the city's three Congregational churches. Since 1831 each of these churches had experienced "protracted meetings" or revivals that gathered in new converts and renewed religious fervor. At the Beneficent Congregational Church in August 1831 future abolitionist Stephen S. Wardwell heard the noted evangelist Charles Grandison Finney preach "on the subject of the free moral agency of man, in which it was conclusively shewn [sic] that man has the power to choose either good or evil as he is disposed to [and] is therefore accountable to God for the choice he makes." In 1839 Congregational laymen, believing that "slavery is a sin, in which the churches have largely and criminally participated," established the Union Congregational Anti-Slavery Society in order to "purify" the church of any remaining connection with slavery.[58]

Another fifth of the abolitionists, including all five clergymen in the sample, were Baptists. Like Deacon Thomas Northup, who signed the call for the state convention, many of them had been converted during recent revivals. In his three years as pastor of the Pine Street Baptist Church from 1834 to 1837, John Blain, one of the

[56] Federal Manuscript Census for Rhode Island, 1850, RIHS; J. R. Cole, *History of Washington and Kent Counties, Rhode Island* (New York: W. W. Preston & Co., 1889), 1338.

[57] They differed in this respect from the secular workingmen who signed abolitionist petitions in New York City. See John B. Jentz, "The Antislavery Constituency in Jacksonian New York City," *Civil War History* 27 (June 1981): 101-22.

[58] Wardwell diary, vol. 11, 18 August 1831; Union Congregational Anti-Slavery Society, *Constitution, with an Address to the Beneficent, Richmond-Street and High-Street Congregational Churches* (Providence: H. H. Brown, 1839), 3-4. Anne C. Loveland emphasizes this link in "Evangelicalism and 'Immediate Emancipation' in American Antislavery Thought," *Journal of Southern History* 32 (May 1966): 172-88.

delegates to the state antislavery convention, baptized more than 250 persons—the greatest revival in the church's history. Like the Congregationalists, with whom they differed only on the issue of infant baptism, these Baptists distrusted sensuality, license, and a life without restraint. In observing prohibitions against the use of alcohol, Sunday travel and recreation, and frivolous amusements written into their church covenants, they too practiced rigorous self-discipline. Church members who strayed from the fold were admonished, suspended from fellowship, and occasionally excommunicated.[59]

Still other local abolitionists came from churches that had opened their doors to antislavery speakers between 1832 and 1836. Although this sample from 1836 includes only three Methodists, there is evidence of a much larger Methodist antislavery contingent. When abolitionists requested the use of the Chestnut Street Church for antislavery meetings, the trustees insisted that any blacks who attended be segregated in the gallery. Chafing at this racial prejudice, Deacon William F. Hammond, a carpenter, and other antislavery Methodists withdrew in 1841 to from the Wesleyan Methodist Church, "based on antislavery principles, with no bishop and no presiding elder."[60]

Of the ten Unitarians in this sample, all but one worshiped at the Westminster Church, whose minister, Frederick A. Farley, attended antislavery meetings in Boston. Only one of the Unitarians among the anti-abolitionists seems to have worshiped there.[61] For a number of abolitionist Unitarians, men like William M. Chace and George L. Clarke, partners in a dyestuffs firm, Joseph J. Cooke, a real estate developer, Joseph A. Barker, a hardware dealer, Christopher Greene, a teacher, and Thomas Davis, abolitionism marked a way station on the road to Transcendentalism and the "universal broth-

---

[59] *The Centennial Services of the Central Baptist Church, Providence, Rhode Island* (Providence: Remington Printing Co., 1906), 24.

[60] "Trustees' Book of the [Chestnut Street] Methodist Society," 1817-1902, 17 September 1838, 2 December 1839, Vestry of the Trinity Union Methodist Episcopal Church, Providence; William F. Hammond, "A History of the Foundation Street Wesleyan Methodist Church," *Narragansett Historical Register* 6 (1888): 37-46; Donald G. Mathews, *Slavery and Methodism: A Chapter in American Morality, 1780-1845* (Princeton: Princeton University Press, 1965).

[61] *Liberator*, 6 June 1835; Westminster Unitarian Church, Records of the Society, vol. 1, 28 October, 2 November 1839, 4 June 1844, RIHS.

erhood" and "universal church" of Fourierism. In the 1840s Davis, Chace, Greene, and Clarke lived briefly at Holly Home, a utopian "cottage" on the outskirts of Providence, where "they dwel[t] in anti-slavery simplicity" and published their own Transcendentalist newspaper, the *Plain Speaker*.[62]

The abolitionists were far more likely than their opponents to belong to the moral reform societies that were busy remaking the antebellum North along Christian lines. Some, like Amos Barstow and Stephen Wardwell, were Sunday school teachers and superintendents. The eight abolitionists who were members of the Providence Religious Tract Society combatted both religious indifference and the abhorrent doctrine of universal salvation preached by the Universalists.[63] Sixteen abolitionists opposed war as members of the Rhode Island Peace Society; only three anti-abolitionists did so. The Reverend Thomas Williams, James Eames, John Prentice, and attorney Samuel S. Ashley were among the charter officers of the Providence Graham Society. Like dietary reformer Sylvester Graham, who had lectured in Providence in January 1834 on "the Science of Human Life," they believed that self-control could be achieved through vegetarianism, avoidance of coffee, tea, and other stimulants, and sexual continence. Samuel Ashley, William Chace, and Thomas Davis crusaded against capital punishment as spokesmen for the antigallows movement in Rhode Island. Significantly, at least fifty-eight of the abolitionists had taken the temperance pledge. Only one, however, Henry Cushing, had been among the charter members of the Society for the Encouragement of Faithful Domestic Servants.[64]

[62] Leo Stoller, "Christopher A. Greene: Rhode Island Transcendentalist," *Rhode Island History* 22 (October 1963): 103. See also Charles R. Crowe, "Utopian Socialism in Rhode Island, 1845-1850," ibid. 18 (January 1959): 20-26; ibid., "The Religious History of a Christian Socialist: Joseph J. Cooke's 'A Personal Relation,'" ibid. 23 (July 1964): 81-89; and Anne C. Rose, *Transcendentalism as a Social Movement, 1830-1850* (New Haven: Yale University Press, 1981), 128n, 140-61.

[63] Providence Association of Sabbath School Teachers, MS Records, 1827-54, RIHS; *Twelfth Annual Report of the Providence Religious Tract Society* (Providence: H. H. Brown, 1837), 2.

[64] *Graham Association* (n.p., n.d.), 5; Stephen Nissenbaum, *Sex, Diet, and Debility in Jacksonian America: Sylvester Graham and Health Reform* (Westport, Conn.: Greenwood Press, 1980); Abzug, *Passionate Reformer*, 157-60; Philip English Mackey, "'The Result May Be Glorious'—Anti-Gallows Movement in Rhode Island, 1838-1852," *Rhode Island History* 33 (February 1974): 19-30.

Because the abolitionists were drawn from each of the city's six wards, as well as from a variety of occupations and churches, the antislavery society played a crucial role in forging an identity based on common interest and devising a language with which to defend it. Joining an antislavery society linked state abolitionists to similarly inclined individuals in other parts of the nation. Their network of agents and societies enabled them, whenever necessary, to bypass uncooperative local elites. This is precisely what they had done in 1835-36.[65]

In a long report published shortly after their state convention in 1836, the abolitionists attempted to dispel their public image as reckless fanatics bent on disrupting the Union. Invoking the rich heritage of the American Revolution, they portrayed themselves as the righteous defenders of republican liberties. Abolitionism, they contended, signified more than "the restoration of men from the condition of 'chattels' to the condition of rational beings." Rather, "to defend *by* principle, and *on* principle, the right of free discussion, is to be an Abolitionist *in* principle and *practice*." Here they identified immediate emancipation and other root-and-branch reforms with a broad producers' community, consisting of all those who worked with both their hands and their brains, whether self-employed or still wage earners—an identification that would become commonplace in the North by the 1850s. "Have the laboring classes in America," the abolitionists asked, "a right to the present enjoyment of civil and religious freedom?" They recalled how gentlemen had disparaged William Lloyd Garrison's opinion because he was an "obscure mechanic."[66]

Following the example of the temperance movement, the abolitionists relied on voluntary associations to organize the public and to mold its opinion. They too believed in the "power of the truth." As one temperance report had put it, "In this cause knowledge is emphatically power; it dispels ignorance, disarms prejudice, awakens conscience, and thus moves to action."[67] Here was the formula for action that all such reformers invoked: carry the self-evident

---

[65] On the ability of abolitionists to circumvent local elites, see Richards, *"Gentlemen of Property and Standing,"* 166-68; and Bender, *Community and Social Change*, 100-108.

[66] *Proceedings of the Anti-Slavery Convention*, 40, 57, 39, 31.

[67] *Total Abstinence: A Report of the Board of Managers of the Providence Association for the Promotion of Temperance* (Providence: W. Marshall & Co., 1832), 9.

principles of one's cause to the public, appeal to its conscience, and the middle classes would quickly take up the reform. Lectures, tracts, and petitions circulated by voluntary associations would "correct public opinion, and arouse public feeling in New England." The abolitionists were just as convinced as temperance spokesmen that their cause "requires only to be understood, to receive the approbation of all who justly estimate the value of moral influences."[68]

Once this information had been disseminated, the abolitionists felt confident that their fellow northerners would quickly come to regard the slaveholding South as the very antithesis of a free labor and Christian society. Slavery, they contended, abrogated "the family condition," invited "the sensual of all colors to wallow in the mire of her impurity," made "labor disreputable" by expropriating the slave's product and, by "inducing idleness," led to "intemperance and gaming." In sum, it threatened domesticity, self-discipline, industry, and self-improvement—all values dear to the hearts of middle-class northerners. Abolitionists thus appropriated the millennial rhetoric of evangelicals like Francis Wayland. They simply substituted slavery for intemperance as the evil so "multiform" that it was "an imperative moral duty to exert all lawful and practicable means to banish it from the earth." In the process, they went far beyond advocates of temperance in explicitly identifying the cause of moral reform with the middle classes.[69]

Whereas the state temperance movement could normally depend on accustomed channels of communication like the press and pulpit to disseminate information, few clergymen and even fewer newspaper editors in the 1830s were willing to advocate the immediate emancipation of the slaves. Although practically all the city's clergymen spoke on behalf of total abstinence and even formed a Clerical Temperance Association to promote the cause, only a few Congregationalist and Baptist preachers joined the antislavery movement. Of the state's principal newspapers, only one, the *Pawtucket Chronicle*, reported abolitionist proceedings or commented fa-

---

[68] *First Annual Meeting of the Providence Anti-Slavery Society*, 8; Providence Association for the Promotion of Temperance, *Quarterly Report of the Committee, for July, 1830*, 7.

[69] *Proceedings of the Anti-Slavery Convention*, 21, 23, 24; *Providence Journal*, 2 February 1835. For a provocative analysis of the "cultural components of antislavery," see Walters, *Antislavery Appeal*, 70-128.

vorably on antislavery speakers. When the other newspapers took notice of the abolitionists, it was to cast aspersions.

With their message either ignored or denounced as subversive, the abolitionists had to rely on agents and a network of auxiliary societies. Agents carried letters of introduction to prominent citizens of the towns they visited requesting that a meetinghouse or a schoolroom be made available for an antislavery lecture. They suffered frequent harassment. While lecturing in East Greenwich in September 1835, for instance, Henry B. Stanton was served with a writ as a vagrant. In Newport, the following month, he claimed to have been mobbed. No wonder the abolitionists charged that at the bidding of "respectable gentlemen" who impugned the public's right to know, "the revellings of a bacchanalian mob" had broken up "large congregations of industrious *farmers and mechanics*, with their wives and children," who had assembled to discuss immediate emancipation.[70]

In casting Stanton and other antislavery agents as foreign emissaries, the anti-abolitionist resolves of 1835 missed the point. State abolitionists were not bent on simply substituting one group of notables for another, as their opponents frequently alleged, but rather on molding public opinion and mobilizing the middle-class public. "What is able to overthrow the present system of Slavery?" asked the abolitionists. "An enlightened, consolidated and wisely directed *public opinion*." And "how shall this be secured? By disseminating *light*," they answered, "by preaching the *truth*." Precisely there lay the real threat to deference and the traditional distinction between the gentry, who led, and the people, who followed. Indeed, the abolitionists annulled this distinction. They appealed instead to middle-class northerners whose claim to social superiority rested on their morality and the identity between their class interests and the public interest.[71]

As the crisis provoked by the postal campaign in the fall of 1835 subsided, the antislavery movement in Rhode Island faded from the public spotlight. Abolitionists continued to undertake controversial initiatives, quizzing political candidates about their views on slavery,

[70] John Prentice to Silas Weaver, 22 September 1835; Henry B. Stanton to Silas Weaver, 9 January 1836; announcement of a town meeting, East Greenwich, Rhode Island, 24 September 1835, Silas Weaver Papers, RIHS; Stanton, *Random Recollections*, 50-53; *Proceedings of the Anti-Slavery Convention*, 35.

[71] *Pawtucket Chronicle*, 31 January 1834.

indicting churches for "their connivance at Slavery," toying with the
idea of a third party, and even appointing a committee on woman's
suffrage.[72] But in holding annual conventions and raising money
through fairs and tea parties, the movement came more and more
to resemble other antebellum moral reform crusades. By 1846 the
state antislavery convention in Providence could "hold its sessions
day after day without attracting any notice." "Radicalism," commented the *Providence Journal*, "raves to empty benches."[73]

Yet in the meantime, as the *Journal* observed, "the moral sentiments of the community" had "grown deeper and stronger in their
abhorrence of the institution of domestic slavery." The very
churches that abolitionists had come out of only a few years earlier
were by this time taking strong stands against the peculiar institution. In 1844 the First Universalist Church adopted an antislavery
resolution proposed by its minister, and the Providence District
Conference endorsed the plan of separation that split the Methodist
Episcopal Church along sectional lines. The following year, the Reverend Dr. Edward B. Hall was among the 173 Unitarian ministers
who signed "A Protest against American Slavery."[74] Community opposition to slavery mounted after the passage of the Fugitive Slave
Act in 1850. When Congress adopted the Kansas-Nebraska Act in
1854 over Thomas Davis's opposition, more than fifteen hundred
citizens assembled at a public meeting to register their outrage.[75]

Though never attracting as many followers or raising as much
money as they had hoped, Rhode Island abolitionists nonetheless
formulated a distinctive view of northern society in a new middle-
class language twenty years before it became commonplace. Since

[72] *Providence Journal*, 31 July 1837, 18 November 1839, 8 January 1840, 13 November 1841; Lawrence J. Friedman, " 'Historical Topics Sometimes Run Dry': The State
of Abolitionist Studies," *Historian* 43 (February 1981): 177-94.

[73] *Providence Journal*, 19 November 1846.

[74] Ibid.; First Universalist Church, Records of the Church, 13 May 1844, RIHS;
Providence Conference Minutes, 1841-51, 3 July 1844, Vestry of the Mathewson
Street Methodist Episcopal Church, Providence; *Providence Journal*, 21 October
1845; Samuel J. May, *Some Recollections of Our Antislavery Conflict* (1869; reprint, New
York: Arno Press, 1968), 335-45. See also John R. McKivigan, *The War against Pro-
slavery Religion: Abolitionism and the Northern Churches, 1830-1865* (Ithaca: Cornell
University Press, 1984).

[75] *Proceedings of a Public Meeting of the Citizens of Providence, Held in the Beneficent Congregational Church, March 7, 1854, to Protest against Slavery in Nebraska* (Providence:
Knowles, Anthony & Co., 1854).

the antislavery cause "began with the stable middling class of society, and remains in their hands," editor William Goodell noted in
accounting for the strength of antislavery sentiment in Providence
and its vicinity, "its growth is therefore solid—not swollen with the
fickle tide of those who follow in the wake of the great and
wealthy."[76] The abolitionists thus defined a moral community of
producers that transcended sectarian, partisan, and even regional
distinctions. They envisioned a classless, homogeneous society, a
middle-class America, consisting of industrious, frugal, sober shopkeepers and artisans, whose values set them conspicuously apart
from the presumed idleness, extravagance, and dissipation of both
the rich and the poor. Though a product of social and economic differentiation, middle-class consciousness reflected a widespread
yearning for social and cultural homogeneity in a mobile, heterogeneous, and stratified society.[77]

It was precisely this morality that distinguished middle-class
northerners from the rich and the poor. After all, they were the
ones who supported such controversial reforms as immediate
emancipation, prohibition, and the remodeling of traditional patterns of work and leisure. They also proved the mainstay of the
public schools and such institutions of self-improvement as lyceums
and mechanics' institutes. Thus when Robert C. Pitman, justice of
the Supreme Court of Massachusetts, proclaimed at the annual
meeting of the Rhode Island Temperance Union in 1874, "You will
find in this battle as in any other great moral reform, that it is the
middle class that is to fight it," he echoed a morality-based definition
of the middle classes first expounded by abolitionists almost forty
years earlier. "The final victory" of any great reform, Pitman reminded his audience, was "not to be obtained through wealth,
through politicians, through appetite, but through morality alone."
Needless to say, it was the morality of the middle class that prevailed
in the mid-nineteenth-century North.[78]

[76] *Emancipator*, 2 June 1835. Arline Kiven estimates that between 1835 and 1838
from 1,500 to 2,000 Rhode Islanders joined antislavery societies. *Then Why the Negroes*,
59.
[77] Walters, *Antislavery Appeal*, 129-45; Donald G. Mathews, "The Second Great
Awakening as an Organizing Process, 1780-1830: An Hypothesis," *American Quarterly*
21 (Spring 1969): 39-40.
[78] Pitman quoted in the *Seventh Annual Report of the Rhode Island Temperance Union*
(Providence: Providence Press Co., 1875), 14.

2 MIDDLE-CLASS CULTURE IN THE PROCESS OF FORMATION

"SOCIETY," declared the Select Committee of the Providence Association of Mechanics and Manufacturers in 1852, "is composed of three classes—the rich, the poor and the middling. In New England, a smaller proportion of the first two classes are to be found than in any other place. It is the influence, therefore, which is exerted by the middling class," among which the members of the Mechanics' Association proudly numbered themselves, "that is most felt in the community." This celebration of the antebellum North as a middle-class society, rare in the 1830s, had become commonplace by the 1850s. In the previous two decades master craftsmen, shopkeepers, and other middle-class northerners who profited from an expanding domestic economy had begun to assert themselves in an effort to attain social status and political power commensurate with their economic success. As they grew more self-confident, they attempted to democratize and evangelize the industrial North. Thanks to the strong organizational networks they forged, their values—sobriety, strict Sabbath observance, domesticity, self-improvement, and the purposive use of spare time—eventually prevailed as cultural norms. A middle-class culture thus coalesced to complement the middle-class consciousness first expounded by the abolitionists in the 1830s.[1]

Providence, like other New England cities, grew at its most rapid rate ever in the years leading to the Civil War. Between 1832 and 1860, the city's population tripled from 17,000 residents to 51,000, almost 30 percent of the state's population. By then Rhode Island was the most urbanized state in the Union; more than two of every three of its citizens were living in incorporated communities of

---

[1] Records of the Providence Association of Mechanics and Manufacturers, vol. 5, 12 April 1852, RIHS.

2,500 inhabitants or larger. The consequent need for the social and cultural organization of rapidly growing cities like Providence prompted attempts to redefine the meaning of "community" and to restructure the social order around internal sanctions that would replace attenuated external restraints. Colonial Providence had enshrined a hierarchical order resting on social and cultural homogeneity and on deference to a merchant elite. But this traditional pattern foundered in the face of substantial in-migration, industrial development, and the rise of class consciousness. No longer able to depend on what sociologists were later to call the "face-to-face community," which tended to be restricted to family and neighborhood, city residents had to formulate new notions of community.[2]

Some people, particularly members of the Providence elite, attempted to revitalize paternalism. Others, particularly members of the city's middle classes, formed a host of new voluntary associations that proved crucial to the bonding of such a diverse population. Middle-class northerners saw in the mutual support and vigilance afforded by these associations an antidote to social disorder. Aided by their associational networks, they sought to remodel customary patterns of leisure they considered profligate, frivolous, and immoral. Their quest for a more "rational" sociability generated the characteristic cultural institutions of the mid-nineteenth-century industrial city—Sunday schools, young men's associations, public schools, lyceums, libraries, museums, and parks.

Around 1840, industrial development began to accelerate in Rhode Island. Over the next two decades, the state's industrial labor force doubled while output and productivity increased significantly in the cotton and woolen industries. Providence boomed, attracting a disproportionately large share of the state's business. In the process it became the unchallenged "second city" of New England after Boston. Guidebooks commonly described the city, "one of the most extensive manufacturing communities in the country," as "a bee hive of industry." Though profits from textile production flowed into Providence, making it one of the richest cities per capita in the country, few mills actually sprang up within the city limits. As late as 1850, Providence claimed only five of the state's 174 cotton mills and only two of its 52 woolen factories.

[2] Jeffrey G. Williamson, "Antebellum Urbanization in the American Northeast," *Journal of Economic History* 25 (December 1965): 592-608.

The Providence Athenaeum, c. 1870 (courtesy of the Rhode Island Historical Society)

Far more important to the city's future was the development of its "Five Industrial Wonders of the World," five companies that brought fame and prosperity to Providence. In 1831 the world-famous Gorham Manufacturing Company got its modest start when its founder, Jabez Gorham, began to manufacture silverware. In 1833 mechanic Joseph R. Brown entered the jewelry business with his father. Twenty years later, when Brown's former apprentice Lucian Sharpe became his partner, the firm was still quite small, employing only fourteen workmen. But as the manufacturer of precision tools like the Vernier Caliper, which Brown had invented, Brown & Sharpe expanded to become the city's largest employer. By 1849 the American Screw Company, founded eleven years earlier, had pioneered in the mass production of pointed screws on its way to becoming the largest screw manufacturer in the United States. During the Civil War, the Nicholson File Company, which had been founded by William T. Nicholson in 1839, mechanized the production of quality files. The Corliss Steam Engine Company, incorporated in 1857 by Providence inventor George Corliss, was the only machine shop in the country capable of producing, on short notice, a special turret for the USS *Monitor*. Corliss, who had migrated to Providence in 1844, received forty-eight patents in his lifetime and twelve more posthumously. He was most famous for the huge engine he designed to power the Centennial Exposition at Philadelphia in 1876.[3]

An expanding domestic economy created new opportunities, not only for the city's shopkeepers and mechanics, but also for nearby farmers. In 1850 there were almost half again as many boot- and shoemakers, tailors, leather goods workers, and other tradesmen in Providence as there had been only five years earlier. Yet another

[3] John C. Thompson, *Illustrated Hand-book of the City of Providence, R.I.* (Central Falls, R.I.: E. L. Freeman & Co., 1876), 95; B. Michael Zuckerman, "The Political Economy of Industrial Rhode Island, 1790-1860" (Ph.D. diss., Brown University, 1981), 206; Kurt B. Mayer, *Economic Development and Population Growth in Rhode Island* (Providence: Brown University Press, 1953), 37-48; George H. Kellner and J. Stanley Lemons, *Rhode Island: The Independent State* (Woodland Hills, Calif.: Windsor Publications, 1982), 67-69; Henry Dexter Sharpe, *Joseph R. Brown, Mechanic, and the Beginnings of Brown & Sharpe* (New York: Newcomen Society, 1949), 7-17; Robert W. Kenny, "George H. Corliss: Engineer, Architect, Philanthropist," *Rhode Island History* 40 (May 1981): 49-61. On the city's impressive wealth, see Edwin M. Snow, *Census of the City of Providence, Taken in July, 1855* (Providence: Knowles, Anthony & Co., 1856), 54-56; and the *Providence Journal*, 5 March 1856.

measure of artisanal prosperity was the greater wealth of members of the Mechanics' Association relative to the city as a whole. In 1833 only 15 percent of the resident members of the Mechanics' Association ranked in the upper fifth of the city's taxpayers; by 1857 the proportion had almost doubled to 29 percent.[4] The city's growth also encouraged the rapid commercialization of agriculture within the market radius of Providence. By 1840 local farmers were draining marshes, reclaiming land, and raising record crops of onions, carrots, turnips, and potatoes.[5]

The expansion of the domestic economy, in turn, lay behind "the political revolution of the 1850s," in which Amos C. Barstow and other "men of business" replaced professionals and merchants of "rank, style and station" as officeholders. In electing Barstow as their first businessman mayor in 1852, Providence voters followed the example of New Haven voters, who had elected Philip Galpin, a carpet manufacturer, mayor ten years earlier. Businessmen were also "politicized" in Springfield, Massachusetts, where the number of merchants, tradesmen, and manufacturers who sat on the Board of Aldermen rose by almost half between the 1850s and the 1870s.[6] Barstow's election set a pattern that lasted until 1892. With the single exception of his successor, Walter R. Danforth, a Democratic attorney and former newspaper editor, Providence mayors would be Republican businessmen. Barstow's election also foreshadowed the phenomenal success of Republican candidates across the North after 1854. Campaigning against both northern aristocrats and southern slaveholders, they appealed, in the words of Samuel

[4] Thomas Eric Mark, "Industry and the Irish in Providence, 1850" (undergraduate history paper, Brown University, 1973), 12-16, RIHS; *A List of the Members of the Providence Association of Mechanics and Manufacturers* (n.p., 1833); *Charter, By-Laws, Rules and Regulations of the Providence Association of Mechanics and Manufacturers* (Providence: Knowles, Anthony & Co., 1857). I have traced members of the association to the city tax lists for 1833 and 1857, respectively.

[5] Charles T. Jackson, *Report on the Geological and Agricultural Survey of the State of Rhode Island* (Providence: B. Cranston & Co., 1840), cited in Percy W. Bidwell, "The Agricultural Revolution in New England," *American Historical Review* 26 (July 1921): 688-89.

[6] The term "men of business" comes from the *Providence Patriot*, 23 October 1830; Robert A. Dahl, *Who Governs? Democracy and Power in an American City* (New Haven: Yale University Press, 1961), 25-31; Michael H. Frisch, *Town into City: Springfield, Massachusetts, and the Meaning of Community, 1840-1880* (Cambridge: Harvard University Press, 1972), 241-46.

Bowles, partisan editor of the *Springfield Republican*, to "the great middling interest class," those who "work with their own hands, who live and act independently, who hold the stakes of home and family, of farm and workshop, of education and freedom." Abraham Lincoln's victory in 1860 solidified the Republicans' hold on Rhode Island politics, which was not relinquished until 1935. Their success, together with Rhode Island's adoption of statewide prohibition in 1852, testified to the hegemony of middle-class values in the antebellum North.[7]

Amos C. Barstow and other middle-class reformers had good reason to be proud on the eve of the Civil War. After a long struggle, they had largely succeeded in remodeling customary patterns of recreation. By the 1850s it was common to contrast the decorum and restraint of their recreations with the promiscuity and disorder of more traditional amusements. Commenting on the quiet and dry celebration of the Fourth of July in 1857, the *Providence Journal* asked the rhetorical question, "Who cannot remember when the village taverns were the chief theatres for the exhibition and the stimulus of patriotism on the glorious fourth, when brutal games were the amusements of the populace, and when the number of wounded fighters at the close of the eventful day was fully equal to our loss at any battle of the revolution?" Since then, a new pattern of more rational and respectable sociability had emerged. "Not only are our towns and villages comparatively free from riotings and revellings, but they are enlivened by social gatherings, by picnics in the groves, by good old Rhode Island clambakes, by floral processions, by the public exercises of musical or other societies." No doubt the *Journal* took some literary license in order to dramatize the contrast between the past and the present, and to encourage its readers to conclude that Americans were indeed "progressing." But the editors were right in calling attention to the family-oriented, whole-

[7] Bowles quoted in Paul Goodman, "The Politics of Industrialism: Massachusetts, 1830-1870," in Richard L. Bushman et al., *Uprooted Americans: Essays to Honor Oscar Handlin* (Boston: Little, Brown & Co., 1979), 164. On the political revolution of the 1850s, see Eric Foner, *Free Soil, Free Labor, Free Men: The Ideology of the Republican Party before the Civil War* (New York: Oxford University Press, 1970); Michael F. Holt, *Forging a Majority: The Formation of the Republican Party in Pittsburgh, 1848-1860* (New Haven: Yale University Press, 1969); ibid., *The Political Crisis of the 1850s* (New York: John Wiley & Sons, 1978).

some recreations that temperance, antislavery, and other middle-class reform movements had propagated.[8]

Spurred by the revivals of the Second Great Awakening, middle-class reformers took the lead in attacking popular amusements that they associated with self-indulgence, Sabbath-breaking, and immorality. Their hostility to traditional patterns of leisure meshed well with the demands of an industrializing economy for a new labor discipline and for a punctual, industrious, and sober work force. Once amusements had taken place in small, homogeneous communities where they promoted social cohesion, enjoyed the patronage of gentlemen, and were not yet distinguished from work. As industrialization regularized the workday and workweek, however, work and leisure no longer mixed well. Eventually they separated and evolved into separate spheres. The middle-class attack on popular amusements hastened this process of separation.[9]

Until the temperance movement, launched in the late 1820s and

---

[8] *Providence Journal*, 11 July 1857. Stephen Yeo writes about Reading, England, that "what impressed those in Reading with a sense of before-and-after in relation to 'the great change' between early and mid- to late nineteenth-century Reading was the violence, disorderliness, and intermittency of pre-1840 Reading culture. Events were the focus of activity rather than associations, May Day Fairs rather than Temperance Festivals." *Religion and Voluntary Organisations in Crisis* (London: Croom Helm, 1976), 37.

[9] Much has been written on the contrast between pre-industrial and industrial leisure patterns. British works on this subject include Robert W. Malcolmson, *Popular Recreations in English Society, 1700-1850* (Cambridge: Cambridge University Press, 1973); Brian Harrison, "Religion and Recreation in Nineteenth-Century England," *Past and Present* 38 (December 1967): 98-125; Peter Bailey, *Leisure and Class in Victorian England: Rational Recreation and the Contest for Control, 1830-1885* (London: Routledge & Kegan Paul, 1978). Cf. Hugh Cunningham, *Leisure in the Industrial Revolution, 1780 to 1880* (London: St. Martin's Press, 1980), which, to a much greater extent than the preceding works, stresses the continuity between pre-industrial and industrial recreations. American works include Paul G. Faler, *Mechanics and Manufacturers in the Early Industrial Revolution: Lynn, Massachusetts, 1780-1860* (Albany: State University of New York Press, 1981); Alan Dawley and Paul Faler, "Working-Class Culture and Politics in the Industrial Revolution: Sources of Loyalism and Rebellion," *Journal of Social History* 9 (June 1976): 466-80; David Montgomery, "The Shuttle and the Cross: Weavers and Artisans in the Kensington Riots of 1844," *Journal of Social History* 5 (Summer 1972): 411-46; Eric Foner, *Tom Paine and Revolutionary America* (New York: Oxford University Press, 1976), 45-56; Paul E. Johnson, *A Shopkeeper's Millennium: Society and Revivals in Rochester, New York, 1815-1837* (New York: Hill and Wang, 1978); Jill Siegel Dodd, "The Working Classes and the Temperance Movement in Ante-Bellum Boston," *Labor History* 19 (Fall 1978): 510-31; Bruce Laurie, *Working People of Philadelphia, 1800-1850* (Philadelphia: Temple University Press, 1980).

culminating in the early 1850s when almost every northern state adopted statewide prohibition, drink figured prominently in the work and leisure of Americans of all social classes. As one local resident recalled, merchants commonly greeted each other with "Good morning, Mr. A. or B., won't you walk in and take a glass of brandy or gin?" "Up to the modern era of total abstinence," reminisced former mayor Walter R. Danforth, "the most sober men would occasionally put aside their gravity and relieve the labors of the day with festivity and a little dissipation, and not a few who generally walked upright *during the day* would sometimes *at night* return to their homes with a *stone in their hats*." John Howland, president of the Mechanics' Association, defied the prevailing custom in 1827 when he persuaded the carpenters who were putting up his new house "to accept an equivalent in money for the customary supply of liquor" they normally received as partial payment for their services.[10]

Drink also lubricated virtually every social occasion. President George Washington drank wine and punch during his official visit to Providence in August 1790. So too did the Marquis de Lafayette on his triumphant return to the United States in 1824. On both occasions militiamen who had mustered for the occasion were treated to rum. During the 1820s wine flowed freely at banquets thrown by the Society of Cincinnati and at "Cotillion parties" held by the city's merchant elite. Even those critical of this pattern of sociability felt obliged to observe it. When Stephen S. Wardwell buried his mother in 1825, he noted sadly in his diary that, "I must say that I do not approve of the custom at funerals of having liquors to drink after the funeral and of having a large supper. It was not congenial with my feelings this afternoon, but such is the custom."[11]

Despite the success of the temperance movement, those at the

---

[10] William J. Brown, *The Life of William J. Brown, of Providence, R.I.* (Providence: Angell & Co., 1883), 93; Clarkson A. Collins, 3rd, "Pictures of Providence in the Past, 1790-1820: The Reminiscences of Walter R. Danforth," *Rhode Island History* 10 (April 1951): 47; Edwin M. Stone, *The Life and Recollections of John Howland, Late President of the Rhode Island Historical Society* (Providence: George H. Whitney, 1857), 227.

[11] Joseph K. Ott, "John Innes Clark and His Family—Beautiful People in Providence," *Rhode Island History* 32 (November 1973): 124; "An Old-Time Gala Day: The Visit of Lafayette to Providence in 1824," clipping in Sidney S. Rider, comp., "Contributions to the Local History of Rhode Island," Rider Collection, Brown University Library; receipt from Leon Chappotin for a dinner catered to the Society of Cincin-

margins of middle-class respectability clung to traditional values. Wine and other expensive fermented beverages were common at the salons and clubs of the rich and well-born. The merchants and professionals who joined the Providence Club in the late 1850s furnished their club with an ample stock of choice wines and liqueurs.[12] Unlike the wealthy and fashionable who sipped wine, the city's workingmen guzzled hardier drinks like whiskey. Indeed, for the city's volunteer firemen, copious amounts of alcohol "distributed gratuitously by shop and public bar keepers in the vicinity of the fire," were necessary to fortify them against "the inclemency of the weather" and the "imminent dangers from falling beams and crashing walls." Since fire companies enrolled brawny young men "notorious as pugilists and fighting characters," fights were common. Investigating a brawl between two rival companies that left a young Irish immigrant dead in 1853, a coroner's jury ruled that "the prime cause of the whole affray" had been "the free and intemperate use of intoxicating liquors." In the aftermath of the fatal brawl, the municipal government replaced the volunteers with paid firemen, whom it strictly prohibited from drinking on the job.[13]

Hopes for rooting out intemperance receded even further as thousands of immigrants arrived in the city. Irishmen first came to Providence in the late 1820s to build the Blackstone Canal, and stayed to lay the track bed for the railroads entering the city after 1835. By the late 1840s they had begun to move into the mills. From a scant two hundred in 1828 their numbers grew to more than ten

nati, 4 July 1821, Miscellaneous Uncatalogued MSS, RIHS; Elisha Dyer, "The Old Taverns of Providence," *Narragansett Historical Register* 5 (1886): 136-38; Almon D. Hodges, Jr., ed., *Almon Danforth Hodges and His Neighbors* (Boston: privately printed, 1909), 148, 324-29; Stephen S. Wardwell, Diary, 1818-39, vol. 6, 8 September 1825, Vestry of the Beneficent Congregational Church, Providence. For the pervasiveness of drink in pre-industrial society, see Brian Harrison, *Drink and the Victorians: The Temperance Question in England, 1815-1872* (Pittsburgh: University of Pittsburgh Press, 1971), 37-63; John Allen Krout, *The Origins of Prohibition* (New York: Alfred A. Knopf, 1925), 26-50; W. J. Rorabaugh, *The Alcoholic Republic: An American Tradition* (New York: Oxford University Press, 1979), 23-57; and Ian R. Tyrrell, *Sobering Up: From Temperance to Prohibition in Antebellum America, 1800-1860* (Westport, Conn.: Greenwood Press, 1979), 16-32.

[12] Providence Club, MS Records, RIHS.

[13] Letter from A. [Zachariah Allen], *Providence Journal*, 3 March 1854, quoted in Franklin C. Clark, "History of the Providence Fire Department, 1754-1904," typescript, 184, RIHS; Paul Gould, "Murder in Back of the Fire Department," typescript, 6, folder 558, David Patten Papers, RIHS.

thousand in 1855, or 22 percent of the city's population, nearly one and a half times their percentage (16 percent) of the state's population. Their influx accelerated by the famines of the 1840s, most arrived in Providence destitute, without industrial skills, and feared by many Protestants for their fervent Catholicism.[14] During the 1840s temperance spokesmen noted that these immigrants furnished "five-eighths of the criminal business before our Municipal Court," comprised "the majority among the inmates of our Jail and Asylum," and made up "almost the entire rank and file of our street beggars!" Yet these same spokesmen denounced the greed of native-born rum sellers, who preyed on the immigrants' poverty, and hailed the work of Catholic priests like Father John Corry in organizing parish societies for total abstinence. They also conferred their blessings on Father Theobald Mathew, the famous Irish "Apostle of Temperance," when he visited Providence in September 1849. After dining with the mayor and receiving the blessings of the city's Protestant clergymen, Father Mathew administered the pledge to an estimated three thousand Irishmen, many of whom were operatives enjoying a rare holiday.[15]

Although chiefly concerned with suppressing intemperance, which seemed to be the common denominator of all the city's social problems, middle-class reformers also attacked other popular pastimes at cross-purposes to religion. They particularly objected to the ways in which many of their fellow townspeople spent the Sabbath. Identifying the preservation of the republic with strict Sabbatarian observance, they insisted that Sunday be "a day of intellectual and moral improvement" conducted under religious auspices and not "a mere holiday for amusement and dissipation" or even "a mere day of rest and nothing more." As one local minister put it, "if this nation falls, *Sabbath Breaking* will be one cause of the awful catastrophe."[16]

---

[14] Snow, *Census of the City of Providence, Taken in July, 1855*, 16; Patrick T. Conley and Matthew J. Smith, *Catholicism in Rhode Island: The Formative Era* (Providence: Diocese of Providence, 1976).

[15] Rhode Island State Temperance Society, *Temperance in Rhode Island. Address of the State Society, for 1849* (Providence: Amsbury & Newton, 1849), 12; *Providence Journal*, 19-21 September 1849.

[16] "The Observance of Sunday," *Providence Journal*, 4 June 1870; Rev. Daniel Filmore quoted in the Records of the Providence Association of Sabbath School Teach-

Once the residents of Providence had kept the Sabbath strictly. Their "general and honorable regard for morality and a general performance of its duties" impressed Timothy Dwight, president of Yale University, when he visited Providence in 1796. Until the 1820s "Sabbath visiting," or "profaning the Sabbath, by visiting, recreation and inattention at meeting," was confined to mill towns like Smithfield where churches were weak. But as textile mills began to crop up on the outskirts of Providence, violations of the Sabbath became more common. Factory jobs tempted parents to pull their children out of school at an early age and send them to work to supplement the family's income. Youth loitered on street corners, drank, and even gambled on the Sabbath. "The holy Sabbath," lamented the Rhode Island Sunday School Union in 1830, "is hailed by this youthful throng, not as a season set apart for the worship of God, but as a day of relaxation from the severe and continued toils of the week, and is spent in slothful inactivity, or sports and recreations."[17]

For years, Protestant clergymen harped on the necessity for strict Sabbath observance. But there was powerful opposition to a return to the so-called Puritan Sunday. Lobbying Congress in the late 1820s to end Sunday mail delivery failed ignominiously, as did six-day barge and stage lines that refused to convey passengers on the Sabbath.[18] Although rebuffed by Congress and by travelers, Sabbatarians eventually triumphed by molding public opinion. In the 1830s and 1840s Baptists and Congregationalists added clauses to their church covenants that prohibited business, travel, and recrea-

---

ers, 1827-54, 21 August 1837, RIHS. The best analysis of nineteenth-century Sabbatarianism is Roy Zebulon Chamlee, Jr., "The Sabbath Crusade, 1810-1920" (Ph.D. diss., George Washington University, 1968).

[17] Timothy Dwight, *Travels in New England and New York*, ed. Barbara Miller Solomon, 4 vols. (Cambridge: Harvard University Press, 1969), 2:17; report from a Sabbath school teacher in Smithfield, Rhode Island, quoted in *Third Annual Report of the Providence Female Tract Society* (Providence: H.H. Brown, 1818), 6-7; *Fifth Annual Report of the Rhode-Island Sunday School Union* (Providence: H. H. Brown, 1830), 11.

[18] For attempts to rescind the Post Office Act and to set up six-day stage and barge lines, see Whitney R. Cross, *The Burned-over District: The Social and Intellectual History of Enthusiastic Religion in Western New York, 1800-1850* (Ithaca: Cornell University Press, 1950), 132-37; Charles C. Cole, Jr., *The Social Ideas of the Northern Evangelists, 1826-1860* (New York: Columbia University Press, 1954), 105-109; John R. Bodo, *The Protestant Clergy and Public Issues, 1812-1848* (Princeton: Princeton University Press, 1954), 39-43; Bertram Wyatt-Brown, "Prelude to Abolitionism: Sabbatarian Politics and the Rise of the Second Party System," *Journal of American History* 58 (September 1971): 329-35; Johnson, *A Shopkeeper's Millennium*, 83-88.

tion on the Sabbath. Even such a pious man as Wyllys Ames, who made a career of reform, was briefly suspended from the High Street Congregational Church in 1839 after he confessed to traveling on Sunday. Sabbatarian sentiment mounted until 1845, when liberal Protestants and evangelicals pooled their efforts in the Rhode Island Sabbath Union and endeavored to persuade "all persons to abstain from worldly business, travelling and amusements, and to attend the public worship of God on the Lord's Day." The *Providence Journal*, which in 1829 had ridiculed the Sabbatarian campaign to prevent Sunday mail delivery, praised the Sabbath Union's nonsectarian efforts. Within another decade, strict Sabbath observance had become a cultural norm in the industrial North. "I do not know as it is quite right to visit on Sundays," a city resident who was obviously wrestling with his conscience wrote in his diary in 1858, "but in this case the visit was not for any jollity or mirth."[19]

The city's Protestants also waged a long struggle against the theater, which they denounced as a nursery of vice whose "auxiliaries" included brothels, grog shops, and gambling dens. From the opening of the town's first theater in 1795, critics seized every opportunity to discourage theater-going. In 1812, after a disastrous fire in a Richmond, Virginia, theater, five hundred townspeople petitioned the General Assembly to close the Providence Theatre. "The performances of the Theatre," they charged, "have a tendency to corrupt the morals, especially of our youth; to repress industry and sanction idleness; to discourage virtue by diminishing its charms, and encourage vice by adding to its allurements." But just as in 1795, when the prominent merchant John Brown positioned a cannon in front of the embattled Providence Theatre and threatened to fire on trespassers, the patronage of the gentry protected the institution. Until the 1820s, "the theatre was made the scene of fashionable reunion, the place of full dress, of elegant demeanour, and of polite intercourse." But theater-going fell out of favor as the gentry began to spurn the company of boisterous workingmen in the

[19] High Street Congregational Church, Records of the Church, vol. 1, 6 August–3 December 1839, passim, included in the Records of the Union Congregational Church, RIHS; *Preamble and Constitution of the Rhode-Island Sabbath Union* (n.p., 1846); *Providence Journal*, 12 February 1829, 12 April 1845; Christopher T. Keith, Diary, 1854-71, vol. 1, 31 January 1858, RIHS.

audience. In 1832 the Providence Theatre closed its doors for good because of declining patronage.[20]

When a group of investors built a new theater in 1838, Samuel W. Wheeler, a Unitarian abolitionist who kept a temperance grocery, circulated a petition urging the Board of Aldermen not to grant a license. The petition, signed by more than six hundred (or a third) of the city's freemen, alleged that the proposed theater would set the wrong example for the city's youth. The theater's proprietors secured a license, but only after they promised not to sell "ardent spirits" on the premises, admit "persons of bad character," or schedule performances on Saturday evening or the Sabbath. Keeping up the fight against theatrical entertainment, the nearby Pine Street Baptist Church rang its bell during performances and invited Elder Jacob Knapp, an itinerant preacher, to threaten the actors with perdition. By this time most of the city's Baptist and Congregational churches had added clauses to their covenants that prohibited members from attending "theatrical and circus performances, balls and dancing parties," all "considered of evil and demoralizing tendency." Elder Knapp's prayers were evidently answered in 1844 when a fire destroyed the theater. Even before then, an English visitor to Providence remarked on the "grave taste of its inhabitants" in reporting that "the theatre is but rarely opened, and is then but very little frequented."[21]

In their campaigns against drink, Sabbath desecration, and theater-going, critics formulated new norms for the use of leisure time. As the annual report of the Rhode Island State Temperance Society explained in 1843, "we are *not* opposed to relaxation and amusement, either for the poor or the rich. By no means. But let it be re-

---

[20] Records of the Providence Association of Sabbath School Teachers, 1827-54, 19 January 1852, RIHS; Charles Blake, *An Historical Account of the Providence Stage: Being a Paper read before the Rhode Island Historical Society, October 25th, 1860* (Providence: George H. Whitney, 1868), 100, 76; Sally W. Barker, "The Story of the Stage in Rhode Island," typescript, RIHS; Edward M. Fay, "Providence Theatre," typescript, folder 125, David Patten Papers, RIHS; *Providence Journal*, 23 March 1832. For contemporary prejudice against theatrical entertainment, see Neil Harris, *Humbug: The Art of P. T. Barnum* (Boston: Little, Brown & Co., 1973), 36, 41.

[21] *Providence Journal*, 6, 14, 20 June 1838; Blake, *Historical Account of the Providence Stage*, 222-24, 243-47; *Constitution, Confession of Faith, Covenant, &c., and a List of Members of the High Street Congregational Church, Providence, R.I.* (Providence: Knowles & Vose, 1846), 16; J. S. Buckingham, *America, Historical, Statistic, and Descriptive*, 2 vols. (New York: Harper & Brothers, 1841), 2:431.

laxation and amusement that *shall* be rational and innocent. Let it put no blight on intellect, no shame on virtue, no sting on conscience." By "rational recreation," middle-class reformers insisted that the same values govern leisure as governed work. Like work, leisure should strengthen self-discipline, build character, and elevate morality. It was axiomatic, as Unitarian minister Dr. Edward B. Hall put it, that "all pleasures are forbidden that injure body or mind, that disqualify or disincline for pure gratifications, that divert the individual or others from religion and usefulness." Other amusements were "objectionable," according to the Reverend S. R. Dennen, "on account of the expense in time or in money, which they necessitate." The Reverend Edwin Stone proscribed still other amusements because of the bad example they set for the "laboring classes," who were wont "to 'live up to their means,' without thought for to-morrow." Extravagant dress, expensive amusements, and rowdy pleasure excursions were all examples of prodigality. In sharp contrast, rational recreation would be purposive, devoted to self-improvement, to mastering the skills of one's trade, and to learning more about the world.[22]

Rational recreation would also be family-centered, in accord with new definitions of gender roles. The cult of domesticity divided the world into male and female spheres. Middle-class men went out into the amoral business world to earn a livelihood and to advance their careers, while middle-class women stayed home to rear the children according to Christian precepts. No temperance tract, it seemed, was complete without depicting a broken home, where a destitute mother and her children or distraught parents anxiously awaited the return of the prodigal male tarrying at the local grog shop. Reformers constantly deplored the search for amusement outside the home. As the Reverend Mr. Stone complained, "Amusement is sought everywhere but at the fireside."[23] The cult of domesticity,

[22] *Report of the Rhode-Island State Temperance Society, for 1843* (Providence: B. T. Albro, 1844), 17; Edward B. Hall, D.D., *A Lecture on the Pleasures and Vices of the City* (Providence: Knowles, Anthony & Co., 1856), 10; "Discourse on the Tendencies of Amusement," *Providence Journal*, 11 November 1867; *Thirteenth Annual Report of the Ministry at Large* (Providence: Knowles, Anthony & Co., 1855), 20. Daniel T. Rodgers calls attention to "the Victorian concern with scarcity, with the economic necessity of constant doing" in *The Work Ethic in Industrial America, 1850-1920* (Chicago: University of Chicago Press, 1978), 10.

[23] *Ninth Annual Report of the Ministry at Large* (Providence: Albert C. Greene, 1851),

which made the home the locus of morality and women its custodians, thus set a home-centered, middle-class respectability against an aristocratic world of fashion and the promiscuous sociability of the poor. The home became a new source of values, from which respectability was to radiate through society.[24]

When not centered in the home, rational recreation took place in the churches and moral reform societies that had proliferated in the wake of the revivals of the Second Great Awakening. Following his conversion in 1820, when he swore off the theater and other "vain amusements," Stephen S. Wardwell spent his evenings at the Beneficent Congregational Church, where he was organist, choirmaster, and Sunday school superintendent, and at meetings of the antislavery, temperance, and tract societies to which he belonged.[25] But the strategy of enveloping the individual in protective networks of associations worked only for those who, like Wardwell, were already regular churchgoers. Something had to be done for the large proportion of the city's population who were "unchurched." To meet this need, the city's Protestants developed an impressive array of institutions targeted at different age groups.[26]

Sunday schools were the first such Protestant missions. Introduced to this country by Samuel Slater in 1796, they originated as interdenominational charity schools designed to teach poor children how to read and write as well as to draw them "from sport,

21. On the cult of domesticity, see Kathryn Kish Sklar, *Catherine Beecher: A Study in American Domesticity* (New York: W. W. Norton & Co., 1973); Nancy F. Cott, *The Bonds of Womanhood: "Woman's Sphere" in New England, 1780-1835* (New Haven: Yale University Press, 1977); and Mary P. Ryan, *Cradle of the Middle Class: The Family in Oneida County, New York, 1790-1865* (Cambridge: Cambridge University Press, 1981).

24 In several works Richard Sennett has provocatively raised the issue of privatization. See *Families against the City: Middle Class Homes of Industrial Chicago, 1872-1890* (Cambridge: Harvard University Press, 1970); and *The Fall of Public Man* (New York: Random House, 1978).

25 Stephen S. Wardwell, autobiographical account, in "Material Relative to Providence Sunday Schools," RIHS; Arthur E. Wilson, *Paddy Wilson's Meeting-House in Providence Plantations, 1791-1839: Being an Account of a Genial Irish Parson Who Shaped a Community's Culture and Life* (Boston: Pilgrim Press, 1950), 156-74.

26 On the networks of voluntary associations centered on the church, see Gregory H. Singleton, "Protestant Voluntary Associations and the Shaping of Victorian America," in *Victorian America*, ed. Daniel Walker Howe (Philadelphia: University of Pennsylvania Press, 1976), 47-58; Donald M. Scott, *From Office to Profession: The New England Ministry, 1750-1850* (Philadelphia: University of Pennsylvania Press, 1978), 43-45; and Mary P. Ryan, "The Power of Women's Networks: A Case Study of Female Moral Reform in Antebellum America," *Feminist Studies* 5 (Spring 1979): 66-85.

amusement and dissipation" on the Sabbath. Although their sponsors had to rebut criticism that the schools were meant only for the
poor, desecrated the Sabbath, or heralded the union of church and
state, these schools multiplied in the wake of the revivals of 1816-20.
Their pedagogy was simple. "We went there to study the Bible and
the New England Primer," reminisced Amos C. Barstow, who had
attended Sunday school at the Beneficent Congregational Church.
"We had no library, no lessons, no children's papers, no children's
hymns or music, and but little singing. The chief thing was the rep-
etition of Scripture, which often extended to several long chapters,
learned and recited by individuals." Industrious students received
books as rewards for memorizing prodigious numbers of verses. As
the children of artisans and shopkeepers entered the schools in
large numbers, and as evangelical Protestants came to stress the ca-
pabilities of children, Sunday schools became nurseries for future
church members. Soon they featured libraries stocked with children's literature, singing classes, juvenile temperance, benevolent,
and antiswearing societies. By the 1840s they even celebrated
Thanksgiving and Christmas with gala fetes.[27]

As sectarian institutions attached to particular churches, Sunday
schools appealed primarily to the children of church members.
How to reach out to the city's poor, who stayed away from Sunday
services because they could not afford the pew rents, were embar-
rassed by their tattered dress, or preferred secular pursuits, posed
a more difficult challenge. The city's Protestants tried to reach the
urban masses in a number of ways. Beginning in the 1820s, evangelical women employed a city missionary to visit the poor, distribute clothing and fuel (but never money), and refer them to jobs. He

[27] *Report of the Board of Trustees of the Bible Society of the State of Rhode-Island and Prov-
idence Plantations* (Providence: Miller & Hutchens, 1816), 5; "Annals of the Sunday
School," MS, Records of the Third Baptist Church, RIHS; Barstow quoted in James
Gardiner Vose, *Sketches of Congregationalism in Rhode Island, with Special Reference to the
History of the Beneficent Church* (New York: Silver, Burdett & Co., 1894), 166-67. For
interpretations of the Sunday school movement, see Anne M. Boylan, "Sunday
Schools and Changing Evangelical Views of Children in the 1820s," *Church History* 48
(September 1979): 320-33; Joseph F. Kett, *Rites of Passage: Adolescence in America, 1790
to the Present* (New York: Basic Books, 1977), 116-21; J.F.C. Harrison, *Learning and
Living, 1790-1960: A Study in the History of the English Adult Education Movement* (To-
ronto: University of Toronto Press, 1961); and Thomas Walter Laqueur, *Religion and
Respectability: Sunday Schools and Working Class Culture, 1780-1850* (New Haven: Yale
University Press, 1976).

also encouraged his wards to take the temperance pledge. In 1841 Unitarians and evangelicals collaborated in establishing a seamen's bethel; but their collaboration ended acrimoniously when the evangelicals charged the Unitarians with using the Sunday school to disseminate their heterodox doctrines. Several Protestant denominations also maintained free churches, which did not assess pew rents. In 1842 Episcopalians established Christ Church as a mission among the city's blacks. The following year, Stephen S. Wardwell was among those who helped organize the Free Evangelical Congregational Church.[28]

In the most ambitious mission to the city's poor, Unitarians, following the example of members of their denomination in Boston, dispatched a minister at large to the city's North End, where many poor day laborers and "those who have neither profession nor trade" presumably wallowed in poverty and vice. Edwin M. Stone, minister at large from 1847 until 1877, described his ministry as a "peculiar" one, covering "the whole ground of moral and social reform." To familiarize himself with the habits and needs of his poor neighbors, Stone walked between six and ten miles a day. Among the first things he did was to set up a Sunday school staffed by well-heeled volunteers from the city's two Unitarian churches. This school, Stone explained, stood "in the relation of helper to home instruction." Volunteers taught plain sewing to young girls and instructed their mothers on personal health and family diets. Periodic entertainments—concerts "strictly devotional and free from the features of exhibitions," tea parties, and floral fairs—were designed to wean neighbors from objectionable amusements.[29]

Evening schools, like the one maintained by the Ministry at Large, were designed to instill in youth, particularly those "without suitable parents or guardians," the "habits of sobriety and industry." Stone urged the city to establish age-specific institutions that would segregate the deviant from the rest of the community. So too did the

[28] Secretary's Book of the Providence Female Domestic Society, 1824-28, RIHS; "Mariner's Bethel Church," MS, RIHS; Christ Church, Records and Correspondence of the Vestry, 1842-51, RIHS; Free Evangelical Congregational Church, Records of the Society, 1843-78, RIHS.

[29] *Ninth Annual Report of the Ministry at Large*, 4; *Twelfth Annual Report* (Providence: Knowles, Anthony & Co., 1854), 3; *Nineteenth Annual Report* (Providence: Knowles, Anthony & Co., 1861), 13; *Twenty-Third Annual Report* (Providence: Knowles, Anthony & Co., 1865), 16.

Mechanics' Association, which in 1847 memorialized the city council on the need for a municipal "institution for the Confinement, Instruction and Reformation of idle and vicious persons." Shortly thereafter, it began to keep its library open six nights a week. Its petition led to the establishment of a municipal reform school in 1850.[30]

Middle-class reformers adopted a totally different strategy to deal with the thousands of single young men migrating to Providence in search of jobs. In April 1853 Unitarians and other liberal Protestants founded the Providence Young Men's Christian Union (YMCU), which made no distinction among young men on the basis of their religious affiliation. Characterizing itself as a secular institution with no relation to any organized church, the YMCU sought to promote an "elevated standard of *public Christian morality*." It thus reflected the Unitarian preference for ethics over doctrine. "The conversion of souls," declared one of its pamphlets, was "the peculiar province of the Churches." Spurning cooperation with liberal Protestants, evangelicals established a rival institution, the Providence Young Men's Christian Association (YMCA), which restricted active membership to young men who attended evangelical churches and whose officers represented the city's Baptist, Congregational, Episcopal, and Methodist churches. Like other YMCAs in England and the United States, it was specifically dedicated to proselytizing Christianity. Although informed by opposing interpretations of practical Christianity, both the YMCA and the YMCU consciously nurtured "home-like" atmospheres, placed young men in respectable boarding houses, and purveyed rational recreation in the form of libraries, lectures, and concerts. Within a year, the two organizations claimed more than seven hundred members each.[31]

[30] Edwin M. Stone, "Some Account of the Evening School connected with the Ministry at Large," clipping, 1849, Rider Collection, Brown University Library; *Providence Journal*, 15 January 1848; Records of the Mechanics' Association, vol. 4, 11 May 1847, RIHS; David J. Rothman, *The Discovery of the Asylum: Social Order and Disorder in the New Republic* (Boston: Little, Brown & Co., 1971); Christopher Lasch, "Origins of the Asylum," in his *The World of Nations: Reflections on American History, Politics, and Culture* (New York: Alfred A. Knopf, 1973), 3-17.

[31] Young Men's Christian Union, *An Appeal to the Citizens of Providence in Behalf of Young Men* (Providence: n.p., 1853), 4, 1; *Constitution of the Providence Young Men's Christian Association* (Providence: A. Crawford Greene, 1854), 11-12. On the YMCA see Paul S. Boyer, *Urban Masses and Moral Order in America, 1820-1920* (Cambridge: Harvard University Press, 1978), 108-120; Allan Stanley Horlick, *Country Boys and*

The supporters of the YMCU professed the modest aim of res-
cuing the city's young men from the snares of temptation; the evangelicals, however, viewed the YMCA as an instrument in their attempt to evangelize the city. In 1854 Amos Barstow, the YMCA's
first president, dedicated its new building to the cause of "evangelical religion," by which he meant "gospel religion, a religion that is
consonant with the principles and precepts of the gospel of Jesus
Christ." Other speakers at the dedication ceremony exulted in the
triumph of interdenominational cooperation and institution building that the YMCA represented. Francis Wayland looked forward
to the imminent "subjection of the whole city to Christ." Methodist
Elder Robert Allyn hailed the new institution as a sign of spiritual
awakening among the city's businessmen. "We want laymen to go
out and do *business* for God, and thus introduce the principles and
practices of christianity into every day business life." For Gilbert
Richmond, the occasion evoked memories of the spontaneous revivals in the early 1830s that had sent him, Barstow, and many other
converts into the temperance and antislavery movements. He too
expected the YMCA "to promote the revival of God's work in this
city."[32]

The general religious awakening that these evangelical spokesmen so eagerly anticipated occurred four years later. Practically all
the denominations in Providence had experienced revivals before
1858. Even the Unitarians had gathered in new members in the winter of 1841-42 when Elder Knapp conducted "protracted meetings"
at the Third Baptist Church in Providence.[33] But these revivals were

---

Merchant Princes: The Social Control of Young Men in New York City (Lewisburg, Penn.:
Bucknell University Press, 1975), 226-43; Marion L. Bell, *Crusade in the City: Revivalism in Nineteenth-Century Philadelphia* (Lewisburg, Penn.: Bucknell University Press,
1978), 169-99; Charles Howard Hopkins, *History of the Y.M.C.A. in North America*
(New York: Association Press, 1951); and Gregory Anderson, *Victorian Clerks* (Manchester: Manchester University Press, 1976), 74-88. Middle-class moralists, worried
over how mass migration dislodged youth from the stable moorings of family life,
produced a voluminous advice literature. See Karen Halttunen, *Confidence Men and
Painted Women: A Study of Middle-Class Culture in America, 1830-1870* (New Haven:
Yale University Press, 1982).

[32] *Dedication of the Rooms of the Providence Young Men's Christian Association* (Providence: Thompson & Crosby, 1854), 5, 21, 18, 27-28.

[33] First Unitarian Church, Records of the Church, 1819-1960, 19 January 1842,
RIHS; E. H. Johnson, *History of the Third and Brown Street Baptist Churches, of Providence, R.I.* (Providence: J. A. & R. A. Reid, 1880), 14. On Elder Jacob Knapp, see Jacob Knapp, *Autobiography of Elder Jacob Knapp* (New York: Sheldon & Co., 1868), esp.

intermittent and never citywide. Contemporaries had never seen (and would never again see) anything like the wave of revivals that engulfed Providence and other northern cities in the spring of 1858. For three months, the city was awash with religious enthusiasm. At noontime businessmen left their offices and shops "to engage for an hour in social devotions." These spontaneous noonday prayer meetings, led by laymen, were the hallmark of the urban revivals. Years afterward, the Reverend James G. Vose of the Beneficent Congregational Church recalled this awakening as the highwater mark of religion in the nineteenth-century North, when revival measures became institutionalized in every denomination and evangelical Protestantism became practically coterminous with northern culture. "Large numbers confessed their faith in Christ," he said, "and so extensive was the work that the whole city was moved. In fact, there never was, in the history of the country, a more wide-spread and personal interest in religion than that which prevailed in these years."[34]

But the most noteworthy aspect of the urban revivals was the way in which they overcame the sectarian quarrels that had formerly divided the city's Protestants. Unitarian minister Hall, who had earlier dismissed Knapp's preaching as "of doubtful usefulness on the whole," pronounced the awakening one "with less of the human, [and] more apparently of divine agency, than [any] we have known before." The Second Universalist Church added forty-four new members, thirty more than in the preceding year. Union prayer and conference meetings on Sabbath evenings at the chapel of the Min-

---

122-24; and Timothy L. Smith, *Revivalism and Social Reform: American Protestantism on the Eve of the Civil War* (1957; reprint, Baltimore: Johns Hopkins University Press, 1980), 47-48.

[34] *Providence Journal*, March-May 1858, passim; Vose, *Sketches of Congregationalism in Rhode Island*, 146-47. Perry Miller characterizes the antebellum revivals as "a central mode of this culture's search for national identity" in *The Life of the Mind in America, from the Revolution to the Civil War* (New York: Harcourt, Brace & World, 1965), 6. On the annus mirabilis of 1858, see Samuel W. Dike, "A Study of New England Revivals," *American Journal of Sociology* 15 (November 1909): 375-76; and Smith, *Revivalism and Social Reform*. For overviews of antebellum revivals, see William G. McLoughlin, *Modern Revivalism: Charles Grandison Finney to Billy Graham* (New York: Ronald Press, 1959); George M. Marsden, *The Evangelical Mind and the New School Presbyterian Experience: A Case Study of Thought and Theology in Nineteenth-Century America* (New Haven: Yale University Press, 1970); and Richard Carwardine, *Transatlantic Revivalism: Popular Evangelicalism in Britain and America, 1790-1865* (Westport, Conn.: Greenwood Press, 1978), 3-56.

istry at Large drew representatives from five denominations. "My effort to promote a Union based on *Spirit* rather than *dogmas*," wrote Edwin Stone, "has been cordially met by individuals of different religious creeds." The ecumenical spirit fostered by the urban revivals of 1858 set the stage for the coalescence of a middle-class culture.[35]

It is doubtful, however, whether Protestant churches and auxiliaries like the YMCA could by themselves have remodeled traditional patterns of leisure. Fortunately, they did not have to do so. Crucial to the remaking of the antebellum North along middle-class lines was the establishment of a system of popular education and its propagation of an ideology of self-improvement. This ideology stemmed from the widely held belief that the diffusion of useful knowledge would lead to the moral renovation of society. "If we neglect the temperance cause," Congregational minister Nathaniel S. Folsom told the Rhode Island State Temperance Society in 1839, "we shall abandon one of the most efficient auxiliaries to the diffusion of knowledge." Folsom contended that "the disuse of intoxicating drinks has been attended with an improvement in the means of livelihood. This improvement has redeemed time for other purposes than those of toil for the necessaries of life. It has provided leisure and means for acquiring knowledge."[36]

Folsom was not alone in positing a connection between the diffusion of useful knowledge and self-improvement. Popular education had long been one of the chief concerns of the Mechanics' Association, whose members exercised a proprietary influence over the public schools. In 1799, after previous efforts by clergymen, gentlemen, and other local notables had proved unavailing, the association petitioned the General Assembly to establish free schools. Although a republican government, as everyone knew, depended on "a general diffusion of knowledge among the people," Rhode Island suffered youth "to grow up in ignorance, when a common education would qualify them to act their parts in life with advantage to the public and reputation to themselves." The petitioners por-

[35] First Unitarian Church, Records of the Church, 1819-1960, 21 November 1841, January-April 1858, RIHS; Clerk's Book of the Second Universalist Church, 1849-71, 30 December 1858, RIHS; Records of the Ministry at Large, 1841-61, 19 April 1858, RIHS.

[36] Nathaniel S. Folsom, *Discourse before the Rhode Island State Temperance Society* (Providence: Knowles, Vose & Co., 1839), 23.

trayed themselves not as upwardly mobile men in search of opportunities for self-improvement, but rather as virtuous republicans who spoke for "the great majority of children throughout the State, and in particular those who are poor and destitute—the son of the widow and the child of distress." After the General Assembly passed enabling legislation in 1800, Providence quickly established the first free schools in the state. Open to "all [white] children of both sexes," these schools taught English grammar, composition, spelling, penmanship, and simple arithmetic. Students also learned how "to conduct themselves in a sober, orderly and decent manner, both in and out of school."[37]

But these schools soon disappointed their supporters. Bowing to rural pressure in 1803, the General Assembly repealed the enabling act; thereafter, schools had to charge their students tuition to pay for supplies and fuel. Attendance remained low. As late as 1828, only about "one-tenth of the whole number of children" in Providence regularly attended school. After studying the situation, a committee chaired by Francis Wayland called for reorganization to make the public schools more attractive to "the middling classes, and the poor." In particular, it recommended grading the schools by age and opening a high school. "Such an education as we propose the rich man can give, and will give his son by sending him to private schools," the Wayland Committee explained. "But the man in moderate circumstances cannot afford to incur the heavy expenses of a first-rate school, and if no such provision be made, the education of his children must be restricted to the ordinary acquisition of a little more than reading and writing." If the schools were reorganized, however, the same man "would be enabled to give his child an education which would qualify him for distinction in any kind of busi-

[37] *Charter, By-Laws, Rules and Regulations of the Providence Association of Mechanics and Manufacturers. With a List of Members, and the Address of John Howland, Esq., delivered before the Association, January 10th, 1825* (Providence: A. C. Greene, 1850), 11-12; School Committee Records, 7 October 1800, Providence School Department, quoted in Francis X. Russo, "John Howland: Pioneer in the Free School Movement," *Rhode Island History* 37 (November 1978): 120; Charles Carroll, *Public Education in Rhode Island* (Providence: E. L. Freeman Co., 1918), 53-68, 77-83; William G. Shade, "The 'Working Class' and Educational Reform in Early America: The Case of Providence, Rhode Island," *Historian* 39 (November 1976): 1-23. See also Carl F. Kaestle, *The Evolution of an Urban School System: New York City, 1750-1850* (Cambridge: Harvard University Press, 1973).

ness." Reorganization of the town's school system soon followed, but the construction of a high school was postponed indefinitely.[38]

School attendance, however, continued to lag behind population growth. A census taken in 1836 revealed that of 5,295 children of school age in Providence only 1,456 attended public schools. Another 2,235 were enrolled in private schools. The other 1,604 children did not attend any school. These circumstances elicited another memorial from the Mechanics' Association in 1837, this time to the Providence city council. In contrast to the deferential tone of its earlier petition, the association now spoke as the self-appointed representative of the city's middle-class property owners. Claiming to voice the opinions of a "large portion of the heads of families of the city," the master craftsmen demanded that the council do something about the deplorable state of the public schools. Overcrowding and low teachers' salaries, they complained, forced the city's "middling classes" to send their children to private schools. "Unless a more liberal system of public education is pursued," they warned, "the children of the poorer classes must grow up in comparative ignorance; and that the laxity of morals, and loss of an honest pride in their own capacities, which would result from this state of things, would more than outweigh the increased expense which would be necessary to arrest it." Because financial necessity forced many children to leave school at the age of twelve or thirteen to go to work "with a very superficial knowledge" of those branches "so necessary for obtaining a livelihood in any business," the city should establish "intermediate" schools that would teach "Reading, Writing and Arithmetic only."[39]

In response to the association's petition, Providence became one of the first cities in the country to appoint a school superintendent and the first community in Rhode Island to open a high school. By 1841 public school enrollments had surged ahead of those of the city's private schools. At long last, declared the *Providence Journal*, the city's public schools had become "sufficiently *popular* for all classes [of society] to patronize."[40]

[38] Wayland Committee's report quoted in Carroll, *Public Education in Rhode Island*, 97-99.
[39] Records of the Mechanics' Association, vol. 4, 4 February 1837, RIHS; Carroll, *Public Education in Rhode Island*, 116-17.
[40] *Providence Journal*, 4 December 1840.

Thus the city's public schools, which the Mechanics' Association had sponsored in 1799 as "republican" institutions necessary for an educated citizenry, had by the 1830s become middle-class institutions that taught students the three R's and promoted upward mobility through the inculcation of self-discipline. What Tocqueville called "the principle of self-interest rightly understood" helps account for the association's interest in public schools. In memorializing the city council, the Mechanics' Association was simply extending its program of adult education. In 1821 it had opened a five-hundred-volume library for its members and their apprentices, designed to awaken in the young "a desire for mental improvement." Since then, it had also sponsored lecture series on applied science, with the purpose of withdrawing youth "from the haunts of idleness, and the allurements of temptation and vicious indulgence" and giving "them a taste for scientific enquiries."[41]

In addition to protecting men and women from the temptations of sensual indulgence, education held out the promise of self-improvement. Once self-improvement had meant the cultivation of public virtue, but as manufacturing multiplied the opportunities for master craftsmen, self-improvement came to signify social mobility as well. By placing a premium on useful knowledge, mechanization enhanced the master craftsman's status in the community: the country's technological progress necessarily led to his self-improvement. "Convinced that man sustained his rank solely from the improvement of intellect," the members of the Mechanics' Association envisioned an open, meritocratic society. This conception grew stronger and more clearly articulated as these master craftsmen rose in social status. In its role of awakening intellectual curiosity and stimulating achievement, public education promoted social mobility.[42]

[41] Alexis de Tocqueville, *Democracy in America*, trans. Henry Reeve, ed. Phillips Bradley, 2 vols. (New York: Vintage Books, 1945), 2:129-32; Records of the Mechanics' Association, vol. 3, 14 October 1822, 13 April 1829, 13 October 1823, RIHS.

[42] Walter R. Danforth, *An Oration delivered before the Providence Association of Mechanics and Manufacturers, April 8, 1822, Being the Anniversary of the Election of Officers* (Providence: Miller & Hutchens, 1822), 18. On the ideal of the "scientific mechanic," in whom theory and practice were joined, see Bruce Sinclair, *Philadelphia's Philosopher Mechanics: A History of the Franklin Institute, 1824-1865* (Baltimore: Johns Hopkins University Press, 1974), 5-15; Hugo A. Meier, "Technology and Democracy, 1800-1860," *Mississippi Valley Historical Review* 43 (March 1957): 618-40; A.F.C. Wallace,

Outside the compact boundaries of Providence and Newport, however, popular education was slow to take root. Only during Henry Barnard's tenure as state school superintendent from 1843 to 1849 did public schools spread throughout the state. A distinguished educator who later became the first United States commissioner of education, Barnard stressed the connection between the diffusion of useful knowledge and self-improvement for the masses. Establishing schools, libraries, and other educational institutions, he argued, would "furnish the means of self-culture to all, whatever may have been their opportunities of acquiring knowledge." Barnard looked forward to the day when "every large village" would have "a course of popular lectures," if not a library, to create "a taste," form "habits of reading in the young," and diffuse "intelligence among all classes." To broadcast this message to rural Rhode Islanders, he dispatched the colorful W. S. Baker and his "circus," a wagon loaded with minerals, insects, and students. In the state's more densely populated areas, Barnard arranged for hundreds of educational meetings and lectures and distributed thousands of pamphlets to drum up community support for the public schools. His vision of education as the glue bonding the diverse classes and ethnic groups of an industrial society was to captivate middle-class reformers for the rest of the nineteenth century.[43]

As reformers like Barnard had begun to realize, the remaking of society along respectable, middle-class lines required more than the suppression of objectionable amusements. Rational amusements, "counterattractions" to the barroom, theater, and other nurseries

---

Rockdale: The Growth of an American Village in the Early Industrial Revolution (New York: W. W. Norton & Co., 1978), 211-39. Stephan Thernstrom has argued that mechanization enhanced economic opportunity for skilled craftsmen in "Urbanization, Migration, and Social Mobility in Late Nineteenth-Century America," in *Towards a New Past: Dissenting Essays in American History*, ed. Barton J. Bernstein (New York: Vintage Books, 1969), 171. So too has Bruce Laurie in *Working People of Philadelphia*, 22-23. B. Michael Zuckerman presents similar evidence for Rhode Island in "The Political Economy of Industrial Rhode Island, 1790-1860." Compare Newark, New Jersey, where even before the Civil War industrialization fractured the pre-industrial mechanics' community by arraying journeymen against master craftsmen. See Susan E. Hirsh, *Roots of the American Working Class: The Industrialization of Crafts in Newark, 1800-1860* (Philadelphia: University of Pennsylvania Press, 1978).

[43] Henry Barnard, *Report on the Condition and Improvement of the Public Schools*, 1 November 1845, reprinted in the *Journal of the Rhode Island Institute of Instruction* 1 (1845-46): 15; *Providence Journal*, 17 August 1846; Carroll, *Public Education in Rhode Island*, chap. 4; Robert B. Downs, *Henry Barnard* (Boston: Twayne, 1977), 30-31.

of vice, were also necessary. As the Reverend Hall pointed out in 1856, it was incumbent on critics of customary amusements to "build up" as well as to tear down. "They are to elevate, positively and genially, the whole standard and estimate of pleasure," he announced. "They should aim to furnish, in the city and community, all possible facilities and attractions for whatever is good, improving, exalting and cheering."[44]

Lyceum lectures epitomized the purposive recreation that educated while it entertained. Rapidly becoming the most popular agency of self-improvement in the antebellum North, lyceums were instrumental in disseminating middle-class values. Ralph Waldo Emerson inaugurated the lyceum movement in Providence in 1839 when he delivered six lectures on "Human Life" before the Franklin Lyceum, a young men's debating society organized eight years earlier. Public response encouraged the lyceum to institute an annual winter lecture series. The Mechanics' Association quickly followed suit. The Franklin Society, founded in 1821 to generate public interest in science, also sponsored lecture series, as did the YMCA, the YMCU, and the Brownson Lyceum, a Catholic young men's literary society. The city's middle-class women organized their own lyceum. In 1850 eighty women, the wives and daughters of mechanics and shopkeepers, formed the Providence Physiological Society. Until the society disbanded in 1862, members assembled periodically to listen to lectures, frequently by Paulina Wright Davis, on "the sciences of Anatomy and Physiology."[45]

In 1843 Emerson predicted that "the Lyceum will be the church of future times. Here only can one find a convertible audience—who are, as a body, unpledged to any system, and unapprized of what is to be said. It is the most elastic and capacious theatre of our times." Emerson might have added that it was also a far more respectable pastime than theater-going in antebellum Providence. The middle decades of the nineteenth century bore out Emerson's prediction. As a relatively cheap form of entertainment, with ad-

44 Hall, *A Lecture on the Pleasures and Vices of the City*, 19.

45 *Charter, Constitution, By-Laws, and Catalogue, of the Franklin Lyceum, Providence* (Providence: A. Crawford Greene, 1871), 4; Robert J. Taylor, "The Providence Franklin Society," *Rhode Island History* 9 (October 1950): 124; "The Brownson Lyceum," *Providence Visitor*, 15 April 1899; Providence Physiological Society, MS Records, 1850-62, RIHS; Amy L. Nathan, "Paulina Wright Davis" (history honors thesis, Brown University, 1977), 43-48, RIHS.

mission ranging from $1.50 to $2.00 for an annual series or twenty-five cents for a single lecture, lyceum lectures drew large audiences composed of ambitious young men and women. As many as two thousand persons hungry for "facts" and starved for respectable entertainment on long winter evenings flocked to lectures on current issues, history, and travel, and to occasional concerts. Although the first lecturers tended to be eminent local citizens, soon a corps of professional lecturers emerged. According to their sponsors, lyceum lectures mixed "intellectual entertainment" with amusement. As the lecturer Carl Schurz recalled, "it was expected that the lecturer would discuss serious objects in a serious way—which, of course, does not mean that a joke was not appreciated in a scientific address or even in a sermon. But the prevailing desire," Schurz added, "was that the lyceum audience should be told something worth knowing, that their stock of information and ideas should be enlarged, and that their moral sense should be enlightened and stirred." In his travels on the antebellum lyceum circuit Schurz witnessed "the middle-class culture in process of formation."[46]

Popular lectures, though, were never sufficient to bring about the moral renovation of society. As Barnard had urged, every town in the state needed a library or reading room that would serve as a year-round center of rational recreation for the entire community. This goal took much longer to attain. In 1836 Providence took its first step toward the establishment of a public library when over three hundred proprietors, drawn from the wealthier families of the city, purchased shares for fifteen dollars each in the Providence Athenaeum. Its directors, who characterized the institution as a "public" library, always hoped to attract "the industrious, hard-working classes of the community." They boasted that the Athenaeum was "the cheapest institution of its class in the country." Compared with similar institutions in Boston and Salem, the cost of joining the Athenaeum was indeed inexpensive.[47] For at least one

[46] Emerson quoted in *Providence Journal*, 8 April 1843; Carl Schurz, *The Reminiscences of Carl Schurz*, 3 vols. (New York: McClure, 1909), 2:158. For discussions of the lyceum movement, see Carl Bode, *The American Lyceum, Town Meeting of the Mind* (New York: Oxford University Press, 1956); and Donald M. Scott, "The Popular Lecture and the Creation of a Public in Mid-Nineteenth-Century America," *Journal of American History* 66 (March 1980): 791-809.

[47] *Sixth Annual Report of the Directors of the Providence Athenaeum to the Proprietors* (Providence: Knowles & Vose, 1841), 15; "Historical Sketch," in *Catalogue of the Li-*

observer, however, there was "an air of exclusiveness and aristocratic pretension surrounding it." The necessity of paying fifteen dollars to become a proprietor, the annual membership fee of five dollars, and the fact that the library was rarely open in the evening, explained why so few of the industrious classes belonged.[48] The library's acquisition policy may also have limited its appeal. Distinguishing itself from a lending library, which catered to "the public taste such as it is," the Athenaeum defined its role "as a public educator, in some measure representing the culture of Providence." For many years, its directors waged war against contemporary fiction, or "that class of literary productions which inflames the passions and perverts the moral sentiments." Yet as late as 1871, they still hoped to dispel the impression that the Athenaeum was "an exclusive institution which has received its generous benefactions and accumulated its treasures of learning solely for its own proprietors."[49]

Instead of functioning as a true public library open to all city residents, the Athenaeum played a much narrower role: refining the sensibility and strengthening the self-discipline of the upwardly mobile. Francis Wayland, who gave the address at the dedication of the Athenaeum's Classical Greek building in 1838, hailed the library as a bonding force in the community, "the means for the universal diffusion of knowledge, of knowledge in its most extensive signification, among the citizens of Providence." Wayland pictured America poised on the brink of "a crisis in the progress of civilization." Wellnigh universal literacy had "created in the whole community a desire for intelligence, and that desire must be gratified." The challenge thus facing Americans was to "render knowledge, valuable

brary of the Providence Athenaeum, to which are prefixed the Charter, Constitution, and By-Laws and an Historical Sketch of the Institution (Providence: Knowles, Anthony & Co., 1853), xxxi. Compare the cost of joining the Providence Athenaeum with the much more exclusive Boston Athenaeum, whose shares cost three hundred dollars each and whose membership was limited to a thousand proprietors. See Ronald Story, The Forging of an Aristocracy: Harvard and the Boston Upper Class, 1800-1870 (Middletown, Conn.: Wesleyan University Press, 1980), 13-16.

[48] Letter from "A Shareholder," Providence Journal, 9 April 1853.

[49] Nineteenth Annual Report of the Directors of the Providence Athenaeum to the Proprietors (Providence: Knowles, Anthony & Co., 1854), 21; Thirty-Fifth Annual Report (Providence: Hammond, Angell & Co., 1870), 14; First Annual Report (Providence: Knowles & Vose, 1842), 9; Thirty-Sixth Annual Report (Providence: Hammond, Angell & Co., 1871), 20.

knowledge, accessible to the whole community."[50] Without popular
access to useful knowledge, Americans would fall prey to sensual indulgence, or the "opportunities" that the country's wealth multiplied "for the gratification of passions." The ensuing inequality of
wealth would provoke class conflict by intensifying the "feeling of
estrangement between the rich and the poor." Fortunately, "intellectual cultivation" of the type afforded by the Athenaeum "opens
to men a new path to social distinction," whereby wealth "becomes
in a less degree an object of envy" and more secure. In this way, the
Athenaeum rescued the city's "population from the dominion of the
senses," lured "men away from the fascinations of refined self-grat-
ification," and allayed "the bitterness of [political] party rancor."[51]

Lyceums, libraries, and similar educational institutions were all
products of an ethos of self-improvement that eventually came to
inform the new civic culture of Providence. "There was a time
when, too large for a village and too isolated to boast of metropolitan advantages, Providence was in that state of betweenity which is
always embarrassing and often not a little ludicrous," the *Providence
Journal* observed in 1867. It was no longer enough for Providence
boosters to point to the impressive wealth of the city's manufacturers. Before Providence could be initiated "into the sisterhood of cities," it had to exhibit an urban identity through civic architecture
and a whole range of cultural institutions requisite for any true city:
a public library, an art gallery, a museum of natural history, and
perhaps even a music conservatory.[52] These institutions, which reflected an ambitious attempt to graft an urban civilization to a developing industrial base, were also designed to serve as agents of
cultural assimilation, bringing together members of various social
classes and ethnic groups in the common pursuit of self-improve-

[50] Francis Wayland, *A Discourse, delivered at the Opening of the Providence Athenaeum,
July 11, 1838* (Providence: Knowles, Vose & Co., 1838), 4-5, 10, 11, 12.

[51] Ibid., 22, 28-30, 34.

[52] "Hotels," *Providence Journal*, 26 March 1867. Geoffrey Best writes that "conspicuous among those requirements [of "modern" mid-Victorian city life] was a proper
presentation of the public buildings, civic ornaments and palaces of commerce which
should embody and represent the city's proud sense of its own identity. This desire
to make a good civic showing was rather a new thing about the middle of the century." *Mid-Victorian Britain, 1851-1875* (New York: Schocken Books, 1972), 61-62.
See also Daniel Boorstin, *The Americans: The National Experience* (New York: Vintage
Books, 1965), 113-68; Frisch, *Town into City*, 133-56; and Asa Briggs, *Victorian Cities*
(London: Oldhams, 1963), 22-23.

ment. Self-culture would promote both upward mobility and cultural consensus. As Matthew Arnold pointed out in *Culture and Society*, the word "culture" denoted both self-cultivation and the system of values that bonded the heterogeneous groups of the industrial city.[53]

During the 1860s, city boosters began to redefine the role of the municipal government. Instead of the limited role many of them had formerly insisted on, they insisted that city authorities anticipate future needs of the city. These needs included water works, sewage systems, and even parks. Wealthy Providence could well afford improvements that would make the city a better and more attractive place to live. Moreover, these ornaments of urban civilization—whether libraries, museums, water systems, public parks, or even hotels—would not only raise property values but "attract population and visitors to Providence." "It is hardly necessary," commented Dr. William F. Channing, son of the Unitarian divine William Ellery Channing and one of the city's foremost advocates of municipal parks, "to present the opposite side of this picture. A city which refuses to inaugurate public works stamps itself with inferiority, and continues to all intents and purposes a village, overgrown indeed, but not otherwise improved." Under the helm of Thomas A. Doyle, an advocate of liberal spending who served eighteen terms as mayor between 1864 and his death in 1886, the city government constructed a municipal water system, installed sewers, and built a new city hall. It also developed Roger Williams Park, a 102-acre farmstead bequeathed by Betsey Williams, a descendant of the city's founder.[54]

[53] Helen E. Meller points out that, for Matthew Arnold, the word "culture" denoted both "a socially cohesive force" (that is, civic culture) and "the means towards an individual's personal fulfilment" (self-culture) in *Leisure and the Changing City, 1870-1914* (London: Routledge & Kegan Paul, 1976), 50-51. See also Raymond Williams's discussion of the changing meaning of the word "culture" in *Keywords: A Vocabulary of Culture and Society* (New York: Oxford University Press, 1976), 76-82. On the "bonding" function of culture, see Thomas Bender, *Toward an Urban Vision: Ideas and Institutions in Nineteenth-Century America* (1975; reprint, Baltimore: Johns Hopkins University Press, 1982), 95-128; Neil Harris, "Four Stages of Cultural Growth: The American City," in Arthur Mann et al., *History and the Role of the City in American Life* (Indianapolis: Indiana Historical Society, 1972), 30-34; and Robert Lewis, "Frontier and Civilization in the Thought of Frederick Law Olmsted," *American Quarterly* 29 (Fall 1977): 385-403.

[54] Letter from W.F.C. [William F. Channing], *Providence Journal*, 16 February 1867;

The municipal government did not act alone in fashioning a civic culture. Important partners in this scheme of municipal betterment were the voluntary associations that took the initiative in endowing Providence with many of the cultural amenities a true city required. Although they were private organizations that were limited to fee-paying members and governed by self-perpetuating boards of trustees, they claimed to represent the public interest. "Under a republican government and among a republican people, where the laws of primogeniture and of entail are unknown, and where wealth, of course, seldom accumulates in large masses," as the proprietors of the Athenaeum explained, "associated elements in behalf of these institutions are specially required."[55]

Voluntary associations like the Athenaeum vivified the community for urban dwellers and strengthened their local identification. In Kingston, New York, and other towns that the antebellum transportation and communications revolutions had transformed from sleepy backwaters into bustling commercial centers, localism intensified as new institutional structures developed. So too in Springfield, Massachusetts, did an abstract sense of community, or areas of public concern distinct from private interest, become stronger between 1840 and 1880. In fact, it was precisely this "corporate sentiment" that distinguished a city from a mere village. In "a village," wrote William F. Channing, "the business revolves around a few very prominent, perhaps very rich, men. The avenues of enterprise are few and isolated." But a city possessed "a net work of intercommunication, by which all enterprises help each other." A city's "prosperity" thus depended on the development of a transcendent sense of the public interest, "when the inhabitants cease to test measures by the question 'what individual benefit shall I derive from this,' but, on the contrary, ask 'how will it affect the general prosperity,' with the instinctive conviction that that which adds most to the common wealth, best promotes individual gains."[56]

Frisch, *Town into City*, 157-75. For assessments of Doyle's tenure as mayor, see Robert Grieve, "Modern Providence," *New England Magazine* 8 (February 1896): 777-78; Howard Kemble Stokes, *The Finances and Administration of Providence* (Baltimore: Johns Hopkins University Press, 1903), chap. 6; William R. Morris, "The Long and Twisted Life of the City of Providence" (independent study project, Department of History, Brown University, 1976), 62-79, RIHS.

[55] *Second Annual Report of the Directors of the Providence Athenaeum to the Proprietors* (Providence: Knowles & Vose, 1842), 9.

[56] W.F.C. [William F. Channing], "The Present and Future of Providence," *Provi-*

The new civic culture, which took shape between 1850 and 1880, rested on institutions of self-improvement. The museum movement in Providence is a case in point. In 1854 the Rhode Island Art Association began to hold annual exhibitions of paintings, statuary, and other works of art in the hope of endowing a permanent art gallery and an attached school of design. Led by wealthy manufacturers, the new association aimed at creating "a purer taste," developing "a more correct appreciation of what is beautiful," and establishing "a close union between beauty and utility." This last aim was particularly important for manufacturers. At London's Crystal Palace in 1851 American-made products had earned the praise of European critics for their "mechanical proficiency," but they were not yet considered the equals of European products "in the sphere of elegance and taste." If American exports were to compete in foreign markets, they had to be as beautiful as they were practical. "It is not enough that his [the American manufacturer's] article is as good or as useful as his rival's: if it is more beautiful it secures the prize, if less it is driven from the field."[57]

The Art Association proposed a mutually beneficial alliance between art and manufacturing, beauty and utility. "As Art advances, manufacturers and commerce advance with it," it contended. Manufactures advanced because the proposed school of design would instruct artisans in the ornamental arts. Art advanced in turn because the city would gain a permanent art gallery, and its citizens a better appreciation of architecture. Though supported by some of the wealthiest men in Providence, the Art Association depended on public patronage or attendance at its exhibitions to realize its goal. As the *Providence Journal* explained, "In so small a place as this, the wealthy are too few to undertake the enterprise, except by an outlay that could not be reasonably expected of them," but "people of moderate means, who might do much if they pleased, would, for the most part, be quite satisfied with an investment of [a] quarter of a dollar for a ticket to the exhibition." Public interest soon languished, however, and the Art Association disbanded. The proposed school

---

dence Journal, 23 February 1869; Thomas Bender, *Community and Social Change in America* (New Brunswick, N.J.: Rutgers University Press, 1978), 86-95; Stuart M. Blumin, *The Urban Threshold: Growth and Change in a Nineteenth-Century American Community* (Chicago: University of Chicago Press, 1976); Frisch, *Town into City*.

[57] *Circular and Constitution of the Rhode-Island Art Association* (Providence: Knowles, Anthony & Co., 1854), 7-8, 20.

of design was not established until 1878, and then without an art gallery, by women whose interest in the decorative arts had been piqued by the Centennial Exposition at Philadelphia.[58]

Eben Tourjée also invoked the values of self-improvement when, in 1864, he proposed moving his musical conservatory from East Greenwich to Providence. Unlike the art gallery's supporters, Tourjée did not need to generate enthusiasm for music. In 1850 more than two thousand music lovers had purchased tickets to hear the "Swedish Nightingale," Jenny Lind, sing. Brass bands had entertained the public in an "unobjectionable and cheap" manner at Saturday afternoon concerts and local choruses performed the oratorios of Handel and Mendelssohn.[59] Leaving nothing to chance, however, Tourjée solicited testimonials from the city's clergymen to the effect that his conservatory could "hardly fail to raise the standard of devotional music in our churches." In addition to furnishing "every opportunity for a thorough and systematic mastery of the science [of music] in all its parts and relations," Tourjée predicted that his conservatory would bring out the "religious element that exists in music." Music would then "become the handmaid of the Church in christianizing the world." It was "essential," he said, "that the *masses of the people* be educated to appreciate the higher class of music." Tourjée promised to place before his students "such music as is elevating in its tendency and aids in the formation of a correct taste." After only three years in Providence, he set out for the greener pastures of Boston, where he founded the New England Conservatory of Music.[60]

[58] Ibid., 23; *Providence Journal*, 30 August 1854; Records of the Rhode Island Art Association, 1854, RIHS; John R. Frazier, *A History of Rhode Island School of Design* (Providence: Rhode Island School of Design, 1961). Similarly, the founders of the Boston Museum of Fine Arts collected "the most diverse group of objects, chronologically and geographically," in order "to make the fine arts more popular, stimulate native art schools and improve industrial design by the availability of models." Neil Harris, "The Gilded Age Revisited: Boston and the Museum Movement," *American Quarterly* 14 (Winter 1962): 558, 562.

[59] *Providence Journal*, 5-11 October 1850, 26 October 1855, 19 March 1856. See also Harris, *Humbug*, chap. 5.

[60] A. Huntington Clapp, pastor of the Beneficent Congregational Church, quoted in Eben J. Tourjée, *Proposition for Establishing a Musical College or Conservatory in Elmwood* (Providence: n.p., 1864); 8; *Annual Catalogue and Circular of the Musical Institute, Providence, R.I., July, 1866* (Providence: Pierce & Budlong, 1866), 10-11. See also Edward J. FitzPatrick, "Eben Tourjée's Rhode Island Roots," *Rhode Island History* 36 (August 1977): 81-91.

Men like Tourjée obviously believed that the rational recreation purveyed by such innocent amusements as libraries, lectures, art exhibitions, and concerts cut across class and even ethnic lines. They thus viewed libraries both as focal points of the new civic culture and as ornaments of a wealthy industrial city. The opening of the first free libraries in the city by the YMCA and YMCU during the 1850s briefly postponed the demand for a public library. After the Civil War, however, it became increasingly clear that no truly public library existed in Providence. The Athenaeum, critics charged, had "never been a public library in the common meaning of the word. The common people of the city have had very little to do with it." Nor were the libraries maintained by the the Mechanics' Association, the YMCA, and the Union for Christian Work, a Unitarian social service organization established in 1868 as successor to the YMCU, reaching the people most in need of a public library. "For the past decade the lack of a public library has been rather a reproach to Providence," lamented the *Providence Journal*. "Cities of less than one-third her size possessed stately library buildings, well stored with books, and containing, besides books, collections of curiosities or specimens of natural history." Visitors to the city were "in the habit of asking for the public library in about the tone they would have used in inquiring about the depot. When informed that Providence had no public library," these visitors exclaimed, "Why, don't people read in Providence?"[61]

In 1870 Quaker physician and amateur scientist Dr. Welcome O. Brown launched the drive that culminated, eight years later, in the establishment of the Providence Public Library. Urging that the Providence Franklin Society become the nucleus of a public library, Brown enlisted the help of woolen manufacturer Zachariah Allen and Reuben Guild, librarian of Brown University. Together with other public-spirited citizens, they requested a charter from the General Assembly for "a Free Public Library, Art Gallery, and Museum." As originally conceived, this combination library, art gallery, and museum of natural history was to be "a stately edifice" with

[61] "Our Free Library," *Providence Journal*, 4 February 1878. On the establishment of the Providence Union for Christian Work, the first in the country, see William B. Weeden, *An Address on the Relations of Church and People in Our Cities: Read at the Late Meeting of the National Conference of Unitarian and Other Christian Churches in New York* (Boston: Alfred Mudge & Son, 1868).

rooms "devoted to the uses of scientific and literary societies." The Mechanics' Association offered to contribute its library, which by then amounted to more than six thousand volumes. The Franklin Lyceum and two other improvement societies—the Rhode Island Horticultural Society, sponsor of annual exhibitions of flowers and fruit, and the Rhode Island Society for the Encouragement of Domestic Industry, host of the annual state fair—also expressed an interest in the project. In return for receiving rooms in the proposed building, each of these organizations agreed to share its collection with the public.[62]

Leading the drive for a public library were men long identified with self-improvement. Zachariah Allen, Amos Barstow, and file manufacturer William T. Nicholson represented the Mechanics' Association. Representatives from the Rhode Island Horticultural Society included Joseph R. Brown of Brown & Sharpe, Merrick Lyon, principal of Providence's foremost preparatory school, and Dr. William F. Channing. Former abolitionist Joseph A. Barker, who had prospered in the hardware trade, helped launch the library with a gift of ten thousand dollars and a promise of fifteen thousand more. Joseph R. Brown later left a bequest of ten thousand dollars.[63]

Some of these men were also members of the Rhode Island Educational Union, then in the midst of a campaign to establish evening schools, free libraries, and reading rooms in manufacturing communities for "the intellectual and social improvement of the industrial population of this State." Libraries and other agencies of rational recreation, they contended, were "a more efficient means of preserving *public order* in a community, than the best appointed police." Such a warning seemed timely in light of the Paris Commune, which underscored the fragility of industrial cities. Providence, "a city so largely composed of persons of foreign birth," urgently required a free public library "for the purpose of increasing the means of diffusing knowledge." In a veiled reference to the Roman Catholicism of nearly half the city's population, Zachariah Allen, Edwin Stone, and Welcome Brown suggested that a public library

[62] Zachariah Allen et al., *Free Public Library, Art-Gallery, and Museum, in the City of Providence, R.I.* (Providence: Hammond, Angell & Co., 1871); Zachariah Allen, Diary, 1853-81, vol. 5, passim, RIHS; Thomas Durfee, "Address," in *The New Building of the Providence Public Library* (Providence: Snow & Farnham, 1901), 5-6; John H. Stiness, "Historical Sketch of the Early Years of the Library Movement," in ibid., 39-47.

[63] "Our Free Library"; Stiness, "Historical Sketch," 45-46.

would prevent "the domination of the ecclesiastical over the civil power of the world, by keeping the people in ignorance."[64]

But the timing of this grandiose project was inopportune. Its ambitious plans had to be scaled down after the panic of 1873 threw many city residents out of work and reduced municipal revenues. The city council, which had earlier promised a vacant lot for the new library, refused to deed over the land. In addition, only a little more than forty thousand of the estimated one hundred thousand dollars needed to establish the library had been raised by 1874. Reluctantly, the trustees decided to amend the charter. Although the amateur scientists among the trustees, particularly Zachariah Allen and Welcome Brown, continued to push for a polytechnic institution combining science and art with a library, a majority bowed to financial exigency. Combining three institutions in one, they decided, "seemed too great an undertaking, and likely to frustrate the leading object which many had in view, viz: the establishment of a free public library." The city could hardly afford to maintain an institution the size of the Boston Public Library, Reuben Guild pointed out, "requiring an immediate expenditure for building and books of at least three-quarters of a million dollars, and an annual draft upon the city treasury of $125,000 and upward." Was there really any need for such an elaborate and expensive institution, he asked, when "the choice and costly collections of Brown university and the Providence Athenaeum are practically open to the scholarly student, and the patient investigator of scientific truth"? Even if it were open on a limited scale, Guild claimed, the library would still serve as "a natural supplement to the excellent school system of Providence." The art gallery, museum of natural history, and rooms for self-improvement societies could be added later. Yet the narrowing of the scope of the plan dampened the enthusiasm of some of the original sponsors.[65]

When the Providence Public Library at last opened its doors to

[64] Rhode Island Educational Union, Minutes, 1867-72, 20 June, 11 December 1867, RIHS; *The Rhode Island Schoolmaster* 14 (February 1868): 35; *Free Public Library, Art-Gallery, and Museum*, 20. By 1874 more than half of the city's population was of foreign stock; first- and second-generation Irish Americans comprised 37 percent. See Edwin M. Snow, M.D., *Census of the City of Providence, May 1, 1874* (Providence: Hammond, Angell & Co., 1874), 10.

[65] Reuben A. Guild, "Public Library's Birth," *Evening Telegram*, 4 March 1900; Welcome O. Brown, *The Providence Franklin Society: An Historical Address* (Providence: J. A. & R. A. Reid, 1880), 23-24; *Providence Journal*, 19 May 1890.

the public in 1878, it was not in the stately edifice once envisioned, but in rented rooms so cramped that no public exercises could be held to commemorate its opening. The volumes donated by the Mechanics' Association made up almost two-thirds of the new library's collection. Not until 1889 did the library receive its first municipal allocation, the small sum of thirty-five hundred dollars. For many years, the Providence Public Library remained what was essentially a private library, largely dependent on income from its endowment and on private contributions to meet operating expenses.[66] Yet its history illustrates how the meaning of the word "public" changed as the city's population grew larger and more heterogeneous. In antebellum Providence the term had been practically synonymous with voluntarism. Even the Athenaeum, a private corporation, considered itself a public institution. Unlike comparable proprietary libraries in Boston and Salem, it sought to be inclusive by keeping its fees low and not limiting the number of its shareholders. Similarly, the Mechanics' Association, the Franklin Lyceum, and other improvement societies sponsored lectures that as quasi-civil institutions were intended to encompass all the members of the community, creating, as Emerson had predicted, an inclusive, nonsectarian, nonpartisan northern public. Even in its much scaled-down version, the Providence Public Library advertised itself as a place "where books of popular and instructive character can be had by all our citizens irrespective of age or color, without money and without price."[67]

Yet all these associations suffered from the same fatal flaw. As voluntary associations, organized peer groups separated from the rest of the city's population by their membership requirements and fees, they could never function as truly public institutions. The Athenaeum, for instance, could hardly claim to be a public library when few workingmen or immigrants browsed through its shelves or borrowed its volumes. Though intended to include all city residents, the public life or civic sphere of Providence was in reality limited to those inhabitants who were joiners. In Providence, as in midcentury Kingston, Cincinnati, and Jacksonville, Illinois, only a small propor-

[66] William E. Foster, *The First Fifty Years of the Providence Public Library, 1878-1928* (Providence: Providence Public Library, 1928), 15-18.

[67] Guild, "Public Library's Birth"; Scott, "The Public Lecture and the Creation of a Public in Mid-Nineteenth-Century America," 793.

tion of the adult male population belonged to at least one voluntary organization. Still fewer belonged to more than one association. The basic requirement for participation seems to have been middle-class standing in the community. For middle-class northerners, mechanics' institutes, lyceums, library companies, and other voluntary associations did cut across established ties of family, friendship, and work to forge a larger community. Indeed, they were instrumental in the coalescence and propagation of a distinctive middle-class culture in the second third of the nineteenth century.[68]

But even in the 1860s this civic sphere did not include the thousands of workingmen and immigrants who were too poor and too transient to join voluntary associations, or Catholics alienated by the associations' Protestantism. The civic sphere was to become even less inclusive as Providence became more heterogeneous. Partly for this reason, the term "public" would come to mean something quite different in the last third of the century. No longer synonymous with voluntarism, it would come to designate the common people of the city. As associations like the Athenaeum became more privatized, the municipal government gradually assumed many of the public functions that the associations had once performed.

In the middle third of the nineteenth century, middle-class values set the tone for the new civic culture in Providence and other industrial cities in the United States and England. But the hegemony of rational recreation and the purposive use of spare time it enshrined were short-lived. The asceticism of this culture reflected its origins in the early industrial economy of the antebellum period when economic success seemed to depend on hard work, thrift, and self-discipline. The institutions it spawned rested on self-improvement, domesticity, and other common values. In the last third of the century, however, the nature of work (and leisure) changed dramatically for many urban dwellers. The broad antebellum producers' community fragmented as the gap between self-employment and wage labor widened, and as sundry producers defined for themselves narrower, more exclusive, occupational identities. By the 1880s, when

[68] Blumin, *The Urban Threshold*, 166-89; Walter S. Glazer, "Participation and Power—Voluntary Associations and the Functional Organization of Cincinnati in 1840," *Historical Methods Newsletter* 5 (September 1972): 151-68; and Don H. Doyle, "The Social Functions of Voluntary Associations in a Nineteenth-Century American Town," *Social Science History* 1 (Spring 1977): 333-55.

3 CAPITAL AND LABOR

ANTEBELLUM middle-class consciousness presumed a harmony of interests among all producers, whether self-employed or wage earners with aspirations to self-employment. Typical of this producerism was the Mechanics' Association, whose 508 members in 1857 represented more than 110 different trades. But this presumed harmony of interests splintered after the Civil War. After growing to number more than 750 members in the early 1870s, the Mechanics' Association declined rapidly. Even before the panic of 1873, its annual lecture series lost money and was suspended. The generous gift of its library to the embryonic Providence Public Library removed one of the major attractions of the association. The severe depression of 1873-78, which threw many mechanics out of work, made matters worse. Few young members could afford to pay the association's annual fee of three dollars. Many fell into arrears and their names were dropped from the rolls. The city's leading organization on the eve of the Civil War, the Mechanics' Association had become moribund by 1880.[1]

But the decline of the Mechanics' Association also reflected large-scale changes in the nature of work that fractured the antebellum producers' community. In the 1870s a new distinction between "brain work" and manual labor arose to supplant the antebellum ideal of the "scientific mechanic" in whom theory and practice were joined. Even before then, Zachariah Allen charged, artisans had come to be regarded as the "mudsills of Society." "It is because they have indulged in sensual pleasures and dissipated habits, and have performed their labors as mere machines, working with their hands and not with their brains," he wrote in his diary in 1869. Allen was unduly hard on his fellow artisans. He failed to take into account the fact that their loss of social status was not entirely of their own making. Industrialization, in particular the ongoing division of labor,

[1] Records of the Providence Association of Mechanics and Manufacturers, vol. 6, 13 April 1874, 12 April 1875, 10 April 1876, RIHS.

had dealt an irreparable blow to the antebellum view that wage labor was only a temporary stage in one's advance toward self-employment. The industrial revolution, in fact, was creating a permanent class of wage earners whose very presence called into question the view celebrated by the Mechanics' Association in 1852 of a classless producers' community.[2]

Had it come through the panic of 1873 unscathed, the Mechanics' Association would have been an anomaly. As a diffuse producers' organization it ran counter to the post–Civil War trend toward the proliferation of professional societies, boards of trade, unions, and other more specialized occupational groups. As Americans increasingly became aware of their distinct and frequently antagonistic economic interests, they organized a bewildering variety of job-related associations. These associations were formed for a number of reasons: some revolved almost exclusively around sociability; others existed for purposes of job control and occupational regulation; still others were established to fend off state regulation. Organization by the self-employed and salaried middle classes prompted workingmen to organize in self-defense. All these new organizations abetted the segmentation of the work place, as exclusive occupational identities replaced the more inclusive category of "producer." Ironically, this heightening of occupational identity occurred at the same time that the work ethic, an article of faith for antebellum northerners, attenuated.[3]

Although the Civil War generally retarded the nation's economic growth, it ushered in an age of industrial prosperity for Rhode Island. As producers of fine print cloth rather than coarse fabrics, Rhode Island textile manufacturers suffered less from the wartime disruption of sources of supply and markets than did their counterparts in Massachusetts. After the war, the state's textile industry expanded rapidly. Between 1865 and 1880 its labor force grew from 15,800 to 22,600 workers and the number of spindles in operation almost doubled. Similarly, the Civil War fueled the growth of pre-

[2] Zachariah Allen, Diary, 1853-81, vol. 4, 16 September 1869, RIHS. On "the increasing association of nonmanual work with middle-class status," see Stuart M. Blumin, "Black Coats to White Collars: Economic Change, Nonmanual Work, and the Social Structure of Industrializing America," in *Small Business in American Life*, ed. Stuart W. Bruchey (New York: Columbia University Press, 1980), 100-121.

[3] Daniel T. Rodgers, *The Work Ethic in Industrial America, 1850-1920* (Chicago: University of Chicago Press, 1978).

Market Square looking west up Westminster Street, c. 1872 (courtesy of the Rhode Island Historical Society)

cision manufacturing in Providence. The Burnside Rifle Works, Providence Tool Company, and Schubarth Company all profited handsomely from producing munitions for the Union army. The Corliss Company and Providence Steam Engine Company built marine engines and boilers for the navy. Builders' Iron Foundry cast heavy ordnance, including 11-inch and 13-inch Dahlgren guns.

With the return of peace, the Burnside Rifle Works retooled to make locomotives and the Providence Machine Company devoted itself to making tools and sewing machines. The Providence Tool Company continued to manufacture guns, filling large contracts for the Turkish government. Brown & Sharpe, which as late as 1853 had only fourteen employees, became the world's largest manufacturer of machine tools. From a small workshop on the East Side it expanded to a large factory at the foot of Smith Hill, covering three blocks and employing 2,500 workers by 1900. The city's manufacturing jewelers did even better. By 1880, when jewelry overtook cotton manufacturing as the city's leading industry, upwards of 150 different firms made Providence the jewelry capital of the world. In Gorham Providence boasted the largest silver-plate manufacturer in the United States. The American Screw Company, Providence Tool Company, and Nicholson File Company also boasted the largest plants of their kind in the country. So extensive was the city's manufacturing base that, according to one observer, "less disaster befell it during the years of financial distress" occasioned by the panic of 1873 "than almost any [other] city in the Union." In spurring the rapid growth of new industries like machine tools and jewelry, industrial expansion accentuated occupational consciousness.[4]

Even before the Civil War, professionals had begun to organize in

[4] The quotation is from Wilfred H. Munro, *Picturesque Rhode Island* (Providence: J. A. & R. A. Reid, 1881), 218. On the city's industrial development between 1860 and 1880, see Theodore Collier, "Providence in Civil War Days," *Rhode Island Historical Society Collections* 27 (October 1934): 102-104; Kurt B. Mayer, *Economic Development and Population Growth in Rhode Island* (Providence: Brown University Press, 1953), 42-48; George H. Kellner and J. Stanley Lemons, *Rhode Island: The Independent State* (Woodland Hills, Calif.: Windsor Publications, 1982), 63-73. Peter J. Coleman has argued that the panic of 1873 marked a watershed in Rhode Island's economic development. Following the panic, the state's factory labor force grew at a much slower rate than previously and bank capital declined dramatically. "The Entrepreneurial Spirit in Rhode Island History," *Business History Review* 37 (Winter 1963): 319-20. On the Civil War's impact on the national economy, see W. Elliot Brownlee, *Dynamics of Ascent: A History of the American Economy* (New York: Alfred A. Knopf, 1974), 179-84.

Providence. In the absence of state licensing agencies, antebellum professional societies in law and medicine prescribed the length of apprenticeship, licensed practitioners, and defined orthodox practice. Beginning in 1795, the state's lawyers or "Gentlemen of the Bar" met once a year to draw up "Rules of Practice," regulate admission to the bar, set fees for tuition and legal services, promote "Harmony among the Members," and support "the Honor of the profession." Aspiring practitioners served an apprenticeship by reading law for a couple of years with an established lawyer, who then recommended his students to the Bar with the assurance that they had "complied with the Rules of the Bar respecting the qualifications of candidates." The Bar also enforced a code of practice by banning the solicitation of clients and requiring its members to have nothing to do with lawyers who did not abide by its rules.[5] Doctors in antebellum Providence organized themselves as professionals in order to define "orthodox" medical practice. The Providence Medical Association, which, like the American Medical Association was founded in 1848, excluded not only any "proprietor or vendor of patent medicines" but also "any empirical or irregular practitioner." Shunned by allopaths, homeopathic physicians countered by forming their own association in 1850. Nonetheless, the professional activities of both medical societies were remarkably similar. Each drew up fee tables, subscribed to medical journals, collected technical libraries, and held prize competitions for scholarly papers.[6]

Among both doctors and lawyers, concern for their professional status, threatened by sheer growth in the number of practitioners and the emergence of competing schools of practice, prompted organization. Under these new conditions, acquaintance, common social background, and tacit agreement on the conventions governing practice no longer sufficed to maintain the social status of the practitioners. Occupational identity came instead to depend on formal

[5] Providence County Bar Meeting, Minutes, 1795-1844, 1-3, 11, RIHS; *Rules and Regulations of the Bar in the County of Providence* (Providence: Miller, Goddard & Mann, 1814), 4-6; *Articles of Association and By-Laws of the Providence County Bar. Adopted October 3, 1849* (Providence: Joseph Knowles, 1849), 7-11.

[6] Providence Medical Association, *Constitution and By-Laws, with a List of Members* (Providence: Providence Press Co., 1870), 6; Roland Hammond, John E. Donley, and Peter Pineo Chase, "The Providence Medical Association, 1848-1948," *Rhode Island Medical Journal* 31 (January 1948): 15-33; *Constitution and By-Laws of the Rhode Island Homeopathic Society. Adopted May 15, 1850* (Providence: A. C. Greene, 1850).

networks that linked similarly trained attorneys and physicians together. The democratization of a profession, reflected by the entry
of dozens of often ill or unconventionally trained practitioners,
made it less likely that status inhered in the practitioners themselves
as gentlemen. Only by regulating entry into their profession could
practitioners enhance their own social status.[7]

Following the Civil War, new occupational groups began to define
themselves as professions. In 1875 some of the city's most ambitious
architects established the Rhode Island Chapter of the American
Institute of Architects. Members, who included "gentlemen of taste
and education who are lovers of the fine arts generally, or amateurs
in architecture," met monthly to discuss topics ranging from a fee
schedule for professional services to the use of metric measure-
ments. At the request of the city council, they drafted the city's first
comprehensive building code. Members of the Providence Association of Mechanical Engineers, organized in 1894, maintained a
clubhouse, delivered papers, and took summer outings.[8]

Although interested in diffusing "useful knowledge" and en-
hancing the professional status of their members, other occupa-

[7] On the ways in which professionalization affected particular middle-class occupations, see Daniel H. Calhoun, *Professional Lives in America: Structure and Aspiration,
1750-1850* (Cambridge: Harvard University Press, 1965); Joseph F. Kett, *The Formation of the American Medical Profession: The Role of Institutions, 1780-1860* (New Haven: Yale University Press, 1968); Donald M. Scott, *From Office to Profession: The New
England Ministry, 1750-1850* (Philadelphia: University of Pennsylvania Press, 1978);
Burton J. Bledstein, *The Culture of Professionalism: The Middle Class and the Development
of Higher Education in America* (New York: W.W. Norton & Co., 1976); and Geoffrey
Millerson, *The Qualifying Associations: A Study in Professionalisation* (London: Routledge & Kegan Paul, 1964), esp. 47-87. For attempts to define what constitutes a
profession, see William J. Goode, "Community within a Community: The Profes-
sions," *American Sociological Review* 22 (April 1957): 194-200; ibid., "Encroachment,
Charlatanism, and the Emerging Profession: Psychology, Sociology, and Medicine,"
ibid. 25 (December 1960): 902-914; Rue Bucher and Anselm Strauss, "Professions in
Process," *American Journal of Sociology* 66 (January 1961): 325-34; Bernard Barber,
"Some Problems in the Sociology of the Professions," in *The Professions in America*, ed.
Kenneth S. Lynn (Boston: Houghton Mifflin Co., 1965), 15-34; and Monte A. Cal-
vert, *The Mechanical Engineer in America, 1830-1910: Professional Cultures in Conflict*
(Baltimore: Johns Hopkins University Press, 1967), esp. xv-xvi.

[8] *By-Laws of the Rhode Island Chapter of the American Institute of Architects* (Providence:
J. A. & R. A. Reid, 1875), 4; Rhode Island Chapter of the American Institute of Architects, Minutes, 1875-87, 5 January 1876, 18 January 1877, RIHS; John Hutchins
Cady, "Some Reminiscences of the Rhode Island Chapter of the American Institute
of Architects," typescript, Cady Papers, RIHS; Luther D. Burlingame, "The Providence Engineering Society," *Providence Magazine* 30 (May 1918): 240-42.

tional associations existed primarily for sociability or "the promotion of better acquaintanceship and friendly relations." This was especially true of several small, intimate clubs in which social life revolved around members' professional pursuits. The Providence Bar Club, established in the winter of 1881-82 for the purpose of maintaining "the honor, dignity and usefulness of the profession of the law" and for cultivating "social intercourse among its members," arranged banquets and clambakes for the small number of lawyers privileged enough to be admitted. Since its meetings soon became exclusively social, the club left "matters of policy and ethics" to the state bar association. The Providence Clinical Club, organized in 1885 by "a few bright young men with brilliant ambitious minds," inclined toward bohemianism. Dissatisfied with the Providence Medical Association, where papers were long, unoriginal, and "smacked of ancient methods, of abandoned theories [and] practices," fifteen physicians decided to form their own circle. Informal luncheons in members' homes, at which papers were "strenuously" discussed, avoided the expense of catered banquets. Beer and coffee promoted sociability, as did singing popular songs of the day.[9]

Still other occupational associations were formed to protect their members from illness and death. Even white-collar workers in relatively unhazardous occupations saw the value of mutual benefit associations, which helped satisfy the yearning for security that family and kin filled in less mobile societies.[10] Typical of the associations that combined mutual benefit with occupational advancement was the Bank Clerks' Mutual Benefit Association, established in 1871, which held annual banquets "to promote better acquaintance and friendly relations." In return for annual dues ranging from six dollars upwards, depending on age, it paid substantial funeral benefits of five hundred dollars to next of kin and provided annuities for elderly and infirm members.[11]

    [9] "Bar Club's Final Decree," *Providence Sunday Journal Magazine*, 26 May 1929; "History of the Providence Clinical Club," MS, 1-4, RIHS.

    [10] See Michael Anderson, *Family Structure in Nineteenth-Century Lancashire* (Cambridge: Cambridge University Press, 1971). Indeed, F.L.K. Hsu contends that only in voluntary associations do Americans find the sociability, security, and status that Chinese find in their clans. *Clan, Caste, and Club* (Princeton: Van Nostrand, 1963), 192-231.

    [11] *Constitution of the Bank Clerks' Mutual Benefit Association of the City of Providence* (Providence: Knight & Remington, 1881), 4.

The prospect of state regulation accounts for the formation of a final group of occupational associations. The state's pharmacists began to define themselves as a profession after the General Assembly, at the instigation of the Rhode Island Medical Society, passed a "Medicine and Poison Act," which provided for the licensing of pharmacists and the creation of a State Board of Pharmacy. The Rhode Island Pharmaceutical Association, founded in 1874, not only organized the sociability of its members by arranging annual banquets, summer excursions, and other social occasions. It also monitored legislation affecting the druggists' trade since, as purveyors of alcohol for "medicinal purposes," they frequently came under close police scrutiny. The association also claimed credit for the establishment of a state college of pharmacy, which promised to raise professional standards.[12]

Professionals were not the only members of the city's middle classes who turned to more specialized organization following the Civil War. In 1868 Amos C. Barstow was among the prominent businessmen who founded the Providence Board of Trade "for the purpose of promoting trade and commerce in the city of Providence and vicinity." Through its affiliation with the National Board of Trade, purportedly "the most forceful organization in this Country, excepting the Federal Congress," the Board of Trade linked its members to an emergent national business community. As a powerful lobby, it voiced the sentiments of the city's business community.[13]

Later businessmen's organizations, more homogeneous in membership than the Board of Trade, represented more specialized interests. In 1884 manufacturing jewelers, who by this time had be-

[12] Frank A. Jackson, "Some Outstanding Activities of the Rhode Island Pharmaceutical Association," in *Official Souvenir Book, Fiftieth Anniversary of the Rhode Island Pharmaceutical Association* (Providence: n.p., 1924), 16-34. In 1909 an observer reported that the city's drugstores were doing "a thriving traffic" on Sundays "even in other things than medicines, cigars, and soft drinks." Lester Bradner, "Religion," in *A Modern City: Providence, Rhode Island, and Its Activities*, ed. William Kirk (Chicago: University of Chicago Press, 1909), 343.

[13] "Providence Board of Trade," *Providence Journal of Commerce* 5 (March 1897): 25-28; W. Lloyd Warner and Desmond D. Martin, "Big Trade and Business Associations," in Warner et al., *The Emergent American Society*, vol. 1: *Large Scale Organizations* (New Haven: Yale University Press, 1967), 317-25; Robert H. Wiebe, *Businessmen and Reform: A Study of the Progressive Movement* (Cambridge: Harvard University Press, 1962), 33.

come fairly numerous in Providence, established their own board of trade to protect members "from fraud, or unjust and unlawful exactions." Similarly, the city's manufacturing chemists joined a national trade association for "protection against unwise legislation and unjust freight discrimination." Wholesale grocers, milk dealers, and newspaper dealers also formed their own associations, often, as in the case of the city's pharmacists, because of the prospect of state regulation.[14] Regardless of why they were formed, few of these associations neglected the social life of their members. Most arranged banquets, picnics, baseball games, excursions, and balls for their members. The members of the Butchers' and Marketmen's Association, for example, made annual summer excursions to nearby shore resorts on Narragansett Bay, where there were "all kinds of games and pastimes," and sponsored winter concerts and balls that, they claimed, were "patronized by the elite of the city."[15]

Toward the end of the nineteenth century, rising concern over Providence's high freight rates prompted local businessmen to band together in boosters' clubs. The Advance Club, organized in 1890 "for promoting the business and material interests of the city of Providence and for social and literary culture," published pamphlets on municipal issues ranging from the city's water supply to street railways and parks.[16] The Rhode Island Business Men's Association, also organized in 1890, extended membership to firms and corporations as well as to individual businessmen interested in securing better railroad facilities for the city and in ending what were considered discriminatory freight rates. In its efforts to promote the city's commerce, the Business Men's Association lobbied for a new federal post office for Providence and helped mount an impressive state exhibit at the World's Columbian Exposition in Chicago.[17]

By 1900 builders and traders, fruit and produce dealers, real es-

[14] *Constitution and By-Laws of the Manufacturing Jewelers' Board of Trade* (Providence: E. A. Johnson & Co., 1888), 7; *Constitution and By-Laws of the Manufacturing Chemists' Association of the United States* (Providence: Snow & Farnham, 1894), 3.

[15] "Butchers' and Marketmen's Day," 15 May 1883, broadside, Rhode Island Scrapiana, Rider Collection, Brown University Library.

[16] *Organization, Constitution, By-Laws and Membership of the Advance Club, Providence, R.I.* (Providence: E. A. Johnson & Co., 1893), 3-4.

[17] *Manual of the Rhode Island Business Men's Association, 1890-1907* (Providence: Nathan A. Briggs & James B. Littlefield, 1907), 8-9.

tate agents, lumber dealers, market gardeners, retail and wholesale grocers, master carpenters, masons, and plumbers had all organized. The definition of these and other new occupational communities came at the expense of the broad antebellum producers' community. Men who had formerly thought of themselves as "producers" now defined themselves as members of specialized occupational groups—as architects, manufacturing jewelers, bank clerks, and so forth. What had once been a unitary "middle class" of producers had fragmented into more particularistic, though better organized, groups of professionals, white-collar workers, and businessmen.[18]

The same trend toward greater organization proceeded, though at a somewhat slower rate, among the city's workingmen. Also concerned about job control, they joined unions after the Civil War in an attempt to prevent mechanization and the subdivision of tasks from diluting their job skills. Other workingmen sought mutual benefit and class solidarity in credit unions, lyceums, mutual savings associations, and neighborhood clubs. Typically, these workingmen's associations attempted to meld the work and leisure of their members, scheduling festive balls and springtime outings to promote class consciousness.[19] This proliferation of working-class organizations, which paralleled the greater organization of business and professional groups, fanned fears among spokesmen for a middle-class America of heightened class conflict between capital and labor.

Workingmen's associations were the products of the profound changes wrought in artisanal culture by industrialization. Outside of a few precociously industrialized cities like Lynn, Massachusetts,

[18] David C. Hammack has shown how the proliferation of business and professional organizations in late nineteenth-century New York "diffused" the "formidable economic resources" of their members. Because of these numerous competing organizations, businessmen could rarely agree on common policy, even on such fundamental issues as transportation. *Power and Society: Greater New York at the Turn of the Century* (New York: Russell Sage Foundation, 1982), 52.

[19] On the unions' role as purveyors of entertainment, see Daniel J. Walkowitz, *Worker City, Company Town: Iron and Cotton-Worker Protest in Troy and Cohoes, New York, 1855-84* (Urbana: University of Illinois Press, 1978), esp. 156-77; John T. Cumbler, *Working-Class Community in Industrial America: Work, Leisure, and Struggle in Two Industrial Cities, 1880-1930* (Westport, Conn.: Greenwood Press, 1979); and Roy Rosenzweig, *Eight Hours for What We Will: Workers and Leisure in an Industrial City, 1870-1920* (Cambridge: Cambridge University Press, 1983).

and Newark, New Jersey, the economy of the antebellum North
centered on the small workshop, where wage earners worked along-
side their masters. Apprenticeship regulated entry into a trade by
prescribing a term of years for adolescent boys who apprenticed
themselves to master craftsmen from whom they received an education in the skills of the trade, normally along with room, board,
and paternalistic supervision. Lucian Sharpe of Brown & Sharpe,
for example, served an apprenticeship of nearly five years with Joseph R. Brown before becoming Brown's partner in 1853. Although
antebellum mechanization eroded some skills, it put a premium on
many others. Knowledgeable about machinery, both in theory and
practical application, many artisans profited from opportunities
spawned by industrialization. Not surprisingly, a producers' ethos
that recognized no permanent or irreconcilable differences between an employer and his employees held sway, with many journeymen looking forward to the day when they too would become
masters. After the Civil War, however, the trend toward ever larger,
more impersonal units of production and the erosion of job skills
widened the gap between employers and their employees. The waning of paternalism, the entry of large numbers of women and children into the work force, and a combination of lower wages and
longer working hours prompted workingmen to join unions.[20]

Although they appealed to entirely different groups of producers
than did professional and trade associations, unions performed
many of the same functions. They too set occupational standards,
mapped boundaries, regulated apprenticeship, protected their

---

[20] Henry Dexter Sharpe, *Joseph R. Brown, Mechanic, and the Beginnings of Brown &
Sharpe* (New York: Newcomen Society, 1949), 10-11. In some industries, notably machine manufacturing, apprenticeship persisted into the twentieth century. See Luther Burlingame, "An Example of the Modern Development of the Apprenticeship
System," *Engineering Magazine* 26 (January 1904): 511-19; Calvert, *The Mechanical
Engineer in America.* For evocations of artisanal culture and careful examinations of
the changes wrought by industrialization, see Paul G. Faler, *Mechanics and Manufac-
turers in the Early Industrial Revolution: Lynn, Massachusetts, 1780-1860* (Albany: State
University of New York Press, 1981); Susan E. Hirsch, *Roots of the American Working
Class: The Industrialization of Crafts in Newark, 1800-1860* (Philadelphia: University of
Pennsylvania Press, 1978); Bruce Laurie, *Working People of Philadelphia, 1800-1850*
(Philadelphia: Temple University Press, 1980); Sean Wilentz, *Chants Democratic: New
York City and the Rise of the American Working Class, 1788-1850* (New York: Oxford Uni-
versity Press, 1984). Eric Foner delineates the producers' ethos in *Free Soil, Free Labor,
Free Men: The Ideology of the Republican Party before the Civil War* (New York: Oxford
University Press, 1970), 11-39.

members from illness and death, and promoted sociability. Many of Providence's earliest unions, which often originated as mutual benefit societies to provide relief during seasonal lags, were wary of strikes. As time passed, however, they shed their aversion to direct action and adopted more aggressive tactics, either becoming chapters of national unions, or affiliating with other local unions in citywide federations. Increasingly they resorted to strikes, boycotts, and similar weapons to advance working-class interests.

Unions formed before 1880 in Providence commonly resembled secret societies, employing passwords and extracting vows from their members not to reveal union business. The Providence House Painters' Protective Association, established in 1864, required its members to pledge that they would "not divulge the proceedings"; a sergeant-at-arms admitted "no one without the password." The Providence Typographical Union, organized in 1857, attempted to regulate wages among journeymen, set the length of apprenticeship, and prevent the employment of scabs. "Organization is necessary," its members explained, "not only to ensure a fair remuneration for labor, but to establish a regular system in offices, and to elevate the character of the profession, which has too long suffered from the incursions of 'rat-dom.' " The corresponding secretary kept a "Black Book" in which he entered the names of journeymen printers reported as "rats" by unions in other cities, and the local union circulated pictures of these scabs. Below each picture was "matter descriptive of the 'rat's' character, replete in derogatory detail." Although the union twice struck employers who refused to pay its wage scales—first in 1860, and then again in 1872—it generally sought to avoid strikes. One reason was that in 1872 "some of the men most responsible for the Union's embroilment gathered their belongings and left this city, leaving the Union to settle the difficulty as best it could." Indeed, the Providence Typographical Union claimed credit for defeating a proposal made in 1868 to establish a national strike fund.[21]

Other workingmen's associations resembled fraternal lodges in

[21] *Constitution and By-Laws of the Providence House Painters' Protective Association* (Providence: Thurston, 1870), 3, 9; Providence Typographical Union, *Printers and Printing in Providence, 1762-1907* (Providence: Providence Printing Co., 1907), 53, 78, 85, 91; *Constitution and Rules of Order of the Providence Typographical Union, No. 33* (Providence: Providence Press Co., 1870), 7.

their emphasis on thrift, sobriety, and mutual benefit. The constitution of the Providence Cigarmakers Association, formed in 1860, stipulated that "no smoking or refreshments, except cold water, shall at any time be allowed in the Association rooms." In 1867 journeymen tailors organized a protective union with 110 charter members; though making no provisions for sickness, it did pay funeral benefits of fifty dollars to next of kin. Five years later, team drivers also organized a benevolent society "to provide for each other[']s temporal welfare." They too subscribed to the pervasive midcentury ethic of temperance and self-improvement, fining members for intoxication and disorderliness at meetings.[22]

Both practical and ideological considerations help explain why these early workingmen's organizations expressed more interest in mutual benefit provisions than in direct action. Few local unions and even fewer nationals then possessed ample strike funds. Without them, striking workers had to rely on voluntary loans or contributions from sympathetic unions—a precarious base upon which to wage a protracted strike. In addition, many workingmen clung to the antebellum dream of producers united against monopolists, speculators, liquor dealers, and other nonproducers. They thus frequently proclaimed their common interest with employers. Although pledging to defend its interests against "any employer who shall be known to depreciate our trade," the Journeyman Masons' Association, for example, "discountenance[d] the least malicious spirit towards employers, except self-preservation should demand it, being fully sensible that in the prosperity of the employer [the interest of] the employed is found." These journeymen obviously regarded strikes as a last resort, taken only "when all other means shall fail to effect a redress of grievances."[23]

In banding together for purposes of mutual benefit, workingmen took the path of least resistance. Employers could hardly criticize them for following the example of bank clerks and other white-collar workers. On more than one occasion employers themselves took

[22] *The Constitution and By-Laws of the Providence Cigarmakers Association, for Mutual Assistance* (Providence: Henry L. Tillinghast, 1860), 16; *Second Annual Report of the Commissioner of Industrial Statistics* (Providence: E. L. Freeman & Son, 1889), 93-94; *Constitution and By-Laws of the Teamers' Union Benevolent Society, of the City of Providence* (Providence: Franklin Office Print, 1872), 5, 8.

[23] *Constitution and By-Laws of the Journeyman Masons' Association, of Providence, R.I.* (Providence: A. Crawford Greene & Son, n.d.), 4-5.

the initiative in organizing such societies to head off unionization. In 1894, for example, the Union Railroad Company established the Street Car Mutual Benefit Association for its employees to preempt the organization of a local of the Amalgamated Association of Street and Electric Railway Employees. In return for a five-dollar initiation fee and yearly dues of eight dollars, automatically deducted from their wages, the employees received sick benefits of five dollars a week and funeral benefits of one hundred dollars. But they did not receive any assistance in collective bargaining, for the constitution of the new society declared that it "has no affiliation with union labor, as such, and nothing in its principles or practice has any reference to wage questions, terms of employment, or any other of the numberless topics of discussion that arise between the employer and the employed." Indeed, the company shrewdly hired a former union business agent to head the new society.[24]

Until the mid-1880s Providence escaped the labor unrest that affected other parts of the country undergoing rapid industrialization. The national railroad strikes of 1877, precipitated when railroads pared wages while lengthening workdays, gave middle-class Americans their first frightening glimpse of the class conflict that accompanied the increasing organization of capital and labor. After city and state authorities proved unwilling or unable to suppress the disturbances that had spread from Martinsburg, West Virginia, to practically all the other major railroad terminals in the Northeast and Midwest, President Rutherford B. Hayes dispatched federal troops to break the strike. Although Providence was spared, city residents could hardly ignore the signs of an emergent labor movement that forcefully championed workingmen's class interests. They had only to look to nearby Fall River, Massachusetts, which Providence boosters always hoped to make an industrial satellite. Fall River's skilled English mechanics were notorious for their union proclivities. Another hotbed of labor unrest was even harder to ignore. Olneyville, a compact mill village of about five thousand inhabitants, most of them skilled English and Irish artisans, was only two miles west of Providence's central business district. There, for three weeks in 1873, textile operatives and their families

[24] *Official Souvenir and History of the Street Car Mutual Benefit Association* (Providence: Journal of Commerce Co., n.d.), 41; Scott Molloy, *Division 618: Streetcar Employees Fight for a Union in Rhode Island* (Providence: n.p., 1977), 8.

marched in torchlight parades to agitate for a ten-hour day until the onset of the depression of 1873-78 dampened their protest. In the winter of 1875-76 wage cuts and longer hours sent workers in Ashton, Lonsdale, and other mill towns in the Blackstone Valley out on strike. Economic recovery toward the end of the decade emboldened workers to demand that their wages be restored to predepression levels.[25]

In the 1880s, however, a combination of circumstances rechanneled this growing worker militancy into political action. First, political scandals weakened the Republican party, which had dominated state politics since the mid-1850s. In 1880 several thousand voters bolted the GOP after General Charles Brayton, state party "boss," was accused of embezzling postal funds. By 1884 even the partisan *Providence Journal* had been converted to the cause of independent politics. At the same time sentiment mounted in favor of eliminating the property requirement (of $134 in real estate) that effectively disfranchised most of the state's naturalized citizens. A petition bearing four thousand signatures presented by the Equal Rights Association compelled the General Assembly's Committee of the Judiciary to hold hearings on broadening the suffrage in 1881. Among the opponents of the property requirement was former congressman Thomas Davis. The Irish-born Davis had lost his right to vote a year earlier when his jewelry firm failed.[26]

The arrival of the Knights of Labor in Rhode Island, with their emphasis on replacing the wage system with industrial cooperation, also accounted for the shift toward political action. Formed in 1869

[25] Editha Hadcock, "Labor Problems in Rhode Island Cotton Mills, 1790-1940" (Ph.D. diss., Brown University, 1945), 159-80; Paul Buhle, "The Knights of Labor in Rhode Island," *Radical History Review* 17 (Spring 1978): 45-48. See also Melvyn Dubofsky, *Industrialism and the American Worker, 1865-1920* (New York: Thomas Y. Crowell, 1975), 54-61.

[26] Jerome L. Sternstein, "Nelson W. Aldrich: The Making of the 'General Manager of the United States,' 1841-1886" (Ph.D. diss., Brown University, 1968), 143-47; Equal Rights Association, *The Constitution of Rhode Island and Equal Rights* (Providence: Equal Rights Association, 1881); Mary Cobb Nelson, "The Influence of Immigration on Rhode Island Politics, 1865-1910" (Ph.D. diss., Harvard University, 1954), 67-69. From 1842 until the adoption of the Bourn Amendment in April 1888, naturalized citizens could not vote in Rhode Island unless they possessed at least $134 in real estate. Native citizens who did not meet the property requirement could vote if they paid an annual registry tax of one dollar, which political parties often paid for them. Registry voters, however, could not vote in elections for city councilmen or on tax or money questions.

as a craft union by Philadelphia garment cutters, the new organization first adopted the ritual and "vow" of a secret society. Led by "Master Workman" Terence V. Powderly, the Knights set out to enroll all producers in a mass organization. Everyone except bankers, lawyers, liquor dealers, speculators, stockbrokers, and other non-producers could join. Because of criticism from the Roman Catholic Church, the Knights eventually discarded their secret vow. By February 1882 they had reached Rhode Island, stirring interest among boilermakers, tailors, stonecutters, housepainters, and longshoremen in Providence. Later that year, the Knights chartered their first assembly in the state when an "Industrial Association" or lecture club in Olneyville clandestinely affiliated with the national organization. Meetings were secret, announced by word of mouth or by coded messages on sidewalks and outside meeting halls.[27]

The Knights spread rapidly throughout the state. Critical of the "exclusiveness" and strong sense of "caste" of existing craft unions, they hoped to organize "a union of large growth" where "men and women in all trades and occupations would be bound together for the common weal." Advocates of both temperance and self-improvement, they opened reading rooms for wholesome recreation. By 1885 there were enough Knights in Rhode Island to establish a state assembly, centered in Providence, and to publish a newspaper, the *People*. A year later, at the peak of their strength in the state, the Knights claimed more than twelve thousand members. The great majority of these recruits were unskilled weavers, loomfixers, spinners, and other textile operatives who were organized into mixed assemblies. Three thousand were women who, attracted by the Knights' emphasis upon equality and temperance, had joined "ladies' locals." The few skilled workers in the union belonged to "trade locals." The Knights were strongest in the industrial villages of Olneyville and Wanskuck, in Ashton, Lonsdale, and other mill towns in the Blackstone Valley, and in Westerly at the southwestern tip of the state.[28]

[27] *Providence Journal*, 20 February 1882; William M. Jackson, "The Development of Labor Unions in Providence: 1875-1905" (undergraduate history paper, Brown University, 1973), 3, RIHS.

[28] "The Knights of Labor: History of the Order in Rhode Island," *People*, 8 May 1886; *Second Annual Report of the Commissioner of Industrial Statistics*, 86-89; Buhle, "The Knights of Labor in Rhode Island," 49-60. For interpretations of the Knights of Labor, see Norman J. Ware, *The Labor Movement in the United States, 1860-1895: A*

Ever since their inception, the Knights had been wary of strikes, preferring political action to direct action. In a speech before several thousand workingmen in Providence in 1886, Master Workman Powderly insisted that his union was "not a striking machine." Turning to "those who have looked upon us as such in the past," he declared that the Knights "most emphatically stand against strikes." Critical of the wage system and industrial capitalism, the Knights urged cooperation between wage earners and their employers. In 1883 they revived the movement for a ten-hour day, moribund since the mid-1870s. To bring pressure to bear on a conservative General Assembly, they held public meetings and circulated petitions. The assembly, which rejected the first bill to come before it in 1884, eventually decided that it could not long afford to ignore petitions in favor of shorter hours bearing as many as sixteen thousand signatures. "To get it [a shorter working day] out of the way in politics," legislators passed a weak 10-hour act in 1885. Under the terms of the act, manufacturers could only be punished for willful violations. The Knights then turned their attention to extending the suffrage.[29]

The Knights were not alone in their attempts to organize the state's workers. As Rhode Island's economy slowly recovered from the depressed conditions of the 1870s, skilled workers began to band together in craft unions. Journeymen bricklayers and masons, whose wages had plummeted because of the depression from $3.75 to $1.25 for a ten-hour day, unionized in 1880. Carpenters, painters, and plumbers quickly followed their example. Finally, in March 1884, representatives from both craft unions and the Knights of Labor met to form the Rhode Island Central Trades and Labor Union, which preserved "the industrial autonomy and distinctive character of each trade and labor union and without doing violence to their faith or traditions, blends them all in one harmonious whole." Al-

Study in Democracy (New York: D. Appleton & Co., 1929); Gerald N. Grob, Workers and Utopia: A Study of Ideological Conflict in the American Labor Movement, 1865-1900 (Chicago: Northwestern University Press, 1961); Leon Fink, Workingmen's Democracy: The Knights of Labor and American Politics (Urbana: University of Illinois Press, 1983); Susan Levine, "Labor's True Woman: Domesticity and Equal Rights in the Knights of Labor," Journal of American History 70 (September 1983): 323-39.

[29] Powderly quoted in Hadcock, "Labor Problems in Rhode Island Cotton Mills," 162n; Providence Journal, 29 May 1885, quoted in Buhle, "The Knights of Labor in Rhode Island," 49.

though promising financial aid for any member union conducting a "just" strike, the new federation officially discountenanced resort to strikes and boycotts. It shared the Knights' preference for political action.[30]

This surge of unionization, in turn, prompted counterorganization among manufacturers and masters. In February 1886, as organized labor launched its drive to amend the state constitution, textile manufacturers representing all but two of the largest firms in Rhode Island founded the Slater Club, named after the pioneer manufacturer Samuel Slater. Quickly pooling a huge $4 million strike fund to employ scabs in the event of strikes or walkouts, these mill owners challenged unions to tests of strength. In 1887 the Gorham Company used Slater Club funds to crush a walkout by one of the Knights' largest locals outside the textile industry. The success of the Slater Club in breaking unions inspired employers in other industries to organize their own protective associations. Although organized in 1903 ostensibly "for the purpose of engaging in the business of fostering, encouraging, and promoting closer social and business relations among its members," the New England Manufacturing Jewelers' and Silversmiths' Association really existed to maintain the open shop. Master teamsters, lumber dealers, and lithographers also formed protective associations for mutual aid in the event of strikes.[31]

The increasing organization of capital and labor called into question the traditional belief, as expressed by the *Providence Journal*, "that the interests of labor and capital are mutual and interdependent to the greatest degree, involving also the welfare and prosperity of the entire community." In particular, this disturbing development forced commentators, in defense of a middle-class America

[30] "History of Bricklayers' and Masons' Union, No. 1, Providence, R.I.," in *20th Century Illustrated History of Rhode Island and the Rhode Island Central Trades and Labor Union and Its Affiliated Organizations* (Providence: Rhode Island Central Trades and Labor Union, 1901), 246-47; R. A. Ripley, "Sketch of the Providence Central Trades and Labor Union," in Providence Central Trades and Labor Union and Building Trades Council, *Official Labor Day Journal, 1903* (Providence: Franklin Press, 1903), 12; Jackson, "The Development of Labor Unions in Providence," 6-7; Buhle, "The Knights of Labor in Rhode Island," 50.

[31] *Organization, Members and Officers of the Slater Club, 1886* (Providence: Rhode Island Printing Co., 1886); Slater Club, Agreement for a Strike Fund, RIHS; Buhle, "The Knights of Labor in Rhode Island," 63; William Kirk, "Labor," in *A Modern City*, ed. Kirk, 127.

apparently threatened from both sides, to reexamine one of the principal tenets of the antebellum free-labor ideology, the assumption that all hard-working, thrifty, and sober wage earners would eventually become their own bosses. The specter of strikes and other forms of class conflict, either on a national or local level, portended a Europeanized society in which the unorganized public would find itself caught between two antagonistic extremes, plutocrats above and proletarians below. The Knights' newspaper, the *People*, put it this way: "The industrial evolution has developed American Society into classes very similar to those of Europe. The disinherited, the wage earners are practically powerless politically, industrially and socially. The owners of the means of production, factories, lands, mines, &c., are absolutely masters of the people and all their interests."[32]

Among those disturbed by the emergence of a permanent class of wage earners, destined never to rise into the ranks of the self-employed, were Protestant clergymen, who customarily interpreted national trends for their congregations. They spoke in their official capacity as representatives of churches that still purported to be inclusive organizations, resisting the general trend toward segmentation. By this time some of these men were already formulating the doctrines of what was soon to be known as the Social Gospel, in which a large and influential group of Protestants turned away from individualistic views of salvation and ethics to stress the immanence of God and the relevance of applied Christianity to pressing social problems. In attempting to avert class conflict, they explored ways in which to preserve the broad antebellum producers' community.[33]

The prospect of imminent class conflict led the Reverend J. S. Swain, minister of the Union Baptist Church, to reaffirm the ante-

[32] "The Action of the Slater Club," *Providence Journal*, 29 January 1886; "Political Action," *People*, 12 November 1887.

[33] On the Social Gospel, see Charles Howard Hopkins, *The Rise of the Social Gospel in American Protestantism, 1865-1915* (New Haven: Yale University Press, 1940); Henry F. May, *Protestant Churches and Industrial America* (1949; reprint, New York: Harper & Row, 1967), 170-265; Winthrop S. Hudson, *Religion in America* (New York: Charles Scribner's Sons, 1965), 310-15; Sydney E. Ahlstrom, *A Religious History of the American People*, 2 vols. (Garden City, N.Y.: Image Books, 1975), 2:250-73. William R. Hutchison, *The Modernist Impulse in American Protestantism* (New York: Oxford University Press, 1976) is especially good on the theological currents that predisposed Protestant clergymen to social action.

bellum ideal of the dignity of labor. "In the North especially," he said, "it is considered disgraceful to be idle. Labor is dignified in our land, and every man who works shares in the honors and rewards that the land affords." Yet "the frequency of strikes" suggested that workingmen's "condition is not all that it should be." Although quick to express sympathy for the plight of workingmen, Swain condemned strikes, which "unsettle business, create confusion," and "are not in harmony with the kingdom of Christ." Instead he urged workingmen to "bear witness with the truth, to expose evil wherever it may exist, and to remember the pen and the voice are mightier than the sword." Swain's counsel may well have been tempered by the prominent role men like Thomas B. Ross played in his congregation. The anti-union pronouncements of Ross, a building contractor, so angered workingmen that they thwarted his bid for re-election to the Board of Aldermen.[34]

Other Protestant ministers endorsed industrial cooperation. At the venerable First Baptist Church, where a number of Brown University faculty worshiped, the Reverend T. Edwin Brown delivered an extraordinary series of Sunday evening lectures during the winter of 1885-86, later published as *Studies in Modern Socialism and Labor Problems*. Taking as his premise that "there is a social question," Brown asked, "Has Christianity," or "the Church," or "the Christian ministry anything to do with it?" In an appeal to "the responsibilities of wealth," Brown proposed profit sharing and other forms of industrial cooperation, or "democracy applied to labor," as means to reconcile labor and capital. Brown's depiction of strikes as "declarations of economic war, sometimes foolish, sometimes criminal, always costly, but not always inexpedient or unjust" expressed the ambivalence of middle-class Americans alarmed by the specter of class conflict. Brown concluded his lectures by upholding the church's traditional role as a bulwark of a classless society. "Nothing can take the place of the church," he declared. "Class brotherhood, whether in exclusive rich churches, or in labor unions, is not the broad, fair, universal brotherhood taught by Christ." For "society is more than a class," Brown insisted. "Lawyers always consorting with lawyers, preachers with preachers, members of any trade or profession always consorting together, are of necessity men narrowed and so far

[34] *Providence Journal*, 9 March 1885; *People*, 2 October 1886.

degraded." True brotherhood was only to be found in the church, where "rich and poor meet together in the presence of the Lord."[35]

A third group of clergymen, Christian socialists like the Reverend Frederic A. Hinckley, aligned themselves with the fledgling labor movement. In a lecture aptly entitled "Dynamite," delivered in February 1885 to his congregation of liberal Protestants at the Free Religious Society, Hinckley observed that there was "a growing feeling that we are coming to have a permanently degraded labor class in this country, membership in which means that a man is defrauded by something which belongs to him by natural right." The promise of unlimited social mobility, an article of faith among antebellum northerners, had faded by 1885. "You know and I know," Hinckley said, "that the chances are that ninety-nine out of every one hundred of our operatives will remain in the labor ranks; that most of their children are doomed to the same misfortune, and that for this fate there is to them practically no means of redress." Hinckley's lectures on "Competition," "Arbitration," "Co-operation," and other industrial topics won him a large and devoted following among workingmen, even though few if any of them belonged to his congregation.[36]

As the timing of these lectures suggests, many observers were then bracing themselves for another wave of strikes like those of 1877. The Haymarket bombing in Chicago in May 1886, for which eight anarchists were later sentenced to death, only heightened their anxiety. Yet once again Providence was largely spared the strikes that plagued many other industrial centers. Although tailors, weavers, bricklayers and masons all briefly turned out during the

[35] *Providence Journal*, 26 October 1885; T. Edwin Brown, *Studies in Modern Socialism and Labor Problems* (New York: D. Appleton & Co., 1886), 14, 162, 137, 121, 212-13; *People*, 5 December 1885; May, *Protestant Churches and Industrial America*, 179-80.

[36] *Providence Journal*, 16 February 1885; *People*, 2 January 1886. David Montgomery has labeled men like Hinckley Sentimental Reformers, heirs of antebellum radicalism who still believed in the "ideological syndrome" of free moral agency, self-improvement, temperance, and unlimited social mobility. *Beyond Equality: Labor and the Radical Republicans, 1862-1872* (1967; reprint, New York: Vintage Books, 1972), 387-424. Eugene Debs also shared this legacy of antebellum producerism, evangelical reform, and preference for political action. As an advocate of the traditional goal of social harmony, Debs responded to the concentration of corporate capital by emphasizing the need for the organization of the producing classes as producers, not as a permanent class of wage earners. See Nick Salvatore, *Eugene V. Debs: Citizen and Socialist* (Urbana: University of Illinois Press, 1982).

year, the most ominous threat to the city's social harmony came not from manual workers but from dry goods clerks in their drive for early closing. Though also classified as wage earners, the dry goods clerks enjoyed far more support from the city's clergymen than did their blue-collar counterparts. That was because they pursued less radical goals, opted for ad hoc rather than permanent organization, and appealed to the public conscience instead of turning out on strikes. Moreover, their desire for early closing overlapped the traditional clerical concern for strict Sabbath observance.[37]

For many years, the city's dry goods establishments, then on the verge of developing into modern department stores, had stayed open very late on Saturday evenings: until 10 P.M. six months a year, and until 9 P.M. the other six months. Led by a young Irish-American, about three hundred clerks formed the Dry Goods Clerks Early Closing Association in March of 1886. In addition to distributing 30,000 handbills, 400 large posters, and 1,000 circulars urging the public not to shop after 6 P.M. on Saturday evenings, the clerks solicited the assistance of influential middle-class spokesmen. At a grand mass meeting held later that month, Professor E. Benjamin Andrews of Brown University welcomed the "practical union of different organizations [and] different stores" as "a token of a new order of things in the world of wage earners."[38]

Also endorsing early closing were a number of Protestant and Catholic clergymen. Some, like Methodist minister Nicholas T. Whitaker, criticized late closing of depriving "the clerks of opportunities for social and intellectual improvement." Others pointed out that shopping on Saturday evenings abetted flagrant immorality downtown. "It is difficult to place this aspect, in plain language in public before a mixed audience, but there is a degree of immodesty and indecency found on Saturday evening that is a snare and a trap," declared David H. Greer, rector of Grace (Episcopal) Church. "It would be less harmful," he asserted, "for many a young woman to go through the sewer that runs under the street than the one that runs on top of it." A proponent of the Social Gospel, Greer had already organized a number of clubs designed to appeal to the tran-

[37] *Ninth Annual Report of the Commissioner of Industrial Statistics* (Providence: E. L. Freeman & Sons, 1897), 84-85; W. Jackson, "The Development of Labor Unions in Providence," 8-9.

[38] *Providence Journal*, 6, 23 March 1886.

sient boardinghouse population of downtown Providence. He had also supported parish women in their efforts to maintain a day nursery for the children of working women in the heart of the Olneyville mill district. After being called to New York's St. Bartholomew's Church in 1888, Greer built a magnificent parish house and presided over one of the most famous institutional programs in the country.[39]

Still other clergymen expected early closing to promote church attendance. As Congregational minister J. H. Larry remarked, "the masses cannot be expected to go to church, when they go to bed at 12 o'clock Saturday night." For men like Larry, who clung to the antebellum notion that the health of the republic depended on strict Sabbath observance, this was sufficient reason indeed to support the early closing movement. Reflecting this same Sabbatarian impulse, the New England Southern Conference of the Methodist Episcopal Church adopted resolutions in favor of granting workers Saturday afternoon as a half-holiday and giving them their pay on weekdays.[40]

The clerks' moderation also appealed to the city's clergymen. Instead of turning out against their employers, the clerks attempted to appeal to public opinion in the time-honored fashion of public meetings and petitions. Reverend Brown was quick to distinguish between such attempts at suasion and what he regarded as more coercive measures. "This early closing movement," Brown told the clerks, "will be promoted in the best way only by the persuasive force of public opinion, such as has been manifested here to-night. Force or threat of strike, or boycott," he warned, "will injure your cause." The conservative character of the clerks' protest helps explain why ministers who had little sympathy for an eight-hour day were willing to endorse early closing. This impressive support from the clergy notwithstanding, the early closing movement came to

[39] Ibid., 23 March 1886; *People*, 17 April 1886, 23 April 1887. For Greer's ministry in Providence, see Henry Barrett Huntington, *A History of Grace Church in Providence, Rhode Island, 1829-1929* (Providence: privately printed, 1931), 97-114; and Charles Lewis Slattery, *David Hummell Greer: Eighth Bishop of New York* (New York: Longmans, Green & Co., 1921), 47-90.

[40] *People*, 24 April 1886. Brian Harrison has argued that "nineteeth-century sabbatarianism flourished on a genuine coincidence of interest between evangelicals and working men afraid of being exploited." "Religion and Recreation in Nineteenth-Century England," *Past and Present* 38 (December 1967): 105.

nought. Almost twenty years were to pass before the Rhode Island Consumers' League undertook a second and ultimately more successful campaign for early closing.[41]

The Knights initially hailed the early closing movement as a sign of the spread of organization among previously unorganized producers. "The spirit of organization is abroad," proclaimed the *People*, perhaps in the hope that the clerks, by joining the Knights of Labor in one grand union of producers, would blur the emergent distinction between brain work and manual labor that prevented united action. But the newspaper soon had to concede that the clerks felt little if any producer consciousness. "The male portion of the dry goods clerks," it noted, "are not an oppressed class." They worked from nine to nine and a half hours on weekdays and another three to four hours on Saturday, or no more than sixty hours a week. Workingmen, on the other hand, typically labored longer than ten hours a day and till 5 or 6 P.M. on Saturdays. If the clerks wanted workers and their families to shop before 6 P.M. so that they could go home early, they had to help workingmen win a Saturday half-holiday.[42]

Yet another reason for labor's relative quiescence in 1886 was that workingmen channeled much of their energy into political action. This was especially true in Rhode Island, where prohibition, the creation of a bureau of industrial statistics, and modification of the property requirement for voting captured the spotlight. In April 1886 an amendment for statewide prohibition came before the voters. It commanded the support not only of such longtime advocates of prohibition as the Woman's Christian Temperance Union, but also the Roman Catholic Church, the *People*, and the *Evening Telegram*, the official organ of the Democratic party. Surprisingly, the amendment garnered about 60 percent of the vote when submitted to the voters. Many voters apparently voted for it more to embarrass the Republican party, which was closely associated with liquor dealers, than out of genuine conviction. (These same voters quickly turned against prohibition, voting overwhelmingly to repeal the amendment in 1889).[43] Yet prohibition also tapped a deep vein of

---

[41] Compare the views of Methodist minister C. E. Goodell in *Providence Journal*, 23 March 1886 and *People*, 3 April 1886.

[42] *People*, 27 February, 27 March 1886.

[43] *Providence Journal*, 29 May 1886; Robert C. Power, "Rhode Island Republican

antimonopoly sentiment. Among the amendment's most enthusiastic supporters were labor reformers associated with the *People* who
implored workingmen not to "exempt this devil because you like to
drink his broth." The "Liquor Interest," after all, was a monopoly.
As such, it was "an important, if not the most important, organized
corrupting bulwark of capitalism, and *must be recognized as the enemy
of rising labor.*"[44]

The *People*'s endorsement of prohibition was hardly surprising.
The newspaper was the product of a producers' cooperative, the
Rhode Island Co-operative Printing and Publishing Company, incorporated in 1885 as a joint venture between printers and labor reformers. Preaching the virtues of cooperation, the *People* spoke for
the "great productive classes," by whom it meant urban and rural
laborers, artisans, small businessmen, and farmers. As "the organ of
workers," the newspaper propagated the doctrines of "co-operation, and the rightfulness, the duty, and the benefits of labor part-
nerships, or trade unionism as it is sometimes called." The choice of
terms here suggests that its editors looked forward to the organization of workers as members of a broad producers' community
rather than as members of a permanent working class.[45]

During its brief existence from 1885 to 1888, the *People* championed a number of causes reminiscent of the great antebellum crusades for moral regeneration. Reflecting lingering antiparty sentiment, the newspaper decried "old party corruption." It dismissed
the Republicans as "a band of aristocrats." State Democrats were little better—"whining and profuse with promises until you put them
in office," where they too grew "arrogant." Only the Prohibitionists
stood out as a "young vigorous party of reform." They had already
nominated a member of the Knights' Social Science Assembly as a
candidate for a seat in the General Assembly. Moreover, "a very
large and influential portion of the party"—men like Frederic A.
Hinckley and J. H. Larry—were "anti-monopolist in every sentiment and sympathy." Some of the newspaper's contributors even

---

Politics in the Gilded Age: The G.O.P. Machine of Anthony, Aldrich and Brayton"
(history honors thesis, Brown University, 1972), 105-112; Nelson, "The Influence of
Immigration on Rhode Island Politics," 96-102.

[44] "Whiskey," *People*, 25 February 1888.

[45] Charter of the Rhode Island Co-operative Printing and Publishing Company,
Acts of Incorporation, May Session, 1885, Rhode Island State Archives, Providence;
People, 17 December 1887, 5 December 1885.

championed manual education, which had appealed to abolitionists like Theodore Dwight Weld. "The movement to unite industrial with intellectual training," one of them wrote, meant "that we will be no longer satisfied with thinkers who cannot shovel or shovellers who cannot think." Whereas manual education had once been considered therapeutic, designed to bring the mind and body into proper balance, by the 1880s it had become another way to blur the emergent distinction between manual labor and brain work that fractured the producers' community.[46]

Although critical of the typical Protestant church for being "more of a social club than a moral force" in the community and for "ignor[ing] the poor and lowly to whom Christ addressed himself," the *People* had nothing but praise for J. H. Larry, who ministered to a flock of "intelligent and well-to-do working people" at the Free Evangelical Congregational Church. "Some call me a Socialist," said Larry, who also edited the prohibitionist weekly, the *Independent Citizen*. "Well, they may. I believe in the socialism of the New Testament." "So full" of prohibition and labor reform was Larry "that he hardly preaches a sermon that does not bristle all over with [his] 'philosophy of fraternity.' " Other clerics condemned organized labor for its part in inciting the Haymarket riot, but Larry traced the "anarchy" that threatened the country to other sources—"the ballot box corruptions, the class distinctions, the gulf between employer and employee, the modern land system, the modern competitive system of private enterprise and the corrupting power of rum" — and suggested "their removal as the cure."[47]

In defining his role as bringing "the church to the people and to Christ," Larry epitomized the producerist heritage that linked prohibitionists, Single Taxers, Christian socialists, and other spokesmen for a middle-class America. All these critics favored monocausal, moralistic explanations that located corruption in America's decline from the antebellum ideal of a virtuous, sober, classless society where a harmony of interests prevailed between employer and

---

[46] "Political Action," *People*, 12 November 1887; "The Prohibitionists," ibid., 31 March 1888; letter from "Pilgrim," ibid., 10 April 1886; Robert H. Abzug, *Passionate Liberator: Theodore Dwight Weld and the Dilemma of Reform* (New York: Oxford University Press, 1980), 59-69.

[47] *People*, 3 April 1886, 5 December 1885, 31 December 1887, 14 January 1888, 26 November 1887.

employee. All denounced monopolists, rum sellers, and other ben-
eficiaries of special privilege as the agents of this corruption. Accordingly, all expected that once monopolies like the liquor interest
were broken up, other social problems would quickly disappear. As
Frederic Hinckley put it, "in every period of history there is some
great fact which stares us in the face, demanding attention and ultimately removal." Until the Civil War, "that fact was chattel slavery." Since then, it had been poverty, the "natural outgrowth" of
monopoly. "If you seek the strongholds of vice and crime, the
abodes of intemperance and prostitution," Hinckley observed, "you
go straight to the doors of extreme wealth and extreme poverty."[48]

The *People* voiced the views of middle-class moralists like Harry
C. Vrooman, a Christian socialist who edited the newspaper from
October 1887 to May 1888. Never an advocate of strikes, Vrooman
preached the efficacy of "the ballot and the labor organization." His
socialism, like that of Larry, amounted to a "philosophy of fraternity."[49] Henry George's faith that a simple tax on unimproved
land would eliminate monopoly also found frequent expression in
the *People*. Edwin C. Pierce and Robert Grieve, president and secretary respectively of the Rhode Island Co-operative Printing and
Publishing Company, were both Single Taxers. Pierce, a Providence
native, had specialized in real estate law since his admission to the
Rhode Island Bar in 1874. Elected state representative as a Republican in 1888, he introduced legislation mandating the Australian or
secret ballot. After leaving the GOP in 1898 because of his opposition to President McKinley's Philippines policy, Pierce won election
as the first state senator from newly incorporated Cranston. In the
General Assembly he led Democratic reformers in their attempts to
set minimum wages, prevent the attachment of wages in payment of

[48] *People*, 28 April 1888; Frederic A. Hinckley, *The Philosophy of the Labor Movement*
(Boston: George H. Ellis, 1874), 4; ibid., *The Just Demand of Labor, A More Equal Distribution of Wealth* (Boston: American Workman Print, 1871), 4. Herbert G. Gutman
discusses the millennial Protestantism labor leaders drew on to criticize capitalism
and exhort workers to organize in "Protestantism and the American Labor Movement: The Christian Spirit in the Gilded Age," in his *Work, Culture, and Society in Industrializing America: Essays in American Working-Class and Social History* (New York:
Vintage Books, 1977), 79-117.

[49] Ross E. Paulson, *Radicalism and Reform: The Vrooman Family and American Social
Thought, 1837-1937* (Lexington: University of Kentucky Press, 1968), 61-65. Leon
Fink points out the important contribution middle-class radicals made to the labor
movement as editors and propagandists in *Workingmen's Democracy*, 13-14.

debt, and create an industrial accident commission. Grieve, a native of Scotland who immigrated to the United States at the close of the Civil War, had learned the printer's trade in New Bedford and Providence, before becoming a free-lance writer. In pieces contributed to reform journals like the *Arena*, Pierce denounced "corporate capital" for leaving "the toilers only a bare living" by corralling "all the surplus wealth."[50]

John Francis Smith, the *People*'s first editor, was yet another middle-class moralist influenced by the doctrines of both the Social Gospel and the Single Tax. Proprietor of a small printing company in Cranston, Smith authored a number of pamphlets in which he advocated temperance, equal rights for naturalized citizens, equal pay for women, and, like Hinckley, public employment for all those who could not find work in the private sector. Although clearly sympathetic to the aspirations of workers, Smith had little sympathy for strikes. Voting, he predicted, "would directly accomplish the same thing, in greatly shorter time, for less than a thousandth part of the money cost of strikes." Like his fellow Single Taxers, Smith considered monopoly the most formidable threat facing American society. "High life for the few," he declared, "is a hindrance to higher life for the masses." His belief that labor and capital could coexist in harmony only "when labor owns the capital" probably explains his reason for becoming a shareholder of the Rhode Island Co-operative Printing and Publishing Company. In 1894 Smith served as an editor of *Justice*, a newspaper published by the Rhode Island Central Trades and Labor Union in conjunction with the Socialist Labor party.[51]

[50] *Preamble and Constitution of the Free Religious Society, of Providence* (n.p., n.d.); John Buenker, "Urban Liberalism in Rhode Island, 1909-1919," *Rhode Island History* 30 (May 1971): 46; Thomas Williams Bicknell, *The History of the State of Rhode Island and Providence Plantations*, 5 vols. (New York: American Historical Society, Inc., 1920), 5:553-54; Robert Grieve, "Why the Workers Want," *Arena* 14 (October 1895): 262; Rhode Island Scrapbook, vol. 8, 76, microfilm, RIHS; *Brown Alumni Monthly* 25 (November 1924): 111-12. On Henry George, see John L. Thomas, *Alternative America: Henry George, Edward Bellamy, Henry Demarest Lloyd and the Adversary Tradition* (Cambridge: Harvard University Press, 1983).

[51] Smith quoted in Carl Gersuny, "John Francis Smith, Heterodox Yankee Printer," *Rhode Island History* 38 (August 1979), 88; letter from Smith, *Providence Journal*, 15 January 1883. Edwin C. Pierce characterized Smith as a "true radical" in his eulogy, *John Francis Smith—Memorial Address by Edwin C. Pierce at Radical Club, October 19th, 1904* (Providence: n.p., 1904). "John Francis Smith," Pierce said, "would be

But the most distinguished Single Taxer associated with the *People* was Dr. Lucius F. C. Garvin, first president of the Equal Rights Association. A "country" physician, Garvin practiced medicine in the village of Lonsdale, built around Goddard Brothers' principal mill, from 1867 until his death in 1922. He embraced the Georgist nostrum of the Single Tax upon reading *Progress and Poverty* shortly after it appeared in 1879. Appointed to the General Assembly to fill a vacant seat in 1883, and elected in his own right the following year, he authored a bill to create a bureau of industrial statistics, sponsored legislation providing for physiological and hygenic temperance instruction in the public schools, and introduced petitions in favor of the ten-hour day, woman's suffrage, and a state constitutional convention. Elected governor for two consecutive terms in 1903-1904, Garvin used his office as a pulpit from which to thunder against corruption and to call for civic regeneration.[52]

Elsewhere workingmen and their middle-class allies organized "labor parties" and contested elections, as in New York City, where Henry George finished second in a three-way race for mayor. But in Rhode Island organized labor first had to obtain the right to vote for workingmen, many of whom, as naturalized citizens, could not vote. "At present," declared the *People* in December 1885, "the people of this state are manacled by the disfranchisement of a vast majority of the artisan class." According to one estimate, the foreign-born, though a majority of the state's population, comprised less than a fifth of its registered voters. After the General Assembly rejected a motion calling for a constitutional convention to consider abolition of the property requirement for voting, organized labor mobilized petition drives and recruited large numbers of workingmen into equal rights clubs. A flurry of petitions soon forced the assembly to reconsider its decision by submitting the question to the voters. The result was the so-called Bourn Amendment, ratified by a majority of the state's freemen in 1888. Although abolishing the property re-

glad that his eulogist should mingle with a tribute to his memory an appeal for radicalism, an appeal for the bringing together in organization all the true progressives who will stand shoulder to shoulder in the great battle with privilege, monopoly, reactionary toryism, and in this State with an entrenched oligarchy the opening skirmishes of which only have been fought." Smith's pamphlets are in the Brown University Library. Issues of *Justice*, 1893-95, are on microfilm at RIHS.

[52] Carl Gersuny, "Uphill Battle: Lucius F. C. Garvin's Crusade for Political Reform," *Rhode Island History* 39 (May 1980): 57-75.

quirement in elections for mayors and other executives, it retained the property requirement in elections for councilmen and other legislative officers. Yet the amendment enabled the Democrats in 1892 to elect their first mayor in Providence since 1853 and to control the mayoralty thereafter. Elected by the 40 percent of the voters who met property requirements, the city council remained Republican until those requirements were finally abolished in 1928.[53]

The Bourn Amendment quickly made organized labor a force to be reckoned with in state politics. Even before sending the Bourn Amendment to the voters, the General Assembly created a bureau of industrial statistics in March 1887. Republican legislators apparently took this action in order to conciliate workers as well as to redeem their tarnished reputation among voters disaffected by the party's handling of the prohibition amendment. If labor's demand for such an institution epitomized the political program of labor reformers in the 1880s, it also revealed the limitations of their vision. Workingmen and their middle-class allies regarded such bureaus as reform agencies. They believed that to "collect, arrange, tabulate and publish in a report" all of the "facts and statistical details in relation to the condition of labor and business in all mechanical, manufacturing, commercial and other industrial business of the state" would improve workingmen's "advantages for intellectual and moral instruction." They fully expected that shorter working hours, safer and healthier working conditions, and more comfortable homes for the working class would result from the creation of such bureaus.[54]

Although supporters contended that labor bureaus were created "to harmonize the interests of capital and labor, of employer and employe[e]," employers viewed them with suspicion and frequently refused to cooperate. The Slater Club, for instance, charged that the state's Bureau of Industrial Statistics "was being run in the in-

[53] *People*, 5 December 1885; Nelson, "Influence of Immigration on Rhode Island Politics," 151-52; Murray S. Stedman, Jr., and Susan W. Stedman, "The Rise of the Democratic Party of Rhode Island," *New England Quarterly* 24 (September 1951): 339. The best source on the Knights' preference for political action is Fink, *Workingmen's Democracy*.

[54] *First Annual Report of the Commissioner of Industrial Statistics* (Providence: E. L. Freeman & Son, 1888), 3; *Third Annual Report* (Providence: E. L. Freeman & Son, 1890), 1-4; John Ker Towles, *Factory Legislation of Rhode Island* (Princeton: American Economic Association, 1908), 113-17.

terests of the Knights of Labor." When the bureau sent out its first questionnaire concerning "the capital, wages, product and profit" of textile mills, the club's president objected strenuously "on the ground that the State had no right to inquire so closely into the business methods and conditions of private individuals and corporations." The club's members complied only after a new query, much less comprehensive, had been "gotten up."[55]

The Bureau of Industrial Statistics soon disappointed its supporters. From its inception, there were repeated attempts in the General Assembly to abolish the bureau. After the retirement in 1889 of Josiah Bowditch, who as the first commissioner of industrial statistics had been an impartial investigator, his position became a patronage appointment. As a result, the bureau assumed a low profile, often as interested in measuring union strength as in inquiring into the profitability of textile manufacturing. Yet even had Bowditch not retired, it seems likely that the bureau would still not have lived up to its supporters' expectations. As they began to define themselves as a profession, the statisticians who typically manned these bureaus distanced themselves from labor reformers. In 1888 Carroll D. Wright, pioneer statistician and first commissioner of the National Bureau of the Statistics of Labor, told the American Social Science Association that "the point aimed at always in the collection of labor statistics is the truth; and the results must be fearlessly stated, without regard to the theories of the men who collect the information." Wright went on to distinguish objectivity from mere advocacy. "Scientific statistics," he maintained, "are those which tell the actual truth, not those which simply establish our own theories." In Wright's opinion, agencies like the Bureau of Industrial Statistics were never intended to "solve social and industrial problems," though this is exactly why Garvin, Hinckley, and other labor reformers had supported them in the first place.[56]

---

[55] *First Annual Report of the Commissioner of Industrial Statistics*, 6, 14-15; *Second Annual Report of the Commissioner of Industrial Statistics*, 2.

[56] Nelson, "The Influence of Immigration on Rhode Island Politics," 144-45; Carroll Wright's address before the American Social Science Association in Saratoga, New York, 3 September 1888, quoted in *Third Annual Report of the Commissioner of Industrial Statistics*, 10. See also James Leiby, *Carroll Wright and Labor Reform: The Origins of Labor Statistics* (Cambridge: Harvard University Press, 1960); and Mary O. Furner, *Advocacy and Objectivity: A Crisis in the Professionalization of American Social Science, 1865-1905* (Lexington: University of Kentucky Press, 1975).

Labor's disappointment with the legislation that it had worked so hard to enact coincided with a momentous development within the labor movement as leadership shifted from industrial unions and cross-class alliances like the Knights of Labor to craft unions affiliated with the American Federation of Labor (AFL). Reasons for the Knights' precipitous decline in Rhode Island from more than twelve thousand members in mid-1886 to fewer than a thousand only a year later were many, but included their aversion to strikes, internecine disputes that weakened the state organization, and employers' hostility.[57] Unlike the Knights, the AFL accepted the inevitability of industrial capitalism and workers' subordinate status as a permanent wage-earning class within an inequitable economic system. The AFL also generally shunned political action, at least until 1906. Moreover, the federation repudiated attempts to forge broad producers' coalitions in which middle-class moralists like John Francis Smith had important roles to play. Although unionists affiliated with the state AFL continued to press their demands for shorter hours and better working conditions through their elected representatives and even toyed now and then with the idea of a "labor party," they gradually turned their attention from general reform issues that affected them as "producers" to issues that affected them as members of particular crafts—that is, to higher wages, shorter hours, and collective bargaining. As bread-and-butter unionism triumphed, strikes became more and more common.[58]

These upheavals affected Providence in particular as the state's largest city. In 1887 seventy-three horseshoers were partially successful when they struck for two days to demand higher pay. Over the next four years, building workers, tailors, file cutters, compositors, weavers, and railroad truckmen all walked out, some more than once. Between the Homestead strike of 1892 and the Pullman strike of 1894, strikes spread to a number of previously unaffected occupations—to plumbers and nailmakers in 1892, to bleach and dye workers in 1893, and to street laborers, granite cutters, and messengers in 1894. Reasons for these strikes ranged from reduc-

[57] Buhle, "The Knights of Labor in Rhode Island," 62-65.

[58] For talk of the formation of "a labor party," see *Providence Journal*, 11 January 1894. On the rise of the AFL, see Dubofsky, *Industrialism and the American Worker*, 61-64; and Harold C. Livesay, *Samuel Gompers and Organized Labor in America* (Boston: Little, Brown & Co., 1978), esp. 75-108.

tions in wages to demands for higher wages and shorter hours, opposition to piecework and excessive fines, and hostility to capricious foremen. Significantly, an increasing number of the strikes were union-led. By 1894 there were at least twenty-seven unions with more than 2,800 members in Providence.[59]

In self-defense, workers were following the examples of professionals, white-collar workers, and businessmen in turning to more specialized organization. Unions, as the *People* had pointed out in 1887, represented "the embodyment [*sic*] of the centralizing or organizing idea among the masses" and were "the first substantial prophecy of a better civilization." What had changed since then was that workingmen had begun to define their own class interests independently of labor reformers, Protestant clergymen, and other sympathetic middle-class figures. Although this development did not preclude cross-class alliances, it did make much more likely the clash of interests between antagonistic producer groups. It also fanned middle-class fears of class conflict. Organization increased the possibility that workingmen might choose to spurn the counsel of middle-class reformers, dissolve their long-standing alliance with these moralists, and aggressively pursue their own class interests, even when these ran counter to the public interest.[60]

Even more disturbing to middle-class observers was the frequency with which workers resorted to strikes, boycotts, and other class weapons. Eugene Debs, president of the American Railway Union and perennial Socialist party nominee for president, expressed the views of many unionists when he addressed the Central Trades and Labor Union in June 1896. "I know well that in every community there are many intelligent, well-meaning men who are not in sympathy with labor organizations. They say, and I say, that strikes should be averted as a terrible calamity," Debs declared in voicing his well-known aversion to strikes. "But," he added, "in the insatiable greed of some corporation, the workingman finds himself to choose between strike or degradation. When it comes to that, I say, as I have always said, 'strike every time.' "[61]

[59] *Ninth Annual Report of the Commissioner of Industrial Statistics*, 84-93; *Seventh Annual Report* (Providence: E. L. Freeman & Son, 1894), 72-73.

[60] *People*, 15 October 1887.

[61] Debs quoted in the *Providence Journal*, 24 June 1896; Salvatore, *Eugene V. Debs*, 169 and passim.

Debs's speech signaled a new labor militancy in Providence. Earlier that year, journeymen tailors had turned out against members of the Master Tailors' Association, and plumbers were soon to lay down their tools for an eight-hour day. In 1898 more than nine hundred employees walked out of textile mills in the industrial suburb of Wanskuck. The following year, some three hundred molders were led out by union organizers. In 1900 forty machinists briefly quit work at the Providence Steam Engine Company after one of their mates had been discharged, and on May Day the Painters' and Decorators' Union struck local shops that had refused to concede an eight-hour day. After a brief strike in January 1901 printers and pressmen won higher wages. When the following May some two hundred plumbers declined to report to work until they were granted an eight-hour day, most of the city's contractors quickly caved in. Also in 1901, striking machinists won a nine-hour day from several local machine works. This wave of labor militancy crested in 1902.[62]

The year 1902 was "a remarkable one," according to the commissioner of industrial statistics. "Probably never before, with conditions so prosperous and work so abundant, has there been so intense a spirit of unrest among the wage earners." For nine months as many as six thousand weavers turned out in protest against the installation of the two-loom system in Olneyville, which Providence had annexed in 1898. Next, brewery workers demanded a nine-hour day. Then, on May Day, team drivers struck their masters for union recognition. On the one side stood fifty team drivers who, making "much of the fact that they are consumers as well as producers," boycotted stores to which scabs made deliveries. On the other side were the "employers who have never had occasion yet to deal with their employees as forming part of an organized body," especially a branch of a national union. "We have practically paid them [our team drivers] union wages," protested a spokesman for Congdon & Carpenter, a local iron and steel company, whose workers walked out when the company refused to recognize their union, "but no man wants to have his business run by an organization." In

[62]*Providence Journal*, 30 April, 2 June 1896, 11 January 1898, 1 May 1899; *Fourteenth Annual Report of the Commissioner of Industrial Statistics* (Providence: E. L. Freeman & Sons, 1901), 67-68; *Fifteenth Annual Report* (Providence: E. L. Freeman & Sons, 1902), 117, 121-22.

the middle were the company's office workers who, as scabs, risked assault by angry strikers or their sympathizers.[63] Also caught in the middle were consumers, who suffered the inconvenience of the strike and higher prices for goods in short supply. Small business-men felt beleaguered. One grain dealer, fearing that shipments driven by scabs would not be delivered, came to terms with the union before the strike. "The small business man is the most heavily oppressed man there is to-day," he contended, "for capital grinds him on the one hand and labor on the other."[64]

In the most dramatic strike the city had yet seen, conductors and motormen of the Union Railroad Company, which operated all the trolleys in Providence and its vicinity, walked off their jobs on 1 June 1902. A year earlier, some of the railroad's employees had quietly organized Division 200 of the Amalgamated Association of Street and Electric Railway Employees of America. The employees, re-ported the Evening Telegram, were not really angry at the railroad; but they did claim "that there were a number of grievances that ought to be adjusted, and the only way to bring about such a result, in their opinion, was to have the backing of a strong union." In March 1902 the new union presented a list of grievances to the rail-road's general manager, including demands for recognition, a union shop, the arbitration of disputes, and a raise from $2.00 to $2.25 a day. Several weeks later the company publicly rejected the demands, although negotiations between the general manager and the union continued in private. The company's refusal to comply with a new state law mandating a ten-hour day for motormen and conductors sparked the walkout.[65]

Seven hundred of the railroad's thousand motormen and con-ductors walked out. Two hundred and twenty-five older men, hired before the electrification of the streetcars in the early 1890s and earning $2.50 a day, stayed on the job, as did about one hundred of the younger, lower-paid employees. Service was quickly cut in half.

[63] Sixteenth Annual Report of the Commissioner of Industrial Statistics (Providence: E. L. Freeman & Sons, 1903), 129-33; Providence Journal, 2 May 1902.

[64] Providence Journal, 7 May 1902.

[65] Evening Telegram, 25 June 1901. My account of the streetcar strike draws on the Providence Journal, June-July 1902, passim; Sixteenth Annual Report of the Commissioner of Industrial Statistics, 131-33, 138, 140, 150-75; and Scott Molloy, "Rhode Island Communities and the 1902 Carmen's Strike," Radical History Review 17 (Spring 1978): 75-98.

Making use of prearranged wagon service, the strikers encouraged a public boycott of the trolleys. Before the strike was a week old, a committee representing the older employees still on the job told the railroad's general manager that even though "they had no desire to quit," they believed "a considerable portion of the general public was inimical to them because they remained at work." This they knew from "the insulting and abusive language which was showered upon them."[66]

For the first four days of the strike, peace reigned in Providence. On the evening of 5 June, however, some five hundred strikers led by a military band paraded downtown in front of a crowd estimated at twenty thousand. Egged on by some of the marchers, the crowd blocked streetcar tracks with carts, wagons, and bicycles, and stoned the few streetcars running. The city's police commissioners moved quickly to restore order by closing all saloons in the evenings and banning crowds downtown for whatever purpose. As a result, Buffalo Bill's Wild West Show, then visiting the city, had to cancel its traditional parade. At the same time, municipal judges sentenced strikers and their sympathizers convicted of disturbing the peace to the maximum sentence of ninety days in jail. Within a week, full streetcar service had resumed in Providence.[67]

Although striking motormen were more successful in the nearby mill town of Pawtucket, where, according to the commissioner of industrial statistics, "local sympathy with the strikers was strong, and the local police authorities seemed to find it difficult to escape the influence of that sympathy," the days of the strike were numbered after striking carmen in Providence voted to return to work on 5 July. A few days later the holdouts called off the strike. Most of the strikers went back to work for the Union Railroad, though the most militant were not rehired. On 1 August Division 200 of the Amalgamated Association of Street and Electric Railway Employees disbanded.[68] In November, however, the defeated carmen and

[66] *Providence Journal*, 8 June 1902.

[67] Ibid., 6, 7, 10, 14, 22 June 1902.

[68] *Sixteenth Annual Report of the Commissioner of Industrial Statistics*, 132. In towns like Pawtucket citizens frequently sided with workers against absentee corporations. See Herbert G. Gutman, "Class, Status, and Community Power in Nineteenth-Century American Industrial Cities—Paterson, New Jersey: A Case Study," in his *Work, Culture, and Society in Industrializing America*, 234-60. Robert and Helen Lynd reported that in Muncie, Indiana, public support for organized labor lasted until after the turn

other workingmen got their revenge when they went to the polls in record numbers to help elect Lucius F. C. Garvin as only the second Democratic governor in the state since the Civil War. Indeed, Garvin attributed his surprising margin of more than 7,700 votes, after he had lost by 6,500 votes the preceding year, to "feeling against the nonenforcement of the Ten-Hour Law." Having exhausted its court appeals, the Union Railroad finally agreed to comply with the terms of the ten-hour law, which the state supreme court had declared constitutional.[69]

By the first decade of the twentieth century, the segmentation of the work force into exclusive and frequently antagonistic occupational groups had fractured the broad producers' community as well as dealt a devastating blow to the presumed harmony of interests between employer and employee. When employers refused to bargain in good faith, workers struck to press their demands for shorter hours, higher wages, and union recognition. According to the commissioner of industrial statistics, 170 strikes occurred in the state between 1901 and 1905. Of these 93 were reportedly "organized" by unions. As one response to this growing labor militancy, some companies adopted "welfare capitalism." Thus the Gorham Manufacturing Company spent more than twenty thousand dollars to build an elaborate "casino," equipped with a cafeteria, a broad veranda, lounging rooms, bathrooms, and a thousand-volume library for its employees; the Wanskuck Company, a worsted manufacturer, installed a gymnasium for its employees.[70]

Labor militancy also prompted a search for intermediaries, disinterested third parties, who could mediate between the contending groups or, better yet, conciliate them before any more nasty disputes like the streetcar strike occurred. Although noting "the long and varied list of occupations involved" in the strikes of 1903, the commissioner of industrial statistics also pointed to "a growing disposition on the part of the employer and employee to confer and

of the century. *Middletown: A Study in American Culture* (1929; reprint, New York: Harcourt, Brace & World, 1956), 76-80.

[69] *Providence Journal*, 5 November 1902, quoted in Gersuny, "Uphill Battle," 63-64.

[70] *Twenty-Second Annual Report of the Commissioner of Industrial Statistics* (Providence: E. L. Freeman & Co., 1909), 252-57; "Welfare Work in Rhode Island," in *Nineteenth Annual Report* (Providence: E. L. Freeman & Sons, 1906), 186-91; Daniel Nelson, *Managers and Workers: Origins of the New Factory System in the United States, 1880-1920* (Madison: University of Wisconsin Press, 1975), 116.

arbitrate for the settlement of grievances." Two years later, businessmen joined with union leaders in establishing the Providence Branch of the National Civic Federation (NCF). Consisting of seven representatives each from capital, labor, and the public, the NCF sought "to conciliate in advance, thereby preventing the need of arbitration."[71]

For their part, Protestant ministers frequently volunteered their services as arbitrators representing the disinterested public. When in 1905 journeymen carpenters struck their masters, the Right Reverend William N. McVickar, Episcopal bishop of Rhode Island, arbitrated the dispute, awarding the journeymen much of what they had demanded. Two years later, committees from Local no. 147 of the International Association of Machinists visited nearly every clergyman in Providence to solicit support in the machinists' struggle for a nine-hour day. The union, as its secretary explained, hoped to enlist sympathetic clergymen as arbitrators because they were "above interested bias either way" and would "not suffer in a business way if they act according to their best judgment and conscience."[72]

Yet clerical mediation revealed just how much Providence and greater American society had changed since the 1880s, when clergymen like Hinckley and Larry had also intervened in labor disputes. Representatives from the state's Protestant churches reluctantly acknowledged this fact when they discussed the strained relations between organized labor and Protestantism at the First Convention of the Churches of the State in 1909. Although acknowledging that "an alienation between organized Christianity

[71] *Seventeenth Annual Report of the Commissioner of Industrial Statistics* (Providence: E. L. Freeman & Sons, 1904), 101, 103; *Nineteenth Annual Report of the Commissioner of Industrial Statistics*, 177. For another call for arbitration, see "Rhode Island Wage Earners," in *Twenty-Second Annual Report of the Commissioner of Industrial Statistics*, 235-37.

[72] *Nineteenth Annual Report of the Commissioner of Industrial Statistics*, 169; *Providence Journal*, 14 May 1907; Kirk, "Labor," 135-36; J. C. Barrett, "The Labor Movement from a Local Standpoint," *Official Labor Day Journal*, 15. In 1887 Episcopalians sympathetic to organized labor established the Church Association for the Advancement of the Interests of Labor. Among its many activities, the association arbitrated industrial disputes, having "concluded that it would be a good thing in industrial war if there could be a third party who from a disinterested standpoint could amicably adjust matters . . . not in the name of law, but of Christ." Quoted in Clyde Griffen, "Christian Socialism Instructed by Gompers," *Labor History* 12 (Spring 1971): 204.

(the Church) and organized Labor" existed, the Committee on the Religious Needs of Rhode Island insisted that this was simply "an alienation of institutions." After all, since "the ideals of Labor are embodied in the ideals of Christianity," organized labor had "no quarrel with Jesus, the Carpenter." Here the committee echoed the sentiments of Reverend Brown, who more than two decades earlier had also written of "Jesus the carpenter" and declared that "a class church, whether of rich or poor, is so far as it is a class church something less than a Christian church." Similarly inspired by visions of universal brotherhood, concerned Protestants in 1909 proclaimed their belief in a classless society. They traced the apparent alienation between organized labor and the church to workingmen's mistrust of Protestant clergymen as apologists for capital. It was precisely to overcome this suspicion that ministers mediated disputes between capital and labor as the public's disinterested representatives.[73]

Yet by 1909, Protestant churches no longer functioned as inclusive organizations, comprehending all parties—employers, employees, and the middle-class public—within their walls. By this time fewer than one-third of Rhode Island's wage earners had native-born fathers. To the extent that wage earners attended the state's Protestant churches, they were generally clerks, commercial travelers, bank clerks, and other white-collar workers. If members of any church, the state's foreign-born millhands and operatives, with the exception of Swedes and immigrants from the British Isles, were Roman Catholics in the only state in the Union with a Catholic majority.[74]

Just as the broad antebellum producers' community fell victim to industrialization and urban heterogeneity following the Civil War, so too did the civic culture. As clubs and fraternal lodges proliferated, the inclusive civic culture of the mid-nineteenth-century city fragmented into a number of subcultures distinguished from each other by their exclusive leisure associations and activities. The increasing privatization of cultural pursuits meant that rational rec-

[73] *The Proceedings of the First Convention of the Churches of Rhode Island* (n.p., 1909), 24; Brown, *Studies in Modern Socialism and Labor Problems*, 196, 205; Hopkins, *The Rise of the Social Gospel in American Protestantism*, 280-301; Clyde Griffen, "The Progressive Ethos," in *The Development of an American Culture*, ed. Stanley Coben and Lorman Ratner, 2nd ed. (New York: St. Martin's Press, 1983), 176-80.

[74] Kirk, "Labor," 99-100; *Twenty-Second Annual Report of the Commissioner of Industrial Statistics*, 127.

reation, which had once cut across class and ethnic lines to forge a homogeneous community, began to sort people out along lines of neighborhood, ethnicity, sex, and above all class. By 1900 there were even signs of the emergence of distinctive upper and lower middle-class strata. Behind the walls of their exclusive clubs, afflu-ent businessmen and professionals separated themselves from the urban masses. In the meantime their wives and daughters created a national network of literary clubs. Vestiges of the antebellum pro-ducers' community did survive, however, among the shopkeepers, white-collar worker, and skilled workingmen who crowded into the city's fraternal lodges. As leisure became just as segmented as work, antebellum conventions enjoining the purposive use of spare time, sobriety, and strict Sabbath observance attenuated.

4 The Club Idea

"The opening of the twentieth century found the club idea firmly established in the minds of all classes of society, irrespective of nationality, condition or sex," declared the manual of the Congregational Club of Rhode Island in 1910. It had not been so as recently as 1875, when the club was founded. If the late eighteenth century was the heyday of the English club, the years between the Civil War and the First World War marked "the Golden Age of fraternity" in the United States, as clubs, lodges, and other leisure associations multiplied rapidly in cities and towns across the country.[1] Providence was no exception. As late as 1865, the city claimed no incorporated social or athletic clubs and but a handful of fraternal lodges. Only twenty-one years later in 1886, as Providence prepared to celebrate the 250th anniversary of its founding by Roger Williams, one observer counted 1,600 Masons, 2,400 Odd Fellows, and 400 Pythians in the city. In all, as many as 8,500 city residents out of a total population of 120,000 may have belonged to the city's myriad lodges. Hundreds more belonged to the social and athletic clubs formed during the two previous decades. Not to be left out, women joined the auxiliaries of their husbands' lodges, became members of tennis, cycling, and country clubs, and formed a host of literary clubs.[2]

[1] *Manual of the Congregational Club* (Providence: Standard Printing Co., 1910), 9; W. S. Harwood, "Secret Societies in America," *North American Review* 164 (May 1897): 623. For a discussion of clubbing in late eighteenth-century England, see John Brewer, "Commercialization and Politics," in Neil McKendrick et al., *The Birth of a Consumer Society: The Commercialization of Eighteenth-Century England* (Bloomington: Indiana University Press, 1982), 217-30; and Mary Ann Clawson, "Brotherhood, Class and Patriarchy: Fraternalism in Europe and America" (Ph.D. diss., State University of New York at Stony Brook, 1980), esp. chaps. 3 and 4. As Arthur M. Schlesinger noted, "perhaps the most striking upsurge of voluntary associations" following the Civil War "was in the domain of leisure." "Biography of a Nation of Joiners," *American Historical Review* 50 (October 1944): 18.

[2] Welcome Arnold Greene, *The Providence Plantations for Two Hundred and Fifty Years* (Providence: J. A. & R. A. Reid, 1886), 201-219. For estimates of lodge and club

The increasing organization of leisure after the Civil War seems to have been the product of more spare time and disposable income, the formalization of previously informal or casual activities, changing attitudes toward leisure, and Americans' desire to set themselves apart from others who were different in a heterogeneous society. As sociability became more organized, it became more secular, more segmented, and more sharply differentiated from work. Churches and moral reform societies, which for an earlier generation had been the principal purveyors of organized recreation, faced increasing competition from secular voluntary associations. The improving, purposive, family-centered amusements prescribed by rational recreation gave way to free-and-easy entertainment, normally segregated by sex and often accompanied by drink. Leisure, once viewed as a common bond among the heterogeneous inhabitants of industrial cities like Providence, increasingly sorted people out along lines of neighborhood, ethnicity, and class. As middle-class Americans flirted with leisure, they reconsidered their earlier allegiance to the purposive use of spare time, sobriety, and strict Sabbath observance.[3]

Providence residents' growing interest in leisure stemmed in part from the city's substantial population growth, geographical dispersion, and residential segregation. In the single decade from 1865 to 1875 the city's population jumped from 68,904 to 104,850, as Providence nearly tripled in size. Annexing land from both Cranston and North Providence, it grew from a walking city of 5.31 square miles into a dispersed metropolis of 14.76 square miles. As Providence spread out, its residents increasingly segregated themselves by class and ethnic background. The gradual development of a central business district centered on Westminster Street pushed affluent downtown residents further west along Broadway and south along Elmwood. Settlement on the aristocratic East Side expanded toward the Seekonk River along Waterman and Angell streets. Immigrants, who by 1875 made up half of the city's population, con-

---

membership in Providence around 1880, see William B. Weeden, "List of Rhode Island Organizations," MS, RIHS.

[3] For a discussion of sociability, or "a collective pattern of companionable relationships," see Reuel Denney, "Feast of Strangers: Varieties of Sociable Experience in America," in *On the Making of Americans: Essays in Honor of David Riesman*, ed. Herbert J. Gans et al. (Philadelphia: University of Pennsylvania Press, 1979), 251-69.

centrated near the wharves in Fox Point, on Smith Hill near the factories that lined the Moshassuck and Woonasquatucket rivers, and
at the western periphery of the city in Olneyville. Yet, until the end
of the century, there was ample room for all of the city's inhabitants.
In 1875 the acreage of the fifty-seven farms then in the city comprised over half its total area. As late as 1900, when there were still
large undeveloped tracts on the city's northwest fringe, less than 6
percent of the city's dwellings housed more than two families.[4]

Organized group leisure under secular auspices had not been
common in Providence before the Civil War. Few social or athletic
clubs existed, and those, without exception, appealed to members of
the city's merchant elite, who flouted the norms of the sober middle
classes. The Narragansett Boat Club, which maintained a boathouse
on the Providence River from its organization in 1838 until it dis-
solved in 1851, attracted "young gentlemen" who sought in rowing
"recreation, health and pleasure." At a time when the temperance
movement directed its fire at the fashionable who continued to observe the custom of the social glass, these gay blades toasted the
newly wed in their company with champagne.[5] Although Philadelphia and New York boasted elite men's clubs as early as the mid-
1830s, Providence had to wait until 1856. The Providence Club afforded "the advantages of a reading room and library," game rooms
for whist and billiards, and a wine cellar. Its stiff admission fee of
fifty dollars, high annual dues of twenty-five dollars, and exclusive
nature restricted membership to merchants from old families, large
manufacturers, attorneys, and a few physicians. Not a single member of the Mechanics' Association belonged.[6]

[4] Theodore Collier, "Providence in Civil War Days," *Rhode Island Historical Society
Collections* 27 (October 1934): 101-102; *The West Side, Providence* (Rhode Island His-
torical Preservation Commission, Statewide Preservation Report P-P-1, 1976), 20-21;
Elmwood, Providence (Rhode Island Historical Preservation Commission, Statewide
Preservation Report P-P-3, 1979), 17-24.

[5] Narragansett Boat Club, Minutes, 1838-52, 5 March 1839, RIHS. On the antebellum rowing craze, stimulated by a race on the Hudson River between a champion
British crew and American challengers in 1824, see Benjamin G. Rader, *American
Sports: From the Age of Folk Games to the Age of Spectators* (Englewood Cliffs, N.J.: Prentice-Hall, 1983), 41-42.

[6] *Constitution, By-Laws and Regulations of the Providence Club* (Providence: A. Crawford Greene & Brother, 1856), 3; Providence Club, Minutes, 1856-60, RIHS. I have
compared the club's membership with the *Charter, By-Laws, Rules and Regulations of
the Providence Association of Mechanics and Manufacturers* (Providence: Knowles, Anthony & Co., 1857).

View of Market Square, c. 1889 (courtesy of the Rhode Island Historical Society)

Limited to wealthy merchants and attorneys in antebellum Providence, the club idea spread rapidly through the ranks of the city's middle classes after the Civil War. Three clubs established in 1875-76—the Rhode Island, Union, and Hope clubs—set the pattern for future men's clubs. All three were expensive to join, restricted their membership, and extended the sociability of small groups of friends to embrace much larger numbers of men drawn from the same neighborhood and social class.[7] Later men's clubs served as social centers in new residential neighborhoods, provided downtown athletic and dining facilities, and enhanced professional identity. Both the West Side Club and the Elmwood Club, founded in 1885 and 1887 respectively, were, in the words of the *Providence Journal*, "merely a neighborhood club, used by men living in the immediate vicinity of the club house."[8] The Providence Athletic Association, which opened its doors in 1891 as the city's first downtown athletic club, was distinguished by its large membership and by its turkish baths, swimming pool, and fully equipped gymnasium. It boasted "about everything to be found in the amusement line," from boxing, wrestling, and fencing classes to vaudeville and minstrel shows.[9] The Central Club, established in 1898, offered a downtown location to suburban businessmen who lived too far away to return home for lunch.[10] In the University Club, incorporated in 1900, doctors, attorneys, and other young college graduates mixed on equal terms with their older and wealthier professional colleagues.[11]

After duplicate memberships are taken into account, perhaps fifteen hundred men belonged to these clubs in 1900. The overwhelming majority were white Anglo-Saxon Protestants—in a city where nearly seven out of every ten inhabitants were of foreign stock. No blacks were among these men, and but a few Catholics or

[7] Moses King, ed., *King's Pocket-book of Providence, R.I.* (Providence: Tibbitts & Shaw, 1882), 53, 91, 113. On the increasing organization of leisure activities in the second half of the nineteenth century, see Daniel T. Rodgers, *The Work Ethic in Industrial America, 1850-1920* (Chicago: University of Chicago Press, 1978), chap. 4, esp. 108-109; and Peter Bailey, " 'A Mingled Mass of Perfectly Legitimate Pleasures': The Victorian Middle Class and the Problem of Leisure," *Victorian Studies* 21 (Autumn 1977): 12-13.

[8] *Providence Journal*, 4 September 1898.

[9] *Souvenir Club Book of the Providence Athletic Association* (Providence: Journal of Commerce Co., 1899), 68.

[10] *Providence Journal*, 4 September 1898.

[11] *University Club of Providence* (Providence: Standard Printing Co., 1900).

Jews. Only the University Club, which admitted men on the basis of educational achievement, and the Providence Athletic Association, whose elaborate facilities required a large membership to sustain, were open to more than a handful of upwardly mobile non-Protestants.[12] Largely excluded from the other clubs, well-to-do Jews and Catholics eventually established their own elite social organizations.[13]

Prohibitive membership fees further limited the size of these clubs. Annual dues at the Hope Club, the most exclusive of the men's clubs in Providence, doubled from twenty-five dollars in 1876 to fifty dollars in 1882, then rose to sixty dollars in 1903, at a time when the average wage earner in the state earned less than $450 a year. Even the least expensive, the West Side Club, assessed a fifteen-dollar admission fee, later raised to twenty-five dollars, and charged twenty dollars in annual dues. In addition, there were the not inconsiderable expenses incurred while dining, drinking, or playing at the clubs; not surprisingly, members came from the ranks of the city's manufacturers, large proprietors, and professionals.

In joining one of these clubs, men purchased shares in well-appointed facilities where they could relax, meet associates, and entertain friends. They were also attracted, no doubt, by the exclusive male camaraderie, for the men's club served as a refuge from what its members must have regarded as the oppressive domesticity of the middle-class home. (Only the Providence Athletic Association opened its facilities to women.) Ensconced in comfortable armchairs, members relaxed, read out-of-town newspapers and peri-

[12] I have linked membership lists from the Hope Club and the Central Club for 1899, the University Club for 1900, the West Side Club for 1902 (partial), the Elmwood Club for 1890, and the Providence Athletic Association for 1896. *Hope Club, Providence, Rhode Island* (Providence: R.I. Printing Co., 1899); *Providence Central Club, 1899* (Providence: J.F. Greene Co., 1899); *University Club of Providence* (Providence: Standard Printing Co., 1900); *West Side Club* (Providence: Whittemore & Colburn, 1902); *Constitution and By-Laws of the Elmwood Club, Providence, R.I.* (Providence: Chadsey & Clarke, 1890); and *Charter, Constitution, By-Laws and House Rules of the Providence Athletic Association, Providence, Rhode Island* (Providence: Livermore & Knight, 1896).

[13] In 1901 Jewish business and professional men incorporated the Oxford Club for "fraternity and social enjoyment." By 1914 reportedly every prominent Catholic layman in Providence had joined the Catholic Club, established five years earlier with Bishop Harkins's encouragement. "Chartered Organizations," *Rhode Island Jewish Historical Notes* 2 (June 1956): 33; *Providence Visitor*, 27 February 1909; *Providence Magazine* 26 (September 1914): 633.

odicals, or passed time playing checkers and chess, gambling for small stakes, and bowling. Few restrictions seem to have been placed on members except that their behavior not embarrass the club. In 1876 the board of directors of the Hope Club reluctantly expelled a member who, after becoming "intoxicated," made himself "thoroughly obnoxious," and was "violent" when removed. Most of the clubs also featured restaurants whose table d'hôte lunches and dinners were generally cheaper than those at downtown hotels. In all but the West Side and Elmwood clubs, both of which were dry, members could choose from ample stocks of fine wine. Indeed, profits from the sale of food, alcohol, and tobacco proved an important source of revenue for the clubs, supplementing the income derived from annual dues.[14]

Clubs like these were especially important in ascribing social status in a wealthy industrial city. As Max Weber observed of the early twentieth-century United States, "at the present time, affiliation with a distinguished club is essential above all else." Indeed, "he who did not succeed in joining was no gentleman." Until the Civil War, the city's evangelical churches had closely scrutinized the credentials of would-be members. Admission to a Protestant church in antebellum Providence required convincing the brethren that the prospective member had undergone a genuine conversion experience. Membership in the club was similarly based on what Weber called "recruitment by ballot." But admission depended, not on religious experience, but rather on "proving [one]self to be a gentleman," as well as demonstrating one's "credit worthiness." Clubs thus functioned as "vehicles of social ascent into the circle of the entrepreneurial middle class"—a function especially appreciated by the upwardly mobile who clamored for admission to bastions of privilege like the Hope Club. The proliferation of clubs in post–Civil War Providence also reflected the secularization of American society, as

---

[14] Hope Club, Minutes of the Regular and Special Meetings of the Board of Governors, 1875-86, 18 November 1876, RIHS; Dixon Wecter, *The Saga of American Society: A Record of Social Aspiration, 1607-1937* (New York: Charles Scribner's Sons, 1937), 252-88; E. Digby Baltzell, *Philadelphia Gentlemen: The Making of a National Upper Class* (Chicago: Quadrangle Books, 1971), 335-63; and David C. Hammack, *Power and Society: Greater New York at the Turn of the Century* (New York: Russell Sage Foundation, 1982), 65-77. In 1904 the average wage earner in Rhode Island earned $443. Henry W. Mann, *Manufacturing in Rhode Island* (Providence: Rhode Island State Planning Board, 1937), 58.

club membership became more important in determining social status than denominational affiliation.[15]

By the turn of the century a hierarchy of clubs had risen in Providence to parallel those in New York, Philadelphia, and other cities.
Since Providence was too small to spawn separate hierarchies of
clubs along lines of wealth, ancestry, and culture, clubs in this medium-sized city seem to have admitted men primarily on the basis of
wealth and ethnicity. At the top was the patrician Hope Club, three-
quarters of whose members lived on the fashionable East Side. Just
below were the University Club and the Central Club, both of which
functioned as downtown clubs. On the next tier were found the
Elmwood and West Side clubs, neighborhood clubs that served as
"social centers" for rapidly growing suburban districts. At the bottom of this hierarchy came the Providence Athletic Association,
which, "as far as club atmosphere and chumminess goes," was
"more of a hotel than a club."[16]

Many of these same businessmen and professionals paid as much
as three hundred dollars each to become proprietors of Squantum,
Pomham, Hauterive, and the other exclusive shore clubs that flourished after the Civil War. The shore or clambake club preserved an
old Indian custom, which became institutionalized (and commercialized) in the second half of the nineteenth century, of visiting the
seashore to eat shellfish. One afternoon each week during the summer the proprietors repaired by boat, train, or carriage to clubhouses down Narragansett Bay, where they dined on chowder, clam
cakes, sausage, fish, sweet potatoes, and Indian pudding, washed
down with punch and wine. Before returning to their offices, they
relaxed by smoking pipefuls of their favorite tobacco, shooting billiards and pool, and wagering small stakes on "penny-100." As U.S.
Senator Henry B. Anthony described Squantum, "this beautiful
spot is peopled by a company of grave and sober pleasure seekers,
not the jovial fellows who frequent the more crowded and gayer resorts of the bay, but solid and substantial men, mostly middle aged,

[15] Max Weber, "The Protestant Sects and the Spirit of Capitalism," in *From Max Weber: Essays in Sociology*, trans. ed., and with an introduction by H. H. Gerth and
C. Wright Mills (New York: Oxford University Press, 1946), 308-311.

[16] *Providence Journal*, 26 May 1895. On club hierarchies in other cities, see Baltzell, *Philadelphia Gentlemen*, 343-45; Hammack, *Power and Society*, 73-76; and J. Willis
and R. Wettan, "Social Stratification in New York City Athletic Clubs, 1865-1915,"
Journal of Sport History 3 (1976): 45-63.

who leave their business, for a few hours, and return to it refreshed by their brief visit to the sea." With the exception of the family-oriented Home Society, established in 1882 by well-to-do Catholics, these shore clubs were for men only, normally inviting women and children to only a few of their twenty field days each season.[17]

The city's businessmen and professionals also joined the clubs organized by all the city's mainline Protestant denominations between 1871 and 1891. Two imperatives accounted for the organization of these clubs. First was the growth of the city, which scattered adherents of the same religious doctrines. As churches multiplied within each of the denominations, it seemed necessary to have an institution that fostered a citywide denominational identity by bringing together "representative laymen." In 1871, when the Baptist Social Union was organized, there were eleven Baptist churches in Providence, two of them only recently founded. The denominational clubs were also designed to interest the more secular-minded in religion. At quarterly banquets members listened to invited speakers discuss matters of denominational interest or the latest projects for social reform. "A good many of our most prominent and influential members," as attorney Royal H. Gladding, secretary of the Congregational Club, explained to a prospective member, "are not members of the church but only attendants."[18] Because of their relatively low admission fees, in every case less than ten dollars, and moderate annual dues, averaging between four and five dollars, the clubs numbered among their members many teachers, clerks, and other white-collar workers. Even a few artisans belonged. Most of their members, though, were substantial laymen from the wealthiest parishes of each denomination, the same men who were the mainstay of the elite men's clubs. Alone among the denominational clubs, the Baptist Social Union began to admit women in 1892.[19]

[17] Henry B. Anthony, "Squantum," *Providence Journal*, 18 July 1873; Robert E. Anderson, *The History of Squantum on the Occasion of the 100th Anniversary of the Incorporation of the Association* (Providence: Squantum Association, 1972); Records of the Pomham Club, 1887-1902, RIHS; *Providence Journal*, 26 May 1895.

[18] *By-Laws of the Rhode Island Baptist Social Union, with a List of the Constituent Members* (Pawtucket, R.I.: Nickerson & Sibley, 1872), 3; Royal H. Gladding to Rev. William McNair, 12 March 1902, in letter copybook, 1901-1903, Records of the Congregational Club, RIHS.

[19] For membership lists, see *By-Laws of the Rhode Island Baptist Social Union with a List of Members, March, 1899* (Providence: Remington Printing Co., 1899); *Manual, Con-*

Banquets were also put to more secular uses in late nineteenth-century Providence. Unlike the Rotary, Kiwanis, and other twentieth-century "service" clubs, which aimed at "Harnessing the Golden Rule to Business," businessmen's dinner clubs provided common meeting grounds and convivial occasions for their members.[20] The monthly banquets of the Commercial Club, organized in 1878, were intended "to advance the mercantile and manufacturing interests" of the city "by means of social intercourse, and the interchange of opinion among the members." Much more exclusive than any of the denominational clubs, the Commercial Club limited membership to sixty of the city's leading businessmen. For annual fees as high as forty dollars, members were privileged to hear "some of the most prominent men in the country" discuss "all the leading political and business questions of the times." According to attorney John C. Pegram, who addressed the Commercial Club on "The Influence of Clubs" at its monthly meeting in October 1888, these banquets had "the natural effect of wiping out individual selfishness and narrowness, by bringing among its members new ideas and coincidence of relations."[21] While members of the Commercial Club devoted their banquets to promoting the city's commerce, Lucius F. C. Garvin, Robert Grieve, and other Single Taxers discussed Georgist doctrines at the dinner meetings of the Radical Club. The club's

---

gregational Club (Providence: Standard Printing Co., 1900); Churchmen's Club, Diocese of Rhode Island, *Manual Number Three* (Providence: Standard Printing Co., 1899); *Seventh Annual Reports of the Secretary and Treasurer of the Methodist Social Union of Providence, R.I., and Vicinity* (Providence: Snow & Farnham, 1889); Unitarian Club, membership list from 1901, RIHS; *Constitution of the Universalist Club of Rhode Island* (Pawtucket, R.I.: F. E. Wright & Co., 1886).

[20] On the service clubs organized after 1900, see "Harnessing the Golden Rule to Business," *Providence Journal*, 26 December 1920; and Louis Galambos, *Competition and Cooperation: The Emergence of a National Trade Association* (Baltimore: Johns Hopkins University Press, 1966), 33-36. Galambos suggests that the popularity of dinner clubs among businessmen reflected a business "environment which had imposed upon management only the most elementary demands for stabilization, control, and interfirm cooperation . . . [M]ost of the problems that management encountered could still be solved by individualistic, competitive behavior" (p. 36). The dinner club's popularity among religious and political as well as commercial groups in Providence may have simply reflected the emergence of hotels and restaurants capable of accommodating several hundred diners at one time and of well-known caterers like Lloyd A. Tillinghast and Gelb & Norton.

[21] *Organization and Articles of Association of the Providence Commercial Club* (Providence: R.I. Printing Co., 1887); *Club, Bench, Bar and Professional Life of Rhode Island* 9 (March 1898): 8; Pegram quoted in *Providence Journal*, 21 October 1888.

membership, which ranged from university professors and attorneys to blacksmiths and diesinkers, even included a few socialists.[22] At the monthly banquets of the "non-partisan" Economic Club "speakers of national reputation" gave their opinions on "public questions, especially those relating to the harmonization of labor and capital."[23]

Following the Civil War, clubs also organized tennis, golf, and similar sports that required specialized equipment, full-time locations, and codified rules.[24] In so doing, they ascribed social status. To hunt with hounds, to play tennis or golf, or to sail required varying expenditures of time and money. Those sports that required the most expensive equipment and the most extensive space conferred the greatest social honor. Accordingly, country clubs drew their members from the wealthiest strata of the city's population. They were followed in status by tennis and yacht clubs, with cycling clubs at the bottom of the hierarchy.[25]

Since it offered the greatest range of activities and required the most extensive space, the country club was naturally the most exclusive of the sport clubs. It functioned as the American equivalent of an English country house or, in the words of one observer, as "the center of gentlemanly field sports," furnishing "more independent recreation than most hosts are able to provide." Whereas in England "sociability is a by-product of an interest in sport," American country clubs "encouraged" sport "for the sake of general sociability." Providence's first such club, aptly named the Country Club, grew out of the desire of some of the members of the Hope Club to have a country place for riding and shooting. Within a few years of its founding in 1888, the club added tennis courts and a golf course. By 1902 the city's social register listed ten such clubs, most of them only

[22] Radical Club of Providence, membership list, 1903, RIHS.

[23] Committee of Organization to Clarence Saunders Bridgham, 2 March 1905, in envelope of material of the Providence Economic Club, RIHS.

[24] For discussions of sport in late nineteenth-century America, see Foster Rhea Dulles, *A History of Recreation: American Learns to Play*, 2nd ed. (New York: Appleton-Century-Crofts, 1965); Dale A. Somers, *The Rise of Sports in New Orleans, 1850-1900* (Baton Rouge: Louisiana State University Press, 1972); John R. Betts, *America's Sporting Heritage, 1850-1950* (Reading, Mass.: Addison-Wesley, 1974); and Rader, *American Sports*.

[25] Rader, *American Sports*, 46-68; Stephen Hardy, *How Boston Played: Sport, Recreation, and Community, 1865-1915* (Boston: Northeastern University Press, 1982), 127-46.

recently organized, from which affluent residents could choose. All appear to have been more family-oriented than the defunct Country Club, making special provisions for the membership of women and children. In fact, by the turn of the century, some critics regarded country clubs as disreputable haunts where women drank. The "punch bowl is always in evidence," the Reverend Father Walter J. Shanley charged at the annual convention of the Rhode Island Catholic Total Abstinence Union in 1900.[26]

Because of their ample facilities, the country clubs overshadowed the tennis clubs that had sprouted on vacant lots on the East Side and in Elmwood in the 1880s. Tennis owed its appeal to the proximity of Newport, where it had been introduced to America with the imprimatur of some of the nation's most fashionable families. Although no membership lists survive, the city's tennis clubs were undoubtedly expensive organizations to join. The Providence Tennis Club, founded in 1882, charged its members fifty dollars a year for court privileges; shares in the club sold for as much as five hundred dollars each. Tournaments attracted outstanding British and American players from Newport and Saratoga.[27]

Though less exclusive than either riding to the hounds or playing tennis or golf, sailing also sorted out the city's population. Interest in rowing, which had declined in the 1850s, revived after the Civil War. In 1871 the newly incorporated Narragansett Boat Club raised ten thousand dollars for a boathouse replete with billiards room, gymnastic apparatus, and ladies' parlor that it erected on the banks of the Seekonk River. "Composed of the rising young men of Providence," each of whom paid a modest entrance fee of five dollars and steeper annual dues of twenty dollars, the club's six-oared crew won the New England Regatta in 1878 and its eight-oared crew

[26] Caspar W. Whitney, "Evolution of the Country Club," *Harper's New Monthly Magazine* 90 (December 1894), reprinted in *The Land of Contrasts, 1880-1901*, ed. Neil Harris (New York: George Braziller, 1970), 143; George Birmingham, "The American at Home and in His Club," in *America in Perspective: The United States through Foreign Eyes*, ed. Henry Steele Commager (New York: Random House, 1947), 283; Records of the Country Club, 1888-97, RIHS; *The Rhode Island Society Blue Book* (New York: Dau Publishing Co., 1902), 15-23; Shanley quoted in *Providence Journal*, 30 November 1900. By 1899 golfing had "arrived" as an elite pursuit. That year, *Outing* magazine featured a series of articles on country clubs in Boston, Philadelphia, Chicago, and New York City. *Outing* 34 (May, June, July, August 1899): 129-42, 260-68, 354-65, 443-57.

[27] "Constitution of the Providence Tennis Club," 1882, RIHS.

claimed the American amateur championship in 1881. In 1880, in conjunction with a patent medicine company, the club sponsored a regatta that drew eighty thousand spectators, the most ever to see a sporting event in Rhode Island, to the banks of the Seekonk River for a four-mile race between professional scullers. Over the next few years, however, the club's activities shifted from regattas to Gilbert and Sullivan light operas, elegant balls, elaborate fairs, and other social activities. By 1885 it had "identified itself as a social organization in this city almost as decidedly as it has assumed an enviable position among the aquatic clubs of the country."[28]

Its place as an aquatic club was soon taken by yacht clubs, whose boats plied the waters of Narragansett Bay. Athough yachting was generally the pastime of the wealthy, the Providence Corinthian Yacht Club numbered many skilled craftsmen and propertyless white-collar workers among its 159 members in 1894. The composition of the Rhode Island Yacht Club, established in 1886, also varied considerably. Some of its approximately three hundred members in 1900 were wealthy manufacturers who belonged to the city's elite clubs; others were clerks and commercial travelers with little or no property.[29]

Cycling clubs in Providence reached even further down the social scale. A few clubs flourished briefly in the 1880s, when bicycle races were featured as commercial attractions at the state fair. But the popularity of cycling awaited the development of safety bicycles and pneumatic tires. Thanks to mass production, the price of a new bicycle fell to as little as fifty dollars by the mid-1890s. In 1894, according to one estimate, there were more than six thousand "wheels" and at least eleven bicycle clubs in Providence. These clubs catered to discrete groups: to Irish-Americans, Scandinavians,

[28] *Providence Star Tribune*, 12 March 1885; *Providence Journal*, 16 March 1885; clippings from Hop Bitters Regatta, Rider Collection, Brown University Library; Patrick T. Conley and Paul R. Campbell, *Providence: A Political History* (Norfolk, Va.: Donning Co., 1982), 112. The history of the Narragansett Boat Club illustrates the conflict that frequently occurred in the sport clubs between the sportsmen who joined to play a sport and the more socially minded members for whom the club's membership defined what Benjamin Rader has called a "status community." Rader, *American Sports*, 50-51.

[29] *Officers and Members of the Providence Corinthian Yacht Club for 1894* (n.p., 1894); *Constitution, By-Laws, Sailing Regulations, Etc., Etc., of the Rhode Island Yacht Club* (Providence: Eagle Printing Co., 1900).

blacks, and women. In all but the women's clubs, clerks, salesmen, and other white-collar workers made up the great majority of the members. Although some of the clubs maintained clubhouses, most confined their activities to furnishing uniforms and organizing group rides or "runs" for their members. "Hardy souls," for example, made runs from Providence to Narragansett Pier, an exclusive resort thirty-three miles from Providence. Cycling marked the lower boundary of the organized sports activities of the city's upper middle class. Although a few of the younger and more athletically inclined members of the elite men's clubs joined the cycling clubs, businessmen and professionals preferred the Providence Driving Association. For them, the horse and trap took the place of the bicycle in leading the strenuous life.[30]

As exclusive clubs took the place of inclusive civic associations in purveying cultural activities to the public, the midcentury civic culture became privatized and, to a lesser extent, feminized. Once seen as institutions that would bond the diverse groups of the industrial city, institutions like art galleries and libraries now sorted people out according to their social status. In the 1850s the Rhode Island Art Association, led by a civic-minded elite, had appealed for public support to endow a municipal art gallery and school of design. Its spokesmen had stressed the utility of such an institution. Although still hoping to marshal "corporate effort" in an attempt to "increase the general culture of our city," the Providence Art Club, founded in 1880, was as exclusive as its neighbor, the Athenaeum, which, since the opening of the Providence Public Library, had defined itself as a "home library" and was soon to limit the number of its proprietors. Begun by artists, the Art Club quickly became an elite social club composed predominantly of East Side residents. In exhibiting the works of local artists and offering instruction in art, the Art Club tried to counter the influence of "the surreptitious saloon, or even the less noxious, but hardly more elevating shore re-

---

[30] *Programme of the Grand Fair, Narragansett Wheelmen* (Providence: Alpine Print, 1894); *Constitution of the Rhode Island Wheelmen* (Providence: Snow & Farnham, 1891); *The Wheelmen's Directory for Rhode Island and Massachusetts* (Providence: Providence Theatrical Publishing Co., 1896); Gladys W. Brayton, *Other Ways and Other Days* (East Providence: Globe Printing Co., 1976), 61; *Providence Journal*, 3 January 1900. See also Richard Harmond, "Progress and Flight: An Interpretation of the American Cycle Craze of the 1890s," *Journal of Social History* 5 (Winter 1971-72): 235-57; Hardy, *How Boston Played*, 147-67.

sort in the summer and Dime Museum all the year round." But the workingmen who patronized the saloon or frequented the Dime Museum rarely entered the Art Club. Only during semiannual exhibitions did the club open its galleries to the general public.[31]

The feminization of the Art Club—women soon made up more than a third of its members—prompted the artists who had been among its founders to retreat into the A.E. (Ann Eliza or "analyze") Club. Of the first thirty-eight members of this all-male club, organized in 1885, eighteen were artists or "near-artists." The rest were art lovers, art buyers, and critics. Uninhibited by the presence of women, the artists gathered around a keg of beer in their "studio" to engage in boisterous discussions of art works and "innocent hilarity." The club toast, "Success to crime," and the title of its periodical, the *Dredge*, suggest that for its members the club's "bohemian" atmosphere meant the pleasures of male camaraderie.[32]

While clubs organized the sociability of the city's businessmen and professionals, fraternal lodges performed a similar function for shopkeepers, clerks, and skilled workingmen. From only a handful in 1865, fraternal orders multiplied rapidly until, by 1900, there were more than forty in Providence. By then, according to one estimate, there were 568 fraternal orders in the United States, 366 of them founded in the previous decade. Some seventy thousand lodges claimed an aggregate membership of five and a half million "brothers."[33]

Fraternal orders had a long and checkered history in Providence. St. John's Lodge, which Masons established in 1757, appealed to sea captains, merchants like the Brown brothers, and other men with

[31] *Sixty-First Annual Report of the Board of Directors of the Providence Athenaeum to the Corporation* (Providence: Providence Press, 1896), 10-11; *Manual of the Providence Art Club, 1886* (Providence: E. L. Freeman & Son, 1886), 5; *Manual* (Providence: E. L. Freeman & Son, 1888), 4; George Leland Miner, *Angell's Lane: The History of a Little Street in Providence* (Providence: Akerman-Standard Press, 1948), 127-36. On the privatization of urban culture, see Neil Harris, "Four Stages of Cultural Growth: The American City," in Arthur Mann et al., *History and the Role of the City in American Life* (Indianapolis: Indiana Historical Society, 1972), 34-40.

[32] My account draws on G. M. Carpenter, "First Annual Address of the President," MS, 1886; and Walter L. Munro, "Early History of A.E.," typescript, 1935, both in the Records of the A.E. Club, RIHS.

[33] Estimates of fraternal membership nationally are from B. H. Meyer, "Fraternal Beneficiary Societies in the United States," *American Journal of Sociology* 6 (March 1901): 655-56.

close ties to England. Following the Revolution, Masonic rolls swelled as the order enrolled large numbers of shopkeepers and artisans. By 1829 there were nineteen lodges and approximately three thousand Masons in Rhode Island. Then catastrophe struck. The abduction and suspected murder of William Morgan, an apostate from Rochester, New York, who had threatened to reveal the secrets of Freemasonry, unleashed a wave of egalitarian sentiment throughout the Northeast that "seemed to threaten the sweeping away of all the fair prospects of the organization—the complete overthrow of the institution." Critics accused the Masons of subverting republican liberties, abetting intemperance, and wasting money ostensibly collected for charity on "festivals, unmeaning ceremonies, and useless parade." Evangelicals denounced the order's elaborate ritual and its religious trappings. In 1834 the Grand Lodge ignominiously surrendered its charter to the General Assembly, not to be reclaimed until 1861, and recommended that all the subordinate lodges do the same. For the next two decades Masonry withered; neither of the city's two lodges initiated a single new member during the 1830s. Not until the 1850s did Masonry revive. Attracting rising young men like future mayor Thomas A. Doyle and future U.S. Senator Nelson W. Aldrich, the Masons established two new city lodges in 1857 and 1867, and four more between 1876 and 1880.[34]

[34] Henry W. Rugg, *History of Freemasonry in Rhode Island* (Providence: E. L. Freeman & Son, 1895), 88; *Proceedings of the Rhode-Island Anti-Masonic State Convention, September 14, 1831* (Providence: Daily Advertiser, 1831), 9; *By-Laws of St. John's Lodge, No. 2* (Providence: Pierce & Berry, 1860), 11; William Evans Handy, *The Story of Mount Vernon Lodge, No. 4, Free and Accepted Masons, Providence, Rhode Island, 1799-1924* (n.p., 1924), 175. On Antimasonry in Rhode Island, see Susan Porter Benson, " 'A Union of Men and Not of Principles': The Rhode Island Antimasonic Party, 1829-1838" (M.A. thesis, Brown University, 1971). In Connecticut, where Freemasonry functioned as a sort of "counterestablishment" to Congregational orthodoxy, Episcopalians, Unitarians, Universalists, and other latitudinarian Protestants predominated in the lodges. Episcopalians and Universalists were also over-represented in the Masonic lodges of Genesee County, New York. Masons in antebellum Providence, however, were drawn from all denominations. See Dorothy Ann Lipson, *Freemasonry in Federalist Connecticut* (Princeton: Princeton University Press, 1977); and Kathleen Smith Kutolowski, "Freemasonry and Community in the Early Republic: The Case for Antimasonic Anxieties," *American Quarterly* 34 (Winter 1982): 543-61. For the later history of Freemasonry, after it had weathered the Antimasonic controversy, see Lynn Dumenil, *Freemasonry and American Culture, 1880-1930* (Princeton: Princeton University Press, 1984).

Perhaps because of their emphasis on mutual benefit, other fraternal orders aroused far less hostility in antebellum Providence than did Masonry. After establishing a lodge in 1829, which foundered during the Antimasonic crusade, the Odd Fellows returned to the city in force in the mid-1840s. Between 1842 and 1844 they chartered four lodges in Providence and by 1845 claimed almost five hundred members. These Odd Fellows were jewelers, carpenters, tailors, and other artisans between the ages of twenty-one and fifty attracted by the order's insurance provisions. Their lodges paid weekly sickness dues that varied from four to six dollars, "provided, such sickness or disability is not caused by . . . immoral conduct," and funeral benefits of fifty dollars for the death of a member or half that amount for the death of a spouse. Sensitive perhaps to the criticism leveled at the Masons because of their conviviality, the Odd Fellows banned intoxicating drinks from their lodges, expelled drunkards, and pledged themselves to cultivate "habits of industry, sobriety, and economy."[35]

In the late 1840s temperance orders began to spring up in Providence. As the successor to the Washington Total Abstinence Society, which had tried to reclaim inebriates, the Sons of Temperance abolished oaths, "unmeaning rites," and "secret modes of recognition." Its lodges were open to healthy white males, of "good moral character," willing to take vows of total abstinence. Like the Odd Fellows, the Sons emphasized mutual benefit over conviviality and paid substantial sickness and death benefits. Auxiliaries—the Daughters and Cadets of Temperance—enrolled women and youth respectively. When criticized by temperance spokesmen for their "closed" or exclusive lodges, the Sons replied that only group vigilance could prevent reformed drunkards from going back to the bottle.[36]

[35] Constitution, By-Laws and Rules of Friendly Union Lodge, Number One, I.O.O.F. (Providence: Br. W. Simons, 1847), iii, 25; B. F. Moore, comp., The Odd Fellows' Directory (Providence: B. F. Moore, 1845).

[36] Constitution and By-Laws of Channing Division, No. 5, of the Sons of Temperance of the State of Rhode Island (Providence: M. B. Young, 1848), 3, 7; Second and Third Annual Reports of the Rhode Island Temperance Union, 1868-70 (Providence: Providence Press Co., 1870), 15-16. On the Sons of Temperance, see John Allen Krout, The Origins of Prohibition (New York: Alfred A. Knopf, 1925), 208-215; and Ian R. Tyrrell, Sobering Up: From Temperance to Prohibition in Antebellum America, 1800-1860 (Westport, Conn.: Greenwood Press, 1979), 203-218. As late as 1876 ministers still critcized the "antichurch spirit" among temperance orders like the Sons of Temperance. See Rev. William F. Bainbridge, "The Relation of the Churches to the Temperance Cause," in

Still other antebellum fraternal orders sprang up in reaction to the massive Irish immigration to the United States. The Know Nothings, the first such nativist order, were something of an anomaly. As a transitional political party, bridging the gap between the dissolution of the Whigs and the formation of the Republican party in the mid-1850s, they thwarted the bid of Irish-born Thomas Davis for reelection to the House of Representatives. Their manuscript records reveal a strange political party in which secrecy was at a premium. Members were commonly referred to not by name but by the numbers they had been assigned upon initiation. Although enrolling a few attorneys and merchants with political ambitions, the Know Nothings appealed primarily to artisans who viewed the immigrants as potential competitors for jobs. By 1856 the Know-Nothing party had given way to the more conventional Republican party. Its place as a nativist fraternal order was soon taken by the American Protestant Association whose officers in 1865 appear to have been immigrants from Ulster.[37]

Following the Civil War, a host of new fraternal orders established lodges in Providence. The Knights of Pythias, whose first chapter was founded in 1864 in Washington, D.C., to promote sectional reconciliation, and the Improved Order of Red Men, consisting of white men who dressed up like Indians, competed with the Masons and Odd Fellows for the patronage of the native born. The Sons of Temperance, Sons of Jonadab, the Temple of Honor, and other temperance orders protected their members from the temptations of drink. The Elks brought together liquor dealers, actors, theater proprietors, and other service workers. The Grand Army of the Republic held reunions for Union veterans.

Nor was the fraternal impulse limited to the city's Protestants. Jews commonly mixed with Protestants in the city's Masonic and Pythian lodges. Catholics, who owing to papal proscription did not normally join the Masons, Odd Fellows, or Pythians, founded their

---

Eighth Annual Report of the Rhode Island Temperance Union (Providence: Providence Press Co., 1876), 12-13.

[37] Records of the Know Nothings, 1854-56, RIHS; *The Providence Directory for the Year 1865* (Providence: Adams, Sampson & Co., 1865), 240; Charles Stickney, "Know-Nothingism in Rhode Island," *Publications of the Rhode Island Historical Society*, n.s. 1 (1894): 243-57; Larry Anthony Rand, "The Know-Nothing Party in Rhode Island: Religious Bigotry and Political Success," *Rhode Island History* 23 (October 1964): 102-116.

own orders like the Knights of Columbus. Immigrants to the city joined native orders, like the German-language Hermann Lodge of the Knights of Pythias, or established chapters of ethnic American orders. Between 1869 and 1874, Jews organized Haggai Lodge of B'nai B'rith, Scots formed the Providence Caledonian Society, English immigrants banded together in brigades of the Order of Alfredians, the Irish chartered a Hibernian lodge, and the Germans established two lodges affiliated with the German Order of Harugari. Later Italian immigrants to Providence brought with them a spate of mutual benefit societies based on provincial loyalties, a common dialect, a patron saint, and shared social and religious customs. Excluded from white lodges, the city's black males supported their own fraternal orders like Prince Hall Freemasonry. Although admitted to the Sons of Temperance (which now welcomed women), the Knights and Ladies of Honor, and several other mixed fraternal orders, the wives and daughters of the "brothers" generally joined women's auxiliaries like the Daughters of Rebekah, affiliated with the Odd Fellows, and the Daughters of Liberty, the female counterpart of the Order of United American Mechanics.[38]

Three features distinguished these lodges from the city's clubs: cross-class membership, brotherhood reinforced by ritualism and secrecy, and mutual benefit. From their inception in eighteenth-century England, Masonic lodges had provided settings in which gentlemen and artisans could mix on equal terms. Although gentlemen opted for more exclusive clubs in nineteenth-century America, the self-employed commonly socialized with wage earners in lodges of all orders. Nor was it uncommon for businessmen who were members of the city's elite clubs to remain in the Masonic and Odd Fellow lodges that they had joined when they were young men. Senator Nelson W. Aldrich, the "General Manager of the United States," is a good example. A member of the Hope and University clubs and a proprietor of Squantum, Aldrich had joined What Cheer Lodge in 1866 when he was a twenty-five-year-old clerk in a wholesale grocery firm. Aldrich's rapid rise through Masonic ranks

[38] On the transplantation of Italian mutual benefit societies to Providence, see Judith E. Smith, *Family Connections: A History of Italian and Jewish Immigrant Lives in Providence, Rhode Island, 1900-1940* (Albany: State University of New York Press, 1985), chap. 4. See also William A. Muraskin, *Middle-Class Blacks in a White Society: Prince Hall Freemasonry in America* (Berkeley: University of California Press, 1975).

to become Eminent Commander of the Calvary Commandery of Rhode Island in 1870 and the reputation for being a skilled parliamentarian that he won in debates at the Franklin Lyceum furthered his political career.[39]

Almost every lodge contained a few professionals—commonly attorneys, doctors, and dentists—for whom fraternal membership was a good way of adding to one's clientele. Most also contained skilled workingmen, whose regular incomes enabled them to afford the monthly or quarterly dues. Myrtle Lodge, no. 15, Ancient Order of United Workmen, for example, included carpenters, molders, and various smiths as well as clerks and foremen. Few members of Vigilant Council, Order of United American Mechanics, claimed any taxable property in 1896. Most were jewelers, masons, and other artisans; a few clerks and bookkeepers also belonged. Among the union leaders whose biographies were given in a 1901 history of the Rhode Island Central Trades and Labor Union, a number of the native-born were affiliated with the Masons, Odd Fellows, or Knights of Pythias; the immigrants generally belonged to ethnic orders like the Ancient Order of Hibernians, the Alfredians, and the Order of Sons of St. George.[40]

[39] Nathaniel Wright Stephenson, *Nelson W. Aldrich: A Leader in American Politics* (New York: Charles Scribner's Sons, 1930), 21-25; Jerome L. Sternstein, "Nelson W. Aldrich: The Making of the 'General Manager of the United States,' 1841-1886" (Ph.D. diss., Brown University, 1968), 47-51. My discussion of the distinctive features of the fraternal order draws on Clawson, "Brotherhood, Class and Patriarchy."

[40] *Myrtle Lodge, No. 15, Ancient Order of United Workmen* (Providence: Snow & Farnham, 1895); *Pocket Directory of Vigilant Council No. 28, O.U.A.M.* (Providence: Evans & Card, 1896); *20th Century Illustrated History of Rhode Island and the Rhode Island Central Trades and Labor Union and Its Affiliated Organizations* (Providence: Rhode Island Central Trades and Labor Union, 1901), 493-557. Contemporary observers also noted the appeal of fraternal lodges to skilled workers. See Charles Stelze, "How One Thousand Workingmen Spend Their Spare Time," *Outlook* 106 (4 April 1914): 764; Royal L. Melendy, "The Saloon in Chicago," *American Journal of Sociology* 6 (January 1901): 433-37. For analyses of lodge membership in other late nineteenth- and early twentieth-century American cities, see Stephan Thernstrom, *Poverty and Progress: Social Mobility in a Nineteenth Century City* (1964; reprint, New York: Atheneum, 1972), 167-71; Roy Rosenzweig, "Boston Masons, 1900-1935: The Lower Middle Class in a Divided Society," *Journal of Voluntary Action Research* 6 (July-October 1977): 119-26; Brian Greenberg, "Worker and Community: Fraternal Orders in Albany, New York, 1845-1885," *Maryland Historian* 8 (Fall 1977): 38-53; Daniel J. Walkowitz, *Worker City, Company Town: Iron and Cotton-Worker Protest in Troy and Cohoes, New York, 1855-84* (Urbana: University of Illinois Press, 1978), 157-67; John T. Cumbler, *Working-Class Community in Industrial America: Work, Leisure, and Struggle in Two Industrial Cities,*

Although quick to stress the equality of their lodges, most fraternal orders provided for "graduated membership." As the neophyte advanced to higher degrees, the secrets of the order were progressively revealed to him. But the thirty-three degrees of Masonry, the seven degrees of the Odd Fellows, and similar internal distinctions based on achievement or service to the order rather than on a man's status before he became a brother were in accord with the meritocratic conception of society held by members of the Mechanics' Association and other middle-class Americans. Indeed, the lodges preserved vestiges of the antebellum producers' community, particularly the dense network of mutual obligation and the cross-class brotherhood into which members were initiated. In an attempt to promote even further equality within the lodge, a few orders abolished payment for degrees. In so doing, the International Order of Odd Fellows, Manchester Unity, claimed to be "the most equitable society in the world," with "every member on the same footing."[41]

Unlike the city's clubs, lodges rarely limited the size of their memberships. But large lodges in which members felt anonymous defeated one of the prime purposes of becoming a brother. In several instances, Masons withdrew from large lodges with memberships "too large for the mutual acquaintance and social intercourse of all the members" to form smaller, more intimate lodges. Characteristically, the charter members of one of these new lodges described it as "a family lodge," or one "wherein the members might be bound in social ties much more closely than would be possible in a Lodge with a larger membership." This process of "schismatic differentiation" reflected the felt need for fraternal intimacy or social solidarity amid the impersonality of a rapidly growing, heterogeneous, and socially stratified city.[42]

1880-1930 (Westport, Conn.: Greenwood Press, 1979), 44-51; William Toll, *The Making of an Ethnic Middle Class: Portland Jewry over Four Generations* (Albany: State University of New York Press, 1982), 25-41, 140-59; Clawson, "Brotherhood, Class and Patriarchy," chap. 8.

41 *Aims and Objects of the Providence, Rhode Island District. The International Order of Odd Fellows, Manchester Unity* (Providence: n.p., n.d.), 6, 3. On graduated membership, see Noel P. Gist, "Secret Societies: A Cultural Study of Fraternalism in the United States," *University of Missouri Studies* 15 (October 1940): 65-69.

42 Rugg, *History of Freemasonry in Rhode Island*, 549, 572; Gist, "Secret Societies," 46-48.

Ceremony and secrecy also distinguished the lodge from the club. Ritual served to bind the brothers together as one big "family" in a network of reciprocal obligation while at the same time setting them apart from other social groups in the city. All lodges, even those that like the Sons of Temperance dispensed with ritual and regalia, employed passwords and secret codes. Most flaunted their ritual—in initiation rites, installations of officers, and parades to commemorate national holidays, dedicate buildings, and bury deceased brothers. In 1864, for example, the city's Masons marched in all their glory to lay the cornerstone of the Trinity Methodist Episcopal Church. The brothers' sworn oaths to secrecy, fraternal symbols like the "all-seeing eye" of Freemasonry, and arcane language made their activities even more impenetrable to the outsider. Ritual also distinguished one fraternal order from another. During the 1870s the Improved Order of Red Men searched for distinctive ritual that would attract men to its lodges before finally settling on Indian lore. "Tribes" or lodges in Providence assessed monthly dues of "five feet every moon" (or fifty cents). After "adoption" or initiation into the tribe, the "hunter" rose to become a "warrior." The neophyte looked forward to the day when he too would ultimately win recognition as a "chief."[43]

Lodges combined the pleasures of organized sociability and fraternalism with the appeal of mutual benefit provisions. Until the twentieth century, most American insurance companies sold insurance as an investment rewarding longevity, rather than as family protection. The Big Three—Equitable, Mutual of New York, and New York Life—wrote deferred-dividend policies whose premiums had to be paid annually or semiannually. Only Prudential issued policies with smaller fixed premiums that could be paid weekly. No wonder young men just starting businesses and families flocked into fraternal lodges, which insured them against the vicissitudes of life. Because of actuarial considerations, lodges commonly refused to initiate men over the age of forty-five. Most required candidates to be of sound health; some required medical examinations. Practically

[43] Rugg, *History of Freemasonry in Rhode Island*, 137-38; *Constitution for the Guidance of Tribes, By-Laws Wamsutta Tribe No. 7* (Providence: R.I. Printing Co., 1875), 26-29. On the ritual aspects of fraternal orders, see Gist, "Secret Societies," chap. 7; and Georg Simmel, "The Secret Society," in *The Sociology of Georg Simmel*, trans., ed., and with an introduction by Kurt H. Wolff (New York: Free Press, 1950), 345-76.

all offered sickness and death benefits, and a few even provided relief in times of need or during seasonal lags. Larger and wealthier orders like the Odd Fellows and the Knights of Pythias organized statewide beneficial associations that paid premiums up to four thousand dollars—four times the standard amount—on the death of the insured. In fact, many of the orders founded after 1875 subordinated ritualism to the provision of mutual benefit. Typical of these "fraternal beneficiary societies" was the Royal Arcanum, "a Beneficiary Order founded upon business principles," which admitted only white males who lived in regions "free from epidemics" and who had passed a compulsory medical examination.[44]

While providing companionship and economic aid to their members, lodges also took the place of mechanics' institutes and lyceums in purveying recreation to the entire community. To raise money, they frequently staged elaborate balls and fairs. In 1890, for instance, the ladies' auxiliary of Mount Pleasant Lodge of the Odd Fellows introduced the *Jahr Markt*, or annual fair, to Providence. A colorful event, it featured seven booths at which fancy and domestic articles were on sale, a gypsy camp, and "orange trees in full bloom." During the summer, lodges commonly organized excusions to shore resorts on Narragansett Bay. In August of every year, the Providence Caledonian Society organized a field day advertised for days in advance by posters asking "Dinna ye hear it." Thousands of spectators gathered to watch track and field contests like pulling the stone, throwing the hammer, and hitch-and-kick. No "Scotch Day" would have been complete without an exhibition of the Highland Fling.[45]

Fraternal lodges attracted large numbers of shopkeepers, clerks, artisans, and other men from the lower middle class and the upper strata of the working class. For these men, the group experience was paramount. They did not join a lodge, as they would have a club, for the facilities offered. Most of their lodges occupied rented rooms,

[44] Morton Keller, *The Life Insurance Enterprise, 1885-1910: A Study in the Limits of Corporate Power* (Cambridge: Harvard University Press, 1963), 9-11, 56-60; *The Royal Arcanum* (Providence: What Cheer Print, 1888), 3, 5; Abb Landis, "Life Insurance by Fraternal Orders," *Annals of the American Academy of Political and Social Science* 24 (November 1904): 475-88.

[45] "Jahrmarkt, Mt. Pleasant Lodge No. 45, I.O.O.F.," December 1890, Rider Collection, Brown University Library; "Scottish Day on the Shore," *Providence Journal*, 28 August 1879; Henry Thomson, *Review of the Providence Caledonian Society from 1870 to 1920* (Central Falls, R.I.: U.S. Sabourin Co., 1921), 23-31.

and the typical lodge met only once every week or fortnight. They joined instead for the sense of belonging that initiation conferred, for the fraternity of the lodge. Instead of purchasing shares as "proprietors," they were initiated into what was in most cases an exclusively male brotherhood. They became "brothers," members of an extended family, whose mutual benefit provisions compensated for the attenuated kinship bonds of a mobile society. For modest yearly fees, which averaged between five and ten dollars a year, young men just starting families and businesses insured themselves against sickness and death, made business and political contacts, won recognition from their peers, and had a good time.

At the same time that their men were flocking into clubs and lodges, middle-class women created a national network of literary clubs. After being refused admission to a dinner at the New York Press Club in honor of Charles Dickens in 1868, a group of professional women formed Sorosis in 1868. That same year, a group of women reformers in Boston established the New England Women's Club. In endeavoring to extend woman's sphere beyond the home, both organizations served as prototypes for the literary clubs that affiliated with the General Federation of Women's Clubs after 1890. By the turn of the twentieth century, a hierarchy of women's clubs had risen in Providence and other cities to parallel the hierarchies of men's clubs, and leisure had become segmented by sex as well as by class and ethnicity.[46]

The women's club movement in Providence traced its origins to the founding of the Rhode Island Women's Club (RIWC) in 1876. According to its founders, suffragists who had previously been active in the antislavery movement, the RIWC offered "the double advantage of pleasant society and intellectual stimulus." It was intended to be "a social and intellectual centre where ladies of the most varying tastes could find congenial companionship." Membership dues were nominal: two dollars for initiation and three dollars annually. Within a year of its founding, the membership had grown from only five members to ninety-seven, with many more women clamoring for admission. Members included both "the society

---

[46] Karen J. Blair, *The Clubwoman as Feminist: True Womanhood Redefined, 1868-1914* (New York: Holmes & Meier, 1980), 15-38; William L. O'Neill, *Everyone Was Brave: The Rise and Fall of Feminism in America* (Chicago: Quadrangle Books, 1969), 84-90, 103-104, 150-52.

woman whose time is inevitably to a great extent frittered away in petty and irksome social forms" and "the weary and overtasked mother of many children, the greater portion of whose life is spent in the thankless and impossible task of trying to make one dollar do the work of two."[47] There were clear limits to sorority, however. Soon after its founding, Elizabeth Buffum Chace and her daughters resigned when the club refused to admit black women. Nor did it apparently admit either Catholics or Jews.[48]

Perhaps the most distinctive feature of the women's club was its emphasis on self-culture. Literary clubs were never intended as associations to promote women's rights; nor were they intended to be still more of the numerous moral reform societies that women supported in Providence after the Civil War. Outsiders, as the secretary of the RIWC observed, "seem unable to conceive the idea that a considerable number of women can possibly wish to meet together without some work of benevolence or reform in view." As a "departmental club," the Rhode Island Women's Club assigned its members to eight sections, which reflected the broad range of interests among its founders: art, literature, music, science, education, politics, sociology, and domestic economy. At each meeting members read papers on such varied topics as painters and sculptors before Raphael, minstrelsy, and the organization of household labor. Only rarely did the problems addressed touch on woman's suffrage, and then as a question to be debated rather than as a cause to be promoted. When in March 1887 members discussed a proposed constitutional amendment that would have granted women suffrage on the same terms as men, the secretary noted that "it was rather a departure from the usual work of the Club, but as a majority desired it, the meeting was held."[49]

A far more pressing task for clubwomen than advancing the cause of woman's suffrage was to develop their public talents. Recruiting leisured middle-class women normally without college or university degrees, the clubs quietly enlarged the public sphere for

---

[47] *First Annual Report of the Rhode Island Woman's Club* (Providence: John F. Greene, 1877), 4; *Second Annual Report* (Providence: John F. Greene, 1878), 5-6.

[48] Nancy Kathleen Cassidy, "A History of the Rhode Island Woman Suffrage Association" (history honors thesis, Brown University, 1973), 48-50.

[49] *Second Annual Report*, 6; *Twelfth Annual Report of the Rhode Island Women's Club* (Providence: Providence Press Co., 1888), 7.

women. Since the 1830s, moral reform causes had frequently sent
women into public life as custodians of middle-class morality. The
club movement, however, staked out middle-class housewives' claim
to an intellectual life. Much as young men cultivated the skills of oratory and parliamentary procedure in debates at the Franklin Lyceum, women overcame their reticence by delivering papers before
other women. Although frequently addressing the RIWC, men
rarely took part in the discussion of papers. Their presence, it was
felt, would deter "women not accustomed to public speaking." Clubwomen thus gained "experience which would make them exact
thinkers . . . accurate in the presentation of facts" in addition to "the
self-possession to do so before an audience."[50]

In 1890 clubwomen from all over the United States banded together in the General Federation of Women's Clubs, whose object
was "to bring into communication with each other the various Wom-
en's Clubs throughout the world, in order that they may compare
methods of work and become mutually helpful."[51] Federated clubs
proliferated in Rhode Island: from the five charter clubs of the state
federation in 1894 to thirty-four affiliated organizations with an aggregate membership of more than thirty-four hundred members by
1910. These clubwomen were drawn from the middle and upper
middle classes. If married, and most were, their husbands tended to
be the manufacturers and professionals, large proprietors, and
members of the upper middle class who belonged to the city's elite
men's clubs or to some of the Masonic and Odd Fellows lodges. The
status of a particular women's club normally depended on the income, occupation, and ethnicity of its members' husbands and male
kin. At the top of the hierarchy were such exclusive groups as the
Fortnightly Club and the Topsy Club, composed of East Side
women whose husbands belonged to the Hope and University clubs,
which never affiliated with the State Federation.[52] Next came the
Rhode Island Women's Club, Providence's leading federated wom-
en's club; the husbands of its members belonged to the University
and Central clubs. Below were Ardirhebiah, Embreaso, and a num-

[50] The Rhode Island Women's Club of Providence (Providence: n.p., 1893), 47, 46.
[51] Fourteenth Annual Report of the Rhode Island Women's Club (Providence: Snow &
Farnham, 1890), 8-9.
[52] Fortnightly Club Papers, 1881-1926, RIHS; Records of the Topsy Club, 1886-
1950, RIHS.

ber of other small, close-knit clubs that normally met in their members' homes. Both the Edgewood Women's Club and the Elmwood Woman's Club served as social centers for their suburban neighborhoods. Roughly equal in status were the Catholic Woman's Club and the Providence Branch of the National Council of Jewish Women. At the bottom were the Sarah E. Doyle Club, a teachers' organization that included many Irish-American women, and the Four Leaf Clover and Jynko clubs, composed of clerks, stenographers, and other single working women.[53] Excluded because of their race, black women organized their own clubs and federation.[54]

In spite of significant differences in membership and function, men's and women's clubs and lodges multiplied in the late nineteenth century for the same reasons. They were, first of all, products of a substantial increase in disposable income for most urban dwellers. Although the average workday remained ten hours in 1890, only a slight decline from what it had been on the eve of the Civil War, real wages and annual earnings rose over the same period by almost half. As a result, Americans spent smaller proportions of their income on food, housing, and other necessities and had more money to spend on organizational affiliations, insurance, and amusement.[55]

What contemporaries referred to as "the club idea" also followed from the desire of Americans to set themselves apart from others

[53] Rhode Island Women's Club, *Year Book*, 1910-11; Ardirhebiah, *Year Book*, 1910-11; Embreaso Club, *Year Book*, 1907-1908; Providence Fortnightly Club, *Year Book*, 1906; Read, Mark and Learn Club, *Year Book*, 1907; Records of the Saturday Club, 1894-1952, RIHS; Vincent Club, *Year Book*, 1907-1908; Edgewood Women's Club, *Year Book*, 1910; Elmwood Woman's Club, *Year Book*, 1914-15; Catholic Woman's Club, *Year Book*, 1910-11; Providence Section, Council of Jewish Women, *Year Book*, 1912-13; Sarah E. Doyle Club, *Year Book*, 1906-1907; Four Leaf Clover Club, *Year Book*, 1909-10; *Sunday Tribune*, 31 March 1912. All yearbooks at RIHS.

[54] Programs of the Annual Conference of the Rhode Island Union of (Colored) Women's Clubs, 1906-1935, Brown University Library.

[55] For evidence of rising real income following the Civil War, see Clarence D. Long, *Wages and Earnings in the United States, 1860-1890* (Princeton: Princeton University Press, 1960). For discussions of how rising real income affected family consumption patterns, see Louise Bolard More, *Wage-Earners' Budgets: A Study of Standards and Cost of Living in New York City* (New York: Henry Holt & Co., 1907); and John Modell, "Patterns of Consumption, Acculturation, and Family Income Strategies in Late Nineteenth-Century America," in *Family and Population in Nineteenth-Century America*, ed. Tamara K. Hareven and Maris A. Vinovskis (Princeton: Princeton University Press, 1978), 206-240.

who were different in a heterogeneous society. "The word 'club,' "
wrote one observer in 1901, "suggests the group, the circle just beyond the family, to which belong immediate friends and neighbors,
those associated by business ties, by political or by social sympathies." He attributed "the multiplication and development of these
groups" following the Civil War to "the phenomenal growth of urban population." In the "more sparsely inhabited" regions of the
country "the relations are more personal and less artificial," he explained. "But where thousands are thrown together within a limited
area, the social relation must be in groups, to which belong those
whom some common interest unites."[56]

Although joining was hardly a new trend among urban dwellers,
the clubs and lodges they joined in such bewildering numbers after
1865 differed sharply from those which had been common before
the Civil War. The typical antebellum association, whether a temperance society, a lyceum, or even an art union, had been deliber-
ately inclusive, enrolling practically every white male, and often
even female, willing to subscribe to the articles of its constitution. In
contrast, clubs and lodges were invariably exclusive. Their initiation
fees, annual dues, blackballs, and limits on membership excluded
many prospective members. Moreover, they performed a different
function. Instead of integrating the community, these exclusive leisure organizations articulated the urban social structure, sorting the
city's population into groups separated from each other by income,
social status, neighborhood, ethnicity, gender, and race. Protestant
churches also sorted people out, but on the basis of religious conviction, which, the Reverend Brown had insisted, was the basis of "the
broad, fair, universal brotherhood taught by Christ," not "class
brotherhood."[57]

Clubs and lodges, then, reflected the segmentation of leisure. As
the *People* pointed out, "friendly and social societies from their very
nature exercise the same means of unconscious coercion on their
members, and set the fashion for the individual as to his clothes, his
manners, his outgoings and his incomings in many ways that we all
can easily perceive." By the turn of the twentieth century, large busi-

[56] Raymond Calkins, *Substitutes for the Saloon* (Boston: Houghton Mifflin Co.,
1901), 45-46.

[57] T. Edwin Brown, *Studies in Modern Socialism and Labor Problems* (New York:
D. Appleton & Co., 1886), 212.

nessmen and professionals supported an elaborate array of clubs, small businessmen, clerks, and skilled workers crowded into countless lodges, while some of the sport clubs and fraternal orders like the Masons and Odd Fellows mediated between the extremes. Middle and upper middle-class women commonly joined federated clubs, while lower middle-class women favored auxiliaries of their husbands' fraternal lodges. Below the several middle-class strata were workingmen and their families, whose leisure activities revolved around their trade unions, mutual benefit societies, and neighborhood saloons. The leisure activities of each of these groups differed in a number of respects: in the expensiveness of equipment and extensiveness of space, in the extent to which they were privatized, and in the social status of their participants. After the Civil War the more homogeneous population of midcentury Providence, which had largely shared similar recreational pursuits and attitudes toward leisure, fragmented, giving way to distinctive subcultures.[58]

As middle-class Americans discovered play, they reconsidered their allegiance to thrift and hard work, to the purposive ordering of time, and to the insistence that recreation always be "rational" or uplifting. As early as the 1840s critics had expressed concern over the compulsive American busyness that struck visitors to the antebellum United States. "From the time we landed in New England until this hour," the English geologist Charles Lyell wrote upon reaching New Orleans, "we seemed to have been in a country where all, whether rich or poor, were labouring from morning till night, without ever indulging in a holiday." Native observers seconded Lyell's opinion. "The laboriousness of Americans," unexampled in the world except perhaps among "the starving operatives of English factories," led to a scrimped material existence and, what was worse, an "anxiety of mind" that "interferes with sociality," observed the *American Review* in 1845. "We consider the common suspicion which is felt of amusements among thoughtful people to be one of the most serious evils to which our community is exposed." Critics warned that this busyness was just as dangerous as self-indulgence. "The two imminent perils to which our community is exposed, the

[58] "Organizations," *People*, 11 December 1886; R. Q. Gray, "Styles of Life, The 'Labour Aristocracy' and Class Relations in Later Nineteenth Century Edinburgh," *International Review of Social History* 18 (1973): 428-52.

prevalent 'vices' as they often prove," declared the Reverend Dr. Hall in 1856, "are absorption in business and absorption in pleasure." There was "no incongruity between these evils," Hall maintained. "On the contrary, one may lead to the other by a natural law. Excessive business, when controlled by no religious principle, not only tends to consume the man, but tempts him to seek relaxation for his over-strained system in sensuous indulgence."[59]

Criticism of the American addiction to work became far more widespread during the 1870s and 1880s, when doctors began to warn that overwork led to neurasthenia, or nervous prostration. In addition, the Civil War gave birth to a new emphasis on physical exercise and the strenuous life. Some of the exponents of this new athleticism even praised such rough pastimes as sparring and football. General Francis Amasa Walker, one of America's leading economists and president of the Massachusetts Institute of Technology, attributed his "present good temper to sparring as also to a healthy development of my chest and lungs." In a Phi Beta Kappa address delivered at Harvard in 1893, Walker contrasted the "strength of will, firmness of purpose, resolution to endure, and capacity for action" nurtured by athletic contests with the "physical lassitude" and "gnawings of dyspepsia" that had characterized his generation of collegians. Heeding the advice of physicians like George Beard, clergymen like Henry Ward Beecher, and even philosophers like William James, middle-class Americans began to take vacations in the late nineteenth century. No longer considered a luxury for an effete upper class, the vacation became a necessity for professionals, office workers, and other Americans exposed to mental strain. Travel agencies like Thomas Cook & Son were only too happy to help them plan their vacations.[60]

[59] Lyell quoted in Dulles, *A History of Recreation*, 87; "Influence of the Trading Spirit upon the Social and Moral Life of America," *American Review* 1 (January 1845): 95-96; Edward B. Hall, D.D., *A Lecture on the Pleasures and Vices of the City* (Providence: Knowles, Anthony & Co., 1856), 7. For a similar complaint from another Unitarian minister, see Edward E. Hale, *Public Amusement for Poor and Rich* (Boston: Phillips, Sampson & Co., 1857). For a provocative analysis of Americans' "flirtation" with leisure following the Civil War, see Rodgers, *The Work Ethic in Industrial America*, chap. 4.

[60] Walker quoted in the *Boston Sunday Herald*, 8 January 1888; Walker's Phi Beta Kappa address quoted in George M. Fredrickson, *The Inner Civil War: Northern Intellectuals and the Crisis of the Union* (New York: Harper & Row, 1968), 223; Guy Lewis, "The Muscular Christianity Movement," *Journal of Health, Physical Education and Per-*

By the 1880s middle-class Americans were turning away from "the inner-worldly form of asceticism" that had once characterized their lives.[61] Somewhat slower perhaps than clubs, which from their very inception flouted sobriety, lodges became known for their conviviality and departed from their earlier adherence to sobriety and other ascetic conventions. Some, particularly the Odd Fellows and the Elks, admitted liquor dealers and saloon keepers into their ranks and liquor into their lodge rooms.[62] Clubs and lodges also lured men away from family and domestic hearth. By the 1890s numerous complaints were heard about the "jiner," the husband or father who neglected his familial and religious obligations for the male camaraderie of the lodge. "Brother," the Reverend M. L. Greene told his congregation at Trinity Methodist Episcopal Church in 1892, "too much club and too little church, they can't flourish together." Though conceding that clubs were necessary for "recreation," Greene admonished his parishioners not to confuse recreation with "dissipation," which was how the idle rich spent their spare time. "There can be no recreation without previous toil," he explained. "There are thousands who spend their summers at Newport or at Saratoga who don't know what recreation means." Too many members of the "stable, industrious, sober middle classes," it seemed, were aping the fashions of an emergent national upper class and retreating into exclusive clubs and resorts.[63]

Only a generation earlier, middle-class Americans had recog-

---

sonality 37 (May 1966): 27-28, 42; Donald Meyer, *The Positive Thinkers: A Study of the American Quest for Health, Wealth and Personal Power from Mary Baker Eddy to Norman Vincent Peale* (Garden City, N.Y.: Anchor Books, 1966), 3-15. On the spread of the vacation habit among the middle classes, see "How Long Should a Man's Vacation Be?" *New York Times*, 31 July 1910; Neil Harris, "On Vacation," in Alf Evers et al., *Resorts of the Catskills* (New York: St. Martin's Press, 1979), 101-108; Hugh De Santis, "The Democratization of Travel: The Travel Agent in American History," *Journal of American Culture* 1 (Spring 1978): 1-17.

[61] Weber, "The Protestant Sects and the Spirit of Capitalism," 320.

[62] By 1878 Unity Lodge, No. 20, I.O.O.F., had initiated a liquor dealer. Within another three years, liquor was being served in the lodge rooms. *Constitution, By-Laws, Rules of Order and Order of Business of Unity Lodge, No. 20, Providence, R.I.* (Providence: Providence Press Co., 1878); Unity Lodge, Minutes, 1881-85, 12 April 1881, RIHS.

[63] M. L. Greene quoted in *Providence Journal*, 14 March 1892. For complaints about the "jiner," see B. Meyer, "Fraternal Beneficiary Societies," 656. On the emergence of a national upper class, see Baltzell, *Philadelphia Gentlemen*; and Frederic Cople Jaher, *The Urban Establishment: Upper Strata in Boston, New York, Charleston, Chicago, and Los Angeles* (Urbana: University of Illinois Press, 1982).

nized little if any distinction between work and leisure. Indeed, they had insisted that the same purposiveness govern both spheres. Once commentators like Greene began to separate leisure from work, even though they made recreation contingent on "previous toil," they found it increasingly difficult to draw the line on permissible leisure activities. For instance, in staging Gilbert and Sullivan light operas, the Narragansett Boat Club helped popularize theater-going as a respectable entertainment. By the mid-1880s liberal Protestants like Frederic A. Hinckley had come to regard the theater, once condemned as a nursery of vice, as "a means of healthful recreation and of mental and moral culture," and praised drama as both "an educator" and as a source of "re-creation." Prize fights had once been held on the sly in nearby rural towns one step ahead of the police; by the 1890s they took place in the gym of the Providence Athletic Association. Given the free-and-easy atmosphere cultivated by many of their leisure associations, it is hardly surprising that middle-class Americans clung less tightly to the antebellum values of sobriety, self-discipline, and strict Sabbath observance that had laid the foundation for their current affluence.[64]

In fact, the so-called Puritan Sunday was a conspicuous casualty of this growing interest in leisure. For many middle-class Americans, strict Sabbath observance symbolized the identification of religious precept and cultural convention realized by the antebellum revivals. By the Civil War, the Puritan Sunday, with its injunction to set Sunday apart from the rest of the week as the Lord's Day, had become a middle-class cultural norm. In 1878 the city council prohibited the letting of boats and swings and the sale of refreshments on Sundays at Roger Williams Park after Baptist ministers had complained that these secular recreations "tempt the boys and girls to frequent the park when they ought to be in church, Sunday School and at home, remembering their Creator piously." The following year, William E. Merriam, pastor of the Central Congregational Church, reaffirmed the conviction that "the observance of the Sabbath is in a degree the measure of a nation's stability." Sunday, as the *Providence Journal* explained, was "a marked and distinct period of

[64] Frederic A. Hinckley, *The Theatre: Is It "the Gate to Hell"?* (Providence: J. A. & R. A. Reid, 1884), 8, 14, 12.

time as related to or compared with the other days of the week." So long as this traditional assumption persisted, "the only question is, what is a proper, a lawful and a Christian observance of the day."[65]

But as middle-class Americans discovered play, some commentators began to identify "rational Sunday observance" with "rest and refreshment." Following the lead of clergymen like James Freeman Clarke and Henry Ward Beecher, they urged that "innocent healthful recreation" be furnished on the Sabbath "by opening the doors of churches, libraries, galleries of art, museums of natural history, reading-rooms, halls for familiar lectures on literary and scientific subjects, and for music." In the mid-1880s the *Providence Journal* took up the cry for more rational recreation on the holy day. "That the reverence for Sunday is diminishing is very clear," it observed in 1884, "and this, in a greater or less degree, among the native-born population." Over the next decade the newspaper stepped up its attack on what it regarded as an anachronism, the Puritan Sunday. In 1891 it expressed the opinion that "This community has grown to approve of a Sunday outing for those who work hard through the week." By 1895 it was ready to declare strict Sabbath observance a dead letter.[66] In the meantime old prohibitions against Sunday travel, recreation, and worldly amusements that the city's evangelical churches had written into their convenants before the Civil War were either rescinded or allowed to lapse. When the Central Con-

[65] *Providence Journal*, 8 September 1877, 4 January 1878; Merriam quoted in ibid., 9 June 1879; "Sunday Recreation," ibid., 2 July 1884. On Sabbatarianism, see Rev. Wilbur F. Crafts, *The Sabbath for Man*, rev. ed. (Washington, D.C.: Authors' Union, 1894); Roy Zebulon Chamlee, Jr., "The Sabbath Crusade, 1810-1920" (Ph.D. diss., George Washington University, 1968); Henry F. May, *Protestant Churches and Industrial America* (1949; reprint, New York: Harper & Row, 1967), 129-30; Robert T. Handy, *A Christian America: Protestant Hopes and Historical Realities* (New York: Oxford University Press, 1971), 84-88, 145-48; and Francis P. Weisenburger, *Triumph of Faith: Contributions of the Church to American Life, 1865-1900* (Richmond, Va.: Mailing Services, Inc., 1962), 118-33.

[66] James Freeman Clarke, "Rational Sunday Observance," *North American Review* 131 (December 1880): 505-506; "Sunday Recreation," *Providence Journal*, 2 July 1884; "Sunday Games," ibid., 30 July 1891; "The Summer Sunday," ibid., 20 May 1895. Hugh McLeod remarks on a similar decline in strict Sabbath observance in London during the 1880s accompanied by growing interest in Sunday excursions and games. *Class and Religion in the Late Victorian City* (Hamden, Conn.: Archon Books, 1974), 231-39. Also useful on English Sabbatarianism is John Wigley, *The Rise and Fall of the Victorian Sunday* (Manchester: Manchester University Press, 1980).

gregational Church revised its covenant in 1898, it did not incorporate a clause, adopted upon the church's organization in 1852, prohibiting "attendance upon the theater or the circus."[67]

Gradually, rational recreation took precedence over strict Sabbath observance. By 1890 the city council permitted the renting of boats and swings and the sale of refreshments on Sundays at Roger Williams Park, though it drew the line at Sunday baseball. City authorities in Providence were not alone in relaxing their Sabbath vigil. All across the country, reported the *Providence Journal*, cities were throwing their parks open on Sundays and permitting "a variety of amusements." Also in 1890, the Providence Public Library began to open its doors on the Sabbath, which the Boston Public Library had done seventeen years earlier. By 1891 the Providence Art Club was scheduling its public exhibitions on Sundays so that workingmen could attend with their families. Within another three years, bicycle clubs were organizing runs on Sundays.[68]

Strict Sabbath observance fell out of favor as interest in the outdoor Sunday mounted. As early as 1893 clergymen blamed declining church attendance on the popularity of the Sunday excursion. By 1909 fondness for the outdoor Sunday had become so pronounced that few Protestant churches still scheduled afternoon services. "The day," wrote Lester Bradner, rector of St. John's (Episcopal) Church, "is more and more given over to outdoor recreation." A religious survey taken in the spring of 1910 confirmed Bradner's impression. It found that only one-tenth of the city's population attended services on a typical Sunday.[69]

Further evidence came from an interview of "representative" businessmen conducted by the *Providence Journal* in October 1912. Few of those interviewed continued to observe the strict Sabbath. William H. Waite, a manufacturing jeweler, was one of the Puritans for whom the Sabbath remained a day of absolute rest. As he had

[67] *Historical Manual of the Central Congregational Church, Providence, R.I., 1852-1902* (Providence: E. L. Freeman & Sons, 1902), 24, 77-79.

[68] "Sunday and the Public Park," *Providence Journal*, 12 July 1890; ibid., 10 May 1890; *Manual of the Providence Art Club* (Providence: E. L. Freeman & Son, 1892), 5-6; "Col. Pope on Sunday Cycling," in *Programme of the Grand Fair, Narragansett Wheelmen.*

[69] *Providence Journal*, 7 December 1893, 27 October 1912; Lester Bradner, "Religion," in *A Modern City: Providence, Rhode Island, and Its Activities*, ed. William Kirk (Chicago: University of Chicago Press, 1909), 344.

done every Sunday for the past twenty-six years, he attended morning and evening services and taught Sunday school at the Pearl Street Baptist Church. He would neither read the Sunday newspaper nor take his car out of the garage for a spin. But Waite was the exception. Theodore W. Foster, a manufacturing jeweler, liked to read the Sunday newspaper. Felix Wendelschaefer, general manager of the Providence Opera House, went fishing or took his family out for drives. Henry A. Barker, principal architect of the city's park system, told a reporter that he preferred to hear "sermons in stones and running brooks" at his rural bungalow rather than attend Sunday services.[70]

By the early twentieth century, there was no longer any consensus about how the Sabbath should be observed, if at all. Middle-class Americans were of several different minds on the extent to which games and other forms of rational recreation could be accommodated while still preserving Sunday as a day set apart from the rest of the week. For the "Puritans" among them—Baptists, Methodists, and some Congregationalists—strict Sabbath observance remained a moral issue, involving a clear-cut choice between right and wrong. Since they believed that religious precept prohibited travel, labor, and recreation on the Sabbath, they insisted that Sunday be devoted to religious services and self-improvement. Refusing even to read the Sunday newspaper, they limited their recreation on the Sabbath to walking and reading history. Typical were the views expressed by the Reverend John A. Hainer, minister of the Pearl Street Baptist Church, in 1907. Observing that Sundays in Providence were "getting more secularized every year," he traced this secularization to both the presence of a large foreign population and waning piety among churchgoers. "Church in the morning and golf in the afternoon is not right," he insisted. Sunday excursions, whether by the wealthy in their motor cars or by the poor on the trolley, were "dissipations and desecrations" of the true spirit of the day. Hainer professed to see little difference between the "hoodlums who play baseball" on the Sabbath and the "gentlemen who go out to play golf or tennis." It was rather like "two burglars, one who works with bare hands, while the other wears kid gloves." There was only one

[70] *Providence Journal*, 27 October 1912.

"proper way to spend Sunday," Hainer stressed, and that was "attendance at church, reading the Word, and spiritual meditation."[71]

The "liberals" among the city's middle-class residents, predominantly Episcopalians and Unitarians, believed that Sunday could be given over to both religious worship and outdoor recreation. One easy way of doing this was to follow the example of the Roman Catholics in scheduling early morning services, a practice that freed the rest of the day for recreation. Boston reformer Richard Henry Dana broached this idea in an address before the Churchmen's Club in 1895. "Sunday," he declared, "is not a day of prohibitions, but one of large opportunity." In 1907 Edmund S. Rousmaniere, rector of Grace (Episcopal) Church, echoed Dana's opinion when he observed that, in his experience, the outdoor Sunday did not clash with Sabbath worship. Even among the most devout, he noted, "the habit of going to church more than once a Sunday has disappeared." "The observance of Sunday," Rousmaniere asserted, "is not a question of right and wrong." Criticizing the Puritan Sunday as "unnatural," he praised "the movement for out-of-door pleasures on Sunday as a natural outcome of modern life." "No one," he suggested, "can blame a workingman who takes his family out for a day . . . to enjoy the pleasures of a few hours in the country." Indeed, the rector thought that the workingman "gets far more enjoyment and perhaps just as much benefit as he would if he attended church, under the existing circumstances."[72]

A third group of middle-class observers straddled the fence between the Puritans and the liberals. Though quick to condemn baseball and other workingmen's games as desecrations of the holy day, they winked at driving, spending the day at one's cottage, and other middle-class recreational pursuits. Presbyterian minister Gerhart A. Wilson spoke for them when he told the *Providence Journal* in 1907 that he could accept walking and driving, provided that "a man

[71] Ibid., 13 October 1907.

[72] Ibid., 19 February 1895, 13 October 1907. Joseph Lee, president of the Playground Association of America, also advocated the liberalization of the Sabbath. He felt that Sunday, the universal day off from work, was the only day in which workingmen could find opportunities for self-expression and re-creation. "Sunday," he wrote in 1910, "is the day of compensation, the day of fulfilment to those essential purposes of life for which the weekday has left no room." "Sunday Play," *Playground* 4 (October 1910): 226.

went to church part of the day." But he objected to games on Sunday, "for the Sabbath is a day of rest and quiet."[73]

These differences of opinion over the proper way to spend Sunday reflected the corrosive impact of the growing interest in leisure on antebellum values. By the first decade of the twentieth century middle-class Americans no longer subscribed to the same norms governing the use of leisure time. Some continued to insist on strict Sabbath observance; others, though quick to criticize workingmen's games, found nothing wrong with Sunday afternoon excursions in the family carriage or automobile; still others thought that the day could be given over to both religion and recreation. Although most middle-class Americans abstained from alcohol, a growing number imbibed in their clubs and lodges. As members of exclusive leisure organizations, urban dwellers were fashioning distinctive styles of life. New cultural distinctions were arising to fracture the civic culture, separating the city's big businessmen and professionals from its shopkeepers, clerks, and skilled workingmen, and men from women. These distinctions overlaid, but did not always correspond with, the occupational distinctions that fractured the antebellum producers' community. The result was that the values of rational recreation institutionalized in the midcentury civic culture no longer performed their earlier function of bonding the heterogeneous population of the industrial city. Recognizing that the civic culture, like the antebellum producers' community, had fragmented, middle-class Americans began in the 1890s to search for new ways in which to reconstruct their segmented society.

The segmentation of work and leisure aroused considerable anxiety among middle-class Americans. Portraying themselves as representatives of the unorganized public, they formed a host of new voluntary associations, frequently national in scope, to initiate fundamental social and economic reform. The great majority of these new organizations cut across partisan lines. No longer encompassing a broad and undifferentiated producers' community, which had been splintered by the emergence of rival producer groups, these nonpartisan associations would nonetheless attempt to recover the antebellum moral consensus. If the turn-of-the century public did

[73] *Providence Journal*, 13 October 1907.

not constitute a community of producers, it could still act as a community of righteous citizens who, outraged at the corruption of machine politicians and the greed of monopolistic corporations, would rally to the candidacies of Single Taxer Lucius F. C. Garvin and patrician statesman Robert H. I. Goddard.

5 CORPORATE GREED AND PARTISAN EXIGENCY

ALTHOUGH it was the smallest state in the Union, Rhode Island in 1905 boasted a political system "grounded on the lowest layer of corruption" yet uncovered by muckraking journalist Lincoln Steffens. A widely traveled reporter, Steffens had seen a lot of corruption, but it all paled in comparison to the system that flourished in Rhode Island. In other states, he explained, "the corruptionists buy the people's representatives. In Rhode Island, they buy the people themselves." Characterizing Rhode Island as "an oligarchy," Steffens charged that the "best people" had acquiesced in this corruption. Yet many of the state's "best people" were "ashamed" of "their political degradation." Like middle-class Americans all across the country, they had awakened to the collusion between corrupt business interests and venal politicians. To correct the glaring abuses of what Steffens described as "a business man's government founded upon the corruption of the people themselves," they were forging a series of broad coalitions to wrest government out of the hands of a corrupt machine and return it to the people where it properly belonged. In Providence as elsewhere, middle-class voters had joined the Good Government crusade.[1]

Unlike in Wisconsin, the state's independent movement did not spring full-blown in reaction to falling tax revenues and corporate

[1] Lincoln Steffens, "Rhode Island: A State for Sale," *McClure's Magazine* 24 (February 1905): 337-39. This chapter draws on the following works: Daniel T. Rodgers, "In Search of Progressivism," *Reviews in American History* 10 (December 1982): 113-32; John L. Thomas, *Alternative America: Henry George, Edward Bellamy, Henry Demarest Lloyd and the Adversary Tradition* (Cambridge: Harvard University Press, 1983); David P. Thelen, *The New Citizenship: Origins of Progressivism in Wisconsin, 1885-1900* (Columbia: University of Missouri Press, 1972); Richard L. McCormick, *From Realignment to Reform: Political Change in New York State, 1893-1910* (Ithaca: Cornell University Press, 1981); and David C. Hammack, *Power and Society: Greater New York at the Turn of the Century* (New York: Russell Sage Foundation, 1982).

arrogance following the panic of 1893. Nor, as in New York, did it
crystallize after legislative investigations of the insurance industry
revealed a corrupt alliance between businessmen and politicians.
Rather, it developed gradually after 1880, fed by a number of
sources. In 1880 General Charles B. Brayton, Republican "boss" of
Rhode Island, was accused of embezzling postal funds. Independent sentiment mounted in the years 1886-89 when several thousand
Rhode Island voters blamed the failure of a recently enacted prohibition amendment on Brayton's tenure as chief of the state police.
In the 1890s grievances against the behavior of Union Railroad and
other quasi-public corporations fanned this sentiment, as did outrage over the General Assembly's encroachment on Providence's
home rule. By 1895 a Good Government movement had coalesced.
For the next two decades, the themes of nonpartisanship and independent politics dominated political discourse in the city.

But the Good Government coalition consisted of a number of different middle-class groups. All agreed on the need to separate partisanship from administration and on the need to forge a dependa-
ble bloc of independent voters who would cast their ballots for the
man rather than the party. There, however, agreement ended. As
heirs of the antebellum antiparty tradition, Single Taxers, prohibitionists, and other middle-class moralists attempted to mobilize the
community against the monster—whether monopoly, liquor, or unjust taxation—that lay at the root of all the corruption afflicting the
body politic. Alone, however, they were never numerous or powerful enough to bring about the civic regeneration they desired. The
success of the Good Government crusade depended instead on the
entry of hundreds of businessmen into the ranks of the city's independents in the 1890s. These businessmen rejected partisanship
less because it was immoral than because it was inefficient. For them,
nonpartisanship signified not a government free of special privilege, but rather one run on business principles. By the First World
War, their quest for efficiency had led them to embrace a new vision
of community, one embodied in translocal federations. Once again,
the moralists, those who continued to favor root-and-branch solutions like prohibition, antimonopoly, and the Single Tax, returned
to the margins of political life.

The roots of Rhode Island's corruption paradoxically lay in the
great prosperity the state experienced between the Civil War and

View of Providence looking toward State House, under construction, c. 1900 (courtesy of the Rhode Island Historical Society)

the First World War. In those years the "city-state" of Rhode Island earned world renown as "preeminently a manufacturing community." According to the federal census of 1910, Rhode Island ranked third among the states in the production of woolen and worsted goods, fourth in cotton goods, sixth in silk and silk goods, and eleventh in hosiery and knit goods. Often spoken of as "the wealthiest city in the country," Providence, with some 210,000 inhabitants or two-fifths of the state's population, ranked seventeenth among the nation's cities in the value of its products. The foremost jewelry manufacturing city in the country, it also claimed the nation's largest plants in the manufacture of steam engines, tools, files, screws, and silverware. Only Philadelphia and Cincinnati outstripped it as centers of the machine tool industry.[2]

Yet economic expansion concentrated wealth and power in the hands of a very few Rhode Islanders. In 1892 fifteen previously independent rubber companies combined to form the United States Rubber Company; Providence industrialist Joseph Banigan, proprietor of the largest rubber-shoe factory in the world, became the new corporation's first president and general manager. Concentration was just as pronounced in the textile industry. While the number of spindles in operation in the state increased by more than half between 1875 and 1909, the number of cotton mills declined from 135 to 106. Many of those that remained were owned by a few families and corporations. The single firm of B. B. & R. Knight, whose products were marketed with the Fruit of the Loom label, controlled over twenty mills in Rhode Island and Massachusetts, operated 11,000 looms, and employed some 7,000 operatives. This same pattern of concentration was true of other industries as well. Of the state's 1,951 industrial establishments in 1909 only 69, or 3.5 percent, produced output valued at more than $1 million. Yet these same establishments employed 43.3 percent of the state's wage earners and produced 48.3 percent of its total product. By that time, more than three-fifths of Rhode Island's 125,000 wage earn-

[2] *Thirteenth Census of the United States taken in the Year 1910. Abstract of the Census . . . with Supplement for Rhode Island* (Washington, D.C.: Government Printing Office, 1913), 611, 613, 617; *Providence: A Reference Book and Guide to a City of Varied Fascinations* (Providence: Providence Board of Trade, 1910), 4-6; Kurt B. Mayer, *Economic Development and Population Growth in Rhode Island* (Providence: Brown University Press, 1953), 49-51; William G. McLoughlin, *Rhode Island: A Bicentennial History* (New York: W. W. Norton & Co., 1978), 164-66.

ers worked in factories employing at least 250 workers. Brown & Sharpe, Providence's largest employer, employed more than 2,500 workers; Gorham, 2,000; the American Screw Company, 1,500; and Ostby & Barton, the largest jewelry firm in the country, more than 800.[3]

Following the Civil War, strong partisan loyalties, legislative mal-apportionment, and electoral corruption concentrated political power in the hands of a few men. Fending off occasional challenges from urban Democrats, prohibitionists, and independents, the Republican party ruled the state until the Great Depression. Only twice between 1865 and 1900 did the Democrats capture the state-house. Republican dominance stemmed from two sources. The strong attachment of the state's Yankee voters to the GOP dated back to the political realignment of the 1850s. For many Rhode Island Yankees like the prominent attorney Rathbone Gardner, grandson of abolitionist Stephen K. Rathbone, the word "Democrat" was synonymous with "copperhead," a northerner who sympathized with the South during the Civil War. Their distaste for the Democrats only deepened as Irish-Americans took control of the party during the last quarter of the nineteenth century. As late as 1876, there were no Irish names among the delegates to the Democratic ward meetings in Providence; by 1900 Irish-Americans made up almost three-fourths of the delegates, with the greatest increase occurring between 1888 and 1900.[4] Republican dominance

[3] George H. Kellner and J. Stanley Lemons, *Rhode Island: The Independent State* (Woodland Hills, Calif.: Windsor Publications, 1982), 69-71; Alfred D. Chandler, Jr., *The Visible Hand: The Managerial Revolution in American Business* (Cambridge: Harvard University Press, 1977), 433-38; *Thirteenth Census of the United States*, 618-19; Frank Putnam, "What's the Matter with New England?" *New England Magazine* 37 (October 1907): 141; *Manual of the Rhode Island Business Men's Association, 1890-1907* (Providence: Nathan A. Briggs & James B. Littlefield, 1907), 40-45; Mayer, *Economic Development and Population Growth*, 49; Ian S. Haber, "The Rhode Island Business Elite, 1895-1905: A Collective Portrait," *Rhode Island History* 26 (April 1967): 33-48.

[4] Gardner quoted in Mary Cobb Nelson, "The Influence of Immigration on Rhode Island Politics, 1865-1910" (Ph.D. diss., Harvard University, 1954), 289; Elmer E. Cornwell, Jr., "Party Absorption of Ethnic Groups: The Case of Providence, Rhode Island," *Social Forces* 38 (March 1960): 207-208. A number of studies have documented the strong ethnocultural allegiances of late nineteenth-century American voters. Among the best of these are Paul Kleppner, *The Cross of Culture: A Social Analysis of Midwestern Politics, 1850-1900*, 2nd ed. (New York: Free Press, 1970); and Richard J. Jensen, *The Winning of the Midwest: Social and Political Conflict, 1888-1896* (Chicago: University of Chicago Press, 1971). For an astute appraisal of this approach, see Richard L. McCormick, "Ethno-Cultural Interpretations of Nineteenth-Century American Voting Behavior," *Political Science Quarterly* 89 (June 1974): 351-77.

also rested on the malapportioned General Assembly, which vested disproportionate power in the state's small towns. Until 1910 Providence elected only twelve of the lower house's seventy-two representatives and only one of the upper house's thirty-eight senators. In fact, twenty small towns, with less than a tenth of the state's population, controlled the senate.[5]

A notorious machine dominated state politics. The so-called Journal Ring originally consisted of Henry B. Anthony, principal owner of the *Providence Journal* and U.S. Senator from 1856 until his death in 1884; General Ambrose E. Burnside, Civil War hero and the state's junior senator; George W. Danielson, Anthony's successor as editor of the *Journal*; and machine manufacturer Henry B. Gardner. After Anthony's death, Nelson W. Aldrich, who succeeded Burnside as senator in 1881, headed the machine until he retired from the Senate in 1911. The ring's actual manager, its "political technician for hire," however, was General Charles R. Brayton, whom Anthony installed in 1874 as the city's postmaster. Son of a former congressman from Warwick, Civil War veteran, and gregarious Mason, Brayton "organized" both the Republican party and the General Assembly. No state politician was more adept at manipulating party caucuses or at buying the votes of rural Yankees.[6]

Machine rule, however, tarnished the GOP's reputation as the party of morality and swelled the ranks of the state's independent voters. It also attracted the attention of two U.S. Senate investigating committees in the late 1870s. The first, led by Senator William A. Wallace of Pennsylvania, documented the widespread vote buying in Rhode Island. As one witness told the senators, "There would not be an election in Rhode Island, in fact, without money, any more than a funeral without a corpse." Going rates for votes, which normally brought from two to five dollars, ran as high as thirty-five dollars in hotly contested elections. The second committee, chaired by Senator Matthew C. Butler of South Carolina, heard testimony that Brayton dismissed postal employees who refused to contribute to Republican campaign kitties and that he used the Post Office as the

---

[5] Robert Grieve, "Rhode Island's Political Debasement," *Independent* 58 (12 January 1905): 88.

[6] Jerome L. Sternstein, "Nelson W. Aldrich: The Making of the 'General Manager of the United States,' 1841-1886" (Ph.D. diss., Brown University, 1968), 138; Steffens, "Rhode Island: A State for Sale," 346; Sidney S. Rider, *Booknotes* 20 (11 April 1903): 62.

site of wild drinking parties. All these charges came to a head in 1880 when Brayton skipped town for several months after being accused of embezzling thirty-seven thousand dollars in postal funds to repay a bank loan. Although the ring paid Brayton's debts to protect him from criminal prosecution, two thousand voters bolted the Republican party to register their disgust. For the first time, prohibitionists, who had heretofore been a "sometimes rebellious wing" of the GOP, decided to nominate a gubernatorial candidate while supporting the rest of the Republican ticket. In 1884 they broke completely with the GOP to organize their own party.[7]

Brayton's alleged embezzlement was only the first of numerous scandals that spurred the growth of the state's independent movement. In 1886 thousands of respectable citizens were outraged by the so-called May Deal when the General Assembly appointed Brayton to head the new state constabulary charged with enforcing prohibition at the same time that it passed a bill to reorganize the courts. Abolishing the local judiciary system, the act created twelve judicial districts, each supervised by a judge. Of the twelve judges appointed, five sat in the General Assembly and another three were members of its staff. At an "indignation meeting" on 2 June 1886, Amos C. Barstow, George H. Corliss, the Reverend David H. Greer, Brown president Ezekiel G. Robinson, and a number of other prominent Rhode Islanders demanded that the assembly remove Brayton and rescind the judicial reorganization. Even the *Providence Journal*, which since 1884 had been owned by a syndicate headed by textile manufacturer Jesse Metcalf, distanced itself from the GOP, referring to Brayton as "the acknowledged head and chief captain of the Swiss mercenaries of Rhode Island politics." As chief constable from 1886 until 1887, Brayton made an outward show of enforcing prohibition while letting liquor dealers know where his true sympathies lay. Disgusted with the results—arrests for public drunkenness, according to the *Providence Journal*, actually rose under prohibition—voters quickly turned against the amendment, and in 1889 voted overwhelmingly to repeal it. "Rum still rules—the

[7] Sternstein, "Nelson W. Aldrich," 142-49 (quotation at 142); Charles Carroll, *Rhode Island: Three Centuries of Democracy*, 4 vols. (New York: Lewis Historical Publishing Co., 1932), 2:651; Rider, *Booknotes* 28 (15 April 1911): 57-62; Nelson, "The Influence of Immigration on Rhode Island Politics," 54-59; Robert Grieve, "The Rise and Fall of Prohibition in Rhode Island," *Providence Journal*, 23 September 1906.

boss lives," commented the *Independent Citizen*, a prohibitionist weekly edited by the Reverend J. H. Larry.[8]

Public resentment over the special favors accorded street railways, gas and electric companies, and other utilities, or quasi-public corporations, also fed the Good Government crusade. In 1890 the Union Railroad Company, which by this time controlled practically all the horsecar lines in the city, requested permission to electrify its railway lines. Before it would agree to issue $3 million in bonds, however, the company sought assurance from the General Assembly that it would be protected from regulation by the municipalities it served. In response, the assembly authorized cities and towns to grant exclusive franchises to utilities for up to twenty-five years in return for a tax payment not exceeding 3 percent upon gross earnings (in 1898 raised to 5 percent). Under the terms of this act, Providence could tax a public corporation only if it awarded the corporation an exclusive franchise. The General Assembly then granted the Union Railroad an exclusive twenty-year franchise for its lines in Providence.[9]

Thanks to a loan from the American Sugar Refining Company—apparently the Sugar Trust's way of repaying Aldrich for his role in securing adoption of the McKinley Tariff in 1890—the senator and his two associates, attorney William G. Roelker and banker Marsden J. Perry, bought up the Union Railroad's stock and then transferred control of the company to the United Traction and Electric Company, a New Jersey-based holding company. Perry, whom Lincoln Steffens called "Rhode Island's first captain of Finance," owned the Narragansett Electric Company, the city's only electric utility. Then, in 1898, the General Assembly effectively exempted the lines of the United Traction and Electric Company from municipal regulation when it authorized the railroad to exchange its twenty-year franchise for a "perpetual franchise" in return for a promise to pay a paltry 1 percent of its gross earnings to the state treasury.[10]

---

[8] *Providence Journal*, 1-3 June 1886; Grieve, "Rise and Fall of Prohibition"; Sternstein, "Nelson W. Aldrich," 325-35; Nelson, "The Influence of Immigration on Rhode Island Politics," 98-102, 146n; McLoughlin, *Rhode Island*, 159.

[9] Nelson, "The Influence of Immigration on Rhode Island Politics," 213-15. On how resentment toward arrogant corporations fed the Good Government crusade, see Richard L. McCormick, "The Discovery that 'Business Corrupts Politics': A Reappraisal of the Origins of Progressivism," *American Historical Review* 86 (April 1981): 247-74.

[10] Steffens, "Rhode Island: A State for Sale," 347; "Municipal Government," *An-*

Providence became even more helpless in 1902, when Perry consolidated the city's quasi-public corporations—the Union Railroad Company, the Narragansett Electric Lighting Company, and the Providence Gas Company—into the Rhode Island Company, a new corporation controlled by the Philadelphia-based United Gas Improvement Company. Although capitalized at more than $8 million, the company paid municipal taxes on property valued at less than $1.5 million. Four years later, the Rhode Island Company became part of the New Haven Railroad, which by this time controlled all the rail lines serving Providence.[11]

What critics denounced as the cheap bartering away of local franchises and their consolidation into an out-of-state holding company coincided with a growing tendency for the General Assembly to intervene in municipal affairs. Providence, which until the late 1880s had been relatively free from legislative interference, was increasingly subject to statutes that "regulated the most fundamental interests of the city." There were several reasons for this encroachment on home rule. One was the gradual shift of municipal power from the mayor's office, where it had gravitated during the Doyle years, to the city council. From Thomas A. Doyle's death in 1886 until the inauguration of Joseph H. Gainer in 1913, no Providence mayor served more than four years in office. Consequently, day-to-day management of municipal affairs devolved on standing committees of the council and on departments staffed by civil servants. These departments, which had begun to grow during Doyle's administration as the city installed water and sewer systems, laid out public parks, and assumed many other new responsibilities, continued to multiply to a point where by 1909 there were some thirty-eight of them and ten commissions or boards. In addition, partisan politics pitted a Republican city council and General Assembly against a Democratic mayor. A broader franchise, as a result of the passage

nals of the American Academy of Political and Social Science 22 (September 1903): 384; Nelson, "The Influence of Immigration on Rhode Island Politics," 212-23; Scott Molloy, Division 618: Streetcar Employees Fight for a Union in Rhode Island (Providence: n.p., 1977), 4-6; McLoughlin, Rhode Island, 176-79. See also Robert E. Falb, "Marsden J. Perry: 'The Man Who Owned Rhode Island' " (American Civilization honors thesis, Brown University, 1964), RIHS.

[11] Nelson, "The Influence of Immigration on Rhode Island Politics," 223-24; Howard Kemble Stokes, The Finances and Administration of Providence (Baltimore: Johns Hopkins University Press, 1903), 288-91; "Municipal Government," 385.

of the Bourn Amendment in 1888 and the adoption of the Australian ballot, allowed the Democrats in 1892 to elect their first mayor since 1853 and thereafter to control the mayoralty. Yet a property requirement that excluded three-fifths of the electorate kept the City Council firmly in the hands of the Republicans until 1928.[12]

The creation of monopolistic utilities with the connivance of a machine-dominated General Assembly and a partisan city council fueled the growth of an independent movement between 1890 and 1895. The city's independents were a disparate lot, consisting of men generally in favor of nonpartisan administration, home rule for cities, short-term contracts if not outright municipal ownership for quasi-public corporations, and greater power for the mayor and other executive officers. Joining prohibitionists and moral reformers who denounced the corrupt ties between liquor dealers and machine politicians were businessmen who wanted to see the city run along the lines of a corporation and middle-class homeowners who wanted to clean up municipal administration as well as their neighborhoods.

At the core of the city's independent movement were citizens outraged at the corruption they saw around them. In 1890, shocked by the spectacle "of a religious city receiving a revenue from licensing a vice," Robert Grieve, Edwin C. Pierce, and some twenty other prohibitionists called for the formation of a Union party dedicated to the "overthrow of the rum power." Heirs of the antebellum antiparty heritage, these moralists hoped to unite the people against the power of the liquor interest. But Rhode Island's recent experience with prohibition doomed this attempt to bring about civic regeneration.[13] A second attempt to organize the city's moral reformers proved no more successful. In 1893 an ad hoc Committee of One Hundred banded together for municipal reform in a Providence counterpart of the Reverend Charles Parkhurst's much publicized crusade against vice in New York City. Concerned citizens like

[12] James Quayle Dealey, "Government," in *A Modern City: Providence, Rhode Island, and Its Activities*, ed. William Kirk (Chicago: University of Chicago Press, 1909), 149, 162; Stokes, *The Finances and Administration of Providence*, v, 308-311, 313-15. Between 1896 and 1906 an average 20,435 voters cast their ballots for mayor, whereas only 8,163 voted in the aldermanic elections. Murray S. Stedman, Jr., and Susan W. Stedman, "The Rise of the Democratic Party of Rhode Island," *New England Quarterly* 24 (September 1951): 339.

[13] *Providence Journal*, 22, 26 February 1890.

Amos C. Barstow and E. Benjamin Andrews, president of Brown
University, served on short-lived and ineffectual subcommittees
that investigated illegal liquor sales, houses of ill fame, gambling,
and other vices.[14]

Moral reformers achieved more permanent organization in the
wake of the panic of 1893 when they founded a chapter of the
Union for Practical Progress. They modeled their organization on
Baltimore's Union for Public Good, which coordinated the efforts
of more than sixty churches, labor unions, and civic improvement
societies. Similar organizations in Boston, Philadelphia, and some
thirty other cities joined a short-lived national federation that used
B. O. Flower's reform journal, the *Arena*, as its organ. As "a UNION
of the progressive forces of the community," the Providence Union
for Practical Progress attempted "to keep the people thinking systematically upon social questions." Headed by Floyd W. Tomkins,
rector of Grace (Episcopal) Church, the new organization recruited
Protestants, Catholics, and Jews interested in civic regeneration.
After compiling statistics on unemployment in the city, the Union
for Practical Progress channeled its energies into abolishing sweatshops, curbing child labor, and, in conjunction with the Free Kindergarten Association, sponsoring the city's first playgrounds. By
1895, however, its members had come to realize that moral reform
was impossible without first freeing the city from boss rule. In
March of that year the Union for Practical Progress hosted a conference at which Lucius Garvin and other speakers compared the
administration of British, German, and American cities.[15]

The second component of the independent coalition consisted of
the Rhode Island Business Men's Association, the Advance Club,

[14] Ibid., 12 January 1893; Charles H. Parkhurst, "Facts for the Times," in William
Howe Tolman, *Municipal Reform Movements in the United States* (New York: Fleming
H. Revell Co., 1895), 15-23.

[15] *Providence Union for Practical Progress* (n.p., n.d.); *Providence Journal*, 23 July, 23
October 1894, 12 March 1895. See also James B. Crooks, *Politics and Progress: The Rise
of Urban Progressivism in Baltimore, 1895 to 1911* (Baton Rouge: Louisiana State University Press, 1968), 27-28, 166-67; Aaron Ignatius Abell, *The Urban Impact on Amer-
ican Protestantism, 1865-1900* (Cambridge: Harvard University Press, 1943), 103-106;
Arthur Mann, *Yankee Reformers in the Urban Age: Social Reform in Boston, 1880-1900*
(1954; reprint, Chicago: University of Chicago Press, 1974), 172; Ross E. Paulson,
Radicalism and Reform: The Vrooman Family and American Social Thought, 1837-1937
(Lexington: University of Kentucky Press, 1968), 92-97. In Milwaukee, Wisconsin,
Protestant, Catholic, and Jewish clergymen also acted to "federate the moral forces
of the city" against political corruption. Thelen, *The New Citizenship*, 106.

and other boosters' organizations that attempted to revitalize the midcentury civic culture. Like Dr. William F. Channing, city boosters in the 1890s distinguished "corporate sentiment" from narrow self-interest. But they also took into account the substantial growth of municipal administration since the 1860s. Accordingly, they criticized the city council for its failure to rise above partisan and neighborhood interests. At their monthly meetings members of the Rhode Island Business Men's Association discussed such topical issues as "Inequitable Taxation," "The People in Municipal Reform," "The Relation of Business Men to Taxation and Public Affairs," "Better Civic Conditions in Providence," and "Good Citizenship."[16] The members of the smaller, more exclusive Advance Club took an even more active part in improved municipal administration. Club president Hiram Howard, a silverware manufacturer who had been the unsuccessful Democratic candidate for mayor in 1889, believed that municipal improvement depended on fundamental political reform. In *A Plea for Progress*, Howard called for the abolition of property requirements for the suffrage and the enactment of "stringent laws against bribery" as measures designed to "put a stop to the infamous 'boodle' methods that have so long disgraced our State and caused it to be held in contempt by all honest and right-minded people." If his fellow Rhode Islanders failed to correct such abuses, Howard warned, "we are but a short step from anarchy, or what is still worse *plutocracy*, or the rule of wealth as against the people, *dollars* against *men*."[17]

In the early 1890s the Advance Club published a number of pamphlets on issues ranging from municipal economy to utility franchises. All emphasized the conflict between partisanship, or the pursuit of narrow self-interest, and the public interest. In *The Crisis: Shall the Advance of the Material Progress of the City of Providence be Arrested by Political or Factional Interests?*, David M. Thompson, a mill engineer and architect who managed B. B. & R. Knight's textile interests, propounded a new conception of "municipal economy." "In the advancement of the public weal," he declared, "all narrow, self-

---

[16] *The Rhode Island Business Men's Association* (Providence: Livermore & Knight, 1896), 17-19. On the growth of municipal administration, see Jon C. Teaford, *The Unheralded Triumph: City Government in America, 1870-1900* (Baltimore: Johns Hopkins University Press, 1984).

[17] Hiram Howard, *A Plea for Progress*, 2nd ed. (Providence: Rhode Island Printing Co., 1890), 49-50.

ish and partisan interests should yield and give place to the higher and more ennobling elements of human nature." His fellow citizens had too often "witnessed the strife and fruitless effort of strictly partisan measures in the past." Efforts "to economize and retrench in the expenditure of public funds [and] to maintain the lowest possible rate of tax" had inadvertently "retarded the growth of population, depressed the values of real estate, prevented many permanent improvements, and maintained a condition of constantly increasing danger."[18]

Rathbone Gardner echoed Thompson's call for more liberal spending. In a speech before the Advance Club in June 1891, Gardner attributed the relatively slow growth of Providence to "ultra-conservatism on the part of our people and not to official corruption, extravagance or inefficiency." Curiously, Gardner thought Providence "a striking and honorable exception" to the English observer James Bryce's characterization of municipal government as Americans' "one conspicuous failure." Providence succeeded, where other cities failed, because of its restrictive franchise. "What are the essential functions of a municipality?" he asked. "Are they not, or at least, should they not be, those of a purely business corporation?" Property owners and renters were therefore "the only ones who are logically entitled to any voice in its administration." Far from advocating the abolition of property requirements for voting, as Howard had urged, Gardner thought they should be raised, and the terms of the mayor and city councilmen lengthened. "The idea [of] the principle of equal political rights for all, and of universal or manhood suffrage" in municipal affairs he dismissed as "fundamentally absurd."[19]

Its avowed hostility to partisanship helps explain why the Advance Club opposed granting special privileges to street railways

[18] David M. Thompson, *The Crisis: Shall the Advance of the Material Progress of the City of Providence be Arrested by Political or Factional Interests?* (Providence: E. A. Johnson & Co., 1891), 7, 15. The Providence Board of Trade adopted this position in 1900 when it opposed a reduction in the municipal tax rate as "a step in the wrong direction." *Board of Trade Journal* 12 (May 1900): 209. E. P. Hennock contrasts the liberality of big businessmen with the frugality of shopkeepers in a British context in *Fit and Proper Persons: Ideal and Reality in Nineteenth-Century Urban Government* (London: Edward Arnold, 1973), 31-38, 308-334.

[19] Rathbone Gardner, *Projects of Municipal Reform: A Paper read June 3d, 1891, at the Meeting of the Advance Club, Providence, R.I.* (Providence: E. A. Johnson & Co., 1891), 18, 4-5, 11, 13-14; Bryce quoted in Mel Scott, *American City Planning since 1890* (Berkeley: University of California Press, 1969), 40.

and other municipal franchises. One of its pamphlets contended that the high cost of streetcar fares and the Union Railroad's refusal to give free transfers retarded the city's growth by preventing workingmen from moving out of overcrowded inner-city neighborhoods to less crowded suburbs. "The citizens of Providence have a right," maintained another of the club's pamphlets, "to demand public lighting at a low cost by plants under municipal ownership and management, or at a low cost by private corporations under short time contracts."[20]

The third and final component of the independent coalition consisted of middle-class homeowners, members of the improvement associations that sprang up in burgeoning residential neighborhoods across the city—among them Highland Park, Mount Pleasant, Blackstone, and Beacon Hill. Typical was the Blackstone Improvement Society, organized in June 1893, which represented affluent property owners on the East Side. Under its first president, architect Alfred Stone, the new organization concentrated on neighborhood improvement—better streets, improved water and sewer systems, and more frequent trolley service. In May 1895, however, Stone proposed that the association join "the movement for better municipal administration." Rathbone Gardner seconded Stone's proposal. In an address on "Faithful Municipal Representation," Gardner contrasted progressive cities, where officials were selected "in view of their special fitness," with Providence, where "executive functions" devolved on city councilmen, "men of very limited intelligence or doubtful character." Gardner considered it "specially important" that every councilman "be a man of capacity and the highest integrity." Attorney Amasa Eaton agreed. He traced "much of the present trouble to the pernicious habit of bringing national politics into municipal affairs." Swayed by these arguments, members of the society backed a slate of independent candidates for the city council.[21]

[20] Advance Club, *Street Railways* (Providence: E. A. Johnson & Co., 1891), 3-5; *How Should the City of Providence be Lighted? Is It Good Business Policy for the City of Providence to Make Long Time Monopolistic Contracts with Private Corporations?* (Providence: E. A. Johnson & Co., 1891), 11.

[21] Blackstone Improvement Society, Minutes, vol. 1, 1893-99, 14 May, 8 October, 12 November 1895, RIHS. For a discussion of improvement associations in other cities, see Jon A. Peterson, "The City Beautiful Movement: Forgotten Origins and Lost Meanings," *Journal of Urban History* 2 (August 1976): 421-25; and Scott, *American City Planning since 1890*, 65-69.

The Beacon Hill Improvement Association also joined the Good Government crusade. Organized in July 1895, it represented a slightly less affluent area than Blackstone Boulevard. Although interested in such issues of importance to their East Side neighborhood as street lighting, sewers, trees, and landscaping, its members saw an intimate connection between neighborhood improvement and better municipal administration. Some even advocated the municipal ownership of public utilities as a means of reducing the city's expenses (not to mention their own taxes). In a tract on "Municipal Economy," Sidney Sherman, a master at Providence English High School, asked how the city could continue to pay for public improvements like streets, parks, and playgrounds—"in a word, to carry out the mission thrust on it by the conditions of modern life"—without raising the rate of taxation, which had already doubled between 1859 and 1895. Answering his own question, Sherman suggested that the "solution" was "for cities to retain in their own hands the many valuable franchises which they possess and to operate them for the benefit of the public treasury." He predicted that municipal ownership would reduce the cost of lighting the city's streets by more than $100,000.[22]

Sherman's tract underscored some of the differences dividing the city's independents. Unlike Garvin and other Single Taxers, Sherman did not condemn monopolies per se. "Monopolies, with great corporations or trusts to operate them, are the very essence of modern industry as it is unfolding to-day," he said. Like the U.S. Post Office, they provided the public services that Americans had come to expect. Sounding much like Edward Bellamy, whose utopian novel, *Looking Backward, 2000-1887*, had spawned Nationalist clubs in Providence and other cities, Sherman advocated the "socialization" of monopolies so that they would "serve" the public interest. "No other duty," he declared, "is so imperatively laid upon municipality, state, and nation as this of drawing the fangs of monopoly by making it public instead of private." Garvin, in contrast, deemed monopoly "indefensible and intolerable." As a Single Taxer who believed in a cooperative commonwealth of small producers, Garvin

[22] Beacon Hill Improvement Association, *The Beacon* 2 (February 1897); Sidney A. Sherman, *Municipal Economy* (Providence: Snow & Farnham, 1896), 4-5, 9. See also ibid., *Public Utilities of Providence* (Providence: Remington Printing Co., n.d.).

traced "the unjust laws upon which the whole fabric of private mo-nopoly rests" to "the absence of popular sovereignty."[23]

In 1895 these disparate elements—moral reformers, city boost-ers, and neighborhood improvers—coalesced. A month before the municipal elections, more than six hundred citizens attended a mass meeting where they heard prohibitionist James A. Williams de-nounce partisanship in municipal politics, the Reverend J. H. Larry ask "Shall the railroads own us or we the railroads?" and attorney Edward D. Bassett expose tax evasion by some of the city's largest property owners. Bassett drew loud applause when he castigated the Union Railroad for its stubborn refusal to grant transfers. Prov-idence riders had requested free transfers and cross-town lines. Yet because of the company's "narrow-minded policy," they had to put up with irregular service and overcrowded trolleys. Bassett and the other speakers concluded their speeches by exhorting voters to choose candidates on the basis of merit rather than party affilia-tion.[24]

In the fall elections of 1895 these independents threw their sup-port to Good Government candidates on the wealthy East Side. They also rallied to attorney Edwin D. McGuinness. Rhode Island's first Catholic secretary of state and a former alderman, McGuinness had been the Democratic nominee for mayor each of the previous two years. On each occasion an unlikely coalition of liquor dealers, Russian Jews, and the United Order of Deputies, a violently anti-Catholic organization, had combined to overcome McGuinness's support in the heavily working-class and Irish wards of the city's North End. But this time McGuinness was not to be denied. Boldly taking the initiative, he accused the Republican incumbent, Frank Olney, of lax enforcement of municipal statutes regulating the liq-uor trade and gambling. To his neighborhood audiences he also pledged to work for free transfers and cross-town lines. Instrumen-tal in McGuinness's success was his ability to mobilize the city's in-dependent voters. Directing his campaign was an ad hoc Committee

[23] Sherman, *Municipal Economy*, 11-14; *Nationalist* 2 (July 1890): 346; ibid. 3 (Sep-tember, November 1890): 113-14, 279; Garvin quoted in the *Providence Journal*, 1 September 1906. On Bellamy, see Thomas, *Alternative America*.

[24] *Providence Journal*, 9, 20, 25 October, 6 November 1895. The Providence Board of Trade similarly favored free transfers as a means of encouraging suburban devel-opment. *Board of Trade Journal*, 12 (February 1900): 67.

of Fifty. Composed of five delegates from each ward, it included not
only veteran independents like Alfred Stone and James A. Williams,
but such formidable newcomers as manufacturer Amos C. Barstow,
Jr., and Lucian Sharpe, president of Brown & Sharpe. The Good
Government crusade also enjoyed the backing of the *Providence
Journal*, whose editorials urged voters to throw "the spendthrifts
and the tools of corporate greed" out of office.[25]

McGuinness, who had lost by 846 votes in 1893 and 382 votes in
1894, defeated Olney by 887 votes. Republican voters who sat out
the election because of Olney's ties to liquor interests provided his
margin of victory. When McGuinness took office in January 1896 as
Providence's first Irish-Catholic mayor, he announced that "the era
of reform and non-partisan municipal government is upon us." At
the seventh annual banquet of the Rhode Island Business Men's Association later that month, where the featured speaker was reformer
Hazen Pingree, mayor of Detroit, who spoke on "The People's Show
of Guard Duty in Municipal Reform," McGuinness was introduced
as "the Pingree of Providence" and greeted "with deafening applause, accompanied by three rousing cheers." The new city council,
in which independents, Democrats, and Republican reformers
made up a slim majority, attempted to reach an agreement with the
Union Railroad on a system of transfer tickets. The best the railroad
would offer, however, was a promise to issue transfers if the city
would erect, at its own expense, a central transfer station. This was
not acceptable, either to the members of the Blackstone Improvement Society, who went on record against the railroad's proposal
"by an emphatic majority," or to the city council, which broke off negotiations.[26]

In an obvious attempt to prevent McGuinness's reelection, the
General Assembly rescheduled municipal elections in 1896 to co-

[25] *Providence Journal*, 2, 16 November 1893, 15 March 1894, 9, 26-28 November
1895; "Bigotry Rampant," *Evening Telegram*, 24 November 1893; Nelson, "The Influence of Immigration on Rhode Island Politics," 199-200, 229-31; Stokes, *The Finances
and Administration of Providence*, 284-87; "Municipal Government," 140; Elmer E.
Cornwell, Jr., "A Note on Providence Politics in the Age of Bryan," *Rhode Island History* 19 (April 1960): 33-40.
[26] *Providence Journal*, 7, 26 January 1896; Blackstone Improvement Society, Minutes, vol. 1, 12 May 1896, RIHS; Nelson, "The influence of Immigration on Rhode
Island Politics," 231-34. See also Melvin G. Holli, *Reform in Detroit: Hazen S. Pingree
and Urban Politics* (New York: Oxford University Press, 1969).

incide with state and national contests in the hope that voters would vote a straight Republican ticket. But the assembly's flagrant intervention in municipal affairs had the unintended effect of sparking the formation of a permanent nonpartisan organization. In May 1896 businessmen and professionals who believed that Providence should be run as efficiently and as economically as a modern corporation banded together in the Municipal League, one of the many such organizations then being formed across the country. Unlike the Union for Practical Progress and the ad hoc Committee of Fifty, the Municipal League did not attempt to represent the entire city. Believing that any such representative "confederation" would necessarily be weak, it rejected the idea of an executive committee composed of delegates from affiliated organizations or from every ward. Instead, following the example of the Boston Municipal League, which had been organized two years earlier, it limited membership to two hundred prominent citizens. "Absolutely nonpartisan," the league barred all candidates and officeholders from membership.[27]

Business support was crucial to the success of the Good Government crusade in Providence. "The chief cause of the present condition of municipal affairs," declared Thomas W. Bicknell, former commissioner of public schools and president of the Beacon Hill Improvement Association, "is that businessmen are too busy to pay any attention to city affairs." By November 1896 the Municipal League had enrolled 175 members. The great majority of them were professionals and managers, the city's "best men." Befitting their occupational status, many were well-to-do: in fact, a quarter ranked among the top decile of property owners in Providence. More than half came from the East Side, traditionally the base of independent strength in the city. The rest generally hailed from other affluent neighborhoods. Indeed, Rathbone Gardner regretted that "so few wards . . . have taken an active interest in the movement." Significantly, the reform coalition cut across ethnic lines, as Roman Catholics made up perhaps a tenth of the league's charter members—essential in a city where Catholics outnumbered Protestants. The University community was also well represented, with E. Benjamin Andrews heading the Brown contingent. Episcopal bishop William N. McVickar was the most prominent of the five clergymen who were among the Municipal League's charter members.[28]

Over the next seven years the Municipal League mobilized a bloc of six to seven thousand independent voters pledged "to guard the chief city offices from unworthy machine candidates" and "to support the man of independent and conservative views rather than the submissive partisan." This is exactly what happened in the fall elections of 1896. Although Republican presidential candidate William McKinley swept the city by more than seven thousand votes, Edwin McGuinness easily won reelection by an even larger margin as the city's voters split their tickets. In the spring elections of 1897 the Municipal League fused with Democrats to oppose Republican incumbents who had failed to defend the city's interests in the General Assembly when the city sought to compel the Union Railroad to issue free transfers. That fall, the same coalition rallied to the support of William C. Baker, who replaced Edwin McGuinness at the head of the Good Government ticket after McGuinness suffered a nervous breakdown. The *Providence Journal* hailed Baker's victory as the "auspicious beginning" of civic regeneration, when "a number of the brightest and best young men of the city have been encouraged to take hold of practical politics in a clear and open way." If the "leading citizens will only come forward and insist that only upright men shall be placed in positions of trust," the newspaper suggested, "Providence might easily become the model city of the United States." Baker, who served until 1901, was succeeded by another fusion candidate, Daniel L. D. Granger. Former City Treasurer, Granger ran as a nonpartisan candidate "independent of corporations" and as an outspoken advocate of free transfers.[29]

"As a center about which the citizens can rally to resist partisan

[28] *Providence Journal*, 30 May, 18 October, 3 November 1896; "A Municipal League for Providence, R.I.," broadside, 23 May 1896, RIHS. The Milwaukee chapter of the National Municipal League was quickly "captured" by businessmen who wanted to lighten the city's tax burden. In 1897, however, the league's members switched their attention to "corporate arrogance," and began to push for corrupt practices legislation. Thelen, *The New Citizenship*, 158-75. In New York as well, the city's "organized independents" consisted of businessmen and professionals. McCormick, *From Realignment to Reform*, chap. 4.

[29] "The Municipal League: A Short History," 1903, RIHS; *Providence Journal*, 8 April 1897, 7 November 1900.

exigencies and corporate greed," the Municipal League advanced a comprehensive program of municipal reform. Chief among its demands was that "all visible, tangible, personal property," whether owned by individuals or corporations, be taxed. The city's "system of taxation," the league charged, was "needlessly unjust." As much as $40 million in personal property escaped taxation, which shifted the burden of taxation to middle-class homeowners. Moreover, the "perpetual franchise" granted local utilities not only deprived the city of revenue—in 1902 the Union Railroad Company paid the city only $61,092, or 5 percent of its gross revenues—but also meant high rates for customers. The city's electricity rates, which by 1903 stood at $1.71 per capita, were among the highest in the country.[30]

The Municipal League also attempted to defend home rule from the General Assembly's "encroachment." It thus called for a constitutional convention to amend the state's antiquated constitution, which except for the Bourn Amendment had remained virtually unchanged since 1842. In *Constitution-Making in Rhode Island*, Amasa Eaton proposed that the lower house of the General Assembly be apportioned on the basis of population, the assembly be forbidden to interfere in municipal affairs, judges be chosen on non-partisan grounds, and property requirements for voting be abolished. In 1899 Eaton assisted city solicitor Francis Colwell in drafting the city's brief against a piece of legislation then pending before the General Assembly to create a board of police and license commissioners. The city protested that the act was clearly "unconstitutional," because it contravened "the right to local self-government" reserved to Providence since statehood and because it did not allow for the appointment of independents, or those without party affiliation, to the proposed commission.[31]

---

[30] "Municipal League," broadside, 8 June 1903, RIHS; *The Good Government Platform* (Providence: Providence Municipal League, 1903), 1-4, 7-8; Nelson, "The Influence of Immigration on Rhode Island Politics," 257-62; Stokes, *The Finances and Administration of Providence*, 275; Henry Brayton Gardner, "Finance," in *A Modern City*, ed. Kirk, 195-96, 217.

[31] Amasa M. Eaton, *Constitution-Making in Rhode Island* (Providence: E. L. Freeman & Sons, 1899), 69-73; [Francis Colwell], *Brief in behalf of the City of Providence* (Providence: Snow & Farnham, 1899), 77-78. In the 1880s Eaton had been one of a small group of Mugwumps who held that "the routine business of government should be conducted on business principles" and officeholders "should be appointed on account of their fitness for the work to be done." *The Civil Service Reform Association of Providence, R.I.* (Providence: Providence Press Co., 1883), 6.

As a third area of concern, the Municipal League advocated that the city charter, a "conglomeration" of statutes dating back to 1866, be revised. In addition to providing for home rule, the new charter should streamline municipal government by strengthening the mayor at the expense of the city council. It should be thus separate the city's municipal and executive functions, expand the mayor's appointment power, and replace existing legislative committees with executive boards. It should also combine the Board of Aldermen and the city council into a single legislative body. Moreover, a new caucus law was needed to democratize nominations, for under existing conditions voters could "seldom do more by caucus attendance than ratify the nominations presented by the ward committees."[32]

Finally, the Municipal League gave its support to the campaign of the Public Education Association (PEA) to "ensure a non-partisan management" of the city's schools. Organized in 1899, the PEA was an educational lobby composed of Brown faculty, public school teachers and administrators, and East Side residents. According to spokesmen for the PEA, the city's 33-member School Committee, consisting of three members from each ward plus three ex-officio members, was simply too "cumbersome and costly." The School Committee was also a partisan body, "representative of political combinations rather than of the educational interests of the city." After a systematic canvass of school systems across the country, the PEA concluded that a five-member "commission" with members serving unpaid four-year terms to prevent "sudden and ill-advised changes of policy" would be far "more efficient." It similarly recommended that administrative duties be entrusted to a highly paid superintendent, an expert insulated from all partisan influences. Although endorsed by Mayor Granger, the Providence Board of Trade, and the *Providence Journal*, a bill to centralize the city's school system bogged down in the General Assembly. Boss Brayton reportedly killed the bill when it came before the state senate because he feared it would mean the election of five Democrats, all Catholics.[33]

[32] *The Good Government Platform*, 13, 9; Stokes, *The Finances and Administration of Providence*, 309n.
[33] Stephen O. Edwards, James Q. Dealey, Alfred Stone, comp., *Statement and Opinions in Regard to the Bill Substituting a Board of Education for the Present Cumbersome School*

The success of Good Government candidates in municipal elections did little, however, to stem legislative meddling in municipal affairs. In November 1901, at the request of the city council, the General Assembly created a police commission. Although the city had to pay their salaries, the three commissioners were appointed by the governor, with the consent of a Republican-dominated assembly. This measure passed in spite of the strenuous opposition of Mayor Granger, Bishop McVickar, Amasa Eaton, and two thousand other citizens who claimed that it would deprive the mayor of much of his limited power and the city of much of its control over the police. Not all middle-class groups, however, opposed the new commission. The Rhode Island Anti-Saloon League, a Protestant church lobby pressing for statewide prohibition, praised the efficiency of the police commissioners, even though "some of our strongest members condemn on principle the overriding of the rights of the municipality by the state." As the Anti-Saloon League's secretary observed in 1902, "more has been done in less than two months to stop law-breaking on the part of saloon keepers and brewers, and to preserve order and public decency in connection with the liquor traffic, than our organization could have done in ten years."[34]

The General Assembly's failure to enforce the state's ten-hour law during the streetcar strike of 1902 sent still more recruits into the Good Government crusade. Voters "aroused at the arrogance and selfishness of the street railroad monopoly" flocked to the polls later that fall to elect Lucius Garvin governor. Observers credited his victory to a large turnout by organized labor. (The turnout in Providence was almost half again as great as in 1901.) But Garvin's victory did not catch the Republicans completely by surprise. A year earlier, the General Assembly had stripped the governor of practically all of

Committee of the City of Providence (Providence: Remington Printing Co., 1905), 3-4; Public Education Association, Should Providence Have a Small School Commission? (Providence: Snow & Farnham, 1913), 12; The Good Government Platform, 11-12; Providence Public Education Association, Minutes, 1899-1908, 6 February, 23 October 1899, 28 January 1901, 31 January, 28 May 1902, RIHS; letter from Royal H. Gladding, Providence Journal, 1 November 1906. On the PEA in New York, Philadelphia, and other cities, see David B. Tyack, The One Best System: A History of American Urban Education (Cambridge: Harvard University Press, 1974), 137-39, 149, 154-56; Hammack, Power and Society, 259-99.

34 Dealey, "Government," 164-65; Willard C. Selleck, "Secretary's Report," Rhode Island Issue 2 (February 1902), 3; Nelson, "The Influence of Immigration on Rhode Island Politics," 267-68.

his limited appointment power. Under the terms of the so-called
Brayton Act of January 1901, whenever the state senate failed to
confirm the governor's appointments, it could substitute its own
nominees. Only the governor's private secretary was not subject to
senate confirmation. No wonder that Brayton greeted the news of
Garvin's election by asking, "What [are] they crowing about? The
Democrats didn't do anything but elect a governor who can't do
anything but sign notaries' commissions and a lieutenant-governor
who can't do anything."[35]

Brayton was right. Even before Garvin took office, a lame-duck
General Assembly repealed the ten-hour act, whose constitutionality the state supreme court had just upheld. Hamstrung by Republican legislators, Garvin used his office as a pulpit from which
to mobilize the state's independent voters against "abuses of
government." In his first annual message to the General Assembly
in January 1903 he denounced the perpetual franchise granted
quasi-public corporations, the creation of police commissions in
Providence and other cities, and the hastily considered legislation
passed during the closing days of legislative sessions. Among the
numerous reforms he advocated were a modified veto for the governor, abolition of the property requirement in elections for city
councilmen, lower trolley fares, and a new ten-hour law for streetcar workers. Garvin also took every opportunity to champion "Direct Legislation," which, he argued, would "put legislative power
[back] in the hands of the people" and bring an end to "the selfish
rule of machine politicians."[36] Garvin's call for the initiative and ref-

---

[35] *State*, 21 October 1905; *Providence Journal*, 5 November 1902; Brayton quoted in
Nelson, "The Influence of Immigration on Rhode Island Politics," 273; "The Victory
of a Persistent Reformer," *Outlook* 73 (10 January 1903): 94-95.

[36] Lucius F. C. Garvin, "The Constitutional Initiative," in *20th Century Illustrated
History of Rhode Island and the Rhode Island Central Trades and Labor Union and Its Affiliated Organizations* (Providence: Rhode Island Central Trades and Labor Union,
1901), 161. Garvin's belief in the efficacy of such nonpartisan measures as the initiative and referendum was echoed by another Single Taxer, Edwin C. Pierce. In 1907
Pierce told workers that "without first securing direct legislation," organized labor,
upon whom "the salvation of this republic depends," "cannot discharge its responsibility and assure to our own time and to posterity the good things which its power
makes possible." All across America, he said, "the corporations are lining up against
direct legislation and the constitutional initiative. Everywhere organized labor is
marshalling its hosts under the standard." "Constitutional Initiative," in Providence
Central Trades and Labor Union and Building Trades Council, *Official Labor Day
Journal, 1907* (Providence: Franklin Press, 1907), 31-33. See also John D. Buenker,

erendum received the support of both the Municipal League and the state Federation of Labor.[37]

In March 1903 Garvin electrified the state when he delivered an extraordinary message condemning electoral corruption. "That bribery exists to a great extent in the elections of this State is a matter of common knowledge," he declared. So common was the practice "that the awful nature of the crime has ceased to impress." In many towns in Rhode Island, "the money paid to the voter, whether $2, $5, or $20, is spoken of as a payment for his time." Garvin's allegations rested in part on the reports of muckraking correspondents for several out-of-state newspapers. In a series of articles in the *New York Evening Post* Edward Lowry documented the extent of bribery in Rhode Island. Lowry pointed out that contrary to popular wisdom, which traced electoral corruption to the massive influx of immigrants inexperienced in the ways of a democracy, Rhode Island's political degradation originated in fourteen "brazenly corrupt" Yankee towns, or "rotten boroughs," where "debauched" citizens sold their votes for whiskey and money. Most were "dying towns" whose populations were smaller in 1903 than they had been during the American Revolution. Four were "heathen towns" without resident ministers. As Lincoln Steffens put it, "the good old American stock sold out." Assisting Lowry in exposing bribery in Rhode Island were Rathbone Gardner, Brown history professor William MacDonald, and Bishop McVickar. All agreed that the state urgently needed "a campaign of political education." The "public conscience," announced Bishop McVickar, "must be appealed to and aroused, and a public sentiment created which shall be as sensitive and intolerant to crookedness and dereliction in public affairs, as it is now to those same faults—or, rather, crimes—in personal and in private life."[38]

"Urban Liberalism in Rhode Island, 1909-1919," *Rhode Island History* 30 (May 1971): 40; and Carl Gersuny, "Uphill Battle: Lucius F. C. Garvin's Crusade for Political Reform," ibid. 39 (May 1980): 57-75.

[37] In June 1900 representatives from the Iron Moulders' Union, the Painters' and Decorators' Union, and the Central Trades and Labor Union as well as from the Rhode Island Woman Suffrage Association appeared before the General Assembly to support the constitutional initiative. The following year, the Mulespinners' Association and the Plumbers' Union also endorsed direct legislation. *State*, 24 February 1906.

[38] [Edward Lowry], *To the People of Rhode Island: A Disclosure of Political Conditions and*

In the fall of 1904 Garvin fell 856 votes short of winning a third term. Considering the powerful forces arrayed against him, his showing was indeed the "great moral victory" that his private secretary, Robert Grieve, claimed. In the same election President Theodore Roosevelt carried the state by a margin of almost sixteen thousand votes. With Garvin out of office, support for a constitutional convention devolved on the "conservative men of the business and professional classes" who joined a loose coalition of Good Government clubs headed by Professor MacDonald. In "To the Voters of Rhode Island," a broadside issued in 1905, the nonpartisan Rhode Island Citizens' Union charged that the state's archaic constitution had "made possible the growth of a system of political corruption so widespread and so bad as to occasion, among thoughtful citizens of Rhode Island without regard to party, profound and increasing irritation." A "corrupt ring," composed of men "who derive financial profit from favoritism to special interests," controlled the General Assembly. Moreover, the constitution sanctioned the bribery that was rife in the state's small towns. In addition, "outrageous caucus laws" had been "ingeniously contrived to prevent independent nominations."[39]

A new nonpartisan weekly, the *State*, broadcast similar charges during its brief existence from July 1905 until June 1907. Echoing Lincoln Steffens's allegations, the *State* charged that one-party domination of the state since the Civil War had transformed Rhode Island into an oligarchy. Thanks to their huge donations to Republican coffers, the state's quasi-public corporations did not pay their share of taxes. Reflecting the views of editor Sidney Sherman, the weekly called for municipal ownership of public utilities. "Private ownership," it charged, "creates a few millionaires by taking excessive toll from the common people." The *State* also endorsed the direct primary. The redemption of labor must come through political action, it said, for "labor organizations, as shown by the principles they avow and the action they take, are the most authentic spokes-

---

an *Appeal for Their Reform* (n.p., n.d.), 9, 33-34, 3; Lincoln Steffens, *The Autobiography of Lincoln Steffens*, 2 vols. (New York: Harcourt, Brace & Co., 1931), 2:467; Grieve, "Rhode Island's Political Debasement," 86-90.

   39 Grieve, "Rhode Island's Political Debasement," 86; *State*, 8 July 1905; Rhode Island Citizens' Union, "To the Voters of Rhode Island," 1905, Lippitt Papers, Brown University Library.

men of the people. Although they include within their ranks only a minority of wage-workers, yet they are the leaders and the representatives of the unorganized as well." The *State* thus expressed the views of middle-class reformers like Sherman who hoped to rechannel workingmen's discontent from strikes and other forms of direct action, which raised the specter of class conflict, into political action.[40]

Independent strength mounted in 1906, sparked by the General Assembly's decision to transfer the power to appoint the city's police commissioners from the governor to the mayor, subject to confirmation by the city council. The legislature's move prompted fifty prominent men, including textile manufacturers Jesse and Stephen Metcalf and Brown University president W.H.P. Faunce, to sign protests against subjecting the commissioners to partisan pressures. It also breathed new life into the Franklin Lyceum, moribund since 1891. At meetings in the spring of 1906, Lucius Garvin, Edwin C. Pierce, and other members of the lyceum debated the franchise question, public ownership of utilities, and the election of judges. "If the Franklin Lyceum had been in existence," former congressman Henry J. Spooner asked his audience, "do you suppose that the electric railway franchises would have passed the General Assembly almost unquestioned?"[41]

By May 1906 a fusion ticket had materialized to challenge the Brayton machine's control of state politics. At the first nominating convention ever held in Rhode Island, Democrats chose Robert Hale Ives Goddard, "a fine old aristocrat of 70," as their candidate for the U.S. Senate. A millionaire cotton manufacturer, a lifelong Republican in national politics, and an officer of the Municipal League, Goddard was "an irreproachable candidate," his name one of "preeminent respectability." As standard-bearer of a ticket that included members of the Rhode Island Citizens' Union, Democrats, and independent Republicans, Goddard pursued the nomination against two Republicans, incumbent George Wetmore, a New

[40] *State*, 26 August, 22 July, 30 December, 16 September 1905. Similarly, Eugene Debs advocated political action and placed his faith in "the redemptive power of the ballot." Nick Salvatore, *Eugene V. Debs: Citizen and Socialist* (Urbana: University of Illinois Press, 1982), 147-49.

[41] *Providence Journal*, 4 April, 5 January, 6, 13, 27 March 1906; Dealey, "Government," 165-66.

Yorker who summered in Newport, and Samuel Pomeroy Colt, president of the United States Rubber Company. By taking the name of the Lincoln Union party, this ad hoc coalition of concerned citizens hoped to persuade voters "to abandon for the time being their party allegiance," just as Rhode Islanders had done in 1861. To attract the independent vote, the Democratic State Committee insisted that party caucuses "clean house." Men of unimpeachable integrity were recruited to stand as reform candidates for the General Assembly. "No pledge will be asked of you to vote for any candidate, or for, or against, any measure," Goddard wrote attorney John C. Pegram, president of the Economic Club, in urging him to become a candidate. "You are known to be opposed to the Brayton domination[,] in favour of political decency [and] honour in R.I. That is enough."[42]

Although Brayton dismissed Goddard's candidacy as simply a clever ploy by the Democrats to get back into office, more disinterested observers stressed its moral tone. In language reminiscent of the antislavery crusade Goddard urged state voters to throw off "the yoke of slavery and establish democracy in Rhode Island." In his acceptance speech, Goddard portrayed himself as a Christian soldier at the head of "a union of those forces of righteousness which exist in both parties." He called on his fellow Rhode Islanders to do battle against "an insidious foe," the Brayton machine, which was "poisoning the air with its breath, and undermining the foundations of our State Government." "It is time," he announced, "that we should again, my friends of both parties, join forces as was done in 1861, in the sacred cause of political honesty and purity." "Patriotism" must "triumph over partisanship." Goddard concluded his speech with the Old Testament exhortation: "Choose ye this day whom ye will serve—Brayton and his machine or the people of Rhode Island."[43]

---

[42] *Providence Journal*, 24 May, 2 September 1906; "The Lincoln Union," broadside, 1907, Robert Hale Ives Goddard Papers, RIHS; John C. Pegram, Diary, 1885-1909, vol. 4, 10 October 1907, RIHS. See also Erwin L. Levine, "The Rhode Island Lincoln Party and the 1906 Election," *Rhode Island History* 21 (January 1962): 8-15; Nelson, "The Influence of Immigration on Rhode Island Politics," 286-95.

[43] *Providence Journal*, 15 June 1906; *State*, 19 May 1906; Goddard quoted in *Lincoln Party, Resolutions, Etc., Leading to Its Formation* (n.p., 1906), 6-7, 10. Goddard's campaign rhetoric illustrates the Protestant moralism that suffused progressive reform. See Clyde Griffen, "The Progressive Ethos," in *The Development of an American Culture*,

The Goddard crusade attracted a wide following. Goddard's campaign committee included prominent Democrats like James H. Higgins, former mayor of Pawtucket and Democratic candidate for governor, independents like Charles Sisson, a Quaker manufacturer who had been among those calling for the formation of a Union party in 1890, and independent Republicans like Henry D. Sharpe, who had succeeded his father Lucian as president of Brown & Sharpe. Textile manufacturer Stephen Metcalf guaranteed payment of all the campaign's advertising expenses, and offered rewards to those who "furnish information resulting in the conviction of any election officer" guilty of bribery. The *Providence Journal*, which only three years earlier had dismissed Garvin's charges about the extent of bribery in Rhode Island as exaggerated, also endorsed Goddard. Sharpe, Metcalf, and other stockholders had just beaten back an attempt by Senator Aldrich, Marsden Perry, and Samuel P. Colt to gain control of the *Journal* in order to tout Colt.[44]

Also rallying to Goddard were clergymen, moral reformers, members of the Radical and Economic clubs, and organized labor. A number of Providence clergymen, denouncing what one called "boss rule and trust tyranny," urged their congregations to join the Good Government crusade. Goddard supporters plumped his candidacy at church clubs. In a speech on "Good Citizenship" before the Men's Club of the Trinity Methodist Episcopal Church, Patrick J. McCarthy, an Irish-born reformer elected mayor in 1907, charged that Brayton was simultaneously "the agent of men high up in his party" and "the agent, the paid attorney, of corporations which have direct interest in legislation, and who trust to his power, his influence, to procure for them that which they most desire." Rathbone Gardner, senior warden of Grace Church and officer of the Churchmen's Club, impressed upon his audiences "the duty of citizenship," a duty "enjoined upon the people by their very religion." Also important to Goddard's candidacy were the Radical and Economic clubs, which between them contributed at least thirty-four men active in his campaign. Organized labor, angry at the Gen-

ed. Stanley Coben and Lorman Ratner, 2nd ed. (New York: St. Martin's Press, 1983), 144-80.

[44] Records of the Campaign Committee, 2 November 1906, 15 November 1907, Goddard Papers, RIHS; Garrett D. Byrnes and Charles H. Spilman, *The Providence Journal: 150 Years* (Providence: Providence Journal Co., 1980), 238-41.

eral Assembly's refusal to mandate an eight-hour day, similarly endorsed Goddard.[45]

Although Goddard led the balloting in the legislative session of
1907, he was unable to obtain a majority. "If he had been willing to
buy votes," his friends reported, "he could have won in a walk."
When the General Assembly could not decide among the three candidates, it postponed the decision until the next session. Once again,
Goddard stood as the reform candidate for U.S. Senator. This time
a committee of twenty-five—fifteen Democrats and ten Lincoln-Re-
publicans—managed his campaign. In January 1908 Rathbone
Gardner, who had been elected state senator on the Democratic-
Lincoln Union ticket, placed Goddard's name before the General
Assembly. Goddard, he declared, was "a statesman" who represented the public interest, "rather than an adroit manipulator of
schemes for petty benefactions to a locality or to individuals." But,
as in the previous session, the malapportionment that allowed less
than a tenth of the state's population to control the other 90 percent
doomed Goddard's candidacy. After Colt withdrew, the Republican
majority at last reelected Wetmore. Though retiring from the struggle against boss rule, Goddard urged unrelenting advocacy of
"those great questions of political decency and personal independence." "We were prompted by no personal or party ambition," he
explained in a letter of thanks to his supporters, "but solely by a lofty
and patriotic desire to secure cleaner politics and better opportunity
for the expression of the will of the people."[46]

Goddard's efforts had not been completely in vain. Inspired by
the Liberal party's victory in England in 1906, workingmen established a Wage Earners' Club to promote the interests of organized
labor through political action.[47] Moreover, Goddard's running
mate, James H. Higgins, "a man with a backbone," won election as

[45] *Providence Journal*, 29 October 1906, 5 December 1907; circulars and programs
of the Providence Radical Club, 1899-1911, RIHS; miscellaneous material of the
Economic Club of Providence, RIHS. For Gardner's comments on "the duty of citizenship," see *Providence Journal*, 17 April 1905.

[46] Putnam, "What's the Matter with New England?" 151; *Providence Journal*, 1 June
1907, 22 January, 6 February 1908.

[47] *State*, 21 July 1906. The Central Labor Union in Worcester, Massachusetts, established a similar club, which for several years wielded some influence in municipal
politics. Roy Rosenzweig, *Eight Hours for What We Will: Workers and Leisure in an Industrial City, 1870-1920* (Cambridge: Cambridge University Press, 1983), 19.

the state's first Irish-Catholic governor. Immediately upon taking office in 1907, Higgins attempted to honor his campaign promise to drive Brayton, "a disgusting and disreputable character," from the sheriff's office in the state capitol, where the by now almost blind boss managed the General Assembly. Persuaded to leave the capitol by his Republican colleagues, who feared the political consequences if he remained, Brayton nonetheless continued to manage state politics until his death from diabetes in September 1910 at the age of seventy. His death, commented the *Nation*, "takes from the political stage the last of the old-time 'bosses,' " none of whom "went about the routine of their business so directly, so simply and without pretence" as did Brayton.[48]

Higgins's election as governor laid to rest much of the stigma that had attached to the Democratic party since the Civil War. Although they would remain the minority party in Rhode Island until the Great Depression, the Democrats benefited from the decline of partisanship as Yankee reformers like Edwin C. Pierce, Rathbone Gardner, and Theodore Francis Green, who as governor from 1933 to 1937 was to inaugurate a New Deal in Rhode Island, found a home in the party. Henceforth Democrats like Green, unsuccessful candidate for governor in 1912, would carry on the struggle against the "political-commercial oligarchy" that ruled the state in league with the Republican party. At the same time Republicans began to reach out to the state's new immigrants, cleverly playing off French Canadians (and later Italians) against the Irish. In 1908 Aram Pothier, a banker from the mill town of Woonsocket, won election as the first French-Canadian governor of Rhode Island. Over Democratic opposition in 1909-10, the Republicans granted Pothier a limited veto and reapportioned the General Assembly so that Providence now had twenty-five seats in the 100-seat lower house. The redistricting, which was carried out with none of the blatant gerrymandering the Democrats had expected, actually increased the Democratic party's urban representation. Following Brayton's death, the Republican whips in the General Assembly found it more difficult to maintain party discipline. Republican legislators often

[48] *Providence Journal*, 9 March, 11 May 1907, 24 September 1910; Higgins quoted in Byrnes and Spilman, *The Providence Journal*, 265-66; *Nation* 91 (29 September 1910): 279; Erwin L. Levine, *Theodore Francis Green: The Rhode Island Years, 1906-1936* (Providence: Brown University Press, 1963), 40-42.

broke ranks to support social and political reforms, like a 54-hour law for women and children in 1913.[49]

In the meantime the independent coalition splintered as businessmen went one way, moral reformers another. For businessmen, efficient and economical government remained the primary goal. In 1914, inspired by the example of businessmen in Chicago and other western cities, they organized the Voters' League to promote nonpartisanship and efficiency in government. On the eve of the fall elections that year the new organization submitted a copy of its platform to every candidate. Rathbone Gardner explained to the Edgewood Improvement Association that the league stood for three principles: honest candidates, nonpartisanship, and the notion "that the voter, as a rule, knows less than he thinks he does of the character or even record of the men he is asked to vote for." It consisted of three hundred businessmen and professionals who paid annual dues of five dollars each. Several men subscribed much more. Stephen Metcalf contributed $900, as did Henry D. Sharpe. Manufacturer James R. MacColl and attorney Thomas F. I. McDonnell each subscribed $200. Significantly, of the 228 members identified, only seven belonged to the Radical Club, where middle-class moralists debated Georgist (and socialist) principles, whereas sixty-three were members of the nonpartisan Economic Club.[50]

In investigating the records of candidates for municipal and state office, a practice inaugurated by the Municipal League in 1905, the Voters' League hoped to force "the political organizations to nominate for public office honest and capable men, irrespective of party, creed, or class." Reiterating some of the demands made by Theodore Francis Green in 1912, the new organization insisted on an end

[49] Levine, *Theodore Francis Green: The Rhode Island Years*, 42-62.

[50] *Providence Journal*, 17 July, 9 October 1914; subscription book in the Records of the Voters' League of Rhode Island, 1914-19, RIHS. About this time, middle-class Americans began to move away from moralism toward emphasis upon efficiency and expertise. Works that analyze this shift include Barry Dean Karl, *Executive Reorganization and Reform in the New Deal: The Genesis of Administrative Management, 1900-1939* (Cambridge: Harvard University Press, 1963); Samuel Haber, *Efficiency and Uplift: Scientific Management in the Progressive Era, 1890-1920* (Chicago: University of Chicago Press, 1964); and Henry F. May, *The End of American Innocence: A Study of the First Years of Our Time, 1912-1917* (Chicago: Quadrangle Books, 1964). See also Wayne K. Hobson, "Professionals, Progressives and Bureaucratization: A Reassessment," *Historian* 39 (August 1977): 639-58. For a discussion of the bureaucratic impulse, see chap. 7 below.

to dual officeholding, conflict of interest, and the employment of
superfluous staff. As Henry D. Sharpe told the Men's Club of the
Fourth Baptist Church in Providence, "The kind of man the Voters'
League wants to see in office is the man who will tend to the State's
business as though it was his own and when he is through, adjourn."
Sharpe denounced what he regarded as "an increasing tendency to
disorderliness, extravagance and disgraceful scenes in the closing
hours of the session," which the league hoped to stop. In fact, he
thought that affairs had grown worse since Brayton's death in 1910.
"Whatever may be said about Gen[eral] Brayton," Sharpe observed,
"I think he felt a certain pride in the way things were carried on;
there was a certain orderliness; the State met its bills; sufficient taxes
were levied to meet the bills." In a speech before the Olneyville Business Men's Association, Thomas McDonnell attributed the waste
that he and other league spokesmen decried to apathy. "The ordinary business man," he explained, "takes but little, if any, interest in
public affairs. He is sadly lacking in public spirit. He neglects to perform his public duty."[51]

The success of the league's campaign to educate voters about
their officeholders depended on publicity. Just before the fall elections of 1914 the league released its first assessments of candidates
for public office. In February 1915 it rated the General Assembly's
performance. By January 1916 these ratings were appearing
monthly. "We hope," said McDonnell, "to raise the calibre of the
men elected[;] we desire to instill into the minds and hearts of the
citizens of the community that the State of Rhode Island is a great
business corporation, that its citizens should be its directors, and
that the officers should be selected with the same discrimination as
those of a private corporation." As the *Providence Journal* added,
"the Assembly is hamstrung by old-fashioned ways of doing business that an up-to-date commercial concern would not tolerate an
instant." Too many state commissions and boards existed, and their
power and functions frequently overlapped. The responsibility of
the members of the General Assembly was loose and indirect. With
no real budget control or proper system for auditing state expenditures, the legislature wasted the taxpayers' money. There were also

<hr/>

[51] *Providence Journal*, 21, 22 October 1914; Levine, *Theodore Francis Green: The
Rhode Island Years*, 57-58.

numerous cases of dual officeholding. State senator Joseph W. Freeman of Central Falls, for example, was proprietor of the firm that did all the state's printing. Finally, the assembly's clerks were too highly paid and too numerous. In sum, the General Assembly was "pitifully unbusinesslike."[52]

Clearly, for the league's members, nonpartisanship signified a more limited objective than civic regeneration in which the "producing classes" overcame social and economic differentiation to unite in opposition to boss rule. What these businessmen desired was efficient and economical government, not the revival of a broad and inclusive middle-class America. Although not rejecting the principle of "party organization," they did seek to curb its "abuses." "The 'party' fetich [sic]" was "overworked," they declared. "The one big issue is clean, honest and efficient State Government." Yet their league eventually succumbed to the very apathy it deplored. Failing "to secure the public support which it hoped for," and with its members apparently divided in their assessments of candidates, the league disbanded in January 1919. The League of Women Voters, organized after the ratification of the Nineteenth Amendment in 1920, carried on this tradition of limited nonpartisanship. Its "members were bidden to go into the parties of their choice and work intelligently and not as rubber stamps."[53]

Where businessmen sought economy and efficiency in government, the moralists who had earlier been their allies in the Good Government crusade looked forward to "the era of civic and business regeneration." In quest of this vision they moved in and out of a number of short-lived organizations. Many joined the Rhode Island Tax Reform Association, organized in 1908 to advocate "Home Rule in Taxation." George Liddell, the bookkeeper who was the association's secretary, predicted that adoption of the Single Tax would remedy the "inequitable system of taxation," reduce unemployment, undercut the appeal of socialism, and above all revi-

[52] *Providence Journal*, 29 October 1914, 9 February 1915, 4 January, 3 April, 5 May, 18 October, 3 November 1916, 28 March 1917.

[53] Ibid., 24 May 1917; Executive Committee to Geo. L. Shepley, 4 January 1919, Records of the Voters' League of Rhode Island, RIHS; "Beginnings of the Rhode Island League of Women Voters," typescript, 1930, 3, Records of the League of Women Voters, RIHS.

talize community life.[54] In 1911 Lucius Garvin and Edwin C. Pierce
were among the officers of the Union for Public Good, a nonpartisan organization that, in order to preserve a middle-class America
of small producers, attempted to wage "a campaign for righteousness" against "an economic or business tyranny, emanating from the
trusts and combinations, which is rapidly destroying republicanism
and democracy." Rhode Island was "a plutocracy," charged Hiram
G. Vrooman, pastor of the Church of the New Jerusalem, "maintained by wholesale bribery and intimidation." Vrooman blamed
the "high cost of living," then a source of considerable anxiety for
middle-class Americans, on monopolies.[55]

Some of these moralists found a temporary home in the Progressive party, which held its first organizational meeting in Rhode Island in September 1910. Many of the planks of the new party's platform must have sounded familiar: the constitutional initiative,
home rule for cities and towns, and an eight-hour day for municipal
workers. After all, they were the same reforms that Single Taxers,
Christian socialists, labor reformers, and other spokesmen for a
middle-class America had championed since the 1880s. For Professor MacDonald, the Bull Moose insurgents were the last hope for
the Republican party. "The Republicans," he wrote in 1911, "are essentially an aristocratic party, representative of the classes rather
than of the masses." The history of the GOP since the Civil War was
one of decline, he said, echoing the opinion of John Francis
Smith, Edwin C. Pierce, and other moralists who had abandoned
the party. "It is the story of every party, in every country, which has
ceased to be a party of moral ideas and popular appeal, but has become instead a party of class interests, vested rights, and intrenched
wealth." Garvin, despairing of the influence wielded by southern
conservatives in the Democratic party, also joined the Progressives.
So too did several leaders of the Rhode Island Woman Suffrage Association who, according to Sara M. Algeo, believed that "in the formation of the Progressive Party in 1912, came women's first great
opportunity to play politics." The moralists were also attracted by

[54] *Bulletin of the Rhode Island Tax Reform Association* 6 (4 April 1908), 1. See also
Woonsocket Taxpayers (Providence: Rhode Island Tax Reform Association, 1911).
[55] *Providence Journal*, 2 January, 13 February 1911; Paulson, *Radicalism and Reform*,
72-73, 185n. On the "high cost of living," see chap. 8 below.

slogans like "Let the People Rule," "Equal Rights," "Pass Prosperity Around," and "Protect the Laborer." After the Progressive party's demise in 1916, some of them joined the Single Tax party. Others, like Garvin, returned to the Democratic fold.[56]

By 1910 the Rhode Island Tax Reform Association had spawned the People's Forum. Meeting every Sunday evening, the forum modeled itself on the Ford Hall lecture series in Boston. Attendance, though small—sixty was considered a crowd—was lively. An invited speaker typically led off its free-for-all debates with a speech limited to fifty minutes; meetings were then thrown open to audience comment. Speakers had to be on their toes if they were to stand up to the rapid-fire questions that followed. Among those who found a home in the forum was dentist James Reid, the only socialist ever to serve in the General Assembly, whom the Voters' League dismissed as "a demagogue," possessing "an erratic mind with rabid views." Like the Single Taxers, Reid and his fellow socialists subscribed to moralistic explanations, attributing poverty and other social ills to unjust laws.[57]

During the First World War the anticonscription comments of Joseph M. Coldwell, a socialist later sentenced to the federal penitentiary in Atlanta for violating the Espionage Act, drew the fire of patriots. Attendance at the People's Forum swelled as agents from the Department of Justice and the Secret Service, joined by Providence plainclothesmen, took down the names of those in the audience. After the Armistice the forum ran afoul of the American Legion, Veterans of Foreign Wars, and other nativist organizations who accused it of harboring dangerous radicals. "The people of Providence will not tolerate the Forum if it is to become a centre of Bolshevism," wrote the *Providence Journal*. Former governor James H. Higgins called for the forum's suppression as "a public nuisance" because of "the wild-eyed theorists" who preached their "damnable

---

[56] *Providence Journal*, 21 September 1910; William MacDonald, "Can the Republican Party Reform?" *North American Review* 194 (December 1911): 836; Sara M. Algeo, *The Story of a Sub-Pioneer* (Providence: Snow & Farnham, 1925), 131-34. John Francis Smith, a Civil War veteran who had joined the Republican party during the struggle over slavery, argued that, following the war, a "class" of men had gained control of the GOP and had since used it as a means "to employ the machinery of government in colossal schemes for private money-making, and the aggrandizement of a class." "A Public Letter," 21 October 1884, Rider Collection, Brown University Library.

[57] *Providence Journal*, 17 October 1915, 11 December 1938, 29 October 1914.

doctrines" there. Charging that "murder, pillage and outrage are the three passwords used by that traitorous crew," he demanded that Garvin, president of the forum, disavow Coldwell's remarks.[58]

Although he refused to accede to Higgins's request, Garvin did eventually resign from the forum in December 1919, explaining that he no longer felt at home there. After the Armistice the organization had "drifted more into the control of the Socialists" and had "ceased to be an effective agent in bringing about the object sought by the Tax Reformers, to wit: the abolition of taxation—that burden upon civilization which is the underlying cause of bad housing, of the high cost of living, of the war between capital and labor, of poverty itself and its countless brood of vices, crimes and sufferings." Succeeding the former governor as spokesman for middle-class moralism was advertising man Granville Standish, who declared that "the People's Forum is for evolution," rather than violent revolution, through "the instrumentality of free speech, free assembly and a free press."[59]

In the two years left till death overtook him in 1922 at the age of eighty, Garvin continued to search for the hydra lying at the root of all social problems. Throughout his life, Garvin, whom the *Providence Journal* once called the "State's champion dreamer," had been partial to monocausal explanations—whether an inequitable system of taxation, monopoly of land ownership, or alcohol. He consistently tried to chart a middle way between monopoly capitalism on the one side and bureaucratic socialism on the other. Yet, like the socialists who had driven him from the People's Forum, Garvin attributed poverty to the monopolies created by unjust laws. Until his death, he clung tenaciously to the producerist dream held so many years earlier by Christian socialist Frederic A. Hinckley of a middle-class America in which the middle classes played a crucial role in mediating between rich and poor to avert class conflict. "The evils arising from alcoholic beverages," Garvin had written in 1906, "are most rife among the poor and the idle rich. The great middle class is distinguished for its sobriety. If, therefore, the extraordinarily unequal distribution of wealth were to cease, if the social extremes were merged and lost in a greater middle class, then drunkenness

---

[58] Ibid., 11 June 1917, 21 January 1918, 7, 8 April 1919.
[59] Ibid., 9 April 1919, 14 January, 26 February 1920.

would fall to a minimum." He traced the widening gulf between the rich and the poor in modern America to special legislation, "law-made monopoly," which "is nothing else than a privilege given to the few to take toll of some kind from all the rest of the people. The 'unearned increment' of the monopolist," he concluded, "is taken from the earnings of those who produce wealth."[60]

For Garvin as for Henry George, the Single Tax was a peculiarly American (and middle-class) solution to the problems that accompanied rapid industrialization. By rooting out privilege and law-made monopoly, the Single Tax would avert imminent strife between capital and labor. It would also quickly put an end to the "unearned increment" exacted by the monopolist. "The labor-problem," Garvin once declared, "will be solved when wage-earners get and keep all they earn." When that occurred, "labor organizations will become purely social and educational, strikes will become things of the past, and class discontent will cease." Robert Grieve, Garvin's former private secretary, similarly feared that "the concentration of capital and its control of the monopolies, unless checked" would "necessarily" result in bureaucratic socialism. He too believed that the American way lay in "the abolition of all the monopolies."[61]

By the First World War, Garvin, Grieve, and other moralists once again found themselves on the margins of middle-class culture. The social and ethnic differentiation of the twentieth-century city doomed their vision of a moral awakening and revitalized civic culture along producerist lines. Moreover, the businessmen with whom they had once made common cause now worshiped at the altar of efficiency. Many had embraced a new vision of community embodied in the translocal federations then being forged across the country. Men like Henry D. Sharpe saw nothing wrong in praising Boss

[60] Ibid., 30 July 1911; Lucius F. C. Garvin, "The Statesman's Job," *Independent* 61 (27 September 1906): 721-22; *State*, 23 June 1906. In 1871 Hinckley had written that in a society "separated into three great divisions . . . the good things of life are in excess in the middle class, and the bad things preponderate in the other two[;] it follows that the middle class comes nearest to the ideal state." He thus predicted that "the abolition of extreme wealth on the one hand, and extreme poverty on the other, would bring us nearer to a just commonwealth." Frederic A. Hinckley, *The Just Demand of Labor, A More Equal Distribution of Wealth* (Boston: American Workman Print, 1871), 4-5. On the socialists' attribution of poverty to unjust laws, see *State*, 23 June 1906.

[61] Lucius F. C. Garvin, "Solving the Labor Problem," *Arena* 36 (July 1906): 10; Robert Grieve, "Why the Workers Want," ibid. 14 (October 1895): 267.

Brayton for running an efficient legislature. In the meantime the impassioned moralism that fired Garvin and his colleagues waned.

At the same time the moralists' root-and-branch prescriptions for social reform fell out of favor. This had been clear as early as January 1910 when Wallace Hatch, secretary of the Rhode Island Anti-Tuberculosis Association, addressed the People's Forum on "The Uses of the Social Worker." Hatch's environmental analysis of the manifold problems facing urban dwellers did not sit well with his audience. As soon as Hatch concluded his talk, a socialist stood up to denounce the real culprit, the liquor interest. Next, George Liddell demonstrated the futility of social work. "Since this settlement work business started," he charged, "poverty has increased 100 per cent, intemperance has increased 100 per cent, suicide has increased 100 per cent, and ignorance has increased 100 per cent. It isn't settlement work we want," he insisted, "it is a readjustment of present conditions." Garvin then followed with the Single Tax rebuttal. The only remedy to the social ills described by Hatch, Garvin contended, was the Single Tax, which would completely redistribute land and revolutionize taxation.[62]

No wonder Garvin and his colleagues were skeptical. Instead of striking out at root evils, a new generation of reformers, epitomized by settlement workers like Hatch, were now advancing a variety of environmental explanations for poverty, drunkenness, and class conflict. Shunning millennial visions of social reconstruction, they preferred to address these problems on a neighborhood basis and in a piecemeal manner. In their attempts to reconstruct neighborhoods around settlement houses, institutional churches, and other social centers, they crusaded against the commercialization of leisure, not against social parasites. For Single Taxers, prohibitionists, and the other moralists who still hoped to fashion a middle-class America, the enemies were the monopolist, the liquor dealer, and the machine politician who lived off the product of the gainfully employed. Yet Hatch and other settlement workers did share one thing in common with the moralists. In their attempts to propagate rational recreation among the urban masses, they too hoped to blur the distinction between brain work and manual labor that pitted segments of the antebellum producers' community against each

[62] *Providence Journal*, 17 January 1910.

6 SUBSTITUTES FOR THE SALOON

IN 1883 the Reverend Frederic A. Hinckley announced a new strategy in the long middle-class campaign against the saloon. Instead of trying "to suppress the devil," reformers should "undermine him. When he sets up a dance-hall where vice reigns, suppose we set up a dance-hall where virtue reigns. When he sets up a grog-shop, suppose we set up a coffee-room, not in the third story, not where you have to use a telescope to find it, but where it will stare you in the face, invite you in, and make you feel at home." Hinckley was far from the first observer to urge reformers to explore new ways of purveying rational recreation to the urban masses. More than a quarter of a century earlier, Unitarian minister Edward Everett Hale had insisted that "the gospel way to arrest evil is to drive out evil with good." "By refusing to put our hands to the good," he said, "the evil comes in in spite of us." Charles Loring Brace, founder of the New York Children's Aid Society, also saw the need for a broader range of substitutes for the saloon. Reminiscing on his twenty years of social work in New York City, he wrote that "the liquor-shop is his [the workingman's] picture-gallery, club, reading-room, and social *salon* at once." So long as "labor is what it is, and the liquor-shop alone offers sociality and amusement to the poor, alcohol will still possess this overwhelming attraction."[1]

Generations of middle-class reformers like Hinckley, Hale, and Brace had sought to remodel the customary recreational patterns of the working class. Even before the onset of the temperance movement, they had attacked recreations associated with self-indulgence, Sabbath-breaking, and immorality that clashed with emergent mid-

---

[1] Frederic A. Hinckley, "Radicalism: The False and the True," in his *The Practical and the Ideal: Twelve Discourses* (Providence: J. A. & R. A. Reid, 1883), 13; Edward E. Hale, *Public Amusement for Poor and Rich* (Boston: Phillips, Sampson & Co., 1857), 9, 11; Charles Loring Brace, *The Dangerous Classes of New York, and Twenty Years' Work among Them* (1872; reprint, Washington, D.C.: National Association of Social Workers, 1973), 64-65. See also Stephen Hardy, *How Boston Played: Sport, Recreation, and Community, 1865-1915* (Boston: Northeastern University Press, 1982), 49-56.

dle-class values. As the temperance movement gathered momentum, their attack increasingly centered on the saloon and the barkeeper. In place of the public, male-oriented domain of the saloon, they hoped to substitute a more "rational" recreation informed by such values as self-improvement, purposiveness, utility, and domesticity. In the middle decades of the nineteenth century this rational recreation commonly took the form of libraries, art galleries, museums, and other didactic amusements designed to appeal to the whole family and to cut across class and ethnic lines.

Reformers, seeking to instill these rational goals after 1880, discovered that growing public interest in recreation compounded their problems. Once seen as an adjunct to work and governed by the same conventions that ruled in the workshop, leisure emerged as a separate sphere defined as the antithesis of work. For reasons of health, affluence, and craving for social status, leisure became increasingly important to Americans; by 1900 many of them had come to expect it as the reward to which their hard work entitled them. As a result, the focus of rational recreation changed. Instead of designating libraries, lyceums, and other institutions that embodied the civic culture, it came to mean small parks, playgrounds, settlement houses, socialized schools, and other social centers around which neighborhood life could be organized in order to perpetuate under new conditions the traditional ideal of a classless, homogeneous society. At the same time voluntary associations evolved from being surrogates for the municipal government into lobbies that framed policy, trained bureaucrats, and mediated between their members and an administrative state.

Following the Civil War, commercial amusements proliferated as entrepreneurs tapped an expanding leisure market. Rapid industrial development, combined with falling prices, brought a substantial rise in real income for most Americans. Across the country real wages and earnings in manufacturing, according to one estimate, rose by almost half between the end of the Civil War and 1890. Though partially offset by renewed inflation, they rose another 37 percent in the years before 1914. Falling prices for food, rent, and other necessities meant that families had more disposable income to spend on recreation and the so-called luxuries of life. They also enjoyed more leisure time. Between 1850 and 1890 the workweek in manufacturing declined from seventy hours to sixty; it continued to

Exchange Place and the Cove, c. 1880-1890 (courtesy of the Rhode Island Historical Society)

decline until 1914, when it stood at 55.2 hours. Skilled workers increasingly won the right to a Saturday half-holiday. Improved public transportation, especially as electric trolleys replaced horsecars in the early 1890s, brought suburban pleasure grounds within easy reach of many urban dwellers. Technological advances, notably electric lighting and motion-picture apparatus, made new recreational forms possible. These long-term trends converged in the late nineteenth and early twentieth centuries to create a mass market in entertainment. Exploiting these trends were "capitalists" or entrepreneurs of leisure who catered to the apparently insatiable demand for recreation.[2]

Commercial amusements naturally proliferated in late nineteenth-century Providence, a city grown rich on the output of its world-famous textile, machinery, and jewelry plants. Burgeoning interest in amateur theatricals in the late 1850s and the popularity of German and Italian opera troupes who visited the city during the Civil War generated popular demand for a "first-class" theater that would put Providence on the map as a "show town." In 1871 the melodrama *Fashion, or Life in New York,* "selected because it gave the ladies an opportunity to show some handsome dresses," inaugurated performances at the lavish Providence Opera House, built in record time after twenty-eight members of the Board of Trade had subscribed $187,000—more money than had been spent on all the city's previous theaters combined. Another opera house soon fol-

---

[2] Clarence D. Long, *Wages and Earnings in the United States, 1860-1890* (Princeton: Princeton University Press, 1960); Albert Rees, *Real Wages in Manufacturing, 1890-1914* (Princeton: Princeton University Press, 1961); Joseph S. Zeisel, "The Workweek in American Industry, 1850-1956," in *Mass Leisure,* ed. Eric Larrabee and Rolf Meyersohn (Glencoe, Ill.: Free Press, 1958), 145-53. Asa Briggs examines the preconditions for the commercialization of leisure in *Mass Entertainment: The Origins of a Modern Industry* (Adelaide: Griffin Press, 1960), 9-12. Recently American historians have become more interested in commercial entertainment and the origins of mass culture between the 1890s and 1920s. Among the many works treating these subjects are Dale A. Somers, "The Leisure Revolution: Recreation in the American City, 1820-1920," *Journal of Popular Culture* 5 (Summer 1971): 125-47; Robert Sklar, *Movie-Made America: A Cultural History of American Movies* (New York: Vintage Books, 1976); John F. Kasson, *Amusing the Million: Coney Island at the Turn of the Century* (New York: Hill and Wang, 1978); Lary May, *Screening Out the Past: The Birth of Mass Culture and the Motion Picture Industry* (New York: Oxford University Press, 1980); and Lewis A. Erenberg, *Steppin' Out: New York Nightlife and the Transformation of American Culture, 1890-1930* (1981; reprint, Chicago: University of Chicago Press, 1984).

lowed.[3] The theater-going habit spread to the city's middle-class residents with the opening of two concert gardens or summer theaters in 1878. Park Garden, with a two-acre lake enclosed by a natural amphitheater, proved to be an ideal setting for productions of *H.M.S. Pinafore*. San Souci [*sic*], featuring a music pavilion with latticed walls, offered nightly illuminations of scenes from the destruction of Pompeii. Both summer theaters were not far from downtown Providence and easily reached by horsecar. As purveyors of wholesome family entertainment, they sold neither beer nor alcohol on their grounds.[4]

The city's opera houses and summer gardens were at once too expensive and too tame for workingmen. They preferred burlesque theaters, which offered female limbs and ribald humor. At the Theatre Comique, which opened in 1874, workingmen mixed with "the 'fast' element of the educated class." There vendors openly peddled beer in the aisles, cigarette and cigar smoke hung heavy in the air, and no "ladies" were to be found. Workingmen also patronized the dime, freak, and variety museums that mushroomed in storefronts during the 1870s and 1880s. In 1887 the Boston impresario B. F. Keith converted one of these into the family-oriented Gaiety Museum, where he introduced vaudeville to Providence.[5]

The invention of kinetoscopes, vitascopes, and other primitive motion-picture projectors soon revolutionized mass entertainment. Penny vaudevilles, or slot machines, spread rapidly from the Pan-American Exposition in Buffalo in 1901 to city storefronts. By 1906 their popularity had aroused the concern of clubwomen, the Rhode

3 Theodore Collier, "Providence in Civil War Days," *Rhode Island Historical Society Collections* 27 (October 1934): 107; "Providence Club Activities," *Providence Magazine* 26 (September 1914): 622-23; George O. Willard, *History of the Providence Stage, 1762-1891* (Providence: Rhode Island News Co., 1891), 192-97; Sally W. Barker, "The Story of the Stage in Rhode Island," typescript, RIHS; Edward M. Fay, "Providence Theatre," typescript, folder 125, David Patten Papers, RIHS; John Hutchins Cady, *The Civic and Architectural Development of Providence, 1636-1950* (Providence: Book Shop, 1957), 153-54.

4 For descriptions of the summer gardens, see "Popular Amusements—The Drama in Providence," *Providence Magazine* 28 (October 1916): 651-52; Roger Brett, *Temples of Illusion: The Golden Age of Theaters in an American City* (Bristol, R.I.: Brett Theatrical, 1976), 31-38; Patrick T. Conley and Paul R. Campbell, *Providence: A Pictorial History* (Norfolk, Va.: Donning Co., 1982), 113.

5 "The Theatrical License Question," *Providence Journal*, 23 March 1878; Brett, *Temples of Illusion*, 21-23, 29, 47-49, 55-58.

Island Anti-Saloon League, and Protestant clergymen. Baptist minister Edward Holyoke denounced their "offensive pictures" as "pictorial traps to catch the unwary child." But motion-picture theaters, which proliferated in Providence after 1906, quickly drove the objectionable penny arcades from the field. By 1915 there were thirteen theaters boasting a total of twelve thousand seats in Providence. Of these, the nine largest were located downtown. The other four were scattered on Federal Hill, a congested Italian neighborhood, and in Olneyville. Because of their cheap admission prices—as little as a nickel, whereas the cheapest live theater had been the dime museums and the "Ten, Twent', Thirt' Shows," whose admission prices were ten, twenty, and thirty cents—moving pictures soon attracted large immigrant and working-class audiences.[6]

Commercial amusements also flourished on a grand scale on both shores of Narragansett Bay. Sailing down the bay on excursions, a popular though still informal pastime by the 1850s, quickly evolved into the "shore business." As early as 1873 the *Providence Journal* had printed a map of Narragansett Bay showing resorts dotting both shores. "Where is there another Narragansett Bay, with its beautiful islands, its ocean breezes, and its delicious clams?" asked a guide book to Providence and its environs in 1876. While the New York City and Philadelphia elites summered at Newport and Narragansett Pier, middle-class families colonized tent cities and cottage villages nearer Providence. Less affluent excursionists frequented the mass resorts that sprang up along the Bay.[7]

[6] *Providence Journal*, 16 April 1906, 13, 19 May 1907, 24 May 1914; Rhode Island Council of Women, Minutes, 1902-1906, 26 March 1906, RIHS; Cady, *Civic and Architectural Development of Providence*, 203-204, 227; Brett, *Temples of Illusion*, 87, 105-113, 147-65; Francis R. North, *A Recreation Survey of the City of Providence, Rhode Island* (Providence: Providence Playground Association, 1912), 27. On the early history of the movies, see Russell Merritt, "Nickelodeon Theaters 1905-1914: Building an Audience for the Movies," in *The American Film Industry*, ed. Tino Balio (Madison: University of Wisconsin Press, 1976), 59-79; Garth Jowett, *Film: The Democratic Art* (Boston: Little, Brown & Co., 1976); Sklar, *Movie-Made America*; and May, *Screening Out the Past*.

[7] *Providence Journal*, 26 July 1873; John C. Thompson, *Illustrated Hand-book of the City of Providence, R.I.* (Central Falls, R.I.: E. L. Freeman & Co., 1876), 115; "Our Steamboats," *Providence Journal*, 23 April 1877. Two other contemporary guide books to Narragansett Bay are W. H. Fish, *The Summer Resorts of Rhode Island* (Providence: Sanford Publishing Co., 1887); and Robert Grieve, *Picturesque Narragansett*, 3rd ed. (Providence: J. A. & R. A. Reid, 1888). In a study of 180 elite businessmen at the turn of the century, Ian S. Haberman found that the wealthiest had summer

Although never rivaling New York's Coney Island in either size or popularity, Rhode Island's shore resorts nevertheless claimed the distinction of being "the people's playground of New England." The oldest and most famous of these was Rocky Point, twelve miles from Providence, on the western shore of Narragansett Bay. Within thirty years after serving its first clam dinner in 1847 it had grown from a simple picnic ground into a heavily capitalized resort, sporting a spacious dining hall that could feed as many as fifteen hundred diners at one sitting, an ice cream saloon, a camera obscura, and for the children, steam-powered flying horses. Crowds of ten thousand day visitors on Saturdays or holidays were not uncommon during the 1870s. Over the next two decades, Rocky Point's proprietors poured millions of dollars into more mechanized amusements such as a water slide, scenic railroad, and ferris wheel. They also added a vaudeville theater and dancing pavilion. Closed in the past from 6:00 P.M. Saturday until Monday morning, the resort had become by the 1890s a small-scale Coney Island, attracting as many as fifty thousand pleasure seekers on Saturdays and Sundays. The Providence Grays, who represented the city in the International League, played their Sunday baseball games there to evade the city's blue laws.[8] Crescent Park, only six miles from Providence on the eastern shore of the Bay, drew even larger crowds—as many as seventy-five thousand excursionists on hot summer weekends.[9]

Even before the turn of the century, dancing had eclipsed the clam dinner and vaudeville as the chief attraction of Rocky Point, Crescent Park, and other shore resorts. Rocky Point's Midway featured a large band stand as well as an "airy" dance hall where excursionists "trip[ped] the light fantastic." On Saturday evenings at Crescent Park as many as five thousand dancers thronged the Alhambra Ballroom to dance to some of the nation's best-known bands. Rhodes-on-the-Pawtuxet, or Rhodes Casino, which opened just across the Cranston line in 1898, had room for twelve hundred

---

houses at Newport or Warwick Neck; the less wealthy summered at Barrington, Bristol, and Watch Hill. "The Rhode Island Business Elite, 1895-1905: A Collective Portrait," *Rhode Island History* 26 (April 1967): 40-41.

[8] Details come from Horace G. Belcher, "Old Rocky Point," *Rhode Island History* 7 (April 1948): 33-50; and Thompson, *Illustrated Hand-book of the City of Providence*, 116-17. On the Grays' Sunday games at Rocky Point, see Steven A. Riess, *Touching Base: Professional Baseball and American Culture in the Progressive Era* (Westport, Conn.: Greenwood Press, 1980), 147n.

[9] "Crescent Park," *Providence Journal of Commerce* 6 (July 1898): 215-16.

dancers and for three hundred canoes underneath the dance floor. A new casino, built after a spectacular fire destroyed the original in 1915, accommodated as many as three thousand dancers.[10]

Commercialization even affected the state fair. Ever since 1850, the Rhode Island Society for the Encouragement of Domestic Industry had held its annual fair in Cranston. The chief attractions of the early fairs had been cattle shows, plowing and drawing matches, and exhibitions of produce and farm implements designed to stimulate competition among farmers and to disseminate the latest advances in scientific agriculture. Following the Civil War, however, entertainment began to overshadow these exhibits. By 1873, the fair featured horse races for premiums of up to several hundred dollars. Within a few years, bicycle racing had become the central attraction. In 1886, when the "new and interesting entertainment" of dog racing joined the bicycle races as a drawing card, the fair's promoters raised attendance by instituting a different theme for each of the fair's five days, including a School Children's Day and Governor's Day. Other promotions drew even larger crowds. On Grange Day in 1888, an estimated forty thousand onlookers watched a couple exchange wedding vows before taking off on their honeymoon in a balloon. Attendance for the five days that year topped one hundred thousand, where in the past fifteen to twenty thousand had been considered a good turnout.[11]

By 1889 the fair boasted a full amusement bill. In that year, the Amusement Committee announced its intention "to place before the public the strongest attractions ever upon a Fair Ground in New England." Heading the bill were "Professor" Harry M. Parker and his $20,000 cat-and-dog circus, a "balloon ascension" by "Professor" Carl Myers replete with parachute leap by Carlotta, "the most daring lady aeronaut in the world," and a spectacular vaudeville show. For the audience's edification the promoters also displayed "Frog Boy" and "Elephant Boy," two "freaks" normally found in dime museums.[12]

[10] "Rocky Point," ibid., 217-18; Belcher, "Old Rocky Point," 48; Evening Bulletin, 3 September 1969; Providence Journal, 10 February 1935, 14 July 1953.

[11] Providence Journal, 14 September 1853; 28 September 1888; Rhode Island State Fair, premium lists for 1872-85, Rider Collection, Brown University Library; Official Program and List of Exhibits of the R.I. State Fair (Providence: Standard Advertising Co., 1886), 17, 29.

[12] Official Programme and List of Exhibits of the Rhode Island State Fair (Providence: Standard Publishing Co., 1889).

After the Society for the Encouragement of Domestic Industry reorganized as a joint-stock corporation in 1892, the state fair became even more of a heavily capitalized entertainment spectacle. In 1895 it advertised almost $60,000 in premiums, 15,000 exhibits, and 63 massive buildings. Its promoters retained the services of Charles Lovenberg, the manager of B. F. Keith's Variety Theatre in Providence, who spent $20,000 to stage *The New King Cole*, a "colossal spectacular extravaganza." The center of attention at that year's fair, however, was a replica of the famous Midway Plaisance at the World's Columbian Exposition, "with bazaars of all nations"; in Cranston as in Chicago, the sideshows proved far more popular than the educational exhibits.[13] In 1896 the fair opened on Labor Day, ten days earlier than usual, so that workingmen and their families could attend. Fair-goers were treated to a horseless carriage race—"the first event of its kind ever held on a race track or on the grounds of a Fair Association, unique, novel, fascinating." And for the first time ever there were alcoholic beverages openly for sale on the fair grounds. With this new departure, the officers of the Woman's Christian Temperance Union, which had maintained a coffee booth at the fair since 1886, voted to close their restaurant. The Rhode Island Council of Women similarly decided that it was wrong for the public schools to exhibit at the fair when some of the sideshows, "judging by the placards and pictures outside the tents, were extremely demoralizing."[14]

The commercialization of leisure had a profound impact on urban culture. Among the working classes of Pittsburgh, Worcester, and other industrial cities, it undermined a plebeian culture organized around churches, mutual benefit societies, fraternal lodges, and unions.[15] Commercialized leisure affected the middle classes in

[13] The description of the 1895 state fair comes from clippings in Charles Lovenberg, "Scrapbook of Theatre and Music in Providence, 1895-98," Brown University Library. For a description of the authentic Midway Plaisance, see Kasson, *Amusing the Million*, 23-26.

[14] *76th Annual Rhode Island State Fair* (Providence: Livermore & Knight, 1896), 10, 174; *Minutes of the Twenty-Third Annual Meeting also Department Reports of the Providence Woman's Christian Temperance Union* (Providence: John F. Greene, 1897), 13; Rhode Island Council of Women, Minutes, 1894-1901, 28 September 1896, RIHS. See also Rhode Island Women's Club, Minutes—Regular Meetings, 1900-1906, 7 March 1900, RIHS.

[15] Francis G. Couvares, "The Triumph of Commerce: Class Culture and Mass Culture in Pittsburgh," in *Working-Class America: Essays on Labor, Community, and American*

much the same way, undermining the authority of organized groups. When voluntary associations had organized the leisure time of most Americans, belonging to an organized group was virtually a precondition for participation in many activities. Membership, in turn, meant subscribing to the norms set by one's peers. As commercial amusements multiplied, however, the price of admission became the sole criterion for participation. Consequently, organized peer groups lost much of their role in setting social norms to entrepreneurs of leisure. The *Providence Journal* captured this aspect in an editorial on church fairs when it pointed out that, because the object was "to raise money by appealing to the appetites and the cupidity of the general mass," invitations were "not confined to the members of the church," who shared many values in common, but were rather extended "to all and sundry who have money to spend, even though they would not be admitted to the private parlors of the managers of the festival." Commercialized amusements did more than dissolve group ties. As Frederic C. Howe, director of New York City's People Institute, pointed out, they also molded urban civilization—"not as it should be moulded, but as commerce dictates."[16]

The commercialization of leisure, moreover, compelled reformers to formulate new strategies in purveying rational recreation to the urban masses. Realizing the need to meet social segmentation with specialized organization, they turned to clubs that were not only segregated by sex, as Victorian custom dictated, but also targeted at specific age groups. In so doing, they harnessed the new instinct psychology, popularized by the kindergarten and playground movements, which posited the existence of a "social instinct" or natural propensity for companionship. As reformers sought to rechannel this impulse into more "wholesome" outlets, their former em-

---

Society, ed. Michael H. Frisch and Daniel J. Walkowitz (Urbana: University of Illinois Press, 1983), 123-52; Roy Rosenzweig, *Eight Hours for What We Will: Workers and Leisure in an Industrial City, 1870-1920* (Cambridge: Cambridge University Press, 1983), esp. 172, 182-83, 206. In their classic account of Muncie, Indiana, during the 1920s Robert and Helen Lynd noted that "the social function of the union has disappeared in this day of movies and automobile, save for sparsely attended dances at Labor Hall." *Middletown: A Study in American Culture* (1929; reprint, New York: Harcourt, Brace & World, 1956), 78.

[16] "Church Fairs," *Providence Journal*, 13 September 1882; Frederic C. Howe, "Leisure," *Survey* 31 (3 January 1914): 415.

phasis on didactic recreations gave way to efforts to evoke a free-and-easy atmosphere, promote sociability, and entertain. At the same time they lobbied for the municipal provision of parks, kindergartens, playgrounds, and other neighborhood "social centers."

For Mayor Thomas A. Doyle, Dr. William F. Channing, and other mid-century boosters, public parks were urban amenities required of any true city. In 1868 Doyle proposed that the city turn Field's Point, a 350-acre municipal tract on the western shore of Narragansett Bay, into a park. Only two miles from downtown Providence, it could easily be reached by boat. While the city council debated Doyle's proposal, the city inherited a 102-acre farmstead from Betsey Williams, a descendant of its founder. Over the next three decades this plot of land became the showpiece of the city's resorts. Even though the panic of 1873 substantially reduced municipal expenditures on public works, city authorities lavished thousands of dollars on the park in damming a lake, collecting a menagerie, and erecting an expensive statue of Roger Williams. Within a few years, Roger Williams Park was drawing several hundred thousand visitors annually.[17]

The development of Roger Williams Park preceded the emergence of the city's first recreational lobby. Not until 1881, when two of the railroads then serving Providence requested that the city council sell them the Cove Basin as the site of a new terminal, did public sentiment crystallize in favor of the municipal provision of parks and other recreational facilities as counterattractions to the saloon. During the middle decades of the nineteenth century, the Cove, which together with its adjoining marsh lands covered thirty-seven acres, had been the literal and figurative center of a burgeoning city whose residents were in the process of acquiring the "corporate identity" that distinguished urban dwellers. As a result of a compromise between the city council and the Providence & Worcester Railroad in the late 1840s, the Cove, previously the irregularly shaped tidal basin of the Providence River, assumed an elliptical form. In return for being permitted to enter the center of the city, the railroad promised to build a retaining wall. The city council then embellished the promenade with shrubs and walks. Families and

[17] Charles E. Lincoln, "Public Park Association's Notable Work: Chapter I," *Providence Magazine* 28 (August 1916): 516; *Providence Journal*, 17 June 1868, 10 March, 16 October 1869.

their children strolled on the picturesque paths encircling the basin; circuses and revivals pitched their tents on the adjoining lands; and municipal celebrations of national holidays took place on the promenade.[18]

By the early 1880s, however, many city residents had come to believe that Providence had to expand its terminal facilities lest it fall behind Boston and other commercial rivals. In January 1880, when the Commercial Club discussed the future of the Cove Basin, "it seemed to be the unanimous sentiment of the gentlemen present that the time is not far distant when something must be done for the benefit of the business community in this direction." The following year, former governor William W. Hoppin announced that the time had come, that "the Cove must go." The Cove, Hoppin said, could not "remain intact much longer." It would "require many hundreds of thousands of dollars and a generation of time to work up the Cove basin into a 'thing of beauty.' " Without central terminal facilities, Providence would languish, "blocked and retarded in its growth," while Boston, Worcester, and other "neighboring cities" diverted its trade.[19] Early in 1882 a five-man commission appointed the preceding December by Mayor William S. Hayward delivered its report. Known as the Goddard Commission after its chairman, William Goddard, who managed the textile interests of Brown & Ives, it recommended that the city fill in the Cove at its own expense and then sell the railroads all the land they needed. In resolutions adopted by the Providence Board of Trade and the Commercial Club a majority of the city's businessmen soon endorsed the so-called Goddard plan.[20]

Yet the railroads' request aroused a storm of controversy. Shortly after the Goddard Commission made its recommendations, the Providence Franklin Society appointed a Parks Committee. This venerable scientific society had attempted to generate interest in science since 1869 by opening its lectures to the public and extending

[18] My discussion of the dispute over the Cove draws on Mark Brennan, "Providence, Rhode Island, and the Crisis over Railroad Terminal Facilities, 1870-1890" (history honors thesis, Brown University, 1969); and Michael Holleran, "The Providence Cove: Image in the Evolution of Urban Form" (independent honors thesis, Brown University, 1979), RIHS.

[19] *Providence Journal*, 27 January 1880, 19 November 1881.

[20] Ibid., 29 April, 1 May 1882.

membership to women.[21] In January 1883 the chairman of the Parks Committee, Dr. Timothy Newell, read a paper in which he spelled out why the city should preserve the Cove. As a physician, Newell was well acquainted with zymotic theory, which held that "open spaces" like the Cove reduced the likelihood of epidemics by acting as "ventilators" or "breathing spaces" for the city's population. "The great advantage of open spaces in cities," he told his audience, "is, that they supply the densely populated neighborhoods with pure air." If covered by a railroad depot and sidings, the Cove would become "an unhealthy locality" and would raise the temperature in the center of the city. Newell went on to stress the urgent need for recreational facilities convenient for workingmen and their families. "The opportunities of securing interior pleasure grounds are becoming less every year," he pointed out. "The open spaces are being built over rapidly." Commons that until a few years ago had existed on Smith Hill and Federal Hill "are now covered with streets and buildings."[22]

But was there really any need for an "interior" park? Why could not rural Roger Williams Park serve the needs of all the city's residents? The problem, Newell answered, lay in Providence's social geography. Roger Williams Park was simply too far away—approximately 3.5 miles—from the houses of workingmen who lived on Smith Hill, near Brown & Sharpe, Nicholson File, the American Screw Company, and other factories lining the Moshassuck and Woonasquatucket rivers. Moreover, the horsecar fare of ten cents each way made frequent excursions prohibitively expensive. It was also unlikely that workingmen, who worked ten or more hours a day, would ever dwell in the suburbs. "No population of the laboring poor will ever dwell in the vicinity of the majority of the parks of the cities of this country," Newell predicted. "The palaces of the rich will surround and overlook them, and only on occasional holidays can the toiling denizens of the central business marts afford the time and money to visit these distant grounds." The city should thus "spare this priceless inheritance of the people," not for the rich, who

---

[21] Welcome O. Brown, *The Providence Franklin Society: An Historical Address* (Providence: J. A. & R. A. Reid, 1880), 21-27; Robert J. Taylor, "The Providence Franklin Society," *Rhode Island History* 9 (October 1950): 119-29.

[22] Timothy Newell, M.D., *A Paper read before the Providence Franklin Society, Jan. 30, 1883* (Providence: Providence Press Co., 1883), 8-13.

were already in the habit of taking summer vacations, but "for the poor, the laborer, the artisan, and their wives and children who are obliged to remain in the city during the hot months."[23]

The Public Park Association, organized in March 1883, forcefully championed the views of Newell and other proponents of "parks for the people." It consisted of a number of elderly men, well-to-do manufacturers and professionals, who had taken an active part in the earlier campaign to fashion a civic culture. Among them were Amos C. Barstow, now almost seventy years old; machine manufacturer George H. Corliss, a devout Sabbatarian who had refused to permit his engine to run on Sundays at the Centennial Exposition in Philadelphia; retired hardware dealer Joseph A. Barker, whose gift helped launch the Providence Public Library; Thomas A. Doyle, temporarily out of the mayor's office; and Ezekiel G. Robinson, president of Brown University. As men whose lives spanned Providence's rise to industrial eminence, the charter members of the Park Association acted as stewards to save their beloved Cove from the encroachment of the railroads. Those among them who were members of the Rhode Island Horticultural Society may have also acted out of a desire to preserve the only green spot left in downtown Providence.[24]

The Park Association was the first of a new type of voluntary association to appear in the city: the lobby, or single-interest pressure group, which defined a special relationship between itself and government. Unlike the Rhode Island Art Association, the Rhode Island Educational Union, and other mid-century voluntary associations that had also sought to promote rational recreation, the Park Association did not propound voluntarism as an alternative to state intervention. Rather, as a lobby, it formulated policy, furnished vol-

[23] Ibid., 5, 19-20. The Park Association contented that "the value of parks greatly depends upon the convenience with which they are used." As landscape architect Horace W. S. Cleveland explained, "A single acre of trees and grass in the heart of a city, which may be reached by a few minutes' walk when the labors of the day are over, is of more value than an area of one hundred acres at such a distance as it only can be visited on an occasional holiday." Public Park Association, *The Cove Park: Its Economical and Sanitary Importance* (Providence: J. A. & R. A. Reid, 1886), 9-10.

[24] *Providence Journal*, 2 March 1883; annual reports of the Public Park Association, 1883-89, Miscellaneous Uncatalogued MSS, RIHS. The median age of the thirty-four charter members of the Park Association whose ages could be determined was sixty. Befitting their age and social status, twenty-nine ranked among the top decile of the city's taxpayers.

unteers or paid staff for pilot projects, and exhorted municipal and state governments to assume new responsibilities for the social welfare. Although voluntary associations continued to initiate new programs, the emergence of the lobby presupposed a more active role for government. Many of the programs advocated by the Park Association and later recreational lobbies—parks, for example, or kindergartens and playgrounds in every public school—could only be implemented with governmental assistance. Accordingly these associations acted as pressure groups, either applying pressure directly on government or attempting to influence policy indirectly by molding public opinion.[25]

Although united in opposing the railroads' plans to develop the Cove, the Park Association's members did not agree on the fate of the tidal basin. Some, like attorney Amasa Eaton, thought that it should be filled in and the reclaimed land then laid out as an interior park. After all, waste from manufacturing along the Moshassuck and Woonasquatucket rivers flowed into the Cove, where it putrified and stank. Others, like Henry T. Beckwith, a member of the Franklin Lyceum who offered to give the city thirty acres for a park in the North End, only insisted that the basin, whether filled or unfilled, be saved. Still others, like Dr. Edwin M. Snow, Providence's nationally known superintendent of public health, and Amos Barstow wanted to dredge the Cove to restore the basin to its pristine condition. Barstow proved to be an eloquent defender of the Cove. Like his close friend William W. Hoppin, with whom he publicly aired his disagreement over the railroads' proposal in letters to the *Providence Journal*, Barstow considered Boston a model. Hoppin regarded Boston as a commercial rival; Barstow looked instead to the Public Garden and Common as civic improvements that Providence should copy.[26]

[25] In his report to the President's Research Committee on Social Trends, Jesse F. Steiner noted how "a new era in the history of recreation began when the government accepted responsibility for the provision of public recreational activities." *Americans at Play: Recent Trends in Recreation and Leisure Time Activities* (New York: McGraw-Hill, 1933), 11.

[26] Eaton spelled out his position in *Providence Journal*, 28 November 1881; for Beckwith's offer, angrily withdrawn in 1884, see *Providence Journal*, 16 January 1883; for Snow's opinion, see Public Park Association, *Objections to the Majority Report of the Commission on Railroad Terminal Facilities, presented to the City Council, December, 1883* (Providence: Public Park Association, 1884), 8; for a sample of Barstow's views, see *Providence Journal*, 22 November 1881.

Although not ignoring arguments used by earlier advocates that parks raised contiguous property values and served as breathing places for densely populated urban districts, the paternalistic spokesmen of the Public Park Association emphasized other advantages. They were especially concerned with demonstrating that parks served as counterattractions to the saloon. Like other recreational reformers, they believed that "public recreation should never displace but should supplement the home." But, as they were the first to admit, crowded homes encouraged the search for recreation outside. "The laborer or artisan often finds his highest idea of pleasure in the nearest gin-shop around the corner," declared one of the association's pamphlets. "If there was an attractive park convenient, he and his family would seek it as instinctively as the plant seeks the sunlight." Newell, for one, viewed municipal parks as rational amusements that, like the Providence Public Library, would elevate the urban masses from their dreary workday pursuits and protect them from the seductions of the saloon.[27]

To swing public opinion behind its campaign to save the Cove, the Park Association published a series of pamphlets extolling the advantages of interior parks. One pamphlet contained a letter from Catholic bishop Thomas F. Hendricken, who predicted that "in warm summer, men who now spend their evenings in the taverns and dusty streets, will be glad to play with their little ones in these mossy groves." Another gave the opinion of Horace W. S. Cleveland, the famed landscape architect who had laid out Roger Williams Park. "If the railroads were removed and the park tastefully improved," Cleveland contended, the rapid settlement of Smith Hill, still "a neglected waste," would soon follow. Not content with merely educating public opinion, the Park Association attempted to mobilize a park constituency. In the spring of 1884 it campaigned for a People's Park ticket that consisted of candidates who pledged to submit the Goddard plan to city voters in a referendum. The entire slate won. While the General Assembly conducted hearings on the plan, the Park Association organized mass demonstrations in favor of saving the Cove. Bowing to this public pressure, the General Assembly stipulated that the city council ratify any plan for the

[27] North, *A Recreation Survey*, 17; Public Park Association, *The Cove Park: Its Economical and Sanitary Importance*, 12.

Cove as the equivalent of a popular referendum. But the association's best efforts could not overcome the business community's insistence on expanded terminal facilities. Later that fall, the city
council adopted the Goddard plan.[28]

Although it lost its battle to save the Cove from the railroads, the
Park Association did succeed in placing parks on the municipal
agenda. The city's development, as the association's spokesmen
never tired of repeating, rendered the municipal provision of recreational facilities imperative. As Newell had pointed out, vacant
lots and common lands customarily used by city residents for their
recreation were fast disappearing. Rapid population growth and
geographical dispersion raised the value of these lands, tempting
neighborhood property owners to enclose and plat them for residences. Even where they were unable to secure outright title to the
lands, private property owners often succeeded in restricting public
use of open lots. That had already occurred at Dexter Field, a ten-
acre common given to the city in 1824 as a militia training ground.
Because of complaints from the well-to-do property owners whose
homes bordered the field about the noise and disorderliness that accompanied baseball games there, the city council banned field
sports on the parade ground in 1880. "These complainants were
willing to enjoy the sanitary advantages of the fresh air, foliage and
fine prospect from their doors and windows," spokesmen for the
Park Association wryly noted, "but were loath to allow others to enjoy these benefits with a greater need."[29]

Thanks in large part to the association's lobbying, parks multiplied in Providence during the 1890s. In 1891, the same year the
General Assembly authorized the city to borrow up to $500,000 to
purchase park lands, a board of park commissioners replaced the
joint committee of the city council that had formerly administered
the city's parks. By this time public opinion was firmly behind the
development of a municipal park system, as Hiram Howard, David
M. Thompson, and other members of the Advance Club argued
that parks were necessary improvements if Providence was to keep

[28] *Letter from the Rev. Thos. F. Hendricken, read before the Providence Park Association,
December 5, 1883* (n.p., 1883), 3; Horace W. S. Cleveland, *The Cove Park and the Woonasquatucket Valley* (Providence: Providence Press Co., 1883), 7, 8.

[29] Public Park Association, *Interior Open Spaces in Cities: Their Advantages* (Providence: Snow & Farnham, 1889), 59.

up with other New England cities. Between 1891 and 1897 the city spent almost $1.5 million on parks. Most of this money went toward quadrupling the size of Roger Williams Park from the original 102 acres to 428 acres. By the turn of the century, more than a quarter of the park consisted of lakes, on which boats made five-mile circuits. In addition, there were nearly eight miles of paved drives. A splendid new menagerie housed "Baby Roger," an elephant purchased by the children of the city with their pennies; a dromedary given by the Shriners; and General Bannockburn, a bull moose that stood eighteen hands high and weighed eighteen hundred pounds. A natural history museum contained collections of birds, mounted animals, and minerals as well as paintings. The Casino, "a commodious and ornamental structure," offered refreshments and space for dancing. Regularly scheduled brass band concerts drew thousands of listeners during the summer. In 1899 Mayor William C. Baker declared that he had "never seen more orderly gatherings, and the whole effect of the concerts seemed healthful and uplifting. There is no doubt of the good they did and of the rest they gave to the tired workingman, his wife and children."[30]

But Roger Williams Park was too remote for most of the city's workingmen and their families, who lived near the center of the city. At the urging of boosters like Hiram Howard, who favored "a chain or system of smaller parks in different sections of the city," the city began to lay out neighborhood parks. In 1890, for example, city authorities purchased the 35-acre estate of former congressman Thomas Davis on Smith Hill for $75,000. In urging that the city buy the land, architect Alfred Stone pointed out how "this was the one spot to which a manufacturing population of 25,000 people could go for recreation and pleasure." Attorney Charles E. Gorman pre-

[30] Hiram Howard, *A Plea for Progress*, 2nd ed. (Providence: Rhode Island Printing Co., 1890), 26-32; David M. Thompson, *The Crisis: Shall the Advance of the Material Progress of the City of Providence be Arrested by Political or Factional Interests?* (Providence: E. A. Johnson & Co., 1891), 21-24; Henry Brayton Gardner, "Finance," in *A Modern City: Providence, Rhode Island, and Its Activities*, ed. William Kirk (Chicago: University of Chicago Press, 1909), 188-89; *A Souvenir. Baby Roger. A Gift to Roger Williams Park from Children of Providence and Vicinity* (Providence: Providence Journal Co., 1893); *The People's Pleasure Ground. Illustrated Roger Williams Park: Its Beautiful Scenery, Principal Points of Interest, History and Development* (Providence: American Book Exchange, 1897-98); Baker quoted in *Providence City Manual* (Providence: Snow & Farnham, 1899), 25.

dicted that the park would induce workingmen to buy homes in the neighborhood, "the only land that a laboring man can obtain to build a home on." Alderman Edwin D. McGuinness reminded the city council that his constituents had to spend at least half an hour and ten cents just to get to Roger Williams Park. But it was ultimately the petitions of local property owners, who believed that the park would raise the value of their property, that persuaded the council to purchase the estate. In 1893 complaints that the city had not spent "a single dollar" on the park except to employ a keeper for $500 a year prompted the city council to allocate $37,000 for improvements and another $34,000 for the purchase of additional land.[31]

As recreational facilities became a normal expectation of the residents of working-class neighborhoods like Smith Hill, debates broke out over what kinds of facilities the city's parks should contain. In 1900 a proposal by the Providence Driving Association for a municipal speedway at Roger Williams Park aroused cries of "class legislation" from observers who asked why if "the city cannot afford to lay out fields for the boys to play base ball or for their elders to play golf," should it "build a speedway for a few favored residents to trot their fast horses?" So much opposition arose that the city council voted to lay the Driving Association's request on the table. Eventually a compromise was reached, whereby the city added both athletic fields and a speedway to the park. By the first decade of the twentieth century, it was no longer a question of whether the city should allocate money for recreational facilities, but rather how that money should be spent and in whose behalf.[32]

In a significant new departure after the turn of the century, the park commissioners began to lay out playing fields and install gymnastic apparatus in the city's parks. By 1904 matched games on Sat-

[31] Howard, *A Plea for Progress*, 26; *Providence Journal*, 20 February 1890, 20 February 1893.

[32] *Providence Journal*, 3, 23 January 1900; letter from "Looker On," ibid., 25 February 1900. Similar controversies over the location and layout of municipal parks had broken out in Worcester, Massachusetts, during the 1880s. Roy Rosenzweig, "Middle-Class Parks and Working-Class Play: The Struggle Over Recreational Space in Worcester, Massachusetts, 1870-1910," *Radical History Review* 21 (Fall 1979): 31-46; ibid., *Eight Hours for What We Will*, 127-40. Stephen Hardy stresses the role of neighborhood lobbies and other special interest groups in the development of Boston's park system in *How Boston Played*, 73-84.

urday afternoons at Davis Park were drawing thousands of spectators. These new facilities were intended to arrest what spokesmen
for the Park Association characterized as the "gradual physical de-
generacy of the race." Observers like Timothy Newell fretted about
"a decline in the physical vigor of the population." But playing fields
and gymnastic apparatus also reflected the influence of new views
about the role of play in the socialization of the young, particularly
those advanced by "instinct psychology." This new psychology postulated the existence of natural instincts that could not be repressed.
One of the most important, it was held, was the social instinct,
which, though common to the human species, varied by age as well
as by sex.[33]

This instrumental conception of play issued from several sources.
One was the Providence Free Kindergarten Association, organized
in 1884 for "the introduction of the Kindergarten or Froebelian
method of teaching in the public schools." The kindergarten, according to its proponents, "recognizes the tendency to play as the
starting point for the training of other faculties." As the noted educator William T. Harris told a Providence audience in 1884, there
are "well-defined epochs of growth or of education," which, if properly directed, transformed the natural spontaneity of the child into
"rational self-determination." By dint of extensive lobbying, the association persuaded school authorities to set aside heated class-
rooms for its kindergartens, next to increase municipal appropria-
tions, and then to assume full responsibility for the kindergartens.
At the same time volunteers organized the children's mothers into
neighborhood clubs. Teachers commonly visited pupils' homes "to
enlarge a mother's sense of the moral responsibility for her children." This strategy paid off in 1898 when the mothers' clubs
thwarted an attempt by the School Committee to slash the kindergarten budget. By 1900, when the Free Kindergarten Association
disbanded, it had "become the avowed policy of the public school
authorities to introduce kindergartens as fast as possible into every

[33] Public Park Association, *Parks of Leading Cities of This Country. Parks of Providence*
(Providence: Snow & Farnham, 1896), 91; letter from Timothy Newell, *Providence
Journal*, 10 June 1900. Newell echoed the widespread concern about the falling birth
rate among the native-born population. Some observers even warned of race suicide.
See Barbara Miller Solomon's discussion of the views of Francis Amasa Walker, a pi-
oneer American demographer, in *Ancestors and Immigrants: A Changing New England
Tradition* (New York: John Wiley & Sons, 1965), 69-77.

Primary School Building." In 1886 there had been only one kindergarten in Providence; twenty-four were now scattered throughout
the city.[34]

The playground movement, a second source of this more instrumental conception of play, grew out of these kindergartens. In 1893
Providence became one of the first cities in the country to make municipal provision for organized play when the Free Kindergarten
Association, with the help of the Union for Practical Progress,
opened nine summer playgrounds. These early playgrounds consisted of little more than sand piles. Within three years, however,
fourteen kindergarten and secondary school teachers were super-
vising the play of children and adolescent boys in nine school yards,
two of which were "model" playgrounds equipped with gymnastic
apparatus. After the Free Kindergarten Association disbanded, a
Citizens' Playground Committee carried on the work, though intermittently, until 1908, when play workers formed the Providence
branch of the Playground Association of America.[35]

Recreational reformers insisted that playgrounds, like kindergartens, were indeed a municipal responsibility. Assimilating the theories of the pioneer American psychologist G. Stanley Hall, they pictured adolescence as a "dangerous period" in which "emancipation
from the home and school takes place and innocent minds are exposed to vile influences in mill, shop, street, and places of amusement." They echoed Hall's belief that the child, while growing up,
retraced the development of the race or, in Hall's memorable
words, that octogeny recapitulated philogeny. In a city without
playgrounds, observed the secretary of the Providence Playground
Association, "there are thousands of children in whom the play-in-
stinct either is starving for want of inducement and place to give it
expression, or else is running wildly toward the baser allurements
of the city."[36]

[34] *Providence Journal*, 10 April 1884; Providence Free Kindergarten Association,
Minutes, 1884-94, 9 April 1890; Minutes, 1894-1902, 15 October 1898; "Final Report," 1900, all at RIHS. See also Marvin Lazerson, "Urban Reform and the Schools:
Kindergartens in Massachusetts, 1870-1915," *History of Education Quarterly* 11 (Summer 1971): 115-42.

[35] Charles E. Lincoln, "Development of the City Playgrounds," *Providence Magazine*
28 (August 1916): 525-28; Clarence E. Rainwater, *The Play Movement in the United
States: A Study of Community Recreation* (Chicago: University of Chicago Press, 1922),
42-60.

[36] Mary Josephine O'Connor, assistant superintendent of municipal playgrounds,

Play workers in Providence included not only Yankees like Sidney
A. Sherman, master at English High School, and Annie Barus, a
Vassar graduate and former president of the National Association
of Collegiate Alumnae, but also Monsignor Thomas F. Doran, vicar
general of the Diocese of Providence, Mrs. Caesar Misch, president
of the Providence Section, National Council of Jewish Women, and
other members of the city's ethnic middle classes. All agreed on the
importance of the environment in shaping character. "The environment of children living in the poorest wards," they held, "causes
physical, mental, and moral degeneration." Many also shared a rural bias. "Children are properly brought up only in the country,"
Sidney Sherman pointed out. "The next thing to the country is the
city spread out thinly, and the next thing to that is frequent open
and shaded places throughout the crowded city." In order to make
their playgrounds "more attractive than the streets," volunteers
equipped them with swings, seesaws, gymnastic apparatus, playing
fields, and other "features to be enjoyed only in the playground."
Organized games, ranging from croquet to baseball, not only developed a child's self-expression but, more importantly, integrated the
child into an organized peer group.[37] To ensure the success of the

---

quoted in "The Municipal Playground a Builder for Citizenship," *Board of Trade Journal* 25 (September 1913): 351; Providence Playground Association, "Extracts from
the report of Rush Sturges, Secretary," 1915, RIHS. The literature on the play movement is voluminous. It includes George Ellsworth Johnson, *Education by Plays and
Games* (Boston: Ginn & Co., 1907); J. F. Gillin, "The Sociology of Recreation," *American Journal of Sociology* 19 (May 1914): 825-34; K. Gerald Marsden, "Philanthropy
and the Boston Playground Movement, 1885-1907," *Social Service Review* 35 (March
1961): 48-58; Lawrence A. Finfer, "Leisure as Social Work in the Urban Community:
The Progressive Recreation Movement, 1890-1920" (Ph.D. diss., Michigan State
University, 1974); Benjamin McArthur, "The Chicago Playground Movement: A
Neglected Feature of Social Justice," *Social Service Review* 49 (September 1975): 376-
95; Bernard Mergen, "The Discovery of Children's Play," *American Quarterly* 27 (October 1975): 399-420; Mark A. Kadzielski, " 'As a Flower Needs Sunshine': The
Origins of Organized Children's Recreation in Philadelphia, 1886-1911," *Journal of
Sport History* 4 (Summer 1977): 169-88; Cary Goodman, *Choosing Sides: Playgrounds
and Street Life on the Lower East Side* (New York: Schocken Books, 1979); Dom Cavallo,
"Social Reform and the Movement to Organize Children's Play During the Progressive Era," *History of Childhood Quarterly* 3 (Spring 1979): 509-522; ibid., *Muscles and
Morals: Organized Playgrounds and Urban Reform, 1880-1920* (Philadelphia: University
of Pennsylvania Press, 1981); Hardy, *How Boston Played*, 85-106; and Rosenzweig,
Eight Hours for What We Will, 143-52. A good place to start is the review essay by Stephen Hardy and Alan G. Ingham, "Games, Structures, and Agency: Historians on
the American Play Movement," *Journal of Social History* 17 (Winter 1983): 285-301.

   [37] *Vacation Schools and Playgrounds in Providence* (n.p., n.d.), 1, in the Papers of the

playground movement, volunteers adopted the strategy that had proved so effective for the city's kindergarten advocates. They converted school yards in "congested" neighborhoods into pilot playgrounds that they maintained "until such time as the city is in a position to take them over."[38]

Just as reformers began to define a larger role for the municipal government, so too did they formulate new strategies in purveying rational recreation. Coming to terms with the segmentation of leisure activities, they encouraged the formation of self-governing and preferably self-sufficient clubs among the working class. Emphasizing the solidarity of the peer group, they feared that those without any organizational affiliation were especially prey to the temptations of objectionable amusements. The antidote to this demoralization, they believed, lay in harnessing the unorganized individual's social instinct and turning it to higher purposes than mere hedonism or escape. In this way, self-governing clubs would become the vehicles for civilizing the urban masses.

The "club idea" came naturally to middle-class reformers in the late nineteenth century; since the Civil War, clubs and lodges had increasingly organized the leisure of the city's more affluent residents. During the 1880s churches as well established federated clubs like the Christian Endeavor Union and the Epworth League to reach youth too young for prayer meetings.[39] In 1882 the Providence YMCA embraced "muscular Christianity" when it moved into new quarters replete with a fully furnished gymnasium. Yet all of these organizations reached a predominantly middle-class audience. New means had to be found to organize the city's working class.[40]

Providence Public Education Association, RIHS; *Report of the Joint Committee of the Union for Practical Progress and Providence Free Kindergarten Association on Summer Playgrounds* (n.p., 1895), 6-7; *Fourth Annual Report of the Joint Committee on Summer Playgrounds, Providence, R.I.* (n.p., 1897), 9.

[38] "Providence Playground Association," 15 April 1911, RIHS.

[39] For the young people's societies within the churches, see Aaron Ignatius Abell, *The Urban Impact on American Protestantism, 1865-1900* (Cambridge: Harvard University Press, 1943), 210-17; Joseph F. Kett, *Rites of Passage: Adolescence in America, 1790 to the Present* (New York: Basic Books, 1977), 189-98. Stephen Yeo discerns the same "tendency toward division of organisation and activity into separate age groups, occupational groups or class groups" in late nineteenth-century Reading, England. *Religion and Voluntary Organisations in Crisis* (London: Croom Helm, 1976), 177.

[40] For a breakdown of YMCA membership in Providence, see *Thirty-Eighth Annual*

One of the first groups to extend the "club idea" to the unorganized was the Young Woman's Christian Temperance Union (YWCTU). Inspired by purity, sisterhood, and other middle-class ideals of womanhood, its members directed their efforts at young women who worked in jewelry shops, textile mills, and department stores. In 1884 the YWCTU established a tearoom or coffee shop "in the heart of the city" where working girls could bring their lunches or purchase cheap but nutritional meals. Intended "as a counter-attraction to the temptations of the street and *so-called* restaurants," the downtown rooms, though simply furnished at the outset, soon featured lectures and classes, libraries, and even dramatic sketches. Profits from the sale of food and drink supported a vacation cottage on Narragansett Bay where for as little as three dollars a week as many as 150 women a summer "might pleasantly and safely spend their vacations with little expense." If similar tearooms were established in every ward, predicted the Women's City Missionary Society, "many drinking saloons would be closed and the question of license or no license would soon go by default." The tearoom also propagated evangelical Protestantism, as the YWCTU arranged for noonday prayer meetings.[41]

Other middle-class women, "who had many opportunities and some leisure," organized working girls' clubs for "those of their sisters who passed busier days in closer contact with the hardships of life." Modeled on the 38th Street Working Girls' Society established by Sunday School teacher Grace H. Dodge and New York City in 1884, working girls' clubs in Providence offered classes in domestic science, business skills like bookkeeping and stenography, and athletics. According to the *Providence Journal*, they reflected the growing participation of women in "the field of competitive labor." Their

---

Report of the Providence Young Men's Christian Association (Providence: YMCA, 1891), 31; *Fortieth Annual Report* (Providence: YMCA, 1893), 29. See also Benjamin G. Rader, *American Sports: From the Age of Folk Games to the Age of Spectators* (Englewood Cliffs, N.J.: Prentice-Hall, 1983), 149-54; Charles Howard Hopkins, *History of the Y.M.C.A. in North America* (New York: Association Press, 1951); David I. Macleod, *Building Character in the American Boy: The Boy Scouts, YMCA, and Their Forerunners, 1870-1920* (Madison: University of Wisconsin Press, 1983).

[41] *Far and Near* 1 (April 1891): 108-109, Brown University Library; *Eleventh Annual Report of the Young Woman's Christian Temperance Union* (Providence: n.p., 1893), 15; "History of the Rhode Island Woman's Christian Temperance Union," MS, 25-27, box 1, Records of the WCTU, RIHS; *Fifteenth Annual Report of the Women's City Missionary Society* (Providence: J. A. & R. A. Reid, 1882), 8.

founders, "superior women in education, attainments and wealth," were churchwomen who believed that the domesticity of club life would protect working girls from less desirable amusements, promote self-improvement, and reconcile class differences. The founders looked forward to the day when "younger members," or the working girls themselves, imbued with "loyalty to the settlement," would take on the day-to-day management of the nonsectarian, and ideally self-supporting, clubs.[42]

The Mount Pleasant Working Girls' Association grew out of a club organized in 1887 by a Sunday School teacher and her thirteen students at the Academy Avenue Congregational Church. Located in "a neighborhood of comfortable houses, with but little real poverty and with average educational advantages," the new organization grew quickly. By 1891, when it moved into a new clubhouse, it claimed twenty-five teachers and almost two hundred members. The popularity of evening classes explains its rapid growth. Some classes honed housekeeping skills like embroidery, basketmaking, and cooking; others taught penmanship, accounting, and English grammar. Dancing, singing, and ice cream parties provided a good time for all. Gradually, the clubhouse became the home of a number of small clubs and circles who used its rooms for their meetings. Clubs for neighborhood children featured games, singing, and even gymnastics—all designed to promote rational recreation. The Knights of the Round Table, a short story club, admitted boys who promised not to chew, smoke, or swear, and to wash their hands and faces before the weekly meeting. The Domestic Club consisted of the mothers and married sisters of the association's members. By 1900 the clubhouse had become the center of a network of neighborhood clubs.[43]

[42] *Reports of the Mount Pleasant Working Girls' Association, 1887-1902* (Providence: Snow & Farnham, 1903), 3; *Providence Journal*, 19 April 1890; Mrs. Elizabeth H. Haight, head worker of Sprague House, quoted in *Providence Journal*, 18 November 1914. On the working girls' club movement, see Maude Stanley, *Clubs for Working Girls* (New York: Macmillan Co., 1890); Kathy Lee Peiss, "Cheap Amusements: Gender Relations and the Use of Leisure Time in New York City, 1880 to 1920" (Ph.D. diss., Brown University, 1982), 171-96; Joanne Reitano, "Working Girls Unite," *American Quarterly* 36 (Spring 1984): 112-34.

[43] Robert A. Woods and Albert J. Kennedy, eds., *Handbook of Settlements* (New York: Russell Sage Foundation, 1911), 288; *Reports of the Mount Pleasant Working Girls' Association, 1887-1902; Far and Near* 1 (March 1891): 88.

A second working girls' club, the North End Working Girls' Association, "sprang into being" in 1889 after two women physicians in Providence established a dispensary amid the factories of the city's North End. Supported by the ecumenical Women's Christian Association, it admitted girls sixteen and older who paid quarterly dues of twenty-five cents. Members could choose from a variety of classes ranging from sewing and embroidery to reading, writing, and arithmetic. Gym classes were also offered. The clubhouse was open on weekdays for use as a lunchroom and on Saturday afternoons for baths. A number of auxiliaries were soon organized: a domestic circle for female relatives and friends of the members; a senior club for girls sixteen and older; and a smaller junior club for girls twelve to sixteen. When in 1899 one of the managers of the Women's Christian Association paid off the mortgage, the stage was set for the North End Working Girls' Association to become self-supporting. It gradually separated itself from the Women's Christian Association and, in 1904, joined the newly formed Rhode Island Association of Working Girls' Clubs.[44]

Still other groups of middle-class reformers specialized in boys' work. Since the late 1870s, the Union for Christian Work had worked with the city's street urchins. Volunteers sought to teach the boys self-control and "instill in their minds the germs of manly being and upright living." They were not particularly successful. Although furnished with illustrated books, colorful magazines, and simple games, the union's rooms were normally open only two evenings a week, manned by volunteers, and no attempt was made to appeal to the social instinct. Unless channeled into more wholesome outlets, the boys' natural gregariousness found release in gangs.[45]

The Providence Boys' Club, which was established as a separate organization in 1898 after a national organizer visited the city, was more successful in attracting members. Open every day but Sunday

[44] *Far and Near* 1 (March 1891): 88; *Twenty-Third Annual Report of the Young Women's Christian Association* (Providence: J. A. & R. A. Reid, 1890), 6-8; *Thirty-Second Annual Report* (Providence: Snow & Farnham, 1899), 9. See also Dorcey Baker, "Women and Reform, 1865-1900: The Women's Christian Association, Providence" (undergraduate paper, Brown University, 1978), RIHS; Colette A. Hyman, "The Young Women's Christian Association and the Women's City Missionary Society: Models of Feminine Behavior, 1868-1920" (American Civilization honors thesis, Brown University, 1979).

[45] Providence Boys' Club, "A Brief History," 1917, RIHS.

and administered by a full-time paid superintendent, it offered
rooms for reading and typing, manual training classes, printing and
carpentry shops, stereopticon entertainment, a bowling alley, and as
its centerpiece, a fully equipped gymnasium presided over by a
trained instructor. "Our first object," said a spokesman, "is to get the
boy away from the saloons, the cheap theatres and other resorts
where he naturally drifts when he can't stay on the street." To do
this, the club had to "offer him a chance to play." Among the many
activities the club offered were sparring matches. Superintendent
Percy Smith maintained that sparring built character as well as phy-
sique. "Boys naturally admire men like Jeffries, Fitzsimmons, Cor-
bett and the other ring heroes, and would like to emulate them," he
explained. "I tell them of the hard training and clean living these
men have to go through, and they profit by the example." If the club
succeeded in instilling self-discipline in the boys, "an embryo tough"
might one day "make a good citizen."[46]

After spinning off its boys' club, the Union for Christian Work
turned its attention to workingmen. As its "unique contribution" to
the city's "forward movement," it opened a men's club in 1905.
"There is a multitude of men nightly in our saloons," a spokesman
explained, "who are there really in response to the same instinct,
only more imperative in their case, that takes the well-to-do man to
his club, namely, the instinct of sociability." For this reason, the city
needed men's clubs that would compete against the saloon. "As long
as the poor man remains a social being the only way to get him out
of the saloon is to open up another place which attracts him with all
the allurements he finds in the saloon and others which he doesn't
find there." Accordingly, the new club, whose furnishings were at
first limited to papers and a few simple games, soon installed tables
for checkers, whist, and billiards, and added a separate library and
reading room. Indeed, the club's sponsors considered the atmosphere crucial to the success of the experiment. To simulate the

---

[46] *Fifteenth Annual Report of the Providence Boys' Club* (Providence: n.p., 1914), 3;
Smith quoted in the *Providence Journal*, 12 November 1911. In 1909, only two years
earlier, the Rhode Island State Federation of Women's Clubs pressured the police
into suppressing prize fighting at the North Providence Athletic Club. Rhode Island
State Federation of Women's Clubs, *Year Book* (n.p., 1909-1910), 31. On boys' clubs,
see Steven L. Schlossman, "G. Stanley Hall and the Boys' Club: Conservative Appli-
cations of Recapitulation Theory," *Journal of the History of the Behavioral Sciences* 9
(January 1973): 140-47.

"free-and-easy" or "democratic" atmosphere of the saloon, they sold tea, coffee, and "various light eatables." "Eating and drinking," they pointed out, "are great looseners of tongues and spirits, and any social enterprise which ignores that fact is likely to repel and fail." Renouncing any efforts at proselytizing, they defined their role as that of "the saloon-keeper."[47]

While the Union for Christian Work drew the line at providing alcoholic refreshments, a few workingmen's clubs in other cities actually sold beer and unadulterated liquors in the hope of taking the profit out of the sale of liquor. In 1904 reformers in New York City opened the Subway Tavern as a clean and wholesome place where workingmen would "feel impelled to drink little rather than much, where the beverages could be the best of their kind at modest price, and where every influence will discourage rather than induce drunkenness." Although hailed by the Right Reverend Henry Codman Potter, Episcopal bishop of New York, as "in many respects the greatest social movement New York has ever known," this particular counterattraction was almost universally condemned by the religious press. "A man can get drunk at the Bishop's bar just as quickly as at any other," quipped one critic.[48]

In selling alcohol, the Subway Tavern resembled the British workingmen's clubs, which numbered about seven hundred by the end of the century. In 1863 Unitarian minister Henry Solly had established the Working Men's Club and Institute Union with the twofold object of weaning workingmen away from their saloons and promoting class conciliation. But in the following decades disputes over whether the clubs should sell beer or remain dry arrayed workingmen against their aristocratic and middle-class sponsors. By 1884 the workingmen had prevailed in England. Selling liquor enabled their clubs to become independent and self-sufficient. The Union for Christian Work, which still hoped to control the workingmen's leisure activities, must have found the results of the British experiment mixed.[49]

[47] Mary Conyngton, "Philanthropy," in *A Modern City*, ed. Kirk, 312-13; *Manual of the Union for Christian Work for 1905* (Providence: Snow & Farnham, 1905), 14-15.

[48] Harold Underwood Faulkner, *The Quest for Social Justice, 1898-1914* (New York: Macmillan Co., 1931), 225n; Mark Sullivan, *Our Times: The United States, 1900-1925*, 6 vols. (New York: Charles Scribner's Sons, 1926-35), 2:621-22.

[49] Richard N. Price, "The Working Men's Club Movement and Victorian Social Reform Ideology," *Victorian Studies* 15 (December 1971): 117-47; John Taylor, *From*

Although they might disagree over whether drink was necessary in their substitutes for the saloon, the sponsors of these working-men's clubs shared a common awareness of the importance of sociability. Of recent origin, this awareness had not informed the early activities of the Union for Christian Work. Upon opening its rooms in 1868, as the first organization of its kind in the country, the union had installed a billiard table only to discover that "there seemed to be a spirit of license in the game which was out of harmony with the life of the rooms. The same people who would play croquet or backgammon without tendency to wrong, seemed of a different spirit when playing billiards. Perhaps if it were the habit of ladies to use the game at home, their influence would have made a different result." By 1905 the billiards table, long since the staple of the exclusive men's club, seemed indispensable to the success of this counter-attraction.[50]

Moreover, in sharp contrast to paternalistic efforts in 1868 to bring rich and poor together, the volunteers in 1905 described their men's club as "a business proposition." In so doing, they betrayed a heightened sensitivity to patronage. "There must be no patronizing," they warned. "The guest must feel that he is wanted there, not to have good done to him, but to get something out of him. This gives him a chance to buy or to pay, or both, and, by paying, to feel his right to be there and have the freedom of the place." Instead of emphasizing the elevating influence contact with his social superiors would have on the workingman, the union's volunteers spoke of self-government. The workingmen would govern themselves while the union exercised "unobtrusive direction and control" with the help of individual workers who worshiped at the city's Unitarian churches. Within a year after the establishment of the club, the volunteers had turned active management over to the workingmen themselves. Proceeds from the sale of food and nonalcoholic bev-

Self-Help to Glamour: The Working Man's Club, 1860-1972 (Oxford: History workshop, 1972); Gareth Stedman Jones, "Working-Class Culture and Working-Class Politics in London, 1870-1900: Notes on the Remaking of a Working Class," *Journal of Social History* 7 (Summer 1974): 460-508; Peter Bailey, *Leisure and Class in Victorian England: Rational Recreation and the Contest for Control, 1830-1885* (London: Routledge & Kegan Paul, 1978), 106-123.

[50] *Manual of the Union for Christian Work for 1869-70* (Providence: Providence Press Co., 1869), 17.

erages reduced the club's dependence on contributions from the union's wealthy supporters.[51]

In the prospectus for its men's club, the Union for Christian Work rehearsed new explanations for the popularity of the saloon. According to observers like Francis G. Peabody, who taught social ethics at Harvard, the saloon functioned as a social center for the working class. For its patrons the saloon thus played a role analogous to that of the lodge or the club. In an article that appeared in 1896, aptly entitled "Substitutes for the Saloon," Peabody urged reformers to devise substitutes that offered "some degree of sociability without drink."[52] The following year, sociologist E. C. Moore put timely questions to opponents of the saloon. What role did the saloon play, Moore asked, and what kinds of counterattractions would meet the same needs among workingmen? The saloon, he suggested, was the product of "an *unorganized* society" that would wither away if "society can wisely *organize* the needs which it supplies."[53] In 1901 the Committee of Fifty for the Investigation of the Liquor Problem issued its long-awaited report on substitutes for the saloon. For the previous eight years, these academics, clergymen, and reformers had examined the "drink habit," not to advocate "one theory or another," but rather to investigate the "facts without reference to the conclusions to which they might lead." After studying "the contribution of the saloon to sociability," the committee concluded that the saloon was indeed "the poor man's club." Its appeal "does not wholly proceed from its satisfying the thirst for drink. It satisfies also the thirst for sociability." For many workingmen, then, the saloon took the place of the club and fraternal lodge.[54]

[51] *Manual of the Union for Christian Work for 1905*, 14-16.

[52] Francis G. Peabody, "Substitutes for the Saloon," *Forum* 21 (July 1896): 597. On Peabody, see Arthur Mann, *Yankee Reformers in the Urban Age: Social Reform in Boston, 1880-1900* (1954; reprint, Chicago: University of Chicago Press, 1974), chap. 4.

[53] E. C. Moore, "The Social Value of the Saloon," *American Journal of Sociology* 3 (July 1897): 12. Emphasis added.

[54] Charles Dudley Warner, "Editor's Study," *Harper's New Monthly Magazine* 94 (February 1897): 483; Raymond Calkins, *Substitutes for the Saloon* (Boston: Houghton Mifflin Co., 1901), viii; Royal L. Melendy, "The Saloon in Chicago," *American Journal of Sociology* 6 (November 1900): 289-306 and (January 1901): 433-64; George L. McNutt, "Why Workingmen Drink," *Outlook* 69 (14 September 1901): 115-18; Francis G. Peabody, ed., *The Liquor Problem: A Summary of Investigations Conducted by the Committee of Fifty, 1893-1903* (Boston: Houghton Mifflin Co., 1905). See also Jon M.

Along with this discovery of a working-class sociability centered on the saloon came an interest in what the Committee of Fifty labeled the "leisure problem." "Work is not and was not meant to be the whole of life," pointed out one of the contributors to the committee's report. Indeed, "the leisure problem equals in importance the labor problem, and surpasses it in difficulty," he said. The antidote to intemperance, therefore, was not to be found in futile efforts to repress instinctive desires among any segment of the population; prohibition had failed because it had treated only the symptom—the saloon—and not the root cause itself—the low incomes and crowded homes of workingmen and their families.[55] Previous generations of middle-class reformers had proceeded from a mistaken premise. They had assumed that since alcohol was an "appetite," once "temptation in its open and glaring forms" was "removed," "the disposition to drink" would naturally decrease. "Men and women have confessed that they could not resist the open saloon and the smell of liquor," observed the Women's City Missionary Society in 1886. "They drank, because the stuff was right in their path, and they are glad it is gone, giving them a chance to be sober and industrious."[56]

Kingsdale, "The 'Poor Man's Club': Social Functions of the Urban Working-Class Saloon," *American Quarterly* 25 (October 1973): 472-89. By 1919 the Committee of Fifty had reverted to the view that drink was a habitual appetite. Although once the committee had believed that "the solution of the [drink] problem seemed to lie in the effort to extirpate the social features of the saloon, and to develop social substitutes for them," it had since concluded "that the problem of providing the needed social opportunity furnished by the saloon can be successfully undertaken only when the saloon itself has ceased to exist." In other words, the sociability of the saloon could *not* be separated from the alcohol it dispensed. Francis G. Peabody, "Preface to the New Edition," in Raymond Calkins, *Substitutes for the Saloon*, rev. ed. (Boston: Houghton Mifflin Co., 1919), v-vi. See also Robert A. Woods, "A New Synthesis after the Saloon," in ibid., 319-27.

[55] Calkins, *Substitutes for the Saloon*, 1901 ed., 5. See Paul Boyer's contrast between "positive environmentalism" and such "coercive reforms" as prohibition in *Urban Masses and Moral Order in America, 1820-1920* (Cambridge: Harvard University Press, 1978), 205-251.

[56] *Nineteenth Annual Report of the Women's City Missionary Society* (Providence: F. H. Townsend, 1886), 9. Even an opponent of prohibition attributed drink to appetite. "The point at issue," wrote William B. Weeden, the first president of the Union for Christian Work, "is not whether it is wise or unwise for these men [workingmen] to drink liquors, but whether society, as a whole, can absolutely prohibit an appetite which fully one-half of the respectable laboring people consider reasonable." *The Morality of Prohibitory Liquor Laws* (Boston: Roberts Brothers, 1875), 98.

But in its account of why men drank the Committee of Fifty's report pointed to the role of the environment. Workingmen drank less because they thirsted for alcohol than because they thirsted "for fellowship and recreation." In the absence of counterattractions, those who were poor and lived in crowded homes would naturally seek sociability in the saloon. Although the saloon could not be suppressed by legislative enactment, it could be driven out of business. Let reformers plant working-class neighborhoods with all sorts of organized recreation—whether clubs sponsored by voluntary associations or municipal parks and playgrounds—and the saloon would quickly lose its customers. The failure of prohibition when last tried in Rhode Island must have convinced a number of local reformers of the futility of the traditional blue-law approach.[57]

The counterattractions or substitutes envisioned by these reformers had to vie in attractiveness with saloons and other commercial entertainments in satisfying "the social instinct." Although reformers could not arrest the commercialization of leisure, they could do something about the tendency of commercial entertainments, in the absence of competition, to debase the standards of entertainment to the lowest common denominator—often the prurient. In competing with the saloon and other commercial entertainments for customers, counterattractions would elevate entertainment; but, unlike the tearooms established during the 1880s, they would "be unmixed with purposes of missionary zeal." The intrusion of prayer meetings would only drive workingmen away. "In a genuine poor-man's club—as in a rich-man's club—visible signs of religious intention must be eliminated." So too must the least hint of patronage.[58]

These various clubs were the nuclei of the social settlements established in Providence after the turn of the century. Between 1886 and 1911 some 392 settlement houses sprang up in thirty-four states. Modeled on London's Toynbee House, established in 1884, they endeavored to bring rich and poor together. Many were inspired by the vision of Christian brotherhood preached by advocates of the Social Gospel. The most famous of them, Chicago's Hull House, founded by Jane Addams and Ellen Starr in 1889, not only provided a vocation for the first generation of college-educated

[57] Raymond Calkins, "A Summary of Investigations Concerning Substitutes for the Saloon," in Peabody, ed., *The Liquor Problem*, 148.

[58] Peabody, "Substitutes for the Saloon," 603-604.

women, but also profoundly influenced the emergent discipline of urban sociology. Settlements in Providence never seemed to have involved substantial numbers of idealistic college graduates residing as missionaries of middle-class culture among the poor. Perhaps the city was too small for this to be contemplated. Rather, volunteers planted settlements in congested neighborhoods with the intention of promoting neighborhood identity and cohesion among a transient urban population. Each of the city's settlements employed resident workers who were assisted by nonresident volunteers.[59]

In theory, each of the city's settlements became the center of an elaborate network of clubs consisting of all the residents of its neighborhood. Given a skilled head worker and sufficient income or endowment, a settlement would eventually recruit the entire neighborhood from parents down to their young children into organized peer groups. Through integrating the disparate activities of the mobile individuals flowing in and out of inner-city neighborhoods, settlement workers strove to resist the atomization of the industrial city. Among the conditions that "brought settlements into being," explained Professor William MacDonald, were "our class distinctions, our great foreign population, [and] our lack of understanding of one another." "A settlement," MacDonald added, "must furnish a common meeting place for the people of its neighborhood."[60]

[59] A good introduction to the settlement movement is Allen F. Davis, *Spearheads for Reform: The Social Settlements and the Progressive Movement, 1890-1914* (New York: Oxford University Press, 1967). John P. Rousmaniere attempts to account for the interest of college alumnae in the settlement movement in "Cultural Hybrid in the Slums: The College Woman and the Settlement House, 1889-1894," *American Quarterly* 22 (Spring 1970): 45-66. On the settlement movement as the crucible of urban sociology, see Robert M. Crunden, *Ministers of Reform: The Progressives' Achievement in American Civilization, 1889-1920* (New York: Basic Books, 1982), 79-89.

[60] *Providence Journal,* 30 May 1906. On the settlement workers' interest in neighborhood reconstruction, see Roy Lubove, *The Professional Altruist: The Emergence of Social Work as a Career, 1880-1930* (1965; reprint, New York: Atheneum, 1980), 171-80; Don S. Kirschner, "The Ambiguous Legacy: Social Justice and Social Control in the Progressive Era," *Historical Reflections* 2 (Summer 1975): 69-88; David Stratton Locke, "The Village Vision: Goals and Limits in Urban Reform, 1890-1914" (Ph.D. diss., Brown University, 1972), esp. chap. 5; and Davis, *Spearheads for Reform,* 60-83. "A settlement aims to get things done for a given neighborhood," declared the nationally known settlement worker Mary K. Simkhovitch. "It proposes to be the guardian of that neighborhood's interest, and through identification of the interests of the settlement group with the local interests, it forms a steadying and permanent element in a community which is more or less wavering and in flux. To work out the methods by which a neighborhood may become a consciously effective group is . . . the difficult task of the settlement everywhere." Quoted in Davis, p. 75.

The transformation of the Mount Pleasant Working Girls' Association into Sprague House illustrates this organizational imperative. As more and more neighborhood groups began to use its clubhouse, the association decided to throw its facilities open to the neighborhood in 1900. It hired a full-time resident worker, who visited between forty and seventy-five of her neighbors monthly, invited them to tea when she was "at home" on Thursday afternoons, and allowed their children to use the hall and yard of the clubhouse as playgrounds. After its incorporation as Sprague House in 1903, the new settlement began to specialize in work among the Italian immigrants who flocked to nearby Federal Hill. In one of its rooms, it established the city's first branch library, which cultivated a taste for reading among immigrants seeking self-improvement. Home visitors used the settlement as a base from which to disseminate the latest techniques of professional homemaking. In 1910, after three years of planning, Sprague House opened an Italian cultural center. Four years later, the settlement transferred its original Mount Pleasant site to the public library and moved its operations to Federal Hill. As the new Federal Hill House, "a social neighborhood centre, with a resident worker as general director," the settlement added members of the local Italian-American community to its board of directors and launched a fund drive to raise money for a much larger building equipped with gym, special assembly room, and rooftop garden. These facilities were all directed toward the settlement's primary goal of Americanizing the immigrant.[61]

Episcopalian laymen supported two more settlements in Providence, both of which traced their origins to day nurseries and girls' friendly clubs organized by Mrs. Rathbone Gardner and other women from Grace Church while David H. Greer was rector. The Day Nursery Association, which in 1884 opened a nursery in Olneyville for the children of working women, gradually added clubs until it evolved into Nickerson House in 1917.[62] Neighborhood House

[61] *Reports of the Mount Pleasant Working Girls' Association, 1887-1902*, 5-8; *Report of the Sprague House Association and Federal Hill Association* (Providence: C. S. Reynolds, 1914), 6-7; *Report of the Federal Hill House Association, December, 1915* (Providence: C. S. Reynolds, 1915), 5. For further accounts of the settlement's activities, see *Providence Journal*, 31 October 1910, 16 March 1913, 7 June 1914.

[62] Annual reports of the Providence Day Nursery Association, RIHS; Cady, *Civic and Architectural Development of Providence*, 229. Not all middle-class observers approved of the work of the city's day nurseries. Carol Aronovici, head worker of

grew out of a parish mission established in South Providence in 1904. As it evolved into a full-fledged settlement, Neighborhood House added non-Episcopalians to its board of directors and cut its ties to Grace Church. To appeal to its Irish and German neighbors, the new settlement converted its backyard into a playground for neighborhood children, offered classes in cooking, housekeeping, sewing, and dressmaking, and organized social clubs for women and girls, who were "constantly in need of amusement which helps to break the monotony of daily labor and inadequate social life." It also solicited funds for "a large hall with proper floor for dancing and dramatic entertainments" designed as a counterattraction to "the cheap and dangerous dance hall and the low grade theater, which stimulate an unhealthy desire for excitement among girls and boys of the working classes."[63]

The men's club of the Union for Christian Work was the nucleus of yet another settlement, located amid the jewelry shops of South Providence. After hiring Carol Aronovici, a Romanian immigrant who later became a nationally known housing reformer, as its head worker, the Unitarian organization reorganized itself "on a scientific basis" as Union Settlement in February 1908. In order to make the settlement into "a centre of neighborliness," Aronovici and his wife supervised the recruitment of the settlement's neighbors into age-graded clubs. Russian Jews, "who, owing to ignorance of the English language, are compelled to occupy poorly paid positions," studied literature and learned English conversation "through intercourse with Americans." Working girls attended lectures by Brown University faculty on the history of drama and staged *Midsummer Night's Dream* and other "plays of literary and artistic value." Harried mothers who had to feed large families on small incomes received tips on "food values, buying, dietaries, beverages, [and] house sanitation" from an instructor in domestic economy. Neighborhood children spent their Sunday afternoons mounting pictures and telling stories. Ambitious young men and women attended "sys-

Union Settlement, commented that "the opportunity that women find to leave their homes and enter upon some steady employment may, in the case of women with able-bodied husbands, result in permanent injury to the family." "The Charitable and Philanthropic Organizations of Providence," in *Twenty-Third Annual Report of the Commissioner of Industrial Statistics* (Providence: E. L. Freeman Co., 1910), 158.

[63] *Annual Report of Neighborhood House Association for 1911* (n.p., n.d.), 7; Woods and Kennedy, *Handbook of Settlements*, 287-88.

tematic courses of lectures" at the People's Institute designed to "help them keep abreast with modern scientific and social progress." "The philosophy of settlement work," Aronovici declared in summing up Union Settlement's activities, was "the offering of opportunity."[64]

As these brief accounts of the city's settlements suggest, proponents of rational recreation had lowered their sights since the 1860s. Whereas rational recreation had once been considered coextensive with civic culture, by the early twentieth century it denoted neighborhood activities. The civic culture itself had long since fragmented, as reflected by the proliferation of clubs and lodges. Only the neighborhood, contended Robert A. Woods, head worker of Boston's South End House, "is small enough to be a comprehensible and manageable community unit." The city was not and never would be "concretely conceivable" unless "organically integrated through its neighborhoods." It was for this reason that recreational reformers like Woods experimented with social centers designed to foster neighborliness.[65]

Institutional churches supplemented the work of settlement houses in revitalizing declining neighborhoods. Downtown churches whose parishioners were moving to outlying residential areas could not "remain neighborhood institutions, as practically all the Protestant churches in the residential districts are." They faced the choice of either selling their meetinghouses and following their parishioners out to the suburbs or redefining their ministry. Those who chose the latter course added reading rooms, parish houses, athletic facilities, and other institutional programs designed to re-establish their neighborhood base.[66]

[64] Union Settlement, *Annual Report of the Head Worker for 1908* (Providence: n.p., 1909), 5-9; *Providence Journal*, 24 December 1905, 27 March 1908; Carol Aronovici, "Social Settlements in Providence," *Sunday Tribune*, 29 November 1908; Woods and Kennedy, *Handbook of Settlements*, 325-26.

[65] Robert A. Woods, "The Neighborhood in Social Reconstruction," *American Journal of Sociology* 19 (March 1914): 579.

[66] "How the Down-Town Problem Was Met," *Providence Magazine* 26 (August 1914): 581. On the institutional church movement nationally, see Abell, *The Urban Impact on American Protestantism*, 137-65. For the importance of residential proximity to the typical church, see Robert Duncan McKenzie, *The Neighborhood: A Study of Social Life in the City of Columbus, Ohio* (Chicago: University of Chicago Press, 1923), 588-95; Harlan Paul Douglass, *The St. Louis Church Survey: A Religious Investigation with a Social Background* (New York: George H. Doran, 1924); and, for an earlier period,

Episcopalians in Providence as elsewhere took the lead in the institutional church movement. As early as 1893, St. John's, located on the northeastern edge of the central business district, became "an institutional church for a restricted and peculiar field" when it built an elaborate parish house equipped with game rooms, library, and gymnasium, all open to "the unchurched multitude." The Russian Jews who played whist and euchre in the coffee house would certainly have been put off by any attempts at religious conversion.[67] Led by Floyd W. Tomkins, its rector from 1894 to 1899, Grace Church multiplied both the number of services and the number of auxiliary organizations. In 1897 alone more than a thousand services were held in the church, and this figure does not include the many others that took place in private homes. Grace Church also sponsored an impressive number of auxiliary organizations, including ten women's societies, a men's association, two boys' clubs, a Girls' Friendly Society, a Christian Endeavor Union, two Sunday schools, and an employment bureau. Construction of a parish house in 1913 capped its drive to become "the municipal church," making "every possible effort to attract" the downtown's "floating population."[68]

Other Protestant denominations followed the Episcopalians' lead. Faced with the commercialization of its downtown parish, the Mathewson Street Methodist Episcopal Church decided to specialize "as an evangelical institution with a strong social appeal to transients and newcomers." Instead of fleeing to a more suburban location in 1896, the church erected a new meetinghouse in the form of a four-story business block, with a fully equipped physical culture room on the top floor and plenty of meeting rooms for neighborhood clubs. The elders reasoned that the church's commercial front would

Michael S. Franch, "The Congregational Community in the Changing City, 1840-70," *Maryland Historical Magazine* 71 (Fall 1976): 367-80.

[67] "How the Down-Town Problem Was Met," 582; *Annual Reports of St. John's Guild, also Dedicatory Exercises of the Parish House, Thursday, November 9, 1893* (Providence: Snow & Farnham, 1894), 47, 51-52; *Providence Journal*, 10 November 1893. For an analysis of Episcopalian activities in New York City, see Clyde Griffen, "An Urban Church in Ferment: The Episcopal Church in New York City, 1880-1900" (Ph.D. diss., Columbia University, 1960). Griffen summarizes his findings in "Rich Laymen and Early Social Christianity," *Church History* 36 (March 1967): 45-65.

[68] Henry Barrett Huntington, *A History of Grace Church in Providence, Rhode Island, 1829-1929* (Providence: privately printed, 1931), 124-26; Records of the Vestry, 1912-16, Easter 1914, Grace Church, Providence.

make it easier to sell the structure should the need ever arise. Math-ewson Street Church "ought to be a center," explained its pastor, Samuel M. Dick, "and its power through its institutional work ought to so permeate this whole city as to break down the wall of partition between the classes in this city."[69]

"Old Beneficent" Congregational, the downtown New Light church that the abolitionist Stephen S. Wardwell had attended, also specialized in institutional work. In 1896 its longtime minister, James G. Vose, who recognized that "the encroachment of business on the vicinity of our location" portended a decline in membership, inaugurated a series of praise services so that his church might be-come more of a "missionary" than a "home" church. Under his suc-cessor, Asbury Krom, Old Beneficent commissioned neighborhood surveys, established a Christian Service League for young men and women, and maintained a Social Institute for men interested in studying "the vital social problems of the day, in the light of the gos-pel of Jesus Christ, and especially to discover what, if anything, the church can do toward the solution of these problems." In 1912 it be-came the first church in Providence to install a projector. Motion pictures, as the Reverend Mr. Krom pointed out, were one more means of interesting the masses in the church as a "social centre" and ultimately increasing attendance.[70]

By 1912 six churches in Providence had established gymnasiums and several more featured well-equipped parish houses. Still others permitted neighborhood groups to use their rooms. In addition, fully half of the city's churches had organized athletic clubs for boys. There were at least twenty-six baseball teams, twelve basketball teams, and four bowling teams—all of which belonged to church leagues. One reason for these institutional programs was to reestab-lish the parish or territorial base for churches whose parishioners had moved to the suburbs. Another was to stimulate church attend-ance. Beneficent Church, whose membership had declined from

[69] "How the Down-Town Problem Was Met," 582; *Souvenir of the Mathewson St. Meth-odist Episcopal Church of Providence, Rhode Island* (Providence: Snow & Farnham, 1896); Samuel M. Dick, *Semi-Centennial Sermon by the Pastor, Sunday, October 23, 1898* (Providence: Snow & Farnham, 1898), 6-9.

[70] Church Records, 1863-99, 21 May 1896, annual report for 1897; Annual and Quarterly Meeting Records, 1899-1927, 11 February 1909, both at the Vestry of the Beneficent Congregational Church, Providence; Krom quoted in *Providence Journal*, 1 December 1912.

1897 to 1905, enrolled more than a hundred new communicants over the next decade. Thanks to its new programs and parish house, Grace Church boasted the largest Sunday school in the city. Calvary Baptist Church, located in one of the newer residential areas of the city, did even better. Christening itself Calvary Baptist Institute, it added a library of two thousand volumes, a reading room, an evening school, and even a gymnasium. As a result, membership more than tripled from 267 in 1887 to 905 by 1914. Yet such a program was not cheap. In 1914, for instance, it cost twelve thousand dollars to keep the institute's doors open seven days a week. Nor did institutional programs always bring in new communicants. They did not, for example, arrest the decline in membership at the venerable First Baptist Church.[71]

In spite of the heroic efforts of these and other voluntary associations, there simply were not enough privately sponsored neighborhood social centers in Providence for the urban masses. This was the conclusion of a recreational survey commissioned by the Providence Playground Association in 1912. Similar surveys, conducted in cities across the country along the lines of the Pittsburgh Survey of 1907-1909, drew on the resources of the Russell Sage Foundation. Assisted by local volunteers, Francis R. North, field secretary of the Playground and Recreation Association of America, studied "recreation conditions in Providence," particularly as they affected "the play life of children" in poor neighborhoods. Every week, North and his assistants estimated, as many as 43,500 people under the age of twenty-five attended motion-picture shows and theaters. Nearly 24,500 youth made use of the city's 160 poolrooms and 18 bowling alleys; another 8,000 patronized its 35 dance halls. Thus attendance at commercial amusements far exceeded the estimated 6,000 young people who took advantage of recreations sponsored by churches, settlements, and other nonprofit groups. Moreover, according to a report presented to the Rhode Island Council of Women, four out of every five children of school age in the city sought their recreation outside the home.[72]

[71] North, *A Recreation Survey*, 21; Lester Bradner, "Religion," in *A Modern City*, ed. Kirk, 331-34; Edward S. Holyoke, "The Socialized Church," *Providence Magazine* 26 (August 1914): 576-78; C. Allyn Russell, "Rhode Island Baptists, 1825-1931," *Rhode Island History* 28 (May 1969): 37-38.

[72] North, *A Recreation Survey*, 4, 26-32; Rhode Island Council of Women, Minutes,

Echoing similar investigators in other cities, North recommended the provision of more "constructive" reforms. He expressed the views of a new generation of middle-class reformers who were willing to work out a modus vivendi with entrepreneurs of leisure when he wrote that "commercial recreations are good or bad entirely independent of the fact that they are commercial." Among his proposals were the establishment of a recreation commission, the provision of municipal recreation on a year-round basis, the conversion of schools into neighborhood social centers, and the adoption of a policy of "co-operative regulation" toward commercial amusements. "As good recreation can be spoiled in some cases by cupidity or lack of responsibility," North explained, "it must be subject to regulation."[73]

North's recommendations spurred the appointment of a municipal board of recreation in 1913. The new board quickly moved to provide year-round "recreation-spots" in the city's most congested neighborhoods. Following the example of city authorities in Chicago and Boston, it equipped parks with field houses that offered club rooms, assembly halls, and gymnasiums. By 1915 there were even two self-governing "recreation centers," homes for neighborhood athletic, musical, and civic clubs.[74] In addition to assuming responsibility for the playgrounds formerly maintained by the Playground Association, the board opened two municipal dance halls, each with more than twenty thousand square feet of well-ventilated dancing space. Professional dancer Harold E. Thomas pronounced these new facilities "unexcelled." They were "large, modern, easy of

---

1910-13, 27 January 1913, RIHS. Similar studies include Michael M. Davis, Jr., *The Exploitation of Pleasure: A Study of Commercial Recreations in New York City* (New York: Russell Sage Foundation, 1911); William Trufant Foster, *Vaudeville and Motion Picture Shows: A Study of Theaters in Portland, Oregon* (Portland: Reed College, 1914); and John J. Phelan, *Motion Pictures as a Phase of Commercialized Amusement in Toledo, Ohio* (Toledo: Little Book Press, 1919). See also Alan Havig, "The Commercial Amusement Audience in Early 20th-Century American Cities," *Journal of American Culture* 5 (Spring 1982): 1-19.

73 North, *A Recreation Survey*, 4-5, 58; Belle Lindner Israels, "Regulation of Public Amusements," *Proceedings of the Academy of Political Science in the City of New York* 2 (July 1912): 123-26.

74 Lincoln, "Development of the City's Playgrounds," 526-28; Lee F. Hanmer and August H. Brunner, *Recreation Legislation*, rev. ed. (New York: Russell Sage Foundation, 1915), 96-98; "Board of Recreation," *Providence Magazine* 28 (September 1916): 595.

access, [and] splendid in equipment."[75] The board also authorized the "wider use" of the city's public schools. It thus permitted the Immigrant Educational Bureau, successor to the Union for Christian Work, to sponsor extension classes in cooking, embroidery, and athletics, lectures on American history, and talks on baby care and personal health in several schools in the city's North End, and to convert an abandoned school into a neighborhood center equipped with a library, dental and baby clinics, and clubs for the center's Italian neighbors.[76]

The transformation of the public school into "the common gathering place, the head-and-heart quarters" of a neighborhood, reflected the growing tendency among middle-class reformers to identify neighborliness with democracy. "A neighborhood without a forum," declared Mary K. Simkhovitch, "can never arise to full self-confidence." If a park in every neighborhood was not always a feasible proposition, the neighborhood school could easily be "socialized." As early as 1897 volunteers from University Settlement had established boys' and girls' clubs, delivered lectures illustrated with stereopticon slides, and given concerts in New York City's public schools. Since 1907 municipal authorities in Rochester, New York, had promoted grass-roots democracy by opening up schools after hours to clubs and other neighborhood organizations. In 1911 Wisconsin authorized local school boards to convert schools into community centers. The "aim" of what came to be known as the Community Center Movement, declared spokesman Clarence Arthur Perry, was "to organize America into a society with the schoolhouse as the society's home and clubhouse in each local unit." For Frederic C. Howe, who regarded the public school as a potential "people's clubhouse," "the public school as a social center offers the easiest approach for a city-wide, all-the-year-round program of recreation and culture." Others hailed the neighborhood school as a

[75] *Providence Journal*, 8 November 1914. On the pre-war dance craze, see Lewis A. Erenberg, "Everybody's Doin' It: The Pre-World War I Dance Craze, the Castles, and the Modern American Girl," *Feminist Studies* 3 (Fall 1975): 155-70; and Peiss, "Cheap Amusements," chap. 3.

[76] Providence Immigrant Educational Bureau, *Report, 1913* (Providence: Standard Printing Co., 1913), 14-20; *Providence Journal*, 29 September 1920, 4 December 1921. For the activities of a similar agency, see Robert L. Buroker, "From Voluntary Association to Welfare State: The Illinois Immigrants' Protective League, 1908-1926," *Journal of American History* 58 (December 1971): 643-60.

"little democracy." Henry E. Jackson, special agent in community organization for the United States Bureau of Education, predicted that it would foster "the neighborly spirit essential for concerted action."[77]

Even motion pictures, if subject to "co-operative regulation," could promote rational recreation. As early as 1909 Jane Addams had likened the motion-picture theater to a "House of Dreams." "The theater," she said, was for many urban youth "the only place where they can satisfy that craving for a conception of life higher than that which the actual world offers them." In 1910 the *Review of Reviews* went a step farther, declaring that the motion picture "is probably the greatest single force in shaping the American character." By 1912 Providence's motion-picture theaters boasted a seating capacity equal to nearly 4 percent of the city's population. Not satisfied, their proprietors sought to attract an even larger audience, particularly middle-class patrons, with greater publicity, feature films like *The Birth of a Nation*, and elaborate movie palaces. Eight theaters opened in downtown Providence between 1912 and 1919; two of them, the Strand and the Shubert Majestic, built exclusively for motion pictures, accommodated more than two thousand persons each. Given their immense popularity, movies looked like splendid substitutes for the saloon. In 1914, according to one survey, twice as many workingmen in New York City went to the movies as patronized the saloon. Although the same "spirit of democracy" pervaded the motion-picture theater and the saloon, motion pictures provided far more wholesome and family-oriented entertainment.

[77] Edward J. Ward, ed., *The Social Center* (New York: D. Appleton & Co., 1914), 1; Mary Kingsbury Simkhovitch, "The New York Public Library Assembly Halls," *Charities and the Commons* 15 (17 March 1906): 885; J. G. Phelps Stokes, "Public Schools as Social Centres," *Annals of the American Academy of Political and Social Science* 23 (May 1904): 457-63; Perry quoted in Edward W. Stevens, Jr., "Social Centers, Politics, and Social Efficiency in the Progressive Era," *History of Education Quarterly* 12 (Spring 1972): 22; Howe, "Leisure," 416; Henry E. Jackson, *A Community Center: What It Is and How to Organize It* (New York: Macmillan Co., 1918), 14. See also Clarence Arthur Perry, *First Steps in Community Center Development* (New York: Russell Sage Foundation, 1917); Ida Clyde Clarke, *The Little Democracy: A Text-book on Community Organization* (New York: D. Appleton & Co., 1918); John Collier, "Community Councils— What Have They Done and What Is Their Future?" *Proceedings of the National Conference of Social Work, 1919* (Chicago: Rogers & Hall, 1920), 476-79; Jean B. Quandt, *From the Small Town to the Great Community: The Social Thought of Progressive Intellectuals* (New Brunswick, N.J.: Rutgers University Press, 1970), 36-50; Davis, *Spearheads for Reform*, 76-83.

"Next to the daily press and the school," declared Howe, "the movie is probably the most influential educational and recreational agency in our daily life." If properly supervised, "democracy's theater" would elevate the masses and Americanize the immigrant.[78]

Worried that motion pictures were "degrading the minds and the artistic taste of our children," yet recognizing their educational value, middle-class women urged that city authorities censor the films shown in Providence. Chicago, New York City, Portland, Oregon, and other cities had already created municipal review boards, composed of citizen volunteers, who previewed films before they were shown to the public. There was also a National Board of Censorship of Motion Pictures, established by the People's Institute in New York City in 1909, which functioned, according to its chairman, Frederic C. Howe, as "a regulative force between the producers, on the one hand, and the public, on the other."[79] In 1913 the Rhode Island Congress of Parents and Teachers, a federation of

[78] Jane Addams, *The Spirit of Youth and the City Streets* (New York: Macmillan Co., 1909), 75-76; "The Moving Picture and the National Character," *Review of Reviews* 42 (September 1910): 320; Cady, *Civic and Architectural Development of Providence*, 227; Brett, *Temples of Illusion*, 207-236; North, *A Recreation Survey*, 27; Charles Stelzle, "How One Thousand Workingmen Spend Their Spare Time," *Outlook* 106 (4 April 1914): 762; Frederic C. Howe, "What to Do with the Motion-Picture Show: Shall It Be Censored?" ibid. 107 (20 June 1914): 412-13. See also Barton W. Currie, "The Nickel Madness," *Harper's Weekly* 51 (24 August 1907): 1246-47; George Ethelbert Walsh, "Moving Picture Drama for the Multitude," *Independent* 64 (6 February 1908): 306-310; "The Drama of the People," ibid. 69 (29 September 1910): 713-15; Charles Stelzle, "Movies Instead of Saloons," ibid. 85 (28 February 1916): 311; Adele F. Woodard, "The Motion-Picture Theatre as a Saloon Substitute," in Calkins, *Substitutes for the Saloon*, rev. ed., 358-67; Jowett, *Film*, 66-67; Rosenzweig, *Eight Hours for What We Will*, 191-221.

[79] "Report of Committee on Education," Sarah E. Doyle Club, Minutes, 1908-15, 28 May 1910, RIHS; Frederic C. Howe, "What to Do with the Motion-Picture Show," 414; John Collier, "Cheap Amusements," *Charities and the Commons* 20 (11 April 1908): 73-76; ibid., "Moving Pictures: Their Function and Proper Regulation," *Playground* 4 (October 1910): 232-39; Foster, *Vaudeville and Motion Picture Shows*, 17, 22; Robert Fisher, "Film Censorship and Progressive Reform: The National Board of Censorship of Motion Pictures, 1909-1922," *Journal of Popular Film* 4 (1975): 143-56; Kathleen D. McCarthy, "Nickel Vice and Virtue: Movie Censorship in Chicago, 1907-1915," ibid. 5 (1976): 37-55. Even as late as 1926 censorship remained relatively rare. Fewer than a hundred cities, and only seven states, provided for either official censorship boards or censors. See Donald Young, *Motion Pictures: A Study in Social Legislation* (1922; reprint, New York: Jerome S. Ozer, 1971), 60-81; Ford H. MacGregor, "Official Censorship Legislation," *Annals of the American Academy of Political and Social Science* 128 (November 1926): 163-74.

thirty-seven mothers' clubs attached to public and private schools, proposed a civilian censorship board for Providence, with the censors to be drawn from the congress's fifteen hundred members. Volunteers pledged to work "constructively" with theater managers to make "the 'movies' wholesome as well as entertaining." But perhaps because the proposal would have taxed each reel to defray the expenses of censorship, the city council decided to vest authority for censoring movies in the Board of Police Commissioners instead.[80]

The "efficient work" of Sergeant Richard H. Gamble, appointed the city's first censor in 1913, quickly won the praise of the Union Ministers' Meeting and later that of the National Board of Censorship as well. Gamble's successor, Herbert B. Caffrey, was "particular about gun play," "careful of the way in which drug addicts and their practices are presented," and "wary of pictures that go down into the dregs of life on the pretext of pointing a moral." He was also reportedly "death on burglary, murder and other choice crimes." A survey made in 1917 by a group of middle-class women and social workers found that Caffrey did his job well. Fifty-three visitors attended the city's thirteen theaters 135 times. Of the thirty-seven films they viewed that dealt with "sex appeal," only eight were "objectionable in that low ideals in sex relationship were depicted."[81]

Still not satisfied, middle-class women took several steps to improve the quality of the films shown in Providence. They called on theater managers to book only "wholesome and moral" films. They also experimented with children's theater. As the president of the Providence Mothers' Club explained, children's theater represented an attempt "to develop the play principle in children and inculcate moral lessons through the medium of the play itself." By 1922 grammar school children were putting on *Cinderella, The Finding of the Mayflower*, and other plays under the auspices of the Providence Mothers' Club.[82] During the winter of 1922-23, women's groups organized the Better Films Committee of Rhode Island, which met periodically with local theater managers to ensure that

[80] *Providence Journal*, 9 November 1913, 10 January 1914.

[81] Union Ministers' Meeting of Providence and Vicinity, Minutes, 1910-30, 19 October 1914, RIHS; *Providence Journal*, 14 December 1913, 12 December 1915, 4 March, 10 June 1917.

[82] *Providence Journal*, 20 February 1921, 2 November 1922. See also Carl E. Milliken, "The Movie: Has It a Social Obligation?" *Proceedings of the National Conference of Social Work, 1927* (Chicago: University of Chicago Press, 1927), 352-60.

only "the highest type of pictures" played in Providence. The new organization was part of the nationwide "Better Film Movement," which, in the words of Orrin G. Cocks, secretary of the National Committee for Better Films, was "essentially a plan which calls upon the community or the neighborhood as a unit" as well as "recognizes the necessity of special entertainments for young people."[83]

Following the Civil War, middle-class Americans discovered the benefits of play, which they proceeded to organize. Clubs, lodges, and other leisure-time organizations soon sprouted in cities across the country. The discovery of play greatly affected rational recreation, or middle-class attempts to remodel working-class amusements so that they would be purposive, restrained, and above all respectable. Because of the commercialization of leisure, the influence of instinct psychology, and new ethnographic theories of group formation, strategies of rational recreation changed dramatically. From lyceums, libraries, museums, and other citywide, didactic, and voluntaristic institutions, recreational reformers began to emphasize the provision of self-supporting and self-governing clubs among segments of the working class. These clubs were differentiated by age, sex, and neighborhood. Rejecting prohibition and similarly "destructive" measures, a new generation of middle-class reformers turned to more "constructive" reforms that took into account the social instinct or sociability. They also came to terms with the commercial amusements that their predecessors had resisted. At the same time, because of lobbying by both philanthropic associations and neighborhood groups, governmental bodies assumed much of the responsibility for the provision and maintenance of wholesome recreation.

Once intended to cut across class and ethnic lines, to appeal to all age groups, and to involve the whole family, rational recreation had itself become segmented. In organizing recreation on neighborhood lines and targeting it for specific age groups, recreational re-

[83] *Providence Journal*, 8 February 1923, 31 March, 11 October 1929, 22 March 1930; Olivia D. Hammill, *Thirty-Five Years of Accomplishment: The Story of the Rhode Island Council of Women from 1889 to 1924* (n.p.: Rhode Island Council of Women, 1925), 12-13; Federation of Women's Church Societies of Rhode Island, Minutes, 1924-33, 24 January 1928, in the Records of the Rhode Island Council of Church Women, RIHS; O. G. Cocks, "How a Neighborhood Can Improve Its Motion Picture Exhibitions," *Proceedings of the National Conference of Social Work, 1922* (Chicago: University of Chicago Press, 1922), 342.

formers furthered the segmentation of urban culture. This segmentation, or the breaking up of what had once been a socially and
culturally homogeneous society into innumerable organized peer
groups, stemmed from a number of sources: from the emergence
of a permanent working class, from the immigration of large numbers of non-Protestants who did not share the values enshrined in
the midcentury civic culture; from the geographical dispersion of
the city's residents, who sorted themselves out by class, ethnicity,
and race; and most of all from the differentiation of leisure activities. As neighborhood organizations proliferated, a number of middle-class Americans came to believe that a harmonious and well-ordered society depended less on the community life of revitalized
neighborhoods than on systematic and efficient social organization.
From the 1890s on, they forged a number of federations, translocal
associations that would link isolated middle-class groups on the basis
of common interest. For these groups, community no longer carried a spatial dimension, but rather denoted a complex organism
that, much like a machine, had to be organized along functional
lines and administered by specially trained professionals in the public interest.

7 Individualism Run Rampant

In 1911 Frank and Lillian Gilbreth, "partners for life" in industrial engineering, moved their large family to Providence. While Lillian pursued a Ph.D. in Applied Management at Brown, Frank "systematized" production at the New England Butt Company, the manufacturing firm founded in 1842 by abolitionist Nicholas B. Fenner. In his thirteen months at New England Butt, Gilbreth pioneered a number of techniques of "scientific motion study," including the first "route models," or process flow charts, and the first "micromotion" studies. Thanks to his efforts, the time required to perform certain industrial operations was cut by three-quarters. Before coming to Providence, Gilbreth had worked closely with Frederick Winslow Taylor, father of scientific management. Though not of one mind on how to apply the principles of the emergent discipline, Taylor and Gilbreth both thought of themselves as "systematizers." Both broke production down into a series of steps that their time and motion studies were designed to make more "efficient." For both, the key to promoting industrial efficiency lay in devising a system that not only provided for the orderly arrangement of the parts but also, as Taylor put it, brought each part "to its highest state of excellence."[1]

Perceiving what seemed to be an increasingly fragmented society, Taylor and Gilbreth joined many of their contemporaries in turning to new organizational modes that promised more efficiency, coordination, and system. In an attempt to preserve individualism, groups of middle-class Americans insisted that it be subordinated to the public interest or, better yet, integrated into translocal federa-

[1] Edna Yost, *Frank and Lillian Gilbreth: Partners for Life* (New Brunswick, N.J.: Rutgers University Press, 1949), 197-231; Daniel Nelson, *Managers and Workers: Origins of the New Factory System in the United States, 1880-1920* (Madison: University of Wisconsin Press, 1975), 66-68, 73; Taylor quoted in Samuel Haber, *Efficiency and Uplift: Scientific Management in the Progressive Era, 1890-1920* (Chicago: University of Chicago Press, 1964), 21.

tions.[2] In so doing, they qualified the meaning of voluntarism. Long a response to perceived disorder, voluntarism itself seemed by the turn of the century to have become the culprit. Those turning away from the individualist ethic recognized the necessity of imposing some kind of order or system on the individual units of society.

This fear of fragmentation and resultant concern for "system" was rooted in the experience of many Providence residents. From a city of slightly more than five square miles on the eve of the Civil War, Providence had more than tripled in size by 1900. No central body set the pace or determined the contours of the city's growth. Rather, metropolitan development proceeded haphazardly, the product of thousands of uncoordinated decisions by homeowners, real estate developers, and speculative builders. This was especially true after the turn of the century. As late as 1900 Providence remained a city of single- and two-family homes. But as wave after wave of immigrants from Italy, eastern Europe, and Portugal "peacefully invaded the city and made parts of it their own," double- and triple-deckers rose in record numbers in the city's most crowded neighborhoods—Italian Federal Hill, Jewish Constitution Hill, and Portuguese Fox Point. On the eve of the First World War, nine out of every ten new dwellings were tenements. Providence, moreover, had one of the lowest percentages of owner occupancy in the country: less than 22 percent in 1907.[3]

As "new" immigrants from southern and eastern Europe streamed into the city, the city's middle classes fled its overcrowded central wards for spacious suburbs to the south of Roger Williams Park. The electrification of the street railways between 1892 and 1895 accelerated their exodus. By the turn of the century, Washington Park, a 140-acre site between Roger Williams Park and Narra-

[2] I have found Jon C. Teaford's discussion of the "federative metropolis" quite helpful in developing my ideas on the federation movement. *City and Suburb: The Political Fragmentation of Metropolitan America, 1850-1970* (Baltimore: Johns Hopkins University Press, 1979), esp. 105-122.

[3] John Ihlder, *The Houses of Providence: A Study of Present Conditions and Tendencies with Notes on the Surrounding Communities and Some Mill Villages* (Providence: Snow & Farnham, 1916), 18, 30-37; George H. Kellner and J. Stanley Lemons, *Rhode Island: The Independent State* (Woodland Hills, Calif.: Windsor Publications, 1982), 119; "Home Ownership," in *Twenty-First Annual Report of the Commissioner of Industrial Statistics* (Providence: E. L. Freeman Co., 1908), 388-89. On haphazard development in one late nineteenth-century city, see Sam Bass Warner, Jr., *Streetcar Suburbs: The Process of Growth in Boston, 1870-1900* (1962; reprint, New York: Atheneum, 1976).

gansett Bay developed as a single tract by a realty company, sported more than three hundred residences, most of them "modern up-to-date cottages" within the price range of thrifty office workers and workingmen. Further to the south, substantial businessmen, professionals, and other members of the upper middle class employed architects to build homes in fashionable Edgewood, a short distance from their casino and yacht club on the Bay. By 1910 the newly developed residential suburbs of Auburn, Oaklawn, and Arlington, which ringed the city's southern perimeter, were growing much more rapidly than Providence itself. While the city's population climbed 52 percent from 176,000 in 1900 to 268,000 in 1925, that of its neighbors—Cranston, North Providence, Johnston, and East Providence—more than doubled. At the same time the trolley expanded the horizons of city boosters, who envisioned a metropolitan Providence stretching fourteen miles from Lonsdale in the north to Lakewood in the south. In 1920 "the Southern Gateway of New England" officially became a metropolitan district.[4]

Urban decentralization, as the walking city of the 1860s gave way to the metropolis of the 1920s, together with social and economic differentiation, encouraged the creation of translocal networks, or federations, as an industrial society put a premium on organizational modes that forged links between discrete and often geographically separate units. Providence's charity societies federated first in 1892 and then again during the 1920s; women's literary clubs in 1894; Protestant churches in 1901, followed by women's church groups in 1906; and businessmen's organizations in 1914. The fragmentation of the once inclusive civic culture of the mid-nineteenth century into competing interest groups increased the need for formal networks to take the place of the informal modes of cooperation and communication that had previously sufficed. Contemporaries recognized the utility of a more "mechanical" union, an integration as in a machine of the interdependent parts of society. In the process of federating their voluntary associations, middle-

---

[4] Isaac L. Goff Company, "What It Was . . . and . . . As It Is," illustrated brochure of Washington Park, Rider Collection, Brown University Library; Rhode Island Historical Preservation Commission, *Cranston, Rhode Island* (Statewide Preservation Report P-C-1, 1980), 23–29; Kellner and Lemons, *Rhode Island*, 118–19. On "Greater Providence," see Robert Grieve, "Modern Providence," *New England Magazine* 8 (February 1896): 790.

View of Providence from the dome of the Christian Science church, c. 1909 (courtesy of the Rhode Island Historical Society)

class Americans, who had once regarded themselves as the broad and cohesive basis for a stable social order, only to shatter into innumerable special groups organized according to occupation, income, and neighborhood, reconstituted themselves along functional lines.[5]

Bureaucratization was a common response to this perception of uncontrolled growth and fragmentation. The model was "the large vertically integrated, centralized, functionally departmentalized industrial organization." In the years from 1898 to 1902 alone, 2,653 independent firms were consolidated into 269 bureaucratic corporations capitalized at $6.3 billion. State governments created new client-oriented departments, like the Bureau of Industrial Statistics, to collect social statistics and promote industrial growth. Occupational licensing agencies, like the State Board of Pharmacy, also multiplied. At the same time voluntary associations themselves spawned bureaucratic structures consisting of central offices, specialized departments, and professional staffs responsible for planning. Between the 1890s and the 1930s groups of middle-class Americans turned to bureaucracy in part because it seemed an organizational mode ideally suited to perpetuating, under new conditions, the traditional ideal of a harmonious and well-ordered society. Indeed, it promised a middle way between anarchy and extreme centralism.[6]

---

[5] John William Ward has written that "a well-designed machine is an instance of total organization, that is, a series of interrelated means contrived to achieve a single end. A machine consists always of particular parts that have no meaning or function separate from the organized entity to which they contribute and whose interrelationships are marshaled wholly toward a given result. In the ideal machine, there can be no extraneous part, no extraneous movement; all is set, part for part, motion for motion toward the functioning of the whole. The machine is, then, both a perfect instance of total rationalization of a field of action, and of total organization." "The Politics of Design," in *Who Designs America?* ed. Laurence B. Holland (Garden City, N.Y.: Anchor Books, 1966), 76.

[6] Alfred D. Chandler, Jr., "The Beginnings of 'Big Business' in American Industry," *Business History Review* 33 (Spring 1959): 27; ibid., *Strategy and Structure: Chapters in the History of the American Industrial Enterprise* (Cambridge: M.I.T. Press, 1969), esp. 19-51; Alfred D. Chandler, Jr. and Louis Galambos, "The Development of Large-Scale Economic Organizations in Modern America," *Journal of Economic History* 30 (March 1970): 201-217. On the growth of government bureaucracies, see James Q. Wilson, "The Rise of the Bureaucratic State," *Public Interest* 41 (Fall 1975): 77-103. See also Max Weber, "Bureaucracy," in *From Max Weber: Essays in Sociology*, trans., ed., and with an introduction by H. H. Gerth and C. Wright Mills (New York: Oxford University Press, 1946), 196-244.

In centralizing their administrative structures, the city's voluntary associations responded to a number of different imperatives. One was rapid growth. When the Young Women's Christian Association (YWCA) was organized in 1867, its managers consisted of middle-class women "chosen as far as practicable from the different Protestant denominations of the city." In 1906, after years of planning, the YWCA moved into a new building equipped with café and dining room. From two boarding houses, or "homes," with an average of seventy-five permanent boarders and forty transients, it became what was "really a small hotel," with 126 permanent boarders and seventy-nine transients. To manage this vastly expanded plant, a board of directors replaced the volunteer officers, and a ten-person paid staff performed the chores once done by the boarders themselves. Expenses shot up. The annual budget for 1908, $50,000, was triple the figure for 1905; three-fifths of the annual income now came from the profits of the café and dining room.[7]

A second reason for bureaucratization was the multiplication of activities, just as firms centralized their management because of a multiplication of product lines. The Union for Christian Work, which became Union Settlement in 1908, is a case in point. When it was organized in 1868, the union consisted of just four sections—worship, education, hospitality, and benevolence. As new interests developed over the next four decades, committees proliferated. By 1908 it had become truly a multifaceted organization, whose thirteen committees ranged from an executive committee to committees on men's and boys' club work to a recently appointed social settlement committee. That same year, "a somewhat radical change in the management of the Union's work" occurred when it hired Carol Aronovici as head worker "to exercise a general oversight of the activities of the organization." The following year, Aronovici's "single admirable report" took the place of "separate reports from many committees," which were "helplessly disconnected, affording us little of the strengthening sense of being co-operative functions of one

[7] *First Annual Report of the Women's Christian Association* (Providence: Hammond, Angell & Co., 1868), 8; *Fifth Annual Report of the Young Women's Christian Association, Providence, R.I.* (Providence: Snow & Farnham, 1907), 10-11; *Sixth Annual Report* (Providence: Snow & Farnham, 1908), 12; Colette A. Hyman, "The Young Women's Christian Association and the Women's City Missionary Society: Models of Feminine Behavior, 1868-1920" (American Civilization honors thesis, Brown University, 1979), 53-54.

body." The union, declared its president, the Reverend George Kent, had at least come "together as a united living organism." In this way, the consolidation of what had been several committees manned by volunteers into a professional staff transformed the Union for Christian Work into a better coordinated, more efficient body—much like a machine. Like a machine, it was not a simple organism but a collection of highly developed and specialized functions. What had changed was federation at the top, not the differentiation of parts, over the years.[8]

Over-organization was yet a third reason for centralized administration. When the Providence Board of Trade was founded in 1868, there were few trade associations in the city. These mushroomed in the 1870s and 1880s as sundry producer groups began to feel the need for self-regulation or self-defense. In addition, Rotary, Kiwanis, and other service clubs that aimed at "harnessing the Golden Rule to Business" multiplied after 1910.[9] By 1914 there were at least thirty-two different commercial associations in Providence, all primarily concerned with promoting the interests of their respective trades or sections of the city. None, not even the venerable Board of Trade, represented "the whole Metropolitan District" or championed "projects that are for the benefit of all." It was precisely for this reason that the Board of Trade reconstituted itself as the Chamber of Commerce in 1914. Two years earlier, the United States Chamber of Commerce had superseded the National Board of Trade, which, dominated by powerful interest groups, had ceased to speak for the national business community. Editorials in the *Board of Trade Journal* during the months preceding the reorganization pointed out the limitations of more specialized associations. "We must either reorganize on a broader scale or altogether cease to exist," reported a special committee that had studied the situation. Interviews with more than two hundred businessmen and professionals convinced the Board of Trade's officers of the imperative need for change. A rapidly growing metropolis, all agreed, re-

[8] *Manual of the Union for Christian Work for 1869-70* (Providence: Providence Press Co., 1869), 8; *Manual of the Union for Christian Work for 1908* (Providence: Snow & Farnham, 1908), 3; Union Settlement, *Annual Report of the Head Worker for 1908* (Providence: n.p., 1909), 3.

[9] "Harnessing the Golden Rule to Business," *Providence Journal*, 26 December 1920; Charles F. Marden, *Rotary and Its Brothers: An Analysis and Interpretation of the Men's Service Club* (Princeton: Princeton University Press, 1935).

quired "centralized effort by a powerful representative body."[10] The new Providence Chamber of Commerce was intended to be just such a representative body. " 'Corporate limits' and dotted lines," it announced, "should not be recognized in the Metropolitan District of Providence."[11]

The concern for "system" that ran through the reports of the city's voluntary associations after 1890 reflected a dramatic change in epistemology. The faculty psychology taught in the antebellum college by moral philosophers like Francis Wayland had considered truth to be categorical and apprehensible through a well-developed moral sense. But under the combined influence of the German historical school and Darwinian evolutionism, truth came to have a history of its own, varying from place to place and from period to period. This changing epistemology dictated a new approach to social reform. Since society was, in the words of Carol Aronovici, "a dynamic organism growing constantly more complex, more heterogeneous and more highly differentiated in its functions," campaigns of righteousness that appealed to common values gave way to social surveys conducted by trained, impartial investigators. A new generation of reformers, typified by Shelby M. Harrison, one of the staff who conducted the pioneer Pittsburgh Survey in 1907-1909, insisted on the primacy of social facts: reform could proceed only through "the ascertaining of the facts in each particular case," or "the application of the inductive method to social questions."[12]

[10] *Board of Trade Journal* 25 (December 1913): 497; ibid. 25 (November 1913): 445. On the formation of the United States Chamber of Commerce, see Robert H. Wiebe, *Businessmen and Reform: A Study of the Progressive Movement* (Cambridge: Harvard University Press, 1962), 33-41.

[11] *Board of Trade Journal* 25 (December 1913): 497; *Providence Journal*, 15 November 1913. A similar concern about over-organization—or the "sudden multiplication of agencies" during the First World War—lay behind the transformation of community centers into community councils. As this occurred, community organization became functional as well as spatial. See John Collier, "Community Councils—What Have They Done and What Is Their Future?" *Proceedings of the National Conference of Social Work, 1919* (Chicago: Rodgers & Hall, 1920), 476-79.

[12] Carol Aronovici, *The Social Survey* (Philadelphia: Harper Press, 1916), 8; Shelby M. Harrison, *The Social Survey: The Idea Defined and Its Development Traced* (New York: Russell Sage Foundation, 1931), 10-11; Paul U. Kellogg, "The Spread of the Survey Idea," *Proceedings of the Academy of Political Science in the City of New York* 2 (July 1912): 1-17; Steven J. Diner, *A City and Its Universities: Public Policy in Chicago, 1892-1919* (Chapel Hill: University of North Carolina Press, 1980), chap. 3; Ward, "The Politics of Design," 80-82. Thomas L. Haskell contends that "interdependence," a recogni-

Interest in promoting efficiency gave rise to many of the federations forged in Providence. Typical was the Providence Society for Organizing Charity (SOC), organized in 1892. Pioneered in England, the charity organization movement spread to Buffalo in 1877. Inspired by Buffalo's success, leaders of the charity organization movement in Providence hoped to coordinate the "spasmodic and desultory" private alms giving carried on by the city's thirty-three benevolent societies, not to mention its churches and synagogues. Proponents of federation like E. Benjamin Andrews, president of Brown University, believed that the adoption of such bureaucratic (and corporate) features as functional specialization and centralized coordination would make relief work at once more efficient and systematic. They viewed the SOC's work as largely "administrative," designed to enhance the efficiency of participating agencies. "Our office is the 'central telephone exchange' of Providence charities," explained W.H.P. Faunce, president of both Brown University and the SOC, in 1906. "We try to keep the wires from crossing, to keep the 'house of have' in close intelligent touch with the 'house of want.' "[13]

---

tion of the interconnectedness of social phenomena, was the hallmark of this new epistemology, and that this sense of interdependence reflected contemporaries' "concrete social experience in an urbanizing, industrializing society." *The Emergence of Professional Social Science: The American Social Science Association and the Nineteenth-Century Crisis of Authority* (Urbana: University of Illinois Press, 1977), esp. 1-47 (quotation at 14-15). On the impact of the German historical school on American thought, see Jurgen Herbst, *The German Historical School in American Scholarship: A Study in the Transfer of Culture* (Ithaca: Cornell University Press, 1965); James Leiby, *Carroll Wright and Labor Reform: The Origins of Labor Statistics* (Cambridge: Harvard University Press, 1960); Benjamin G. Rader, *The Academic Mind and Reform: The Influence of Richard T. Ely in American Life* (Lexington: University of Kentucky Press, 1966), 28-53; and Morton White, *Social Thought in America: The Revolt against Formalism* (New York: Beacon Press, 1960).

[13] *First Annual Report of the Providence Society for Organizing Charity* (Providence: Snow & Farnham, 1893), 10; *Year Book of the Providence Society for Organizing Charity* (Barrington, R.I.: St. Andrew's School Press, 1906), 6, 3. On the national charity organization movement, see Roy Lubove, *The Professional Altruist: The Emergence of Social Work as a Career, 1880-1930* (1965; reprint, New York: Atheneum, 1980), esp. 1-21; Nathan Irvin Huggins, *Protestants Against Poverty: Boston's Charities, 1870-1900* (Westport, Conn.: Greenwood Press, 1971), 57-81; Kenneth L. Kusmer, "The Functions of Organized Charity in the Progressive Era: Chicago as a Case Study," *Journal of American History* 60 (December 1973): 657-78; Paul Boyer, *Urban Masses and Moral Order in America, 1820-1920* (Cambridge: Harvard University Press, 1978), 143-61; and Kathleen D. McCarthy, *Noblesse Oblige: Charity and Cultural Philanthropy in Chicago, 1849-1929* (Chicago: University of Chicago Press, 1982), 125-48.

While protecting families from unnecessary visitation, repeated questioning, and proselytizing by overzealous Protestants, the new federation eliminated the duplication, waste of time and money, and confusion that tended to "pauperize" recipients of aid, or make them "permanent public charges," instead of placing them in a position where they could become "self-supporting." A strictly nonsectarian agency, the SOC was the first permanent organization in the city to coordinate the work of Protestant, Catholic, and Jewish relief agencies. Indeed, its volunteers attributed the previous "lack of definite co-operation" among the city's relief agencies to "the sturdy individualism which is the peculiar heritage of Rhode Island." In coordinating charity activities, the SOC realized an old dream of volunteers: the division of the entire city into districts and the systematic registration of all charity recipients at a confidential central bureau.[14]

The systematization of charity work in Providence depended on increasing professionalization. With the appointment of James Minnick as general secretary in 1905, the SOC "definitely entered on a broader field of work." Social workers took over most of the administrative duties and even began to dispense alms, or cash relief, which until then had been forbidden by the SOC's constitution. The annual budget, which had averaged slightly less than $2,000, soared to $35,000 by 1917. The number of cases investigated rose over the same period from fewer than 300 each year to more than 1,600. To manage this ever increasing load, the SOC's professional staff divided the city into five districts, each staffed by paid field workers who met once a week to supervise the work of friendly visitors and discuss the treatment of individual families. In 1912 E. Frances O'Neill came to Providence to coordinate the casework of the district secretaries and establish case conferences in each district. As first supervisor of district work, then general secretary, O'Neill made many efforts to increase the number of friendly visitors at a time when volunteers, most of whom were women, felt the pull of new fields of social service. Before coming to Providence, her successor as gen-

[14] Carol Aronovici, "The Charitable and Philanthropic Organizations of Providence," in *Twenty-Third Annual Report of the Commissioner of Industrial Statistics* (Providence: E. L. Freeman Co., 1910), 140; *Annual Report of the Providence Society for Organizing Charity* (Providence: Franklin Press, 1904), 15.

eral secretary, Henry F. Burt, studied sociology at the Chicago School of Civics and Philanthropy.[15]

The gradual professionalization of charity work occurred at the expense of an older belief that friendly visiting and personal contact would promote class reconciliation and social harmony. Since the 1840s, when minister at large Edwin M. Stone began to make his rounds of the North End, it had been considered vitally important for the volunteer to experience the "wretchedness" of the poor first-hand. Friendly visiting, as the women of the Irrepressibles, an employment society, pointed out in 1877, narrowed the gulf between the rich and the poor: the visitor became "more alive to the welfare of the unfortunate" at the same time that the poor themselves benefited morally as well as materially. Moreover, this paternalistic touch kept "the work from degenerating into a mere mechanical routine, which is discouraging and demoralizing to those who are helped, and hardening to those who help."[16]

As a professional staff consisting of the general secretary and trained caseworkers assumed responsibility for the day-to-day management of the Providence SOC, a new rationale for expertise in charity work developed. In 1902 the SOC's annual report reprinted the remarks of Edward T. Devine, secretary of the New York SOC, as "especially pertinent to the present situation in Providence." Warning against "indiscriminate volunteer social service," Devine suggested that some would-be friendly visitors would be well advised to "do their social work by proxy." He added that "a picked band of a hundred devoted, trained and capable workers" would "not only accomplish more than a thousand untrained, unassorted volunteers," but "may actually do more to develop the genuinely spontaneous charitable tendencies of the whole population."[17]

As expertise and efficiency displaced morality in charity work, experts specially trained in the collection and interpretation of social data gradually took the place of the leisured volunteers who had

[15] *Year Book of the Providence Society for Organizing Charity* (Providence: n.p., 1916-17), 8; *Year Book* (Providence: Snow & Farnham, 1913), 8; *Chronicle* 2 (November 1922): 1-4. The *Chronicle* was the SOC's newsletter.

[16] *Fifteenth Annual Report of the Irrepressible Society* (Providence: Angell, Burlingame & Co., 1877), 11; *Eighteenth Annual Report* (Providence: J. A. & R. A. Reid, 1880), 9-10.

[17] Devine quoted in *Annual Report of the Providence Society for Organizing Charity* (Providence: Franklin Press, 1902), 17-18.

been recruited because of their wealth, social standing, or sense of noblesse oblige. These professionals, dedicated to a "scientific" or factual analysis of poverty without the moralizing proclivities of friendly visitors, interposed themselves between donors and recipients at the expense of the personal touch. Nonprofessionals were still wanted because they brought a "freshness" to "the work of family rehabilitation" that was often missing among social workers whose sympathy had been blunted by heavy caseloads. But the volunteers' role changed from bearing the brunt of administering charity, as well-meaning stewards, to contributing money and attending district conferences as tyros in social work. Not surprisingly, their number declined relative to the number of donors. The SOC's annual report for 1913, for example, listed seven caseworkers, fifteen friendly visitors, and seventy-two interested persons who had attended at least one district conference. Financial contributors that year far outnumbered volunteers. Although the number of volunteers subsequently rose to 166 in 1916, they nonetheless took a back seat to the professionals.[18]

Functional differentiation proceeded even further during the 1920s. Henry D. Sharpe, the efficiency-minded president of Brown & Sharpe and the SOC, believed that two further steps were necessary to consolidate the incremental gains made in charity work since 1892.[19] In 1923 Sharpe proposed the creation of a Council of Social Agencies, to be followed by the establishment of a community chest. "Providence," he explained, "needs a Central Organization not so much to develop co-operation, but to better co-ordinate the work of the various Social Agencies." Sharpe's proposal appealed to professional social workers, whose numbers had grown considerably since the turn of the century. They agreed with Sharpe that such a council promised to systematize charity work: each participating agency would henceforth define its work systematically, in relation to the work of other agencies. In May 1923 representatives from thirty social agencies attended the organizational meeting of the Providence

[18] SOC, *Year Book* (1913), 6, 14.
[19] Sharpe was the "principal organizer" of the Providence Governmental Research Bureau in 1932, a fact-finding agency to promote efficiency and economy in local government. *Evening Bulletin*, 30 April 1951. See also Norman N. Gill, *Municipal Research Bureaus: A Study of the Nation's Leading Citizen-Supported Agencies* (Washington, D.C.: American Council on Public Affairs, 1944).

Council of Social Agencies. Composed of two delegates from each affiliated agency, the council sought to promote unity among the city's social workers as well as to enhance their status. Its functions included sponsoring lectures by nationally known experts, making detailed surveys, and acting in an advisory capacity in helping the city's charity societies chart new lines of work.[20]

With the Council of Social Agencies established as a fact-finding agency, Henry Sharpe pressed ahead toward his second goal— bringing the community chest to Providence. By the mid-1920s the idea of a community chest, pioneered in Cleveland in 1913, had spread to Worcester, New Haven, Bridgeport, Springfield, and New Bedford. Only Boston and Providence, the two largest cities in New England, had not yet embraced the idea. Proponents of the community chest contrasted Providence's experience with that of Worcester, Massachusetts. In 1921 fewer than 5,800 individuals out of a population of nearly 240,000 contributed to the upkeep of twenty-three of Providence's major Protestant charities. More than 90 percent of the $224,000 given that year came from the 1,512 individuals who gave at least twenty dollars each. But in Worcester, which was smaller than Providence, there were nearly 40,000 contributors. The difference was that Worcester had a community chest, which tapped modest contributors as well as systematized alms giving.[21]

The organization of the Providence Community Fund in 1925 had a number of far-reaching consequences. At the same time that federation demoted the volunteer to mere financial contributor, it invested leadership in corporate managers like Henry Sharpe, who became its first president. The city's leading businessmen also welcomed the prospect of greater efficiency in charity relief. "It is a *sine qua non*," declared their official voice, the Chamber of Commerce, "that the financial federation be administered by a union of strong business direction and the best social leadership of the community." After renaming itself the Family Welfare Society, the SOC special-

[20] Sharpe quoted in *Chronicle* 3 (June 1923): 1; *Providence Journal*, 27 May 1923, 18 March 1925. By 1916 the Social Workers' Club of Rhode Island was sponsoring annual summer outings. *Providence Journal*, 25 June 1916.

[21] *Providence Journal*, 3 December 1925; Robert W. Burgess, *Statistical Survey of Contributions to Voluntary Community Organizations of Providence* (Providence: Rhode Island Foundation, 1921), 9-10; Providence Chamber of Commerce, *A Report Proposing a Federation for Financing Social Agencies* (n.p., 1925).

ized in "building up the family" through psychiatric aid, legal services, medical tests, and other measures that reflected the growing emphasis in social work on de-institutionalization. The creation of the Community Fund allowed the Council of Social Agencies to specialize as a fact-finding agency. The council thus advised the Children's Friend Society, when it applied for admission to the Community Fund in 1926, to discontinue the orphanage that it had maintained since the 1830s and take up the placement of children instead.[22]

Although it appointed prominent Catholics and Jews to its board of directors, the Providence Community Fund fell far short of systematizing charity work. Catholic agencies, which balked at joining what Bishop Hickey considered a "civic" undertaking, conducted their own fund drives. Jewish agencies were more eager to participate, but their participation had to await the establishment of their own federation. Moreover, a number of Protestant agencies in Providence never joined the federation. As late as 1936 only thirty-eight of seventy-eight private agencies were members. Finally, the Community Fund raised money only for member agencies' normal operating costs, not for building projects and other extraordinary expenses. Nevertheless, the fund broadened the base of support and increased contributions to the city's charities. Contributions went up from $224,000 in 1921 to $474,000 in 1926 and $569,000 in 1927; the number of contributors rose from fewer than 6,000 to more than 33,000.[23]

For all the emphasis on preserving organizational autonomy, federation frequently promoted standardization and conformity. The Rhode Island State Federation of Women's Clubs is a case in point. Until the formation of the General Federation of Women's Clubs in

[22] A Report Proposing a Federation for Financing Social Agencies; Providence Journal, 5 October, 3, 25 November, 3, 4 December 1925, 29 April 1926; Lubove, The Professional Altruist, 183-219; Morrell Heald, "Business Thought in the Twenties: Social Responsibility," American Quarterly 13 (Summer 1961): 134-35. On the SOC's evolution into the Family Welfare Society, see Chronicle 5 (January 1925): 2-4; Providence Journal, 31 October 1924. On de-institutionalization, see McCarthy, Noblesse Oblige, 139-48.

[23] Providence Journal, 3 November 1925, 13 January, 29 April, 31 October 1926, 16 November 1927; The Providence Survey: A Study in Community Planning, May, 1936 (New York: Community Chests and Councils, Inc., 1936), 16-18. Jesse Steiner discusses some of the limitations of the Community Fund in Community Organization: A Study of Its Theory and Current Practice, rev. ed. (New York: Century Co., 1930), 221-22.

1890, women's clubs in Providence were preoccupied with the self-culture of their members. Once federated, their focus gradually shifted from self-culture to Municipal Housekeeping, or the application of what was considered to be women's special sensitivity to community problems. As the state federation announced in 1903, "the Club call to-day is for social service rather than for self-culture." In part, this shift may have been the product of a second generation of clubwomen, who were better educated, possessed more occupational opportunities, and were consequently more active in the public sphere than their mothers had been. It may also have been a product of the depression that hit Providence and the rest of the country in 1893, which sensitized middle-class Americans to the suffering around them.[24]

But this shift from self-culture to reform also accorded with a more general cultural reorientation. Like so many of their contemporaries, clubwomen came to believe that a harmonious and well-ordered society depended less on campaigns of righteousness or on the community life of revitalized neighborhoods than on the systematic collection of data and efficient social organization. Accordingly, they began to pride themselves on their expertise as social investigators. In undertaking myriad social and political reforms, they did not so much reject their former interest in self-culture as build upon the skills they had cultivated in studying cultural topics. Reform was now rooted in the middle-class claim to expertise rather than in its custody of morality.

Sheer growth in the number of federated clubs in the state created a powerful lobby of middle-class women. "No longer is the need of Federation a subject of discussion," declared state president Lula A. Fowler in 1907. Through "investigation" and "united effort," clubwomen were exploring new "opportunities for service which are open to all." If "each club can arouse and educate public sentiment in its own circle," Fowler's predecessor, Margaret Hill Irons, had observed, "how much greater results we should obtain, if all clubs worked at once for one end." Although the clubs remained

[24] Rhode Island State Federation of Women's Clubs, Minutes, Executive Board and General Federation Meetings, 1902-1906, ann. report 1903, RIHS; Karen J. Blair, *The Clubwoman as Feminist: True Womanhood Redefined, 1868-1914* (New York: Holmes & Meier, 1980), chap. 6; David P. Thelen, *The New Citizenship: Origins of Progressivism in Wisconsin, 1885-1900* (Columbia: University of Missouri Press, 1972), 86-99.

largely segregated by religion and ethnicity—the Sarah E. Doyle Club, composed of public schoolteachers, was the most conspicuous exception to this rule—the State Federation of Women's Clubs nevertheless pooled the efforts of Protestant, Catholic, and Jewish women. It also opened up avenues of leadership for members of the ethnic middle classes. Thus Mrs. Caesar A. Misch, the widow of a prominent manufacturing jeweler and former president of the National Council of Jewish Women, served as president of the state federation from 1922 until 1925.[25]

Federation eventually funneled thousands of middle-class women into social reform. In 1900 the Rhode Island State Federation of Women's Clubs took its first hesitant step toward social service when it appointed a Committee on Kindergarten Extension and petitioned the State Board of Education to establish kindergartens in all the mill towns of the state. The committee disbanded after its proposal was opposed by the majority of school superintendents who replied. In 1901 new committees on civil service reform and traveling libraries were organized, and the state federation collaborated with the Rhode Island Council of Women in founding a state branch of the National Consumers' League. Over the next decade, the state federation joined the crusade against child labor, called for state and national laws to protect the American flag from use in advertising, advocated the establishment of a juvenile court system, and championed stricter divorce procedures. Although quick to endorse a metropolitan park system, pure food and drug legislation, and early closing for department stores, the state federation did not join the drive for woman's suffrage until the eve of the First World War.[26]

[25] Lula A. Fowler, "President's Greeting," in Rhode Island State Federation of Women's Clubs, *Year Book* (n.p., 1906-1907), 3; Margaret Hill Irons, "A Word from the President," *Year Book* (n.p., 1905-1906), 3; Eleanor F. Horvitz, "Marion L. Misch—An Extraordinary Woman," *Rhode Island Jewish Historical Notes* 8 (November 1980): 7-65.

[26] Rhode Island State Federation of Women's Clubs, Minutes, Executive Board and General Federation Meetings, 1894-1902, 10 February, 14 April 1900, 16 April, 1 June 1901; 1902-1906, 30 April, 12 July 1904; 1906-1909, 19 May 1906, RIHS. As late as 1916 suffragists complained that "although there are suffragists among the leading officers and members of the Rhode Island General Federation of Women's Clubs, yet it will not pass a resolution endorsing suffrage, nor admit the Rhode Island Equal Suffrage Association to membership." Agnes M. Jencks, "A Brief History of Woman Suffrage in Rhode Island," typescript, 6, Providence Public Library.

While serving as a vehicle for the new civic interest of clubwomen, federation had the unanticipated consequence of reducing the autonomy and standardizing the activities of most of the affiliated clubs. In 1906 the Rhode Island State Federation of Women's Clubs was reorganized so that its committees replicated committees in the General Federation. Committees on arts and crafts and on hospitality reflected the older emphasis on self-culture; others, however, indicated the growing involvement of clubwomen with pressing national concerns like civil service reform, women's education, child labor, and pure food. The state federation even created a Bureau of Information to correspond with a similar bureau in the General Federation. Local clubs were affected as well. Not only did practically all of them adopt a club motto, choose annual work, and review their activities in virtually identical yearbooks; sooner or later, they replicated the committees of the state and national federations—on civil service reform, industrial conditions and child labor, public health, and pure food. As this occurred, clubwomen in Providence increasingly acted in concert with middle-class women in other parts of the country.[27]

For Protestant churches as for women's clubs, federation proved to be a vehicle for social reform. State churches federated less out of any desire to replicate the centralized administration of bureaucratic corporations than as a response to the same conditions that had led firms to consolidate—proliferation of agencies, duplication of effort, and waste of energy. Spokesmen for the Social Gospel, critical of the individualistic emphasis of an earlier generation of Protestants, saw in federation a practical way to forge a social ethic. In the 1890s Josiah Strong, secretary of the Evangelical Alliance and author of the influential work, *Our Country*, proposed that churches band together "for the prosecution of social reforms." The influential Congregational minister Washington Gladden also advocated federation. One of the first acts of the Federal Council of Churches of Christ in America, established in 1908, was to adopt a "Social Creed of the Churches," which extended "the greeting of human brotherhood and the pledge of sympathy and help" to "the toilers of America." While proponents of federation in Rhode Is-

[27] Rhode Island State Federation of Women's Clubs, Minutes, Executive Board and General Federation Meetings, 1906-1909, 23 June, 22 September 1906, RIHS.

land were similarly inspired by the Social Gospel, they also sought to demonstrate that, through federation, the "religious democracy" of Protestantism could be "as wise and efficient as" the "arbitrary authority" or "religious aristocracy" of Roman Catholicism.[28]

A state census taken in 1905 underscored the problems then facing Protestants in "a modern city." First of all, their numbers relative to the city's population as a whole had long been declining. The census counted only 88,000 Protestants in Providence, as opposed to 102,000 Roman Catholics and almost 8,000 Jews. As a dwindling minority, Protestants could hardly claim that their religious identity was coextensive with the civic culture, a claim they had confidently asserted as late as the 1880s. Perhaps even more disturbing, Protestant churches were fast becoming mere middle-class institutions. Few wage earners worshiped there on Sundays.[29]

The same census also revealed that the concentration of their churches—either downtown or in the wealthier residential neighborhoods to the south and east—handicapped the city's Protestants in their attempts to convert the unchurched. "The three wards with the *smallest* population," noted the Reverend Lester Bradner, rector of St. John's Episcopal Church, "contain the *largest* number of Protestant churches. Put in another way, territory containing 26 per cent of the population holds almost 50 per cent of the Protestant churches, and these churches embrace 50 per cent of the total Protestant church membership in the city." While Protestants tilled an arid downtown or retreated to the city's wealthiest neighborhoods, the Roman Catholics concentrated their churches and their energy in the rapidly growing wards to the north and the west. Most Prot-

[28] Union Ministers' Meeting Committee, *To Providence Clergymen. The Federation of Churches* (n.p., 1901), 11-12; Winthrop S. Hudson, *Religion in America* (New York: Charles Scribner's Sons, 1965), 314. On how the Social Gospel promoted ecumenical cooperation, see Robert T. Handy's discussion of "Cooperative Christianity" in his *A Christian America: Protestant Hopes and Historical Realities* (New York: Oxford University Press, 1971), 170-74; ibid., "The Protestant Quest for a Christian America, 1830-1930," *Church History* 22 (March 1953): 15-17.

[29] The state census returns for 1905 are given in the *Providence Journal*, 27 January 1908. On the middle-class character of Protestantism, see Arthur M. Schlesinger, "A Critical Period in American Religion, 1875-1900," *Massachusetts Historical Society Proceedings* 64 (June 1932): 523-47; Paul A. Carter, *The Spiritual Crisis of the Gilded Age* (DeKalb: Northern Illinois University Press, 1971); and Gregory H. Singleton, *Religion in the City of Angels: American Protestant Culture and Urbanization, Los Angeles, 1850-1930* (Ann Arbor: UMI Research Press, 1979).

estant churches, especially those "supported by respectable and well-to-do people," tended "to be self-centred, while past their doors a stream of *les miserables* pours along for which the church can do nothing."[30]

A number of reasons accounted for the malaise that Bradner and other Protestant spokesmen sensed at the turn of the century. One source of what they pronounced a "declension" lay in the immigration of large numbers of non-Protestants—Irish, French Canadians, Italians, Jews, and Portuguese—who could not be converted to Protestantism. Protestant spokesmen also blamed religious indifference, which they rooted in the "material prosperity of the age," the "strenuousness of modern life," and the "increase of distractions and temptations," particularly commercialized amusements. Yet sounding remarkably like proponents of the charity organization movement, they singled out for blame inveterate "Protestant church-individualism," the byproduct of years of voluntaristic activity. Compared to Roman Catholicism, which was "splendidly organized," "Protestantism is not adequately organized; indeed, as a whole, it is not organized at all. Its numerous divisions and subdivisions have resulted in a multiplicity of small churches, many of which have exhibited weakness and decay instead of a vigorous growth." As a result, "duplication of effort and waste of energy have accompanied this fragmentary policy; and the social field has been cultivated haphazardly, the prosperous portions receiving an excess of attention, and the poorer sections suffering deplorable neglect."[31]

This diagnosis called into question the venerable tradition of voluntarism, whereby each church pursued its own interest without any regard for the general interest of Protestantism. Voluntarism not only led "to the establishment of churches among the well-to-do, the moving of churches into the better residence districts, and the abandonment of the 'down-town' and poorer regions of growing cities to chapels," it also fostered sectarian competition for a shrink-

[30] Lester Bradner, "Religion," in *A Modern City: Providence, Rhode Island, and Its Activities*, ed. William Kirk (Chicago: University of Chicago Press, 1909), 325-26; Edward S. Ninde, "The Down-Town Churches of Providence," *Providence Magazine* 26 (August 1914): 579-80; *The Proceedings of the Second Convention of the Churches of Rhode Island* (n.p., 1911), 39.

[31] *The Proceedings of the First Convention of the Churches of Rhode Island* (n.p., 1909), 21-22; Union Ministers' Meeting Committee, *To Providence Clergymen*, 4-5.

ing number of converts. "Sectarianism," as the Right Reverend William N. McVickar, the Episcopal bishop of Rhode Island, conceded, "makes us uncertain. It makes us weak and doubtful as to where we stand. It is altogether wretched." The Reverend George Kent, minister of Westminster Unitarian Church, also deplored "sectarianism and the refusal of churches to compromise for the sake of combination against the forces of mammonism and materialism."[32]

The city's Protestant churches adopted two distinct though not mutually exclusive strategies to cope with the dual problems of segmentation and sectarian rivalry. Some, especially those who decided to remain downtown instead of following their parishioners to the suburbs, experimented with institutional programs. Most, however, continued their pastoral ministries while exploring ways in which they could consolidate their efforts "in the interest of economy and efficiency." After studying the problems facing Protestants in a fragmented metropolis, the Union Ministers' Meeting concluded in 1901 that since "formal, organic union, upon any old basis of doctrinal or ecclesiastical uniformity, is impracticable for the present at least," federation was the only answer. "It is a form of voluntary cooperation that seeks to *organize* the great activities of the Christian churches, even as a charity organization society seeks to organize the existing charities of a given city." Through federation the discrete fragments of Protestantism gained a system, a view of the whole, that, as things stood, eluded the individual churches. "What is needed is *supervision*,—the allying, aligning and directing, in a comprehensive spirit and plan, of the constructive forces of the entire community."[33] Yet this new federation rested on "voluntary cooperation," not centralization. As a "clearing house," or "joint-bureau of information," it provided participating churches with the information they needed to redefine their missions. It also promoted comity among churches of rival denominations. In Providence as elsewhere, some of the most enthusiastic advocates of federation

[32] Union Ministers' Meeting Committee, *To Providence Clergymen*, 5; *Providence Journal*, 2 December 1905. For an incisive discussion of Protestant "voluntarism," see Sidney E. Mead, "The Rise of the Evangelical Conception of the Ministry in America, 1607-1850," in *The Ministry in Historical Perspectives*, ed. H. Richard Niebuhr and Daniel D. Williams (New York: Harper & Brothers, 1956), 207-249.

[33] Bradner, "Religion," 338-39; Union Ministers' Meeting Committee, *To Providence Clergymen*, 3, 10-11.

saw in it an institutional means to social as well as personal salvation.[34]

After an address by J. Winthrop Hegeman, founder of the New York City Federation of Churches, the Union Ministers' Meeting organized the Federation of Churches and Christian Workers of the State of Rhode Island in 1901.[35] Starting "with no cut-and-dried programme," the new organization preferred to copy programs that had worked well elsewhere. Many of these involved harnessing the methods of the social sciences to promote religion, in the process converting the church into a social agency. The Federation of Churches thus commissioned Professor James Q. Dealey and his students at Brown University to conduct a religious census. The "Co-operative Parish Plan" then drew on this information to assign more than sixty Protestant churches responsibility for evangelizing particular neighborhoods.[36]

The culmination of Protestant reorganization came in January 1912 when the Men and Religion Forward Movement held an "eight-day campaign" in Providence "especially devoted to social service." Launched by the Federal Council of Churches in 1911, the movement carried the gospel of Christian brotherhood to more than fifteen hundred communities across the country in an attempt to bring more men into the church. Spearheading the crusade in Providence was a Committee of One Hundred, chaired by Rathbone Gardner, senior warden of Grace Church. The Reverend Bradner headed up a simultaneous community survey that collected social data on a whole range of issues, from the percentage of illiteracy to the density of immigrant population. Once this information had been tabulated, Christian workers would be sent into previously neglected areas of social service.[37] The Men and Religion

[34] Federation of Churches and Christian Workers of the State of Rhode Island, *A State Federation of Churches—What Is It?* (n.p., 1910), 2-3.

[35] *Providence Journal*, 2 December 1905. On Hegeman and the New York City Federation, see Aaron Ignatius Abell, *The Urban Impact on American Protestantism, 1865-1900* (Cambridge: Harvard University Press, 1943), 188-91.

[36] Federation of Churches and Christian Workers of the State of Rhode Island, *Hand Book, January, 1907* (n.p., 1907), 11-14; *Providence Journal*, 2 December 1905. On the church as a social agency, see Charles Howard Hopkins, *The Rise of the Social Gospel in American Protestantism, 1865-1915* (New Haven: Yale University Press, 1940), 257-79.

[37] *Providence Journal*, 13 November 1911; miscellaneous material from the Men and Religion Forward Movement, 1912, RIHS; Orrin G. Cocks, "The Scope and

Forward Movement was a rehearsal for an even more ambitious postwar crusade for "social reconstruction," the Interchurch World Movement. This exercise in "religious planning" involved a five-year program for the state's churches based on extensive surveys. But in Rhode Island as elsewhere, financial contributions fell far short of millennial hopes for a Christian America.[38]

Federation enabled the city's Protestants to come to terms with the fragmentation of urban America into a plurality of competing interest groups. Some, like McVickar, who arbitrated labor disputes, defined a more specialized role for themselves as mediators between antagonistic interests. Others realized that they could no longer presume that municipal and state governments shared their interests. Like many other groups before them, Protestants realized that they too had to organize and forcefully voice their claims—especially on such "moral issues" as the desecration of the Sabbath.

Here the Federation of Churches performed perhaps its most important function—as a lobby. It thus supplemented the work of the Rhode Island Anti-Saloon League, the political arm of the Protestant churches.[39] Composed of representatives from all mainline denominations, even Unitarians and Universalists, who as liberal Protestants were still debarred from active membership in the YMCA,

Value of the Local Surveys of the Men and Religion Movement," *Proceedings of the Academy of Political Science in the City of New York* 2 (July 1912): 63-70; Hopkins, *The Rise of the Social Gospel in American Protestantism*, 296-98. The Men and Religion Forward movement, in turn, inspired a Labor Forward movement led by the American Federation of Labor. See Elizabeth Fones-Wolf and Kenneth Fones-Wolf, "Trade-Union Evangelism: Religion and the AFL in the Labor Forward Movement, 1912-16," in *Working-Class America: Essays on Labor, Community, and American Society*, ed. Michael H. Frisch and Daniel J. Walkowitz (Urbana: University of Illinois Press, 1983), 153-84.

[38] *Program of the Interchurch World Movement. State Training Conference for Rhode Island* (Providence: F. H. Townshend, 1919). For national perspectives on the Interchurch World Movement, see Donald B. Meyer, *The Protestant Search for Political Realism, 1919-1941* (Berkeley: University of California Press, 1960), 8-10; Hudson, *Religion in America*, 358-59; Handy, *A Christian America*, 186-97; Sydney E. Ahlstrom, *A Religious History of the American People*, 2 vols. (Garden City, N.Y.: Image Books, 1975), 2:382-85.

[39] On the Anti-Saloon League as the first "modern" pressure group, see Peter H. Odegard, *Pressure Politics: The Story of the Anti-Saloon League* (New York: Columbia University Press, 1928); K. Austin Kerr, "Organizing for Reform: The Anti-Saloon League and Innovation in Politics," *American Quarterly* 32 (Spring 1980): 37-53. See also Mark L. Asquino, "The Rhode Island Anti-Saloon League, 1899-1916" (seminar paper, Brown University, 1975), RIHS.

the Federation of Churches furnished "a means to voice the common Christian [that is, Protestant] consciousness." Since Protestants comprised "the more cultivated minority," the minority who still dominated the city's economic as well as cultural life, mobilizing Protestant pastors and laymen normally brought quick results. After a successful protest against Sunday amusements, one pastor remarked, "This alone would justify the organization." In another instance, repeated complaints from the Federation of Churches forced the Providence Police Commission in 1912 to cease its customary turkey raffle on Thanksgiving Eve and to warn parents to keep their children off the streets after 9 P.M. In yet a third instance, Protestant agitation closed four gambling resorts within three weeks. By 1912 the Federation of Churches had developed such a reputation for political prowess that legislators commonly called at its office "to learn its probable attitude" on bills pending before the General Assembly. No longer even purporting to speak for the entire community, Protestants had become one more parochial middle-class group—sometimes disinterested, more often than not self-interested—in a fragmented society, and had begun to act accordingly.[40]

The early history of the Federation of Churches illustrates the conditions that federation, as an organizational mode, was designed to overcome: highly decentralized activities pursued by a number of similar organizations often at cross-purposes to each other. In a society that was "over-organized," proponents of federation portrayed it not as a new organization but rather, in the words of the Federation of Churches, as "a joint-committee," indeed an ad hoc arrangement, "to learn all the facts and ally all the factors, in order to overcome our over-lapping, our over-looking, and our over-organizing." In January 1912, after churches representing more than 90 percent of the state's Protestants had joined the state federation, spokesmen declared that "we have steadily overcome the resistance of inertia, indifference, and sectarianism along a definite line,—that line along which our independent churches are moving from isolation or competition to interdependence and co-operation." Al-

[40] Bradner, "Religion," 347; Federation of Churches, *Hand Book*, 15; The Rhode Island Federation of Churches and Christian Workers, *Why It Is Worth Supporting* (Providence: Remington Printing Company, no date), 3; *Providence Journal*, 20 November 1912.

ready, a "Central Group" of Providence churches was cooperating to evangelize the downtown boardinghouse population.[41]

Federation was an organizational response to what was perceived as the over-organization of American society. This response became ever more imperative as churches dispersed. Called on to host a reception for the city's Protestant ministers in 1905, churchwomen realized that "though living in the same city and engaged in the same work, [they] were miles apart [as far] as any acquaintance went, for no two knew each other." In response, they organized the Woman's Auxiliary of the Rhode Island Federation of Churches. The Woman's Auxiliary, which claimed to be the first such society in the country, was clearly intended to promote social service. A questionnaire sent out to participating churches in 1911 asked, "Do you have *separate* Women's Societies for different objects, or *one comprehensive* ('Federated') Society?" Replies revealed that the "greatest problem" facing the women's church society was "the problem of the unenlisted." To drum up participation, the auxiliary recommended an annual "every woman canvass," where churchwomen's interests would be ascertained and met accordingly. Admitted to the Rhode Island Council of Women in 1910, it took an active part in campaigns against Sabbath desecration and for the ratification and enforcement of national prohibition. "Federation," declared the auxiliary's yearbook in 1923, "means church women organized ready for action, to wield the immense power which is theirs when all speak with one accord in 'unity of spirit.' "[42]

At the same time that businessmen, charity workers, clubwomen, and Protestants were forging translocal networks in response to the over-organization of American society, city planners turned to metropolitan federations as means of comprehending the city as a highly differentiated organism. "The improvement of a city the size of Providence is a tremendously complex problem," landscape architect Thomas W. Sears observed in 1911, "but not nearly as complex as it will be 50 years from now, if nothing is done until that time.

[41] Federation of Churches, *A State Federation of Churches—What Is It?*, 1; *What Church Federation Has Accomplished in Massachusetts and Rhode Island* (n.p., 1912), 1, 3.

[42] E. Tallmadge Root, *Local Federation the Next Step* (Boston: Pilgrim Press, 1927), 5; Woman's Auxiliary of the Rhode Island Federation of Churches, "Inquiry Sheet Regarding Women's Church Societies," 1911, Scrapbook, Records of the Rhode Island Council of United Church Women, RIHS; Federation of Women's Church Societies, *Year Book* (n.p., 1923-24), 3.

The need for parks and parkways is now commonly felt because so little was done 50 years ago." Originating as the City Beautiful movement, the crusade to federate Providence and its suburbs gradually expanded its focus from parks and parkways to city plan commissions, zoning ordinances, "thorofare" plans, and ultimately metropolitan regional planning. Throughout, city planners emphasized the need to correct what they regarded as the haphazard development of the past by means of comprehensive and systematic planning for future growth.[43]

The origins of the city planning movement in Providence, as in other American cities, dated back to the White City of the World's Columbian Exposition of 1893, which not only inspired Americans with a vision of a well-ordered and harmonious city but spawned a wave of monumental public buildings as well. Improvement associations, like the Public Park Association, also stirred interest in the City Beautiful.[44] Led by Augustine Jones, principal of the Friends' School, the Park Association pushed for a metropolitan park system in which parks and playgrounds would be developed in a "scientific" manner. Originally composed of elderly public men like Amos C. Barstow, the organization increasingly recruited attorneys, physicians, professors, and other members of the "new middle class." By means of an extensive "campaign of publicity"—which included photographic surveys, detailed maps, civic art exhibitions, student essays, and "post-card petitions"—the Park Association managed to persuade the General Assembly in 1904 to create a metropolitan park commission.[45]

[43] Sears quoted in *Providence Journal*, 13 November 1911.

[44] In 1906 seven organizations interested in "a better and more beautiful Rhode Island" federated as the League of Improvement Societies. Luther D. Burlingame, "State Civic Improvement and Park Association Organized," *Providence Magazine* 34 (August 1922), 405-409. My discussion of the City Beautiful draws on Jon A. Peterson, "The City Beautiful Movement: Forgotten Origins and Lost Meanings," *Journal of Urban History* 2 (August 1976): 415-34; Roy Lubove, "The Roots of Urban Planning," in his *The Urban Community: Housing and Planning in the Progressive Era* (Englewood Cliffs, N.J.: Prentice-Hall, 1967), 1-22; and Mel Scott, *American City Planning since 1890* (Berkeley: University of California Press, 1969), 31-109.

[45] Charles E. Lincoln, "Public Park Association's Notable Work: Chapter II," *Providence Magazine* 28 (September 1916): 589-93; *Providence Journal*, 5 June 1932. I have compared membership lists of the Public Park Association from the 1880s, in the Association's MS Records at RIHS, with a membership list from 1905. *Public Park Association* (Providence: E. A. Johnson & Co., 1905).

Chief architect of Rhode Island's park system was Henry A. Barker. Barker, whose father served as mayor of Providence from 1889
to 1891, had become interested in the City Beautiful while still a student at Brown. After graduating in 1893, he took a job with the
Rhode Island Electric Protective Company, eventually becoming its
president and general manager. He spent by far the greater part of
his time, however, devising plans for civic improvement. Observed
one friend upon Barker's death in 1929, "In all the years of our companionship, I never once saw Mr. Barker do a bit of work for himself." Said another, "It is a matter of common knowledge that Providence has seldom had a citizen so completely devoted to untiring,
unremitting and efficient labors for the upbuilding of Providence as
a community." After visiting Minneapolis in 1900, then in the middle of creating a park system planned by Horace W. S. Cleveland,
the landscape architect who earlier had laid out Roger Williams
Park, Barker launched a campaign for "a system of parks, playgrounds and parkways" that would integrate the city and its suburbs
into a true metropolis, a "Greater Providence." He feared that the
city's pell-mell growth was squandering its natural assets and jeop-
ardizing its individuality.[46]

Although the new commission consisted of officeholders from
the three cities and six towns included in the system and the presi-
dents of interested organizations like the Providence Board of
Trade, it was the five members representing the Public Park Association who framed policy. Likening their "function" to that of "a
board of directors of a great corporation," the commissioners defined their responsibility as maintaining "unity of action among the
agencies which [the commission] controls." Not surprisingly, they
looked to "Greater Boston" as "a model for local guidance." When
created in 1893, Greater Boston comprised thirty-seven cities and
towns and more than a million people. Believing that "park systems,
like other large, complex, and costly creations of human intelligence, should be carefully designed by trained men," the commissioners retained the services of the renowned firm of landscape architects, the Olmsted Brothers, as consultants.[47]

    [46] *Providence Journal*, 9 December 1906, 28 February, 1, 10 March 1929.
    [47] *Fifth Annual Report of the Board of Metropolitan Park Commissioners* (Providence:
E. L. Freeman Co., 1909), 61; *Second Annual Report* (Providence: E. L. Freeman & Sons,
1906), iii, 29, 42-45. The relationship between the Public Park Association and the

In their annual reports to the General Assembly the commissioners invoked the "economy of foresight." Just as the town's founding fathers had failed to reserve open spaces for commons and public parks, finally provided at considerable expense in the 1880s and 1890s, the city fathers of Greater Providence were slighting the recreational needs of future generations because of shortsighted parsimony. Wealthy Providence devoted less than 1 percent of its annual budget to maintaining its parks, whereas the "average city" expended 2.7 percent. The commissioners predicted that rapid population growth would soon lead to the commercial development of the remaining unspoiled "waste spaces" in the vicinity of Providence—rocky hillsides, deep ravines, craggy summits, and swamps—which had so far been spared because they seemed "the least adapted for commercial uses." If commercially developed, however, they would be "occupied by the things that are the meanest and the shabbiest in the city's growth." These waste spaces would repeat the experience of the once scenic Moshassuck River whose lower reaches had become "pestilence bearers" and "open sewers." In short, the commissioners insisted that Greater Providence "be developed logically and artistically instead of accidentally and whimsically."[48]

To demonstrate their contention that Providence and its suburbs constituted one unit, bounded by the five-cent trolley fare, the commissioners prepared detailed maps that showed a Greater Providence stretching nearly fourteen miles from Valley Falls and Lonsdale in the north to Warwick in the south. Although subject to nine different political jurisdictions, all these communities were served by a common system of sixty streetcar lines radiating from Market Square, Providence's civic center. Altogether, 360,000 people lived in Greater Providence, the nation's eleventh largest urban center. The commissioners' plans for wide, tree-lined boulevards, park-

Metropolitan Park Commission illustrates a common twentieth-century phenomenon. In the United States, a country with but a weak bureaucratic tradition, voluntary associations have frequently functioned as nurseries of administrative skills. Once acquired, these skills can easily be transferred from private to public agencies. Instructive in this regard is Robert L. Buroker, "From Voluntary Association to Welfare State: The Illinois Immigrants' Protective League, 1908-1926," *Journal of American History* 58 (December 1971): 643-60.

[48] *[First Annual] Report of the Board of Metropolitan Park Commissioners* (Providence: E. L. Freeman & Sons, 1905), 19, 54-55, 22, 16-17.

ways, and other "connecting links" were designed to federate Providence and its suburbs.[49]

After a nearly forty-year lapse, Providence residents were once again attending to the problems of fashioning a civic culture. Unlike mid-Victorian Providence, Greater Providence would not be built on any presumed consensus of values. Rather, it would be laid out in an orderly manner according to comprehensive plans devised by experts and administered by metropolitan commissions. Emphasis had thus shifted from institutions themselves, embodying a civic culture, to plans, layout, and foresight. "A beautiful city" was "not all sentiment," Mayor Daniel L. D. Granger had declared in 1902, it was also "a good business adventure, but a beautiful city does not continue beautiful without foresight. It costs little more to make a city pleasing to the eye than to make it ugly, but it does require thoughtful care."[50]

In November 1909 Henry A. Barker announced the arrival of the City Efficient, which had superseded the City Beautiful, when he proposed that Providence adopt a city plan. "Providence," he said, "like most cities, has spent millions in street widenings and extensions trying to undo the mistakes caused by the short sightedness of the past, but it has not yet learned any lesson of forethought, and the suburbs and newer quarters all around are growing up in an unregulated and planless way that sadly menaces the treasury of the future." Although "well ordered, well governed and tolerably clean," Providence needed "a carefully studied city plan more than anything else that can be thought of. It suffers greatly from individualism run rampant." The great challenge facing city residents was to "join and harmonize these crazy quilt patches" that had ensued from 273 years of haphazard development. Barker was only the first of many city boosters to insist that the time had come for a "definite scheme" to guide future development.[51]

Of all the civic organizations that took up the refrain for a city

[49] *Second Annual Report*, 3-6, 65-68.

[50] Granger quoted in *Providence City Manual* (Providence: Snow & Farnham, 1902), 33.

[51] Barker quoted in *Providence Journal*, 15 November 1909. My discussion of the City Efficient draws on Richard Piper, "The Beginning of City Planning in Providence" (undergraduate paper, Brown University, 1972), RIHS; John Hutchins Cady, *The Civic and Architectural Development of Providence, 1636-1950* (Providence: Book Shop, 1957), 213-19; Scott, *American City Planning since 1890*, 110-82.

plan, none matched the enthusiasm of the Rhode Island Chapter of the American Institute of Architects. "There must be a plan looking far into the future, for symmetry, harmony and fitness," declared president Franklin Sawtelle. Eleazer B. Homer, former director of the Rhode Island School of Design, agreed. "Nothing in Providence," Homer pointed out, "has ever been laid out in a comprehensive manner. One generation does a job here, and another one there, without very much consideration for permanent results, and the result is wasteful, extravagant and wholly inadequate to the public needs." The prospect of a city planning commission, which would presumably make use of their expertise, promised to strengthen these architects' claim to professional status, a long-standing concern. "There is a higher plane," insisted architect Howard Hoppin in distinguishing architecture from "the business of building things." "If it is a profession, as we so proudly assert, it must be carried on with dignity and highmindedness."[52]

To popularize the City Efficient, the Rhode Island Chapter of the American Institute of Architects sponsored a week-long planning exhibition in the fall of 1911. The exhibition, the first of its kind in New England and only the third to be held in the United States, generated so much public interest that it had to be extended another week. One visitor, Arnold Brunner, a New York architect who had helped draw up city plans for Rochester, Cleveland, Columbus, and Washington, came away with praise for "the natural assets" of Providence. "No other city in America," he commented, "has such charm of individuality, such a varied character of the things worth saving and cherishing as has your own city of Providence." In no other city were "so many things" either "being done" or "about to be done than in this one." The purpose of a city plan, Brunner explained, was not "to make the whole city over in a day," but rather "to lay out obvious work" so that future development might proceed "systematically." Thanks to the the lobbying of architects, business-

[52] *Providence Journal*, 10 March 1910, 5 November, 21 September 1911; Rhode Island Chapter of the American Institute of Architects, Minutes, 1906-1928, 1 February 1911, RIHS; John Hutchins Cady, "Some Reminiscences of the Rhode Island Chapter of the American Institute of Architects," typescript, Cady Papers, RIHS. In 1914 Mayor Joseph H. Gainer credited the chapter with contributing more than any other civic organization to the drive for a city plan commission. Minutes, 1906-1928, 13 January 1914.

men, and park advocates, the city council appointed a city planning commission in January 1914.[53]

The city council charged the new commission with the task of preparing "a comprehensive plan for the systematic and harmonious development of the city." Since the "function" of the commissioners was "to plan and propose, but not to execute," they had to depend on the cooperation of other municipal agencies. That cooperation was rarely forthcoming. Without a suspensive veto, the commissioners lacked the means to compel other agencies to submit proposed improvement projects to them for prior review. Their small budget, which averaged less than $3,000 a year, prevented them from hiring professional consultants. Never functioning as the clearinghouse originally intended, the City Plan Commission did little more than "program" or inventory potential improvements and review plans for the development of residential tracts in the city's sparsely settled "Northwest Territory."[54]

The City Efficient thus fell victim to the piecemeal development that it had been intended to correct. Following the First World War, city planning in Providence as elsewhere narrowed its focus to two issues that commanded overwhelming public support: zoning and traffic plans. "The most vital civic problem involving the physical arrangement of Providence to-day," reported the City Plan Commission in 1919, "is the matter of establishing a comprehensive Zoning Plan." Architect and city planner John Hutchins Cady described the problem that gave rise to zoning ordinances in cities across the country as the "germ of 'commercialitis.' " "The germ," he explained, "first creeps into the neighborhood in a most unobstrusive manner. Perhaps it's a 'rooms to let' sign, a little shop in someone's home or a dress-making card." Whatever the source, "the character of the district begins to deteriorate just a little bit. Other germs soon

[53] *Providence Journal*, 23 October, 6, 30 November 1911, 21 November 1913, 2, 5 January 1914.

[54] *Annual Reports of the City Plan Commission Providence, Rhode Island for the Years 1915-1920* (Providence: Oxford Press, 1921), 6; *Annual Reports, 1922-1928* (Providence: Oxford Press, 1929), 61; *Providence Journal*, 30 January, 12 July 1919, 12 June 1921; Cady, *Civic and Architectural Development of Providence*, 219; Kellner and Lemons, *Rhode Island*, 117. For a complaint about how "little consideration" city authorities normally gave to suggestions made by the City Plan Commission, see League of Improvement Societies in Rhode Island, *Year Book* (n.p., 1920-21), 8-9.

follow—one at a time they come in until the whole district is affected." The history of Elmwood Avenue, a boulevard lined with some of the city's finest dwellings, illustrated the "indiscriminate intermingling of structures having nothing in common." Laid out in the 1890s thanks to the efforts of the Advance Club, its smooth surface attracted car dealerships and automobile-related enterprises. Traffic congestion and limited parking downtown induced retailers to relocate along the boulevard, thereby accelerating its decline as an attractive residential site. Homes gave way to small shops, followed by larger stores and Chinese laundries. "Residents, alarmed at this invasion, moved elsewhere, and their former homes became converted into boarding houses."[55]

The best way to protect other middle-class residential neighborhoods from the invasion of unwanted commercial development involved the rigid segregation of land use. By 1921 zoning, first tried in New York City in 1916, had become a national craze. Without a municipal zoning ordinance, observers predicted that a similar fate would befall Waterman Street, the main artery from downtown Providence eastward to the Seekonk River. Already a ten-story apartment house, "entirely out of keeping with the surrounding single-family houses," had risen in the vicinity of Brown University, and factories were springing up near the river.[56]

Far from hopeful that the City Plan Commission could persuade the city council to enact a zoning ordinance, proponents turned to pressure-group politics. In February 1921 they organized the Citizens' City Planning Association. After the General Assembly passed enabling legislation, the new lobby brought a series of experts to Providence, including George B. Ford, often called the "father" of zoning, to confer with the city council. The *Providence Journal* quickly endorsed zoning as "the pivot of all other city planning, and the 'map' to guide all future expansion." "Will the future Providence expand in an orderly, systematic matter," the newspaper

[55] *Annual Reports of the City Plan Commission for the Years 1915-1920*, 41-45; *Providence Journal*, 5 March 1922.

[56] *Providence Journal*, 5 March 1922, 7 January 1923. Atlanta's famed Peachtree Street went the way of Elmwood Avenue. See Howard L. Preston, *Automobile Age Atlanta: The Making of a Southern Metropolis, 1900-1935* (Athens: University of Georgia Press, 1979), 78-82.

asked, "or will it just grow haphazardly, as it has for over 275 years?"[57]

Much like an earlier generation of boosters, typified by Hiram Howard, David M. Thompson, and other members of the Advance Club, proponents of zoning attributed urban fragmentation to haphazard development. They too insisted that proposed improvements be considered from a citywide rather than a partisan perspective. What had changed since the 1890s was the widely felt need for a comprehensive plan or "map" to guide the city's future growth. By the 1920s, the costs of unplanned growth had become too high to tolerate any longer. Although Providence had almost doubled in population, its central business district had not "materially expanded." Moreover, the population of many residential districts, particularly among the poor, had vastly increased without any commensurate expansion in area. The result was "gross overcrowding," from which stemmed immorality, crime, disease, and other ill effects of "unrestrained city growth."[58]

After practically no public opposition to the idea of zoning arose, the city council appropriated $20,000 and engaged the services of Robert H. Whitten, a planning consultant and author of the Atlanta Zone Plan. On the basis of his report, the council in 1923 promulgated a zoning ordinance that established a five-person review board with broad powers to grant exemptions. Arthur Henius, a dealer in precious stones who since 1919 had been a member of the City Plan Commission, was appointed the board's first chairman.[59]

Designed as a bulwark against neighborhood deterioration, zoning did nothing to relieve the city's traffic congestion, which by this time threatened to strangle the central business district. As late as 1900 automobiles had been rare sights in Providence. By 1904 they had grown numerous enough for the state to begin to register them and to license their drivers. In 1911, after the city council enacted

[57] *Providence Journal,* 5, 15 March 1922; Burlingame, "State Civic Improvement and Park Association Organized," 409-410.

[58] *Annual Reports of the City Plan Commission for the Years 1915-1920,* 44. By the mid-1920s Providence, like many other cities in the Northeast, faced an acute housing shortage. See Division of Industrial and Municipal Research, Massachusetts Institute of Technology, *Industrial Survey of Metropolitan Providence for the Year 1926* (Providence: Akerman-Standard Co., 1928), 9, 74-77.

[59] *Providence Journal,* 7 March, 12 May 1922, 22 May 1923.

its first comprehensive traffic ordinance, the police assigned nineteen men to a traffic squad and replaced the mounted patrol established in 1879 with a motorcycle squad. In the years between 1911
and 1920 the Fire Department was also motorized. In 1921, when
more than 43,000 automobiles were registered in the state, 3,450
traffic accidents resulted in ninety-eight fatalities. The high accident rate, charged John Hutchins Cady, secretary of the City Plan
Commission, reflected the haphazard manner in which streets and
highways had been laid out—along early lanes, rights of way, and
even "cow-paths." He demanded that traffic provisions be made before costly and permanent buildings were erected and while land
was still relatively cheap.[60]

In 1925 Robert Whitten returned to Providence, this time to
study the city's traffic patterns. After "a comprehensive and pains-
taking study and analysis of traffic data," Whitten expressed his
"sincere appreciation" for the city's "unusual personality." He predicted that "wise planning" would "foster and preserve [this] individuality." "Many American cities," Whitten explained, were "essentially cross-roads towns" that had "grown up at the intersection of
two highways." Although fortunately without "the monotonous
standardized appearance" of such cities, Providence was nonetheless "handicapped by traffic congestion." Every day, more than
6,600 streetcars and 145,000 other vehicles converged on its small
central business district. He thus proposed the construction of two
"trunk-line express roads," one running north-south, the other
east-west, as well as a system of arteries that would radiate from the
center of the city to a proposed beltway. Partisan wrangling between
a Democratic mayor and a Republican city council and General Assembly, however, kept Whitten's proposals from being implemented.[61]

Prospects for the metropolitan regional planning of Greater
Providence brightened after 1926. The abolition of the remaining

[60] *Providence Journal*, 8 January 1922; Kellner and Lemons, *Rhode Island*, 112-14;
Patrick T. Conley and Paul R. Campbell, *Providence: A Pictorial History* (Norfolk, Va.:
Donning Co., 1982), 147.
  [61] *Providence Journal*, 30 August 1925; *Providence Traffic and Thorofare Plan* (City of
Providence, November 1926), 3-9; Cady, *Civic and Architectural Development of Provi-
dence*, 242; Kellner and Lemons, *Rhode Island*, 117-18.

property requirements for voting in 1928 and the "Bloodless Revolution" of 1935 eliminated some of the factionalism that had plagued both municipal and state politics, ushering in Democratic rule in both the city council and later the General Assembly. Charter reform in 1939 abolished the Board of Aldermen, the last bastion of the city's GOP. In the meantime federal initiatives stimulated interest in planning. In 1933 the newly created National Planning Board, three experts charged with advising "the President on problems of long-range planning," proposed the creation of a state planning board, whose chairman would represent Rhode Island on a proposed regional planning commission for New England. Governor Theodore Francis Green, a former member of the City Plan Commission, complied by naming a temporary state planning board in March 1934. The following year, the General Assembly made this board permanent and mandated that all other state agencies submit plans for proposed improvements to the board for prior review. The Works Progress Administration furnished professional planners.[62]

"The question is not 'to plan or not to plan,' " declared John Hutchins Cady and Howard K. Menhinick, consultants for the state planning board in 1937. "Every community has to plan, every day." The real issue, they insisted, was "whether this planning shall be done piecemeal, hit or miss, in bits as each problem arises, or whether it shall be done in a broad, comprehensive manner in advance, for the entire city and the surrounding region, so that every time even a

---

[62] John Hutchins Cady, *Rhode Island State Planning Board, Six-Months Progress Report* (n.p.: Rhode Island State Planning Board, 1937), 1-4, 32, 37; *Annual Reports of the City Plan Commission Providence, Rhode Island for the Years 1932-1935* (Providence: Oxford Press, 1936), 35-36; Kellner and Lemons, *Rhode Island*, 127-29; David L. Davies, "Impoverished Politics: The New Deal's Impact on City Government in Providence, Rhode Island," *Rhode Island History* 42 (August 1983): 86-100. On the National Planning Board and the vogue of planning in the 1930s, see Charles E. Merriam, "The National Resources Planning Board: A Chapter in American Planning Experience," *American Political Science Review* 38 (December 1944): 1075-88 (quotation at 1076); R. G. Tugwell and E. C. Banfield, "Governmental Planning at Mid-Century," *Journal of Politics* 13 (May 1951): 152-53; Barry Dean Karl, *Executive Reorganization and Reform in the New Deal: The Genesis of Administrative Management, 1900-1939* (Cambridge: Harvard University Press, 1963), 76-79, 202-203; ibid., *The Uneasy State: The United States from 1915 to 1945* (Chicago: University of Chicago Press, 1983), passim; and Otis L. Graham, Jr., *Toward a Planned Society: From Roosevelt to Nixon* (New York: Oxford University Press, 1976), chap. 1.

small improvement is made it will fit perfectly into the scheme for the whole region, like a piece in a picture puzzle." In 1914, when the City Plan Commission was created, the challenge had been to comprehend the city proper as a vital organism. By 1937, however, planners were looking beyond the boundaries of the city to the metropolitan region. The ubiquity of the automobile, which made political boundaries seem irrelevant, was one reason for this shift toward "regional co-operation." Another was the small size of the city. Providence, less than nineteen square miles in area, was the smallest and most densely populated metropolitan district in the country. In their attempts to steer a middle way between haphazard development and annexation, which was politically infeasible, city planners looked to Greater London as a model. There the London County Council dealt with "common problems," or those affecting the entire metropolis, while "leaving the local or neighborhood ones to neighborhood control."[63]

The irony was that comprehensive planning was not without problems of its own; not only were the empirical data, or "facts," on which the planners based their projections always changing, but the regional scheme or puzzle into which these facts were fitted took on new configurations. Even with the professionalization of city planning and the adoption of increasingly sophisticated fact-gathering techniques, planners were frequently guilty of the same "lack of foresight" for which they reproached previous generations. Like many other products of the zoning craze of the early 1920s, the city's zoning plan vastly overestimated the central business district's rate of growth, reserving far too much land for business and industry and far too little for residential development. Consequently, those residential areas zoned for commercial development into which business failed to expand suffered premature "blight," while city residents fled to the suburbs in search of better housing. By 1934 it had become clear that the city would have to be re-zoned to "stimulate home building and home improvements." By then, too, it had become clear that something had to be done about the city's

[63] John Hutchins Cady and Howard K. Menhinick, *Planning and Zoning in Rhode Island* (Providence: Rhode Island State Planning Board, 1937), 1; *Annual Reports of the City Plan Commission for the Years 1922-1928*, 68-74 (quotation at 74); Teaford, *City and Suburb*, 105-122.

traffic congestion. Although suited to the city's peculiar topography, the radial arteries that Whitten hoped to incorporate into his Thorofare Plan funneled too much automobile traffic into a congested downtown. In 1947 another expert pronounced the city's radial-concentric street pattern to be one of the country's worst. Even while generating a number of programs to guide future growth, planning did not always prevent haphazard and wasteful development.[64]

City planners attempted to federate Providence and its suburbs for many of the same reasons that impelled social workers, clubwomen, and Protestants to forge their own translocal networks. Barker, Cady, and other planners hoped to curb urban fragmentation, which they identified with partisanship, or the pursuit of narrow self-interest. A pluralistic society, they felt, had become too mired in particularism to strive for that corporate sentiment which, as Dr. William F. Channing had pointed out many years earlier, distinguished a city from a village. In the eyes of Barker and his contemporaries, a modern city resembled a machine; it was a complex organism, whose neighborhoods were differentiated not only along class and ethnic lines but also along functional lines. The challenge, then, was to integrate the city and its suburbs into a translocal federation or "federative metropolis." Much like Taylor and Gilbreth in industry, city planners hoped to systematize urban development—first through city planning commissions, then zoning ordinances and "thorofare" plans, and eventually mechanisms for metropolitan government—so that each neighborhood (and suburb), properly ordered, could be brought to its highest state of excellence. Throughout, their concern was with the totality, the metropolitan region, rather than with the parts, the neighborhoods that were so important to recreational reformers.

The notion that the city was a complex organism requiring expert guidance according to scientific plans appealed to middle-class

[64] Frederick L. Ackerman, "Building Cities Without Inventories: A Note With Reference to the Providence Survey," in *Annual Reports of the City Plan Commission for the Years 1932-1935*, 21-25; L. H. Weir, *Report of a Study of Public Recreation in the City of Providence, R.I.* (Providence: n.p., 1934-35), 8; *Annual Reports of the City Plan Commission, Providence, Rhode Island, for the Years 1936-1938* (Providence: Oxford Press, 1939), 14-15; Conley and Campbell, *Providence*, 198; Scott, *American City Planning since 1890*, 192-98.

groups who, like architects, city planners, and businessmen, were in the process of professionalizing and who worshiped efficiency, expertise, and system. But still other middle-class groups—notably housewives, academics, and white-collar workers—subscribed to a different vision. No longer able to define themselves as producers, they joined the consumer movement. Critical of what they regarded as the "functional representation" of well-organized producers, they attempted to persuade the federal government to represent consumers, who, they argued, were more representative of the public interest than any group of producers. In so doing, they relocated a classless, homogeneous society not in the broad producers' community that Lucius F. C. Garvin and other middle-class moralists hoped to re-create, but in consumers' cooperatives.

8 Consumers Organize

In the years between the 1880s and the 1930s, Single Taxers, Christian socialists, prohibitionists, and other kindred spirits championed nonpartisanship and political independence in a vain attempt to re-create the antebellum moral community. Settlement and recreational reformers, adapting themselves to occupational differentiation if not to the pluralism of American society, attempted to reconstruct a fragmented urban society around settlement houses, institutional churches, socialized schools, and other neighborhood centers. Still other middle-class groups, among them businessmen, social workers, architects, and city planners, struggled to reintegrate their society along functional lines. Adopting corporate models, they turned to federation, which appeared to offer all the advantages of centralized administration without the disadvantages of standardization and uniformity. In a fourth version of community, housewives, academics, and white-collar workers defined themselves as consumers, the middle element between organized capital and organized labor.

The consumer movement developed gradually after 1890. Until the First World War, it was limited largely to housewives, who practiced selective buying to bring about protective legislation for women and children and organized consumer boycotts to fight the high cost of living. During the 1920s the movement incorporated academics, white-collar workers, and other members of the "new middle class" who no longer thought of themselves as producers. By 1933 it was strong enough for consumer advocates to demand representation of the consumer interest in the councils of government. The development of the consumer movement reflected in part the evolution of a service economy, the phenomenal growth of advertising, rising concern about food adulteration, and alarm over the high cost of living. But it reflected as well attempts to resolve certain strains within middle-class culture.

The consumer movement was a product of the reorientation of the American economy from the production of goods to the distribution of services. Whereas in 1870 almost four out of every five American workers were engaged in the production of goods, by 1930 the proportion had slipped to slightly more than one in two. While agricultural employment fell from over half of the total work force to a little more than a quarter, those engaged in manufacturing and mechanical occupations increased from 22 to 33 percent, and those engaged in the exchange and distribution of goods doubled from only a tenth of the labor force to more than a fifth. In their contribution to *Recent Social Trends in the United States*, the report issued in 1933 by President Hoover's Research Committee on Social Trends, Ralph Hurlin and Meredith Givens noted the "vast and growing army of workers in wholesale and retail trade, in financial employments and in the public utilities which provide the means of transportation and communication." This expansion of white-collar work particularly affected single young women, who were increasingly employed outside the home. Female stenographers, almost negligible in number in the 1870s, numbered 800,000 by 1930. Rhode Island, with a higher proportion of its workers engaged in manufacturing than any other state in the Union, likewise experienced a substantial expansion of its service sector—from 38 percent of all gainfully employed workers in 1920 to 45.5 percent in 1930 and 46.3 percent in 1940.[1]

Rising real income for most Americans fueled this expansion of the service sector. Adjusted for changes in the price level, real wages increased by half from $1.00 a day in 1865 to $1.50 by 1890. Annual earnings over the same period rose from $300 to more than $425. Even though prices began to rise once again in the late 1890s, real wages continued to climb for many wage earners right up to the eve of the First World War. By 1914 real daily wages stood at $2.00 and annual earnings averaged between $550 and $600 per worker. The income of the typical Rhode Island wage earner rose from $408 in 1899 to $1,157 in 1927, in real dollars a 155 percent increase.[2]

[1] Ralph G. Hurlin and Meredith B. Givens, "Shifting Occupational Patterns," in President's Research Committee on Social Trends, *Recent Social Trends in the United States: Report of the President's Research Committee on Social Trends* (New York: McGraw-Hill, 1933), 268-324 (quotation at 285); Kurt B. Mayer, *Economic Development and Population Growth in Rhode Island* (Providence: Brown University Press, 1953), 62-63. On the committee, see Barry D. Karl, "Presidential Planning and Social Science Research: Mr. Hoover's Experts," *Perspectives in American History* 3 (1969): 347-409.

[2] Clarence D. Long, *Wages and Earnings in the United States, 1860-1890* (Princeton:

Rising real income meant more money spent on goods and services as food, clothing, housing, and the other necessities of life consumed smaller proportions of family budgets. A study of the consumption patterns of working-class families in New York City at the turn of the century found that as their incomes rose, families spent more on "the luxuries of life." A "critical analysis" of the family budgets of various American wage earners concluded that workingmen and their families "were maintaining a higher standard of living in 1918 than they were in 1901."[3]

Quick to capitalize on this substantial growth in discretionary income were the dry goods merchants who converted their establishments into department stores or "palaces of consumption." During the 1850s and 1860s department stores sprouted on both sides of the Atlantic. In 1862 A. T. Stewart opened his Astor Place store in New York City. His example soon inspired a host of imitators, including Rowland C. Macy in New York, John Wanamaker in Philadelphia, Marshall Field in Chicago, and Edward A. Filene in Boston. By 1886, when dry clerks staged their futile campaign for early closing, Providence boasted several immense emporia in what was rapidly becoming the central business district. Stores like Gladding's, which claimed to be the oldest department store in New England, and Shepard's, which by 1900 employed more than 1,400 men, women, and children in sixty-eight different departments, competed for the carriage trade. Manufacturers' Outlet, which adopted the slogan "more for less," catered to working-class customers by lowering its prices, advertising extensively, and providing free trolley transfers.[4]

Princeton University Press, 1960); Albert Rees, *Real Wages in Manufacturing, 1890-1914* (Princeton: Princeton University Press, 1961); Henry W. Mann, *Manufacturing in Rhode Island* (Providence: Rhode Island State Planning Board, 1937), 58-59.

[3] Louise Bolard More, *Wage-Earners' Budgets: A Study of Standards and Cost of Living in New York City* (New York: Henry Holt & Co., 1907), 267; National Industrial Conference Board, *Family Budgets of American Wage-Earners: A Critical Analysis* (New York: Century Co., 1921), 67. See also Elizabeth Ellis Hoyt, *The Consumption of Wealth* (New York: Macmillan Co., 1928), 286-87; Persia Campbell, *The Consumer Interest: A Study in Consumer Economics* (New York: Harper & Brothers, 1949), 40-95; John Modell, "Patterns of Consumption, Acculturation, and Family Income Strategies in Late Nineteenth-Century America," in *Family and Population in Nineteenth-Century America*, ed. Tamara K. Hareven and Maris A. Vinovskis (Princeton: Princeton University Press, 1978), 206-240.

[4] On the city's department stores, see Charles Carroll, *Rhode Island: Three Centuries*

View of downtown Providence from College Hill, showing the Industrial Trust Company under construction, 1928 (courtesy of the Rhode Island Public Library)

The emergence of the department store revolutionized retail practices. The small, highly specialized shop that had previously dominated retail trade gave way to the functionally organized department store. As this occurred, a single-price system replaced the haggling and multiple prices characteristic of earlier modes of retailing. Prices fell as profits came to depend less on high markups than on volume selling and rapid turnover. In the meantime luxury was "democratized." Elaborate window displays and immense assortments of goods for sale disseminated standardized goods, the shopping habit, and a taste for luxury among all social classes, but particularly among leisured middle-class women, who were the stores' best customers.[5]

As America evolved from a goods-producing into a service economy, advertising became increasingly important. Advertising volume, approximately $104 million in 1880, exceeded $256 million only twenty years later. It climbed to $684 million in 1914, then soared to more than $2.9 billion in 1929. In Providence as elsewhere, advertising agencies sprang up to cater to the needs of manufacturers and distributors. From only one listed in the Providence business directory in 1885, they numbered ten by 1900. In 1910 men "interested in publicity and sales promotion" established the Town Criers of Rhode Island. Within two years, the Town Criers boasted more than 500 members and claimed to be one of only two

of Democracy, 4 vols. (New York: Lewis Historical Publishing Co., 1932), 2:916-19; Charles E. Lincoln, "Shops and Stores of Providence," Providence Magazine 29 (January 1917): 18-22; Patrick T. Conley and Paul R. Campbell, Providence: A Pictorial History (Norfolk, Va.: Donning Co., 1982), 176; George H. Kellner and J. Stanley Lemons, Rhode Island: The Independent State (Woodland Hills, Calif.: Windsor Publications, 1982), 114; Sharon Hartman Strom, "Old Barriers and New Opportunities: Working Women in Rhode Island, 1900-1940," Rhode Island History 39 (May 1980): 50-51.

5 See Michael B. Miller, The Bon Marché: Bourgeois Culture and the Department Store, 1869-1920 (Princeton: Princeton University Press, 1981); Daniel J. Boorstin, The Americans: The Democratic Experience (New York: Vintage Books, 1974), 101-109; Neil Harris, "Museums, Merchandising, and Popular Taste: The Struggle for Influence," in Material Culture and the Study of American Life, ed. Ian M. G. Quimby (New York: W. W. Norton & Co., 1978), 140-74; Susan Porter Benson, "Palace of Consumption and Machine for Selling: The American Department Store, 1880-1940," Radical History Review 21 (Fall 1979): 199-221; Gunther Barth, City People: The Rise of Modern City Culture in Nineteenth-Century America (New York: Oxford University Press, 1980), 110-47; and William R. Leach, "Transformations in a Culture of Consumption: Women and Department Stores, 1890-1925," Journal of American History 71 (September 1984): 319-42.

such clubs in the country "to have engaged in a scientific study of the 'Principles of Advertising Arrangement.'" By 1920 there was a Women's Advertising Club.[6]

Advertising was integral to the new service economy. Until the 1890s, ads simply announced goods on hand as advertisers assumed consumer familiarity with the product. After the turn of the century, however, businessmen attempted to persuade shoppers to insist on distinctive brand names. Advertising by producers themselves soon surpassed that by distributors. Food processors, cosmetic manufacturers, tobacco firms, automobile makers, and other capital-intensive companies burdened with high fixed costs relied on advertising to differentiate their products from those of competitors in national markets. In the meantime interest grew in the nature of consumption. Shortly after the turn of the century, Walter Dill Scott began to investigate "the psychology of advertising." During the First World War psychological research and propaganda techniques developed by the Committee on Public Information set the stage for the full-blown emergence of advertising during the twenties. John B. Watson, professor of psychology at Johns Hopkins before becoming vice president of the huge advertising agency of J. Walter Thompson in 1919, formulated "Behaviorism," which provided advertisers with a theory of environmental manipulation. Edward Bernays, a nephew of Sigmund Freud, explored the implications of "mass psychology." During the 1920s, advertisers achieved prominence as salesmen of corporate capitalism. Bruce Barton, founder of the advertising firm Barton, Batten, Durstine, and Osborn, also sold religion. In *The Man Nobody Knows*, a best seller published in 1925, Barton, the son of a liberal Congregational minister, portrayed Jesus Christ as the "founder of modern business."[7]

[6] *Providence Journal*, 24 February 1910, 23 July 1920; *Town Crier. Rhode Island* 1 (December 1912): 2. Figures on advertising volume are taken from Daniel Pope, *The Making of Modern Advertising* (New York: Basic Books, 1983), 26.

[7] My discussion of advertising draws on Otis Pease, *The Responsibilities of American Advertising: Private Control and Public Influence, 1920-1940* (New Haven: Yale University Press, 1958); David M. Potter, "The Institution of Abundance: Advertising," in his *People of Plenty: Economic Abundance and the American Character* (Chicago: University of Chicago Press, 1954), 166-88; Boorstin, *The Americans: The Democratic Experience*, 137-56; Stuart Ewen, *Captains of Consciousness: Advertising and the Social Roots of the Consumer Culture* (New York: McGraw-Hill, 1976); T. J. Jackson Lears, "The Rise of American Advertising," *Wilson Quarterly* 7 (Winter 1983): 156-67; Stephen Fox, *The Mirror Makers: A History of American Advertising and Its Creators* (New York: William

Advertising's importance reflected the salience of a new problem: the imbalance between supply and demand. Whenever supply outran demand, prices fell, competition intensified among producers, and depressions ensued. This is precisely what happened in 1884-86, the first depression that had not been precipitated by a financial panic. Even before then a number of economists had begun to re-examine the doctrines of classical economics. Some, notably William Stanley Jevons, Carl Menger, and other members of the marginal utility school, formulated a subjective theory of value. "The theory of Economics," Jevons declared, "must begin with a correct theory of consumption." American economist Simon N. Patten went even farther, replacing "the assumption of scarcity," upon which classical economics had been premised, "with an assumption of potential abundance."[8]

Consumer consciousness was thus rooted in the structural transformation of the American economy and the growing emphasis placed by sellers, advertisers, and economists on consumption. But it stemmed also from two recurrent sources of anxiety for consumers—the adulteration of food, drugs, and cosmetics; and inflation. Public outcry following the publication of *The Jungle*, Upton Sinclair's exposé of the appalling conditions of meat-packing plants in Chicago, helped persuade Congress to pass the Pure Food and Drug Act in 1906. Of the almost two hundred measures designed to curb the adulteration of food that had been introduced into Congress between 1879 and 1906, only eight had become law. Yet sentiment for federal legislation mounted inexorably. From his post as head of the Bureau of Chemistry in the Department of Agriculture, Harvey Wylie proselytized "the ethics of pure food." The American Medical Association, which in 1899 established a Committee on National Legislation, pushed for pure food legislation. So too did middle-class women. In 1903 the Rhode Island Council of Women went on record in favor of legislation preventing adulteration. Two years

Morrow & Co., 1984); Pope, *The Making of Modern Advertising*. Leo P. Ribuffo brings out Barton's complexity in "Jesus Christ as Business Statesman: Bruce Barton and the Selling of Corporate Capitalism," *American Quarterly* 33 (Summer 1981): 206-231.

[8] Jevons quoted in Hazel Kyrk, *A Theory of Consumption* (Boston: Houghton Mifflin Co., 1923), 133; Daniel M. Fox, *The Discovery of Abundance: Simon N. Patten and the Transformation of Social Theory* (Ithaca: Cornell University Press, 1967), 11; Daniel Horowitz, "Consumption and Its Discontents: Simon N. Patten, Thorstein Veblen, and George Gunton," *Journal of American History* 67 (September 1980): 301-317.

later, the Rhode Island State Federation of Women's Clubs similarly endorsed a pure food bill. Even before the publication of *The Jungle*, most states provided for the regulation of food, beverages, and drugs.[9]

Concern about "the high cost of living" was yet another source of consumer consciousness. In the late 1890s prices began to rise, after having fallen since the end of the Civil War. Between 1897 and 1914 the cost-of-living index rose by approximately 2 percent per year. Food prices rose nationally by 36.7 percent between 1900 and 1913, with the prices of some commodities nearly doubling. In 1902, when advancing prices and the threat of a winter coal shortage prompted Theodore Roosevelt to mediate a national anthracite strike, Providence mayor Daniel L. D. Granger called an emergency conference to devise contingency plans for "a condition which affects all of the citizens, rich and poor alike." Prices rose even more rapidly after 1902. If in 1909 food prices were still lower in Providence than in other New England cities, according to a survey conducted by the commissioner of industrial statistics, by 1917 they were reportedly the highest in the country. The Armistice brought little relief. In 1921 Providence, declared the *Providence Journal*, was "well in the lead among representative cities in which living is regarded as an increasing luxury." By 1926 retail prices were 60 percent higher than they had been in 1913.[10]

<hr>

[9] Rhode Island Council of Women, Minutes, 1902-1906, 26 January 1903, RIHS; Rhode Island State Federation of Women's Clubs, Minutes, Executive Board and General Federation Meetings, 1902-1906, 13, 20 May 1905, RIHS; Robert M. Crunden, *Ministers of Reform: The Progressives' Achievement in American Civilization, 1889-1920* (New York: Basic Books, 1982), 163-99; Peter Edward Samson, "The Emergence of a Consumer Interest in America, 1870-1930" (Ph.D. diss., University of Chicago, 1980), chap. 3.

[10] *Providence Journal*, 3 October 1902, 27 November 1917, 26 November 1918, 20 August 1921, 19 June 1926; "Wholesale and Retail Prices of Food," in *Twenty-Third Annual Report of the Commissioner of Industrial Statistics* (Providence: E. L. Freeman Co., 1910), 1-24; Samson, "The Emergence of a Consumer Interest," 24-25. An industrial survey of metropolitan Providence commissioned in 1926 by the Providence and Pawtucket Chambers of Commerce reported that "food, fuel and clothing are relatively expensive compared with other New England and Northeastern cities." Only local rents were significantly lower. Division of Industrial and Municipal Research, Massachusetts Institute of Technology, *Industrial Survey of Metropolitan Providence for the Year 1926* (Providence: Akerman-Standard Co., 1928), 74. National figures are from Peter R. Shergold, "Wage Differentials Based on Skill in the United States, 1899-1914: A Case Study," *Labor History* 18 (Fall 1977): 505.

Contemporary observers traced inflation, sometimes referred to as "the cost of high living," to a number of sources: to rising alcohol consumption, to monopoly and "the unearned increment," and to "consumers' want of organization." Many viewed rising prices as a threat to thrift, deferred gratification, and other hallowed values. By 1910 a chorus of economists, academics, and social commentators bemoaned the impact of inflation on the legendary self-discipline of the American middle classes. In their eyes inflation encouraged conspicuous consumption. Others thought that inflation explained why middle-class Americans were having fewer children. A few prescient observers, however, noted that inflation promoted consumer consciousness. "As prices continue to rise," observed Patten's student Walter Weyl in 1912, "a new insistence is laid upon the rights of the consumer, and political unity is based upon him." "We are finding," wrote Walter Lippmann in 1914, "that the real power emerging to-day in democratic politics is just the mass of people who are crying out against the 'high cost of living.' " Lippmann predicted that the consumer interest, especially after women obtained the franchise, was "destined to be stronger than the interests either of labor or of capital."[11]

[11] Albert S. Bolles, "Rising Prices: Their Causes, Consequences and Remedies," *North American Review* 191 (June 1910): 795-804; "Washington Notes," *Journal of Political Economy* 18 (October 1910): 637-38; Christine Terhune Herrick, "Concerning Race Suicide," *North American Review* 184 (15 February 1907): 407-412; Frederic C. Howe, *The High Cost of Living* (New York: Charles Scribner's Sons, 1917); Walter E. Weyl, *The New Democracy: An Essay on Certain Political and Economic Tendencies in the United States* (New York: Macmillan Co., 1912), 251; Walter Lippmann, *Drift and Mastery: An Attempt to Diagnose the Current Unrest* (New York: Mitchell Kennerley, 1914), 71; Richard Hofstadter, *The Age of Reform: From Bryan to F.D.R.* (New York: Vintage Books, 1955), 168-73; Samson, "The Emergence of a Consumer Interest," 112-21; Daniel Pope, "American Economists and the High Cost of Living: The Late Progressive Era," *Journal of the History of the Behavioral Sciences* 17 (January 1981): 75-87. Ironically, studies cited by Pope suggest that middle-class Americans, because they tend to have more nominal debt, are in reality less affected by inflation than either the rich or the poor. Nonetheless, by widening the gap in real income between rich and poor, inflation fueled middle-class fears of class conflict (p. 79). In his study of progressive reform in Wisconsin, David P. Thelen argues that a coalition of "aroused consumers and taxpayers" coalesced in the aftermath of the panic of 1893 to challenge "a producer-oriented establishment that constantly thwarted the will of the majority." *The New Citizenship: Origins of Progressivism in Wisconsin, 1885-1900* (Columbia: University of Missouri Press, 1972), 2. In a recent essay, Thelen elaborates on his thesis that "the drive by consumers to restore discipline over productive processes . . . gave distinctive elements to the American progressive movement." Thelen also emphasizes con-

These long-term economic trends help account for the emergence of what can be called a national consumer culture.[12] They do not, however, explain why certain groups of middle-class Americans began to define themselves as consumers. Other factors, particularly the confluence of three separate currents, crystallized consumer consciousness in the first three decades of the twentieth century. The first, coming out of the working girls' club movement of the 1880s, stressed the moral responsibility of the consumer to the worker, particularly the working woman. The second, a product of the home economics movement, looked forward to the professionalization of the home. The third, an outgrowth of the demand for product standardization during the twenties, called for expert help in aiding consumers to cope with the plethora of goods for sale. Once limited to housewives, the consumer movement incorporated members of the new middle class, particularly professionals and white-collar workers, whose numbers had multiplied since 1870. By the mid-1930s enough middle-class Americans had identified themselves as consumers to demand that government represent the consumer interest.[13]

The first two strains of consumer consciousness emphasized the relationship of the home to the marketplace, and of consumption to production. Both attempted to come to terms with what Florence Kelley, secretary of the National Consumers' League, described as "the exodus of manufacture from the home." The ethical control of consumption, exemplified by the National Consumers' League, traced its origins to the antebellum cult of domesticity. It insisted on

---

sumers' attempt "to reunite consumption with production." "Patterns of Consumer Consciousness in the Progressive Movement: Robert M. La Follette, the Antitrust Persuasion, and Labor Legislation," in *The Quest for Social Justice*, ed. Ralph M. Aderman (Madison: University of Wisconsin Press, 1983), 19-47 (quotations at 20).

[12] T. J. Jackson Lears, *No Place of Grace: Antimodernism and the Transformation of American Culture, 1880-1920* (New York: Pantheon Books, 1981); Richard Wightman Fox and T. J. Jackson Lears, eds., *The Culture of Consumption: Critical Essays in American History, 1880-1980* (New York: Pantheon Books, 1983).

[13] On the origins of the consumer movement, see Helen Sorenson, *The Consumer Movement: What It Is and What It Means* (New York: Harper & Brothers, 1941), 3-30; Kenneth Dameron, "The Consumer Movement," *Harvard Business Review* 17 (Spring 1939): 271-89; "The Consumer Movement," *Business Week* 503 (22 April 1939): 39-52; Margaret G. Reid, *Consumers and the Market*, 3rd ed. (New York: F. S. Crofts & Co., 1942), esp. 1-13; and Norman Isaac Silber, *Test and Protest: The Influence of Consumers Union* (New York: Holmes & Meier, 1983), 1-15.

a sharp distinction between the household, whose "function" was, in the words of Dr. Mary Putnam Jacobi, the first woman admitted to the New York Academy of Medicine, "the fulfilment of personal satisfactions, the creation, if possible, of happiness," and the impersonal modern business enterprise whose "function" was "the creation of wealth." From this perspective, the rationale of the consumer movement was to extend the traditional moral guardianship of the housewife to the marketplace.[14]

The second strain classified the home as an economic rather than as a moral institution. Accordingly, it sought to rationalize the home in much the same way that modern business had been rationalized. To some enthusiastic professional homemakers, it did not sound too far-fetched to claim that the principles of scientific management, popularized by the time-motion studies of Frederick Winslow Taylor, Frank and Lillian Gilbreth, and their colleagues, could be applied to the home. Toward this end, housewives took up the consumer boycott—directed at high prices, adulterated food and drugs, and unsanitary conditions of production and distribution.

The first two strains worked within the dualities of home and marketplace posited by the cult of domesticity; the third strain of the consumer movement, however, affirmed an inclusive consumer identity that transcended more particularistic or conflicting producer affiliations. It promised to reconcile home and marketplace, production and consumption, and even organized capital and organized labor.

The first strain of consumer consciousness, the doctrine of ethical consumption, had numerous antecedents. In antebellum Providence it had informed the efforts of the Providence Employment Society and its Unitarian offshoot, Employment Society No. 2, to maintain sewing shops where seamstresses could sell their crafts. These and later employment centers were intended to mitigate the exploitation of working women. By subcontracting sewing to work-

---

[14] Florence Kelley, "Aims and Principles of the Consumers' League," *American Journal of Sociology* 5 (November 1899): 298; Jacobi quoted in Maud Nathan, *The Story of an Epoch-Making Movement* (Garden City, N.Y.: Doubleday, Page & Co., 1926), 31. "The overarching theme of the late nineteenth and early twentieth century feminist movement," Dolores Hayden has written, "was to overcome the split between domestic life and public life created by industrial capitalism, as it affected women." *The Grand Domestic Revolution: A History of Feminist Designs for American Homes, Neighborhoods, and Cities* (Cambridge: M.I.T. Press, 1981), 4.

ing women, patrons hoped to raise their wages. The same spirit informed the efforts of a number of Providence women's organizations after the Civil War: for example, the laundry established by the Women's City Missionary Society and the bakeshop of the Rhode Island Exchange for Women's Work.[15]

Ethical consumption also found expression in the activities of the Women's Educational and Industrial Union of Rhode Island (WEIU), founded in 1884. Like similar organizations in Boston and Buffalo, the WEIU typified the then current phase of the women's movement, "Municipal Housekeeping," which Frances Willard, president of the Woman's Christian Temperance Union, defined as bringing "the home into the world" and thus making "the whole world homelike."[16] The WEIU offered classes in subjects ranging from stenography and dressmaking to literature and foreign languages, scheduled entertainments and "coteries" to promote sociability across class lines, and sponsored hygienic lectures for women on such topics as "tight clothing," "care of children," and the "physical effects of alcoholic beverages." In pursuit of its goal of the "mutual association of persons on equal and friendly terms," the WEIU maintained a handicraft store, where the sale of fancy work, cakes, jellies, and other confectioneries on consignment from women was designed to teach the "dignity of labor" and the "value of thorough work," and a downtown lunchroom, "a neat, inviting and comfortable place where all women, and men also, could find home cooking at moderate rates."[17]

The same spirit of cross-class sisterhood informed the activities of the first consumers' organization, the Consumers' League, which was organized in New York City during the winter of 1890-91 after a public meeting at which shopgirls had described the squalid working conditions of many of the city's department stores: unlimited hours, inadequate pay, mandatory unpaid overtime, and minimal

[15] Susan Porter Benson, "Business Heads and Sympathizing Hearts: The Women of the Providence Employment Society, 1837-1858," *Journal of Social History* 12 (Winter 1978): 302-12.

[16] Frances Willard quoted in Hayden, *The Grand Domestic Revolution*, 5.

[17] *First Annual Report of the Women's Educational and Industrial Union of Rhode Island* (Providence: J. A. & R. A. Reid, 1885), 22; *Third Annual Report* (Providence: J. A. & R. A. Reid, 1887), 7, 10; *Fifth Annual Report* (Providence: Providence Press, 1889), 27; Karen J. Blair, *The Clubwoman as Feminist: True Womanhood Redefined, 1868-1914* (New York: Holmes & Meier, 1980), 73-91.

sanitary facilities. By then it was clear that industrialization had not only separated production from consumption by removing work from the home, but had distanced the employer from his employees, thereby rendering production more impersonal. Modeled on a similar organization formed several months earlier in London, the Consumers' League subscribed to the notion that "a woman's duty and responsibility are not bounded by the four walls of her home," but rather extended to the working girl, for whom reformers were already establishing clubs. "Every department of the home is but a reflection in miniature of the broader departments of the municipality and the world beyond." Numbered among the league's founders were Dr. Jacobi, Josephine Shaw Lowell, founder of the United States Sanitary Commission during the Civil War and later closely identified with the work of the charity organization movement, and Maud Nathan, a member of New York's small but influential Sephardic community. By 1899 consumers' leagues across the country had federated in the National Consumers' League.[18]

The charter members of the National Consumers' League hoped to nurture in consumers a strong sense of moral accountability as "responsible buyers." (Later consumers' organizations were to stress intelligent buying.) "The buyer (consumer) may be, in the very act of buying, a creator," declared John Graham Brooks, Harvard economist and the league's first president. "The shoddy buyer *is* [a] shoddy maker." The consumer who bought "products made by laborers working in unwholesome surroundings" helped "perpetuate those evil circumstances." Brooks described the league as "an association of persons who desire, so far as practicable, to do their buying in such ways as to further the welfare of those who make or distribute the things bought."[19]

To "arouse a public conscience" and to generate "an effective demand for goods made under right conditions," the Consumers'

[18] Nathan, *The Story of an Epoch-Making Movement*, 19. For descriptions of working conditions in department stores at the turn of the century, see Annie Marion MacLean, "Two Weeks in Department Stores," *American Journal of Sociology* 4 (May 1899): 721-41; and Susan Porter Benson, " 'The Clerking Sisterhood': Rationalization and the Work Culture of Saleswomen in American Department Stores, 1890-1960," *Radical America* 12 (March-April 1978): 41-55.

[19] John Graham Brooks, *The Consumers' League: The Economic Principles upon Which It Rests and the Practicability of Its Enforcement* (Cambridgeport, Mass.: Co-operative Press, [1899], 3-4.

League drew up a White List of employers who met its labor standards. This list of recommended goods protected the league from possible legal challenges over boycotts, which the courts had ruled illegal. In 1901 the league introduced the White Label. Unlike the Union Label, which denoted that goods had been made by a union shop or by one that observed union wages and hours, the White Label signified that goods had been made under sanitary conditions, by adult workers who were paid what the Consumers' League considered a living wage. Goods like women's and children's underwear and linen soon bore the label. By buying only labeled goods, as Florence Kelley pointed out, "consumers can decide, within certain limits, the conditions under which the desired goods shall be produced." Ineffectual as individuals, consumers once organized became a counterweight to capital and labor. Exhibitions of labeled goods helped spread this message across the country and overseas. French consumers organized after the Paris Exposition of 1900, where the National Consumers' League demonstrated its work with photographs of American sweatshops. German women followed suit after hearing Maud Nathan recount the league's activities at the Quinquennial Convention of the International Council of Women in Berlin in 1904.[20]

The consumer movement took root in Rhode Island in December 1901, when a small group of persons gathered to hear Maud Nathan declare that the object of the Consumers' League was "the formation of a public opinion which shall lead consumers to recognize their responsibility." Following the lecture they stayed to organize the Consumers' League of Rhode Island. Although the new organization observed prevailing custom by selecting a man as its president, women provided the real leadership and comprised the vast majority of its members. Most, like Annie Howe Barus, were the wives of managers and professionals; Barus, whose husband was a Brown professor, also played a leading role in bringing kindergar-

---

[20] Nathan, *The Story of an Epoch-Making Movement*, 117; Kelley, "Aims and Principles of the Consumers' League," 298, 303. Useful secondary works on the Consumers' League include Louis Lee Athey, "The Consumers' Leagues and Social Reform, 1890-1923" (Ph.D. diss., University of Delaware, 1965); William L. O'Neill, *Everyone Was Brave: The Rise and Fall of Feminism in America* (Chicago: Quadrangle Books, 1969), 95-98, 151-53; and Allis Rosenberg Wolfe, "Women, Consumerism, and the National Consumers' League in the Progressive Era, 1900-1923," *Labor History* 16 (Summer 1975): 378-92.

tens and playgrounds to Providence. A few, though, pursued careers outside the home. Anna Garlin Spencer, minister of the Bell Street Chapel and president of the Rhode Island Council of Women, had taken the initiative in organizing the local branch. Wellesley graduate Alice W. Hunt, the "Jane Addams of Providence," was to have a long and illustrious association with the Consumers' League, serving as its executive secretary from 1908 until 1920 and then as its president from 1930 until it disbanded in 1951. Spencer, Barus, and Hunt were only three of the many suffragists who were active in the Consumers' League.[21]

From its inception, the Consumers' League of Rhode Island pursued three goals: the White Label, early closing, and protective legislation for women and children. In popularizing the White Label, it met with little resistance. Local merchants seemed only too happy to meet the demand for labeled goods. As early as February 1903 thirteen stores in the state carried goods bearing the White Label. Their numbers multiplied rapidly after that. In fact, the league's only complaint over the years was that the stores failed to carry the goods in sufficient variety. It proved much more difficult, however, to persuade these same merchants to close their stores early on Saturday evenings and in the week preceding Christmas. The league took up early closing, which had been moribund since 1886, at the first meeting of its executive board in April 1902, when it appointed a committee to meet with department store clerks. After learning that the clerks had already petitioned their employers for a Friday afternoon holiday, the league appointed a second committee to study the Christmas trade. The latter committee soon reported "that it was considered unwise to take any action." A third committee appointed to confer with department store owners was rebuffed by the owners, who claimed that there was "nothing to discuss."[22]

[21] "A Brief History [of] the Consumers' League of Rhode Island, 1901-1941," typescript, Records of the Consumers' League of Rhode Island, Brown University Library; *Providence Journal*, 9 February 1947; Nathan, *The Story of an Epoch-Making Movement*, 214-21. On the woman's suffrage movement in Rhode Island, see Sara M. Algeo, *The Story of a Sub-Pioneer* (Providence: Snow & Farnham, 1925); and Nancy Kathleen Cassidy, "A History of the Rhode Island Woman Suffrage Association" (history honors thesis, Brown University, 1973).

[22] Minutes of Annual Meetings, 1901-1911, 14 April, 13 October 1902, 5 February, 19 May, 26 October 1903, Records of the Consumers' League of Rhode Island; "Welfare Work in Rhode Island," *Nineteenth Annual Report of the Commissioner of Industrial Statistics* (Providence: E. L. Freeman & Sons, 1906), 191-93.

Perhaps inspired by Florence Kelley's frequent visits to the state, the Consumers' League of Rhode Island settled down in 1904 to a long struggle for early closing. Adopting the slogan "give the sales-people a chance," it urged Rhode Island shoppers not to put off their Christmas shopping until the last four days before the holiday. With the assistance of the National Consumers' League, which was also conducting an early shopping campaign, it inserted advertise-ments in local newspapers, distributed thousands of cards remind-ing consumers to do their Christmas shopping early, and solicited the aid of clergymen. Thanks to these efforts, the traditional rush slackened. In 1907 the league reported a noticeable decrease in the Christmas trade. The early shopping campaign, it said, had "met with decided encouragement" from both the sales clerks themselves and from the local press.[23]

Store owners, however, were not easily persuaded to close earlier, either on Saturday evenings or in the week preceding Christmas. On several occasions, the league negotiated agreements among the larger stores to close early, only to have one store renege, followed by the others, worried lest their competitor get the jump on them. At other times, intense competition among the stores precluded any agreement at all. In 1909, for instance, three of the largest depart-ment stores promised to close an hour earlier—at 9 P.M.—on the four nights preceding Christmas if the fourth large store would do so too. Suffice it to say that the fourth refused to go along.[24] More than four thousand letters from consumers, support from the Rhode Island Medical Society, Federation of Churches, and State Federation of Labor, and the intervention of Mayor Joseph H. Gainer, who summoned representatives from local organizations to a municipal conference on early closing, eventually led to another agreement that three of the city's department stores would close at 6 P.M. on Saturdays, and the fourth at 7 P.M. Yet the depression of 1914 brought a setback, seeming to make it "obligatory" for the stores "to catch every penny." One by one they reverted to their ear-lier 9 P.M. closing hour. "The reason given," reported the league, was "their inability to stand the cost incurred by early closing."[25]

[23] Minutes of Annual Meetings, 1901-1911, 28 November 1904, 27 November 1905, 27 November 1906, 22 November 1907, Records of the Consumers' League of Rhode Island; *Providence Journal*, 23 December 1906.
[24] Minutes of Annual Meetings, 1901-1911, 29 January 1909.
[25] *Providence Journal*, 7 June 1913; Constitution and Records of Annual Meetings

The success of the early closing campaign, however, ultimately depended less on consumer agitation than on producer self-regulation. The league's "educational" work—including prize essay contests in the schools, frequent public meetings, "Shop before six" buttons, "Shop Early" slides at motion-picture theaters, and a wagon fitted up with signs saying, "You don't work Saturday nights, why make others? Shop before six"—failed to persuade the city's merchants to close early. It took the intervention of the Chamber of Commerce and the federal government to do that. In 1916 six representatives from the Chamber of Commerce joined an equal number of representatives from the Consumers' League in an Early Closing Shopping Committee. Next, the federal government mandated early Christmas shopping as a wartime conservation measure. Following the Armistice, the Chamber of Commerce assumed responsibility for enforcing an early closing agreement reached during the war. Closing at 6 P.M. on Saturdays throughout the year and during the Christmas rush became the rule rather than the exception.[26]

It took even longer for the Consumer's League to attain its third goal—protective legislation for women and children and the abolition of child labor. Demands for a shorter working day, the establishment of a minimum-wage commission in every state, and the prohibition of night work for women and children were all part of the "Ten-Year Program" adopted by the National Consumers' League in 1910. In pursuing these goals the Consumers' League of Rhode Island faced formidable obstacles. One was the state's ingrained conservatism. Another was the power of the state's manufacturers. In its treatment of working women and children, Rhode Island was the most "southern" or reactionary of the northern states. According to the federal census, in 1909 women comprised a third of the state's work force—the highest percentage of working women of any state in the Union. (The national average was only 19.7 percent.) The state's textile mills had traditionally employed large numbers of women; other women found jobs in factories mak-

and Annual Reports, 1911-35, annual reports for 1912, 1913, and 1914, Records of the Consumers' League of Rhode Island; Alice W. Hunt, "The Importance of the Early Closing Movement," *Providence Medical Journal* 16 (January 1915): 39-45.

[26] Constitution and Records of Annual Meetings and Annual Reports, 1911-35, reports of the General Secretary for 1915 and 1916; *Providence Journal*, 9 September 1919, 9 December 1920.

ing jewelry, rubber, and paper boxes. All told, more than thirty-six thousand women worked in Rhode Island.[27]

Even more shocking to middle-class observers was the fact that almost five thousand children under sixteen years of age also worked. At a time when child labor was decreasing in the rest of the North, it was increasing in Rhode Island, where children made up 4 percent of the state's work force, the largest percentage of any northern state. An investigation made in 1905 by the National Child Labor Committee (NCLC) found large numbers of children employed in Rhode Island, many of whom were illiterate. The committee also reported that children as young as twelve worked illegally by lying about their ages. Rhode Island, moreover, lagged behind other states in enacting protective legislation for women and children. Other states limited children's work to eight hours a day; Rhode Island allowed them to work up to ten hours daily. It also permitted night work for girls under sixteen, did nothing to prevent children from operating dangerous machinery or working at hazardous occupations, and set lower educational requirements for working children than any other state in New England.[28]

Because of the corrupt alliance between industrialists and the Republican party, the Consumers' League made slow headway against these conditions. The Child Labor Law of 1905, secured through the efforts of the Consumers' League, the Rhode Island Council of Women, and the State Federation of Women's Clubs, prohibited children under fourteen from working at all and children under sixteen from working in factories between 8 P.M. and 6 A.M. An amendment to the Factory Inspection Act increased the power of the state's factory inspectors over mercantile and manufacturing establishments. The league also campaigned for a 56-hour workweek for women and children. Commonly working 58 hours or longer, women had little time for household tasks or rearing children. After

[27] Constitution and Records of Annual Meetings and Annual Reports, 1911-35, annual report for 1914; Mann, *Manufacturing in Rhode Island*, 53; Strom, "Old Barriers and New Opportunities," 43-44.

[28] John Ker Towles, *Factory Legislation of Rhode Island* (Princeton: American Economic Association, 1908), 45-56; Ellen Hartwell, "Political Extremism and the Quest for Absolutes in Rhode Island, 1900-1935" (history honors thesis, Brown University, 1980), 43-45. Rhode Island thus bucked the national trend toward a diminution of child labor. In 1900 26 percent of all boys aged 10 to 15 were employed; in 1930 only 6 percent were. Hurlin and Givens, "Shifting Occupational Patterns," 303-304.

a three-year struggle, the league at last steered a 56-hour act through the General Assembly in 1909.[29]

In its campaign for protective legislation, the Consumers' League of Rhode Island drew on the resources of the National Child Labor Committee. In 1910 it scheduled a child labor meeting in Providence to coincide with the NCLC's annual meeting being held in Boston. When two years later the NCLC reported that messenger boys were doubling as runners for prostitutes, a report subsequently confirmed by the *Providence Journal*, the league drafted a night messenger bill that prohibited messengers under twenty-one from working after 10 P.M. Public pressure forced the General Assembly to pass this bill over determined opposition in the state senate. In January 1913 the league sponsored a week-long child welfare exhibit in Providence, featuring photographs by Lewis Hine, who had visited Rhode Island three times under NCLC auspices. An advocate of "Social Photography," Hine believed that the photo was the perfect medium for promoting reform. "The photograph has an added realism of its own; it has an inherent attraction not found in other forms of illustration," he said. "For this reason the average person believes implicitly that the photograph cannot falsify." Hine's photographs not only emphasized the dignity of labor, one of the league's favorite themes, they also underscored how common child labor was in Providence. To Annie Barus, the photographs provided conclusive proof that young children "were setting stones for some of the manufacturing jewelers of Providence, the work being done at their homes."[30]

The child welfare exhibit kicked off the league's campaign for a 54-hour law for women and children. Petition after petition persuaded the General Assembly to pass a compromise bill in 1913, which limited working hours for women and for children under sixteen to a maximum of ten hours a day or fifty-four hours a week in all enterprises. In 1915 a Street Trades Bill restricting the hours of boys and girls employed as vendors made its way through the assembly, but only after a dramatic late-night session. Over the next two years, a coalition of Democrats led by Edwin C. Pierce and ur-

[29] "A Brief History," 2; Towles, "Factory Legislation of Rhode Island," 50-56; Strom, "Old Barriers and New Opportunities," 47.

[30] "A Brief History," 3; Barus quoted in Stephen Victor, "Lewis Hine's Photography and Reform in Rhode Island," *Rhode Island History* 41 (May 1982): 40.

ban Republicans in the assembly representing immigrant constituencies succeeded in raising the compulsory school age from fifteen to sixteen, banning the use of the notorious suction or "Kiss-of-Death" shuttle, which studies had linked to the spread of tuberculosis, and prohibiting the common cup and towel in the workplace, also thought to spread the disease.[31]

But the American declaration of war dashed hopes for any further reform in the workplace. After being encouraged by the wartime example of the federal government serving as "a model employer," the Consumers' League soon "learned how very strong the forces of selfishness and reaction are in this state." Following the Armistice, the league resumed its efforts to prohibit night work for women, to institute a 48-hour week for women and children, and to establish a state minimum-wage commission. Only on a few occasions did any of these bills ever get beyond committees in the Republican-dominated General Assembly. It took three years of agitation by a statewide children's committee before the General Assembly passed a comprehensive child labor bill in 1923 prohibiting children younger than fifteen from working and barring children under sixteen from hazardous occupations. Not until 1928 did the assembly decree a 48-hour workweek and a 9-hour workday for children and forbid them from working after 7 P.M. But the prohibition of night work for women, the institution of a 48-hour workweek for all workers, and the establishment of a minimum-wage commission had to await the election of Democratic governor Theodore Francis Green in 1932 and Democratic control of the state government, captured in the "Bloodless Revolution" of 1935.[32]

Although overlapping the Consumers' League in membership and pursuing the same goal of protecting the home, the Providence Housewives League represented a second strain in the consumer movement. The Consumers' League stressed the moral responsibil-

[31] "A Brief History," 3-5; John D. Buenker, "Urban Liberalism in Rhode Island, 1909-1919," *Rhode Island History* 30 (May 1971): 45-46.

[32] Constitution and Records of Annual Meetings and Annual Reports, 1911-35, report of the General Secretary for 1918, annual report for 1919, Records of the Consumers' League of Rhode Island; "A Brief History," 5-8; *Providence Journal*, 26 January 1920. For an introduction to the minimum-wage movement, see James T. Patterson, "Mary Dewson and the American Minimum Wage Movement," *Labor History* 5 (Spring 1964): 134-52. On the activities of the National Consumers' League during and after the war, see O'Neill, *Everyone Was Brave*, 218-19, 232-40.

ity of the consumer; the Housewives League aimed at professionalizing the home and training the housewife in intelligent buying.
"Housewives themselves," according to the latter organization,
"were in a measure responsible for the high prices of the necessaries
of life" and "wholly responsible for insanitary conditions in markets
and groceries and for short weight." Until the United States went to
war in 1917, the Housewives League's raison d'être was to fight the
high cost of living. Following the Armistice, its members subscribed
to a new vision, that of "the Industry of Home-making." By this,
they meant that homemaking, "if well oiled by efficient management and the use of modern facilities," will "operate so smoothly
that the 'drudgery' is removed and each task becomes a pleasure."[33]

The Providence Housewives League "sprang into existence" in
October 1912 to fight the high cost of living. Composed of the wives
of businessmen, academics, and professionals, most of whom re-
sided on the city's fashionable East Side, it was part of a "national
uprising of women." Following the lead of clubwomen in New York
City, more than 165,000 housewives across the country had refused
to buy butter at sixty cents a pound, continuing their boycott until
the price fell by almost half to thirty-two cents. Emboldened by this
success, some 300,000 women flocked into chapters of the National
Housewives League, headed by Mrs. Julian (Jennie) Heath, former
president of the New York City Federation of Women's Clubs and a
student of home economics. Once organized, these housewives declared war against inflated prices, investigated conditions surrounding the sale of eggs, milk, and other staples, agitated for public markets, and promoted food conservation.[34]

The Housewives League reflected the influence of home economics. Home economics clubs had proliferated since the World's Columbian Exposition of 1893. Among the participants at the Lake
Placid conferences, which preceded the formation of the American
Home Economics Association in 1909, was Abby L. Marlatt, a

[33] *Providence Journal*, 30 October 1912; *Housewives League Bulletin* 6 (April 1924): 1.

[34] Mrs. Alfred L. Lustig, "Rousing Up Rhode Island," *Housewives League Magazine*
1 (January 1913): 30; *Providence Journal*, 28 September, 20 October 1912; Board
Meetings of the Providence Housewives League, 1912-14, 27 September, 29 October
1912, RIHS; *New York Times*, 19 October 1913; Mary Dudderidge, "Embattled Housewives," *Independent* 73 (28 November 1912): 1230-34; Mrs. Julian Heath, "Work of
the Housewives League," *Annals of the American Academy of Political and Social Science*
48 (July 1913): 121-126; Samson, "The Emergence of a Consumer Interest," 158-78.

teacher at Providence Manual Training High School, who argued for the inclusion of home economics in the school curriculum. The home economics movement represented an attempt by homemakers to come to terms with the impact of functional differentiation on the home. Once a center of production, the home was fast becoming a center of consumption, as technological advance and the ongoing division of labor transferred canning, laundry, baking, and other traditional household tasks from homemakers to service workers. By the first decade of the twentieth century this trend was already pronounced. The federal census of 1910 noted "the transfer to factories of a considerable part of the canning, preserving, etc., formerly done in private houses." "Housekeeping," Jennie Heath declared in 1912, had "become almost a lost art." Far from regretting the technological transformation wrought in the home, however, she looked forward to the day when housekeeping would "cease to be an art at all and rapidly become a science." In her opinion, putting housekeeping on a scientific basis, or making it a full-time profession, promised to extend "the responsibilities of womankind." Sophie Lustig, president of the Providence Housewives League, echoed Heath's sentiments. "It is perfectly proper for work to be done outside of the home," she said. "It is simply a sign of progression in the line of home keeping."[35]

[35] Wolfe, "Women, Consumerism, and the National Consumers' League in the Progressive Era," 379n; Mrs. Julian Heath quoted in *Providence Journal*, 20 October 1912; Sophie Lustig quoted in "Addresses College Girls," clipping, in "Housewifes [*sic*] League," box 6, folder 1, vol. 2, Records of the Rhode Island State Federation of Women's Clubs, RIHS. On the home economics movement, see Emma Seifrit Weigley, "It Might Have Been Euthenics: The Lake Placid Conferences and the Home Economics Movement," *American Quarterly* 26 (March 1974): 79-96; and Barbara Ehrenreich and Deirdre English, *For Her Own Good: 150 Years of the Experts' Advice to Women* (Garden City, N.Y.: Anchor Books, 1979), 141-81. Home economists pointed to the waste inherent in "domestic industry." Charlotte Perkins Gilman, for example, called for "the professionalization of cooking, cleaning and laundry work," in "The Waste of Private Housekeeping," *Annals of the American Academy of Political and Social Science* 48 (July 1913): 95. The previous year, the economist Wesley C. Mitchell had suggested that "a professional class of Doctors of Domestic Science" be developed who could "be employed in organizing households," give "expert counsel to the newlywed," and provide "free dispensaries of advice for the indigent." "The Backward Art of Spending Money," *American Economic Review* 2 (June 1912), reprinted in *The Backward Art of Spending Money, and Other Essays* (New York: McGraw-Hill, 1937), 18-19. Years earlier, in 1896, Edward T. Devine had urged economists to pay more attention to consumption and the woman's role as "wealth expender" in "The Economic Function of Woman," *Annals of the American Academy of Political and Social Science* 5

Members of the Housewives League believed that once freed from the drudgery of routine household tasks, the housewife would naturally take a greater interest in affairs outside the home. When the Consumers' League spoke of extending the responsibilities of middle-class women, it thought in terms of moral responsibility. The Housewives League, on the other hand, championed the development of a science of household consumption and the application of the principles of scientific management to the home. "Spending is the woman's business," Heath pointed out. "When she has learned to spend intelligently and with the same efficiency demanded for success in any other line of business," the housewife would not only reduce "the cost of living to the lowest point compatible with trade or tariff conditions," but she would lose "the stigma of failure which is now attached by many skeptical observers to the profession of housewifery." The divergence of the two organizations mirrored the tension within women's literary clubs between self-culture and social service.[36]

In order to protect "themselves and their families from impure foods sold at prohibitive prices," middle-class housewives across the country adopted the tactic of the consumer boycott or the "buyer's strike." Boycotts by housewives, who controlled an estimated 75 to 90 percent of their families' budgets, were intended to drive prices down by reducing demand. "If one woman goes to the bakery and asks to see how bread is baked she is promptly refused," Lustig told students at the Women's College at Brown. But "if 400,000 women go around and are refused these women will not buy. They are, therefore, welcomed, and this is just what is happening to-day." In-

---

(November 1896): 361-76. On the reorganization and subsequent mechanization of the household, see Siegfried Giedion, *Mechanization Takes Command: A Contribution to Anonymous History* (New York: W. W. Norton & Co., 1969), 512-627. Yet, as Ruth Schwartz Cowan has pointed out, the reorganization and mechanization of the home may actually have increased the drudgery of housework as the servantless housewife had to perform all household tasks previously performed by servants, and as electric irons, washing machines, and other mechanical devices raised standards of cleaning and child-rearing. "The 'Industrial Revolution' in the Home: Household Technology and Social Change in the 20th Century," *Technology and Culture* 17 (January 1976): 1-23. For an extended treatment of the impact of technology on the household, see ibid., *More Work for Mother: The Ironies of Household Technology from the Open Hearth to the Microwave* (New York: Basic Books, 1983).

[36] Mrs. Julian Heath, "What the Housewife Who 'Seemed to Know' Has Accomplished," clipping, in "Housewifes [*sic*] League," RIHS.

deed, immigrants had already demonstrated how effective this tactic could be. In 1910 Jewish women in South Providence boycotted kosher butchers until meat came "down to the prices which the people could afford." The success of Philadelphia housewives, who in 1912 secured a reduction in the price of storage eggs by threatening to go into the egg business themselves unless local dealers lowered their prices, encouraged the Providence Housewives League to challenge "the Egg Corner." Some forty women, each wearing a conspicuous blue-and-white button, which dealers referred to as "that confounded button," investigated markets. When they discovered that marketmen frequently labeled cold-storage eggs or eggs imported from other states as fresh Rhode Island eggs, which were then sold at higher prices, they threatened a consumer boycott. At the mere threat of a boycott, egg dealers cut prices and began to label eggs properly.[37]

Middle-class housewives thus appropriated what hitherto had been considered an alien form of protest. Yet there were important differences between their egg boycott and the ad hoc protests of immigrant Jews. Immigrant women depended on preexisting neighborhood networks to sustain their spontaneous boycotts; middle-class housewives developed permanent organizations that outlived the protest and could be put to other uses. Moreover, the immigrants' protest tended to be confined to their own neighborhoods; the league's campaigns were citywide and depended on prior organization and ongoing publicity.

After winning the "Egg Crusade," the Providence Housewives

[37] Sophie Lustig, "Addresses College Girls"; *Providence Journal*, 20, 21 December 1912; Lustig, "Rousing Up Rhode Island," 30-32. The term "buyer's strike" is from Christine Frederick, *Selling Mrs. Consumer* (New York: Business Bourse, 1929), 264. For an account of immigrant food boycotts in Providence, see Judith E. Smith, "Our Own Kind: Family and Community Networks," *Radical History Review* 17 (Spring 1978): 113-15. For accounts of a meat boycott on New York's Lower East Side in 1902, see Herbert G. Gutman, "Work, Culture, and Society in Industrializing America, 1815-1919," in his *Work, Culture, and Society in Industrializing America: Essays in American Working-Class and Social History* (New York: Vintage Books, 1977), 61-63; and Paula E. Hyman, "Immigrant Women and Consumer Protest: The New York City Kosher Meat Boycott of 1902," *American Jewish History* 70 (September 1980): 91-105. In Europe women traditionally led food protests against merchants accused of engrossing staples or gouging prices. See E. P. Thompson, "The Moral Economy of the English Crowd in the Eighteenth Century," *Past and Present* 50 (February 1971): 76-136.

League launched a similar campaign against adulterated milk. In 1913 volunteers quietly collected samples of milk from dealers for chemical analysis. When almost half of the samples failed to meet acceptable standards, the league charged that "rotten" milk was sold in Providence because of "a regular system of graft" between the municipal milk department and local dealers. It also accused the milk inspector, whom it had first considered the "innocent victim of a powerful ring," of being a party to this graft. Under mounting pressure from the Housewives League that the issue should "be decided in the interest of *the public alone*," an aldermanic committee investigated the milk department. After a preliminary investigation uncovered evidence of malfeasance, the city fired its milk inspector. A second committee then conducted a full-scale inquiry into the city's milk supply. Witnesses testified about widespread bribery, inspectors' dereliction of duty, and dairies' use of formaldehyde as a preservative. Following these spectacular revelations, the aldermen voted to abolish the Office of Milk Inspector and place milk inspection under the control of Dr. Charles V. Chapin, Providence's famed superintendent of health. The city's housewives, exulted Mary C. Brackett, chairman of the league's Milk Committee, had "fought one bitter fight to rescue milk from the field of politics."[38]

The Providence Housewives League, in concert with leagues in other cities, next investigated sanitary conditions in local groceries, markets, and candy stores. Armed with questionnaires, volunteers visited stores, where they inquired about general cleanliness, ventilation, spitting, and sanitary arrangements for employees (including whether washing facilities and towels were provided). Just as in the earlier milk campaign, the assumption was that the housewife, as the family's primary consumer, was responsible for the conditions in which goods were both produced and distributed. Concern about gouging, profiteering, and other unfair marketing practices led the league to entertain proposals for dispensing with middlemen altogether, either through using parcel post for the direct delivery of produce from farmers or through establishing consumer

[38] "Story of the Pure Milk Campaign in Providence," *Housewives League Magazine* 3 (May 1914): 41-46; *Providence Journal*, 22 December 1912, 23 April, 3 November 1913, 7 January 1914; Mary C. Brackett, "The Housewives League," *Housewives League Bulletin* 1 (11 February 1920): 2; Abby Cohen, "Public Health and Preventive Medicine in Providence, 1913," *Rhode Island History* 36 (May 1977): 55-63.

cooperatives. But the housewives eventually settled on a less drastic solution: the establishment of a municipal market, an expedient other cities had already adopted to lower food prices, which facilitated the direct sale of farmers' produce to urban consumers. In 1913 the Housewives League took the lead in "the market agitation." Petitions signed by over four thousand people, the great majority of them women, helped persuade the city council to adopt the plan. No wonder the league adopted the slogan, "The Power Lies in the Hands of the Consumer."[39]

In its fight against the high cost of living, the league received valuable aid from municipal and federal authorities. As early as 1914 concern about "the high prices of the necessities of life" prompted municipal food conferences and investigations by the U.S. Department of Agriculture. A food conference called in August 1914 by Mayor Gainer attracted representatives from a number of interested organizations, including the Chamber of Commerce, women's clubs, and labor unions as well as the Housewives League. Retail grocers, who for years had "been made to bear the onus and the stigma of raising prices," welcomed the inquiry, claiming "there is no honester businessman in the community." As the grocers had hoped, the delegates concluded that the causes for the recent jump in food prices lay outside the city.[40]

Concern about the high cost of living came to a head during the First World War. Wartime investigations revealed that retail prices were higher in Providence than anywhere else in the country. To clamp down on inflation, the Food Administration, headed by the "Great Engineer" Herbert Hoover, solicited the cooperation of food dealers. Since the Lever Food and Fuel Act limited the Food Administration's statutory powers to setting the price of wheat, Hoover emphasized "assembl[ing] the voluntary effort of the people." "We propose to mobilize the spirit of self-denial and self-sacrifice in this

[39] Board Meetings of the Providence Housewives League, 1912-14, 21 January 1913; *Evening Bulletin*, 27 December 1912, 14 January 1913; *Providence Journal*, 11 November 1914, 23 January 1915; "A Notable Year's Work in Providence," *Housewives League Magazine* 3 (January 1914): 29-31. See also Clyde Lyndon King, "Municipal Markets," *Annals of the American Academy of Political and Social Science* 50 (November 1913): 102-117; and John W. Farley, "A Questionnaire on Markets," ibid., 139-52. Questionnaires from the league's investigations of markets and groceries and of candy factories are included in the material of the Housewives League at RIHS.

[40] *Providence Journal*, 19-21, 23, 25, 27 August 1914.

country," he explained. Hoover "reached out to the public" through press releases, newspaper and magazine publicity, and "personal pledge" campaigns. During the war, a new word entered the American vocabulary: "Hooverizing," which denoted voluntary rationing.[41]

Hoover found willing volunteers in the middle-class women of the country. Providence housewives eagerly practiced food conservation. They observed the "wheatless," "meatless," and "porkless" days proclaimed by President Wilson. Adopting the slogan "Save to Win," members of the Housewives League demonstrated "scientific methods of food economy" at downtown department stores, the city's social settlements, Brown University's Arnold Laboratory, and at a portable "Hoover Hut." One member even turned her kitchen into a "canning centre." Other volunteers staffed a "war bread shop," where they publicized wheat substitutes and demonstrated a "four square plan" intended to reduce the cost of foodstuffs by 10 percent.[42] The city's grocers also did their part. Some 385 of them were among 120,000 dealers across the country who pledged fair and moderate prices for their customers. Periodic investigations by Secret Service agents and telegrams from the Food Administration helped keep prices down. So too did the market guides issued by the Bureau of Markets of the Department of Agriculture. In the summer of 1918 the Food Administration named a state food administrator, who in turn appointed a nine-member price-fixing committee. Composed of retail and wholesale grocers as well as two women who represented the city's consumers, the committee issued a weekly "fair price list" and set a "fair profit" for wholesalers and retailers.[43] By the end of the war, the Housewives League had practically realized its goal of intelligent buying. Indeed, Jennie Heath

[41] *Providence Journal*, 27 November 1917; Hoover quoted in David M. Kennedy, *Over Here: The First World War and American Society* (New York: Oxford University Press, 1980), 118; Craig Lloyd, *Aggressive Introvert: A Study of Herbert Hoover and Public Relations Management, 1912-1932* (Columbus: Ohio State University Press, 1972), 45-52; Joan Hoff Wilson, *Herbert Hoover: Forgotten Progressive* (Boston: Little, Brown & Co., 1975), 61.

[42] *Providence Journal*, 8, 20 May, 15, 24 July 1917, 26 February, 27 April 1918; Providence Housewives League, *News Bulletin No. 5*, 15 July 1917, RIHS.

[43] *Providence Journal*, 23, 26 January, 16 February, 12 March, 2 September 1918. The wartime clamor about the high cost of living prompted a number of studies of household budgets. Many of these were conducted by the pro-business National Industrial Conference Board. See, for example, *The Cost of Living in the United States, 1914-1930* (New York: National Industrial Conference Board, 1931).

claimed that "the principles" practiced by the Food Administration "were, in the main, the principles upon which we had worked since 1911." The war had mustered "a body of housewives already trained in conservation and in the economics of buying."[44]

The campaign against the high cost of living entered a new phase after the Armistice. In August 1919 municipal authorities appointed a "Fair Price Committee" to cooperate with federal agencies. Among its members were Mrs. Howard K. Hilton of the Housewives League and Alice Hunt of the Consumer's League. Subcommittees—on milk, boots and shoes, department stores, groceries and meats, fuel, clothing, wholesale groceries, and educational propaganda—included representatives from the producer groups to be regulated as well as public representatives. In addition to issuing weekly fair price lists, the subcommittees investigated complaints of gouging, profiteering, and engaging in other unfair marketing practices. Agents from the Bureau of Investigation of the Department of Justice assisted their investigations. By February 1920 Rhode Island even had its own federal fair price commissioner who had the power to set arbitrary prices. In addition, the Lever Act authorized the prosecution of dealers who charged excessive or unreasonable prices. Thus within eight years of the founding of the Providence Housewives League, consumers had received at least partial representation as a distinct constituency in the municipal body politic.[45]

With the return of normalcy, the Housewives League took up new interests. The challenge of the postwar era seemed to lie in organizing homemakers as a producer group, if not the home as an industry. "Organization is our keynote for 1920," Heath announced, "one organization—one great body—one union." After all, butchers, bakers, grocers, and other producers, many of whom specialized in what were once household tasks, had organized; their organizations, as Heath was the first to point out, had "brought profit to themselves and in so doing often exploited us." Now it was the housewives' turn to organize. "As we were pioneers in establish-

---

[44] *Housewives League Bulletin* 1 (May 1920): 1; *Providence Journal*, 5 February 1919.

[45] *Providence Journal*, 29, 31 August, 12, 28 September 1919, 20 February 1920. In cities across the country, the high cost of living sparked postwar buyers' strikes. Mark Sullivan, *Our Times: The United States, 1900-1925*, 6 vols. (New York: Charles Scribner's Sons, 1926-35), 6:163-67.

ing the recognition of the fact that homemaking is a business—an industry—so are we pioneers in organizing the industry." "There must be no wavering now," she insisted, "consumers must be made class conscious."[46]

The league's concern with organizing housewives reflected attempts during the 1920s by Lillian Gilbreth, Christine Frederick, and other "household engineers" to rationalize homemaking and eliminate waste of energy in "domestic industry." Applying the principles of scientific management to the home, they conducted skill, motion, and fatigue studies, devised precise daily and weekly schedules for the housewife, suggested "efficient" layouts for the kitchen and laundry, and offered instruction on how to keep accurate household budgets. "Home-making," Gilbreth insisted, "is the finest job in the world." Accordingly, her "aim" was "to make it as interesting and satisfying as it is important." Indeed, the housewife coveted praise as a "producer." For Frederick, it was time to move beyond "the capital-labor relationship," already mediated by the consumer, to study the "consumer-distributor-producer relationship."[47]

New activities reflected the league's intention to organize the home as an industry. Following a second campaign for pure milk in 1921, its members established milk stations in the city's most congested neighborhoods. Household visitors exhorted immigrant children to drink milk, avoid coffee and other stimulants, and eat a hearty breakfast before school. In 1922 the Housewives League agreed to sponsor a salvage shop with the Consumers' League and the Girls' City Club, the latter an outgrowth of the working girls' club movement. Intended as "a real thrift shop" where "a dollar goes a long way," the shop sold garments, shoes, and household furnishings discarded by middle-class families to needy families at a substantial discount—a necessary social service at a time when a substantial number of the city's wage earners were out of work because of a temporary business downturn. The shop also propagated thrift

[46] *Housewives League Bulletin* 1 (May 1920): 1-2.

[47] Lillian M. Gilbreth, *The Home-Maker and Her Job* (New York: D. Appleton & Co., 1927), vii, 145; Frederick, *Selling Mrs. Consumer*, 3. Christine Frederick first came to public attention in the autumn of 1912 when she published a series of articles on "The New Housekeeping" in *Ladies' Home Journal*, which evoked an extraordinary response from the magazine's readers.

and other middle-class values among the poor. Proceeds sustained a Home Information Center, which disseminated the latest techniques of scientific housekeeping among middle-class housewives.[48]

Many of the city's housewives were in the midst of adapting themselves to an acute servant shortage. Concern about the scarcity of good servants was nothing new. Since as far back as the 1840s, middle-class women had fretted about household help. But servants in postwar Providence were scarcer than ever before because women who had formerly gone into domestic service chose instead the higher wages, shorter hours, and greater personal freedom offered by factory and clerical employment. Three out of five working women in 1870 had been domestic servants; by 1920 fewer than one in five were. Only black women, excluded from other jobs because of discrimination, still entered domestic service in undiminished numbers. But there were too few of them in Rhode Island. Many housewives, moreover, had no need of live-in servants because their families had moved into apartment buildings or residential hotels, where household tasks devolved on service workers.[49]

As its solution to the problem, the Housewives League proposed to make domestic service "a dignified and worthwhile occupation, limited to industrial hours and so businesslike that intelligent, refined women need not feel it beneath them." A Bureau of Household Occupations, established just before the Armistice, made it possible for the city's housewives to employ "assistants" for "definite hours of work at a fixed price." Servants thus joined the burgeoning ranks of janitors, elevator operators, and other service workers. Overseeing the new bureau was a "household engineer," a specially trained woman "who can go into homes to reorganize their work, advise as to their expenditures, engage their helpers, plan their

---

[48] *Providence Journal*, 28 May, 29 October, 1 November 1921; *Housewives League Bulletin* 1 (17 December 1919): 1; 1 (May 1920): 3; 3 (January 1922): 1.

[49] Strom, "Old Barriers and New Opportunities," 47-48; Hayden, *The Grand Domestic Revolution*, 170-71; Hurlin and Givens, "Shifting Occupational Patterns," 292-94. As early as 1916 John Ihlder remarked on the preference of the city's middle-class families for apartment living in *The Houses of Providence: A Study of Present Conditions and Tendencies with Notes on the Surrounding Communities and Some Mill Villages* (Providence: Snow & Farnham, 1916), 33-34. See also Christine Frederick's discussion of "The Servantless Household" and the "Management of House Workers" in *Household Engineering: Scientific Management in the Home* (Chicago: American School of Home Economics, 1919), 377-448.

menus on dietetic lines, do their marketing, and put their establishments on a well-ordered scientific basis." In January 1927, reflecting its members' interest in professionalizing the home, the Providence League voted to resign from the National Housewives League, whose chief function by that time was "broadcasting recipes over the radio," in order to affiliate with the American Homemakers, Inc. A year earlier, Mrs. Henry D. Sharpe had been one of the incorporators of the latter organization, established to furnish aid and instruction to housewives interested in organizing their homes. The Providence Homemakers soon opened a home information center similiar to those already in operation in Springfield, Holyoke, and Waltham, Massachusetts. Its full-time, paid director instructed housewives on how to budget both their time and their money. During the Depression, the league was to·establish a women's exchange much like the one maintained forty years earlier by the Women's Educational and Industrial Union.[50]

The Providence Housewives League was not the only women's organization concerned with protecting the home during the 1920s. All across the country housewives endorsed prohibition, which they considered a bulwark of the middle-class family. When enforcement began to break down after 1923, they rallied to its defense. In 1924 representatives from the state chapter of the American Association of University Women, the Rhode Island Federation of Women's Church Societies, the Consumer's League, the League of Women Voters, and fifteen other organizations joined forces in the Woman's Rhode Island Committee for Law Enforcement. Later that year, three thousand women turned out for a "March of Allegiance to the Constitution" against what they perceived as the "growing lawlessness in Rhode Island." By 1926 women's organizations with a combined membership of more than fifty thousand had signed petitions opposing any modification of the Volstead Act to permit the sale of light wine and beer.[51]

Prohibition's defenders often portrayed themselves as members

[50] *Housewives League Bulletin* 1 (10 October 1919): 2; *Providence Journal*, 12, 16, 18 November 1918, 14 December 1919, 4 January 1927, 31 May 1931, 7 April 1946; *Evening Bulletin*, 30 October 1928; Providence Housewives League, Minutes of Regular Meetings, 1924-27, 3 January 1927, RIHS; "Radio for Women," *Literary Digest* 87 (28 November 1925): 20.

[51] *Providence Journal*, 26 October 1924, 14 April 1926; Records of the Woman's Rhode Island Committee for Law Enforcement, 1924-32, RIHS.

of the sober middle classes arrayed against "plutocrats" on the one hand and the "proletariat" on the other. Since the ratification of the Eighteenth Amendment, contended Rupert P. Hutton, superintendent of the Rhode Island Anti-Saloon League, membership in the American middle classes had swelled. Millions of the nation's bond-holders were actually "small holders who buy with savings which would not be saved if beer and wine were soliciting deposits in the 'bank of losing.' " "Prohibition," Hutton concluded, "is preventing the class struggle by eliminating class differences." The struggle over the Eighteenth Amendment, Hutton announced on another occasion, was but the latest phase of "the eternal struggle between the faith of the masses and the pride of the classes." He charged that a small group of wealthy citizens advocated the licensing and taxing of liquor, not for the benefit of the workingman but rather to reduce their own income taxes.[52]

There was some truth to Hutton's charge. Opposing prohibition were some of the most prominent men and women in Rhode Island as well as many Catholics and Jews. In 1923 textile manufacturer Stephen O. Metcalf, attorney William G. Roelker, department store owner Joseph Samuels, and other leading citizens organized the Rhode Island Branch of the Association Against the Prohibition Amendment (AAPA) as a "protest against the tyranny of organized fanaticism." In language reminiscent of the anti-abolitionists' reaction to the antislavery crusade, they denounced the Volstead Act as "wholly pernicious." By "its unpopularity and impracticability," it was not only "bringing all law into contempt and disrepute," but was "making law-breaking a pastime—something for the average citizen to 'brag about.' " Though not in favor of reopening the saloons, these critics of the Volstead Act did urge that the sale of beer and light wine be legalized once more. Echoing antebellum critics of prohibition, they maintained that moral suasion would better advance the cause of "real temperance" than would legal coercion.[53] The

---

[52] Hutton quoted in Records of the Secretary of the Rhode Island Anti-Saloon League, 1908-1929, 9 June 1925, RIHS; *Providence Journal*, 1 September 1930. A poll commissioned by the *Literary Digest* in the spring of 1930 pronounced Rhode Island the "wettest" state in the Union. In a referendum the following November state voters cast their ballots overwhelmingly (by a margin of 3.5 to one) for repeal. *Providence Journal*, 11 April, 5 November 1930.

[53] *Providence Journal*, 14 January 1923, 20 November 1929. On the national AAPA, see David E. Kyvig, "Objection Sustained: Prohibition Repeal and the New Deal," in

wives of many of these men were members of the Providence and Newport chapters of the Women's Organization for National Prohibition Reform (WONPR). More radical than the AAPA, the WONPR called for the outright repeal of the Eighteenth Amendment. According to its members, "increased lawlessness, hypocrisy and corruption" had accompanied national prohibition. Visiting factories, cleaning and dyeing establishments, department stores, and other large employers of women, volunteers enlisted working women in the campaign for repeal. By April 1932 the WONPR claimed more than six thousand members in the state, a twofold increase in less than a year. The state branch of the AAPA reported more than twenty thousand members.[54]

At first glance, the struggle over prohibition appeared to evoke cultural configurations reminiscent of the antebellum temperance crusades. It set the abstemious middle classes against the wet upper and lower classes, and Protestants against Catholics and Jews. Yet, for many Protestants, abstinence was no longer a cultural norm. While the Volstead Act was in effect, drinking became a measure of conspicuous consumption or "luxury." Affluent Americans substituted liquor for beer, and respectable women began to drink in public. Social drinking became acceptable on college campuses as well. Though curbing working-class consumption—per capita consumption fell from an all-time high of 1.69 gallons in 1911-14 to .73 gallon in 1923 before climbing to 1.14 gallons by 1930—prohibition had the unanticipated and clearly unintended consequence of encouraging drinking among the more affluent. Changing attitudes toward drink, particularly as they affected middle-class Protestants, contributed to the drive for the modification and eventual repeal of the Eighteenth Amendment.[55]

Alcohol, Reform and Society: The Liquor Issue in Social Context, ed. Jack S. Blocker, Jr. (Westport, Conn.: Greenwood Press, 1979), 211-33. For the AAPA in action, see Larry Engelmann, "Organized Thirst: The Story of Repeal in Michigan," in ibid., 171-210.

[54] The organization of the WONPR in Rhode Island can be followed in the *Providence Journal*, 29 July, 16 August 1930, 22 February, 14 April 1931, 14 April 1932. On the national WONPR, see Grace C. Root, *Women and Repeal: The Story of the Women's Organization for National Prohibition Reform* (New York: Harper & Brothers, 1934); and David E. Kyvig, "Women Against Prohibition," *American Quarterly* 28 (Fall 1976): 465-82.

[55] J. C. Burnham, "New Perspectives on the Prohibition 'Experiment' of the 1920's," *Journal of Social History* 2 (Fall 1968): 59-60, 63; Joseph R. Gusfield, "Prohi-

The debate over the Eighteenth Amendment also involved changing patterns of consumption. Spokesmen for the American housewife, "Mrs. Consumer," expected prohibition to rechannel money formerly spent on drink—estimated at between $1.8 and $2.2 billion each year—into consumer spending. The Eighteenth Amendment, as Christine Frederick pointed out, had "released a vast sum of money for Mrs. Consumer to spend," because the typical housewife, who controlled most of her family's discretionary income, knew that she could use this money "very nicely indeed for the washing machine, vacuum cleaner, piano, furnishings, automobile and new home which she yearned for but couldn't in the old days afford." A number of businessmen supported prohibition until the stock market crash of 1929 for the same reasons. They attributed the prosperity of the 1920s, the fantastic rise in national income from $63.1 billion in 1922 to $87.8 billion in 1929, to the thrift and domestic expenditures encouraged by the Eighteenth Amendment. As the economy declined catastrophically after the fall of 1929, however, businessmen began to reconsider their support for prohibition. Many eventually embraced repeal as a panacea for economic recovery in the hope that permitting the manufacture and sale of alcoholic beverages would generate new revenues for starved federal and state treasuries as well as pump money into the economy.[56]

The storm over prohibition raged at a critical moment in the development of the American economy. In the three decades from 1900 until 1930 the volume of manufactured goods increased by 151 percent, exceeding by almost two and a half times national population growth, which increased only 65 percent. As production

bition: The Impact of Political Utopianism," in *Change and Continuity in Twentieth-Century America: The 1920's*, ed. John Braeman et al. (Columbus: Ohio State University Press, 1968), 273-78; Norman H. Clark, *Deliver Us from Evil: An Interpretation of American Prohibition* (New York: W. W. Norton & Co., 1976), 210-14; Paula S. Fass, *The Damned and the Beautiful: American Youth in the 1920's* (New York: Oxford University Press, 1977), 310-24.

[56] Frederick, *Selling Mrs. Consumer*, 269, 271; Benjamin R. Andrews, "The Home Woman as Buyer and Controller of Consumption," *Annals of the American Academy of Political and Social Science* 143 (May 1929): 41-42. In September 1918 businessmen from all over the state took out a full-page advertisement to urge ratification of the Eighteenth Amendment. *Providence Journal*, 9 September 1918. On why businessmen generally supported prohibition, see James H. Timberlake, *Prohibition and the Progressive Movement, 1900-1920* (New York: Atheneum, 1970), 67-99.

grew more efficient, consumption lagged further and further behind. Around 1922, the market for consumer goods changed from a "seller's" market to a "buyer's" market. "Concealed inflation," manufacturers' failure to pass on gains in productivity in the form of either higher wages or lower wholesale prices, compounded the imbalance between America's capacity to produce and its capacity to consume. What reduction there was in wholesale prices was frequently "absorbed in marketing channels." By 1929, at the height of "New Era" prosperity, an estimated 20 percent of the productive capacity of many important industries remained unutilized. But "excess capacity" also reflected the maldistribution of national income. In 1929 three out of every five American families earned less than $2,000 a year—the minimum annual income considered necessary to afford basic necessities. As architect Frederick L. Ackerman observed, "our economy is so set up that it produces goods at a higher rate than it produces income with which to purchase them."[57]

Instead of lowering prices or raising wages, manufacturers resorted to "high pressure salesmanship and installment credits to induce people to buy more than they could afford." They also promoted "consumptionism," which Frederick defined as "the idea that workmen and the masses be looked upon not simply as workers or producers, but as *consumers*." To drum up consumption, they turned to "household engineers" like Frederick, invested heavily in advertising, extended credit to consumers, and lavished money on welfare capitalism.[58]

For their part, consumers often expressed bewilderment at the cornucopia of goods available on the market. In fact, as Robert and Helen Lynd pointed out in *Middletown*, their classic study of Amer-

[57] Robert S. Lynd, "The People as Consumers," in *Recent Social Trends in the United States*, 857; Pease, *The Responsibilities of American Advertising*, 13; Arthur Feiler, "The Evolution of the Consumer," *Annals of the American Academy of Political and Social Science* 196 (March 1938): 7; Maurice Leven, Harold G. Moulton, and Clark Warburton, *America's Capacity to Consume* (Washington, D.C.: Brookings Institution, 1934), 2, 54; Harold G. Moulton, *Income and Economic Progress* (Washington, D.C.: Brookings Institution, 1935), 54, 142; Broadus Mitchell, "Brief for the Consumer," *Annals of the American Academy of Political and Social Science* 196 (March 1938): 11; Ackerman quoted in Stuart Chase, *The Economy of Abundance* (New York: Macmillan Co., 1934), 11.

[58] Moulton, *Income and Economic Progress*, 153; Frederick, *Selling Mrs. Consumer*, 4-5.

ican life in the 1920s, consumers were quickly becoming "illiterate." Facing "the very plethora of choices bred by the multiplication of ingenious alternative consumption goods by industries anxious to maintain their volume," consumers were no longer able to rely on the same sorts of commonsense or empirical comparisons once available to their parents. Though still able to discriminate among goods on the basis of price, they found it almost impossible to determine the quality of similarly priced goods. "The consumer's problem," noted Robert Lynd, "is one of selection to a degree never before known." A study of the consumption patterns of some 5,000 Milwaukee residents in 1931 found them using 115 different brands of packaged coffee, 76 brands of toothpaste, and 256 brands of toothbrushes.[59]

Consumers were not only befuddled, they were also tempted. Installment buying and other consumer credit plans, in the words of one consumer advocate, were "revolutioniz[ing] the Puritan idea of thrift as a moral virtue" and eroding "the ideal of abstinence and frugality." According to Robert Lynd, Americans were caught between two rival sets of norms: on the one hand, traditional injunctions to abstinence, frugality, and paying cash; on the other, "the new attitude towards hardship as a thing to be avoided by living in the here and now, utilizing instalment credit and other devices to telescope the future into the present." Lynd particularly objected to the way in which advertising sanctioned immediate gratification and identified self-fulfillment with consumption. Instead of practicing thrift, or "cutting one's expenditures to fit one's purse," many Americans had come to believe that "the way to 'get out of the red' is to push one's income up another peg and that 'you've got to spend money nowadays in order to earn it.' "[60]

[59] Robert S. Lynd and Helen Merrell Lynd, *Middletown: A Study in American Culture* (1929; reprint, New York: Harcourt, Brace & World, 1956), 166, 176, 222; Robert S. Lynd, "Family Members as Consumers," *Annals of the American Academy of Political and Social Science* 160 (March 1932): 89, 92.

[60] Paul F. Douglass, "Foreword," *Annals of the American Academy of Political and Social Science* 196 (March 1938): xi; R. Lynd, "The People as Consumers," 867; R. Lynd, "Family Members as Consumers," 89.On the consumer culture of the 1920s, see Lary May, *Screening Out the Past: The Birth of Mass Culture and the Motion Picture Industry* (New York: Oxford University Press, 1980), esp. chap. 8; Elaine Tyler May, *Great Expectations: Marriage and Divorce in Post-Victorian America* (Chicago: University of Chicago Press, 1980); and T. J. Jackson Lears, "From Salvation to Self-Realization: Advertising and the Therapeutic Roots of the Consumer Culture, 1880-1930," in *The Culture of Consumption*, ed. Fox and Lears, 1-38.

While consumers were befuddled, producers were becoming better organized. As secretary of commerce, Herbert Hoover made his
department into a "service unit" for the American businessman. Exploiting the public relations techniques he had mastered during the
war, Hoover exhorted businessmen to reduce industrial waste and
inefficiency as a means of "rais[ing] American standards of living."
Encouraged by the Department of Commerce, trade associations,
which proliferated during the 1920s, promulgated "codes of fair
competition" for their industries. "We are, almost unnoticed, in the
midst of a great revolution, or perhaps a better word, a transformation in the whole super-organization of our economic life," Hoover announced. "We are passing from a period of extremely individualistic actions into a period of associational activities."[61]
Department store magnate Edward A. Filene and other "corporate
liberals" who shared Hoover's vision of industrial "self-government" dreamed of eliminating "the wastes in production and distribution of our modern business system." Filene, who was later to offer $25,000 to the President's Research Committee on Social
Trends to propose ways in which waste could be trimmed, stressed
the fact that a mass production society depended on the buying
power of the masses. Henry Ford, he believed, had pointed the way
by simultaneously lowering the price of his Model T and raising his
workers' wages.[62]

Although still not represented in Washington, consumers were
gradually becoming more aware of their own interest. Significantly,
neither the Consumers' League nor the Housewives League voiced
this growing consumer consciousness. Because of its concern for
protecting working women and children, the Consumers' League
by its own lights was not "a true consumer group," that is, "a group

[61] Herbert Hoover, "Backing Up Business," *Review of Reviews* 78 (September
1928): 279; Lloyd, *Aggressive Introvert*, 124; R. Lynd, "The People as Consumers,"
885. See also Committee on Elimination of Waste in Industry of the Federated American Engineering Societies, *Waste in Industry* (New York: McGraw-Hill, 1921); Arthur M. Schlesinger, Jr., *The Coming of the New Deal* (Boston: Houghton Mifflin Co.,
1959), 88-89; and Robert S. Lynd, "The Consumer Becomes a 'Problem,' " *Annals of
the American Academy of Political and Social Science* 173 (May 1934): 3.

[62] Edward A. Filene, "Foreword," in Nathan, *The Story of an Epoch-Making Movement*, xvii; Filene, *The Consumer's Dollar* (New York: John Day Co., 1934); Karl, "Presidential Planning and Social Science Research," 385; Kim McQuaid, "Corporate Liberalism in the American Business Community, 1920-1940," *Business History Review* 52
(Autumn 1978): 342-68.

of consumers working *for* consumers." Because of its goal of organizing the home as an industry, the Housewives League had joined the ranks of organized producer groups. Leadership of the consumer movement during the 1920s thus devolved on members of the new middle class. As this occurred, the consumer movement embraced new goals, including quality standards, the elimination of waste, and economic security.[63]

Demands for quality standards issued from men like Stuart Chase, a popularizer of Thorstein Veblen's prescriptions for industrial efficiency, and Frederick J. Schlink, an industrial engineer. In their best-selling work published in 1927, *Your Money's Worth: A Study in the Waste of the Consumer's Dollar*, which Robert Lynd called "the Uncle Tom's Cabin of the consumer movement," Chase and Schlink attacked advertising and high-pressure salesmanship and demanded scientific testing and product standards to provide consumers with technical information so that they could indeed buy intelligently. "The consumer," Chase and Schlink asserted, "can be organized by the million to jump through the hoops of the advertiser." The question was, "can he be organized to better his health, increase his real wages, and get a dollar's worth of value for his dollar?" If the federal government saved hundreds of millions of dollars a year through purchasing by product specification, why should consumers not do the same? Why should the Bureau of Standards of the Department of Commerce, which tested and rated products purchased by the federal government, not share its ratings with consumers? Following the publication of *Your Money's Worth*, quality standards and proper labeling for consumer goods became the primary goal of the consumer movement.[64]

Until the the Bureau of Standards disclosed the information it

---

[63] John D. Black, "Preface," in Sorenson, *The Consumer Movement*, x. See also Clark Foreman and Michael Ross, *The Consumer Seeks a Way* (New York: W. W. Norton & Co., 1935), 189-90.

[64] Robert Lynd quoted in "The Consumer Movement," *Business Week* 503 (22 April 1939): 40; Stuart Chase and Frederick J. Schlink, *Your Money's Worth: A Study in the Waste of the Consumer's Dollar* (New York: Macmillan Co., 1927), 256; Robert A. Brady, "How Government Standards Affect the Ultimate Consumer," *Annals of the American Academy of Political and Social Science* 137 (May 1928): 247-52; Robert S. Lynd, "Why the Consumer Wants Quality Standards," *Advertising and Selling* 22 (4 January 1934): 15-16, 46-49; D. W. McConnell, "The Bureau of Standards and the Ultimate Consumer," *Annals of the American Academy of Political and Social Science* 173 (May 1934): 146-52.

collected, consumers had to rely on their own resources, particularly on independent product-testing agencies. After readers of *Your Money's Worth* besieged the authors with requests for product information, Schlink and Chase converted a small consumer's club in White Plains, New York, into Consumers' Research. As a clearinghouse for consumer information, the new agency employed technical experts to test commodities, and then published the results in a monthly research bulletin reaching 43,000 subscribers by 1932. Product testing and buyer guidance were intended to protect consumers from misleading advertising.[65]

Yet consumers comprised such a heterogeneous group that they proved extremely difficult to organize. Most still saw themselves primarily as producers and only secondarily as consumers. The typical consumer, observed social scientist Arthur Feiler, was "much more inclined to apply all means to increase and protect his nominal income as a producer than to defend his real purchasing power as a consumer." Consumers were also unaware of their illiteracy, their need for expert help in buying. It would take a shock to jar consumers out of their complacency and to crystallize consumer consciousness on a national scale. The stock market crash of 1929 and the ensuing depression constituted just such an "earthquake."[66]

It is claiming too much to say that consumer movement was a "child of the depression," as the chairman of the Consumer Conference of Cincinnati asserted in 1939. When the stock market plummeted in the fall of 1929, the movement had been developing for more than three decades. Yet the Great Depression did stimulate the growth of consumer consciousness. The prolonged business downturn dramatized the fundamental economic problem of a mass-production society: inadequate consumer demand. National income, which was low and badly skewed before the Depression, fell even more after 1929. The National Resources Committee Board found in 1935-36 that two out of every three American families and individuals lived on less than $1,450 a year; a third earned under $780 annually. The Depression hit Providence particularly

[65] Sorenson, *The Consumer Movement*, 46-48; Silber, *Test and Protest*, 17-19.

[66] Feiler, "The Evolution of the Consumer," 3; R. Lynd, "Why the Consumer Wants Quality Standards," 46; Ellis W. Hawley, *The New Deal and the Problem of Monopoly: A Study in Economic Ambivalence* (Princeton: Princeton University Press, 1966), 198-200.

hard, throwing more than a third of the city's labor force out of work. In October 1937, according to the Department of Commerce, 63 percent of the city's families had annual incomes of less than $1,500, 41 percent less than $1,000, and 5.2 percent reported no income whatsoever. In addition, excess industrial capacity, a problem even during the prosperous twenties, became far worse after 1929. Falling demand for consumer goods created a vicious business cycle, in which even the best-intentioned companies could not afford to sustain production and wages at pre-Depression levels. Shorter hours and smaller wages, in turn, further reduced consumer demand.[67]

The Roosevelt administration's response to the business downturn was the National Industrial Recovery Administration (NRA), whose aim was, in the president's own words, "to restore our rich domestic market by raising the vast consuming capacity." In designing the NRA structure, General Hugh Johnson established industrial, labor, and consumers' advisory boards to ensure representation of the three parties to "the industrial process." Characterized by Robert Lynd as "something of an afterthought," the Consumers' Advisory Board of the NRA largely owed its existence to the lobbying of Mary Harriman Rumsey, daughter of the railroad tycoon E. H. Harriman and personal friend of both Hugh Johnson and the Roosevelts. But the creation of the board almost certainly reflected agitation during the winter of 1933-34 for the establishment of a Department of the Consumer, a demand voiced by Robert Lynd in his contribution on "The People as Consumers" to *Recent Social Trends in the United States*. It also reflected the impact of *100,000,000 Guinea Pigs*, by Arthur Kallet and Frederick J. Schlink, which in exposing the inadequacies of the Pure Food and Drug Act of 1906 spawned a wave of "guinea pig journalism." As Kallet wrote in 1934, "it should be evident that our profit economy gives the consumer of foods and drugs not the slightest assurance of either good quality or safety."[68]

---

[67] Mrs. Dennis Jackson quoted in Sorenson, *The Consumer Movement*, 10; Robert S. Lynd, "Foreword," in Persia Campbell, *Consumer Representation in the New Deal* (New York: Columbia University Press, 1940), 10; David L. Davies, "Impoverished Politics: The New Deal's Impact on City Government in Providence, Rhode Island," *Rhode Island History* 42 (August 1983): 91; *Providence Journal*, 11 October 1937.

[68] R. Lynd, "The Consumer Becomes a 'Problem,' " 5; Arthur Kallet and Frederick J. Schlink, *100,000,000 Guinea Pigs: Dangers in Everyday Foods, Drugs, and Cosmetics*

In the end, the Consumers' Advisory Board accomplished little. "Spearheads without shafts," as Rexford Tugwell wryly observed, the economists, sociologists, and other consumer representatives on the board spoke for no organized constituency. Rather, as Robert Lynd explained, they tried to see the aims of the NRA "from the point of view of large public interest and social policy." They fought for formal consumer representation, access to corporate books, quality standards, and purchasing power indices. They also tried to mobilize a consumer constituency. The board's Bureau of Economic Education encouraged the formation of about 150 county consumer councils—grass-roots organizations comparable to the farm bureaus organized with the encouragement of the Food Administration during the First World War. One of these, the Providence County Consumers' Council, a branch of the Consumers' Council of New England, investigated high prices, ensured quality standards, and instructed consumers how to buy intelligently. Composed of department store owners and advertising men as well as consumers, its principal purpose was to restore consumer confidence in the economy through "Buy Now" campaigns.[69]

But precisely because it represented such an amorphous group, the Consumers' Advisory Board was not able to keep Johnson and his administrators from "stabilizing" competition by regulating production and prices. Rationalizing production, however, did nothing to restore consumer purchasing power. Indeed, the NRA paid little attention to consumers, whom it tended to treat "as wage earners with their first stake in a wage increase." But as home economist Hazel Kyrk pointed out, consumer problems had to be "conceived not as problems of income, but of price, cost of production, and information." It is hardly surprising that many consumers came to regard the NRA, which sanctioned producer self-government by trade association, as an instrument of monopoly. Schlink denounced it as "definitely anti-consumer in purpose and policy." The

(New York: Grosset & Dunlap, 1933); Arthur Kallet, "Foods and Drugs for the Consumer," *Annals of the American Academy of Political and Social Science* 173 (May 1934): 34; Robert S. Lynd, "The Consumers' Advisory Board in the N.R.A.," *Publishers' Weekly* 125 (28 April 1934): 1607-1608; Schlesinger, *The Coming of the New Deal*, 122-30.

[69] Tugwell quoted in Schlesinger, *The Coming of the New Deal*, 130; R. Lynd, "The Consumers' Advisory Board in the N.R.A.," 1607; *Evening Bulletin*, 18 October, 9 November 1933; *Providence Journal*, 18 November 1933, 3 October 1934.

Consumers' Advisory Board, complained economist Broadus
Mitchell, was "a cruel comedy." Like "the prison chaplain, who
prays with the condemned in the death cell," it was "engaged" in
"the business of execution of the consumer." Its "chief duty," he
added, "was to reconcile the consumer to his fate."[70]

Even so, Robert Lynd hailed the creation of the Consumers' Advisory Board as "virtually the first official recognition in Washington
of the existence of a private consumer problem 'affected,' as the lawyers say, 'with public interest.' " The board, moreover, provided a
forum for such articulate consumer spokesmen as future U.S. Senator Paul H. Douglas, the economist who headed its Bureau of Economic Education, and Robert Lynd, whose Committee of Standards
proposed the establishment of a "consumers' standards board" that
would set standards for all products sold to the "ultimate consumer." In addition, the board and its local auxiliaries raised consumer expectations. In January 1935 Harry E. Miller, economics
professor at Brown, urged Governor Theodore Francis Green to
establish a Department of the Consumer when he reorganized the
state government. "The growing complexity of the goods and services offered for sale and the greater separation of the consumer
from the original producer," Miller observed, "make it difficult for
consumers, in the absence of technical guidance, to buy with intelligence." Finally, the Consumers' Advisory Board stirred interest in
consumer purchasing power. In 1936 the Works Progress Administration sponsored a nationwide survey of family expenditures by
income level in 50 cities, 140 villages, and 66 farm counties. This
study did more than simply collect information not previously available; in Providence, as in the other communities studied, it furnished employment to unemployed white-collar workers of "education, personality and ability."[71]

[70] Hazel Kyrk, "Wastes in the Consumer's Dollar," *Annals of the American Academy of
Political and Social Science* 173 (May 1934): 25; Frederick J. Schlink, "Safeguarding
the Consumer's Interest—An Essential Element in National Recovery," ibid. 172
(March 1934): 116; Mitchell, "Brief for the Consumer," 10; Hawley, *The New Deal and
the Problem of Monopoly*, 75-79, 198-204.

[71] R. Lynd, "The Consumer Becomes a 'Problem,' " 5; Robert S. Lynd, "A New Deal
for the Consumer?" *New Republic* 77 (3 January 1934): 220-22; *Providence Journal*, 27
January 1935, 30 January, 1 February 1936; Mark C. Smith, "Robert Lynd and Consumerism in the 1930's," *Journal of the History of Sociology* 2 (Fall-Winter 1979-80):
119n.

What was more, Congress enacted several pieces of legislation in-tended to protect the consumer. In 1933 Senator Royal S. Copeland of New York introduced a bill to revise the Pure Food and Drug Act and to strengthen the Food and Drug Administration (FDA) by giv-ing the FDA power to prevent false and misleading advertising. Be-cause of vigorous lobbying by drug companies, Franklin Roosevelt's lack of interest, and public apathy, Copeland's bill did not pass Con-gress until 1938, and then in much diluted form, shorn of its pro-visions authorizing the FDA to regulate advertising. It passed, moreover, only after nearly a hundred people died from taking the so-called wonder drug Elixir Sulfanilamide. Far more important to the future of the consumer movement was the Wheeler-Lea Act, also passed in 1938. Introduced three years earlier as a weaker sub-stitute for Senator Copeland's bill, it authorized the Federal Trade Commission (FTC) to regulate advertising. Consumer groups, who were practically unanimous in their opposition to the Wheeler-Lea Act, protested that the FTC with its limited power to issue cease-and-desist orders could not really prevent deceptive advertising. Because of the substantial growth of the American middle classes following the Second World War, however, the FTC came to speak for a powerful consumer constituency.[72]

By identifying itself with the public interest, the consumer move-ment purported to be inclusive. Consumers, wrote consumer econ-omist Persia Campbell, included "all persons who make final or ul-timate use of economic goods," that is, "everyone, whether or not they contribute to production." Consequently, they "do not consti-tute a distinct group as do certain producer, religious, political, or other groups who may develop a specialized group interest. They include members of all groups when engaged in the function of consumption." As Dr. James Peter Warbasse, president of the Co-operative League, put it, "The consumers are no class. They are all."[73]

In reality, though, the consumer movement was fragmented,

[72] Charles O. Jackson, *Food and Drug Legislation in the New Deal* (Princeton: Prince-ton University Press, 1970); Alan Stone, *Economic Regulation and the Public Interest: The Federal Trade Commission in Theory and Practice* (Ithaca: Cornell University Press, 1977), 153-79; Hawley, *The New Deal and the Problem of Monopoly*, 203.

[73] Campbell, *The Consumer Interest*, 1; James Peter Warbasse, "Introduction," in Charles Gide, *Consumers' Co-operative Societies* (New York: Alfred A. Knopf, 1922), xiii.

consisting of a number of scattered organizations whose numbers multiplied after the stock market crash. "As consumers we are 125 million people interested in countless goods and services," declared Professor Harry Miller, "and so diffuse an interest, though it transcends all others in the aggregate, is difficult to organize and has thus far failed to find expression." Among the organizations who, as the sympathetic economist Gardiner C. Means put it, were "in no way committed to the producer point of view," were the General Federation of Women's Clubs, the National Congress of Parents and Teachers, the American Association of University Women, and similar women's organizations concerned with the adulteration of food, drugs, and cosmetics, and with misleading advertising. Another group of consumer advocates, typified by Frederick J. Schlink, identified the consumer interest with intelligent buying. Schlink urged more technical information, expert research, and the establishment of a federal Department of the Consumer. Arthur Kallet and the other staff members who left Consumers' Research after a bitter four months' strike to found Consumers Union in May 1936 perpetuated the tradition of ethical consumption. Until 1938 *Consumers Union Reports* commonly reported on the conditions in which goods were produced as well as on the quality of the goods themselves. To fight fascism in Europe, the magazine advocated the boycott of German-made goods. Membership drives targeted at union workers, low subscription rates, and coverage of topics thought to be of interest to low-income families reflected Consumers Union's attempt to forge a consumer-labor alliance.[74]

Consumer spokesmen like Stuart Chase and Robert Lynd saw the consumer movement as the entering wedge for a planned society to be directed by technocrats like themselves. These experts, as a sympathetic *New Republic* pointed out, would represent "the public interest," not "the capitalists," and production-for-use would take the place of a wasteful, if not irrational, system of production-for-profit. Chase popularized an economy of abundance, in which

[74] Miller quoted in *Providence Journal*, 27 January 1935; Gardiner C. Means, "The Consumer and the New Deal," *Annals of the American Academy of Political and Social Science* 173 (May 1934): 16; Schlink, "Safeguarding the Consumer Interest," 113-22; Frederick J. Schlink, "What Government Does and Might Do for the Consumer," *Annals of the American Academy of Political and Social Science* 173 (May 1934): 124-43; Silber, *Test and Protest*, 23-29.

the "soviet of technicians" envisioned by Veblen would shorten working hours, raise the standard of living, and "utterly abolish poverty, slum dwelling, ugliness and grime." He joined George Soule, editor of the *New Republic*, economist Wesley C. Mitchell, another Veblen disciple, and others in praising the experience of planned societies in the Soviet Union and Italy until events later in the decade discredited these experiments in central planning.[75] Lynd similarly concluded that " 'business as usual' has become an intolerably wasteful luxury for a democracy." In *Middletown* he and his wife had complained of "consumer illiteracy" and the need for consumer reeducation, but Lynd now argued for "an economy operated for ends of engineered consumption rather than for the uncontrolled end of production for individual profit." Questioning the belief that "rational consumer choices" still determined production, he likened the consumer to "a hard-beset mariner willing to make for almost any likely port in a storm." Precisely for this reason, Lynd insisted that the federal government assume the role of "a surrogate responsible for 'the public interest.' "[76]

A final group of consumers, led by Dr. Warbasse, the author Albert Sonnichsen, and the philosopher Horace M. Kallen, envisioned a middle-class America that consisted not of independent producers, but rather of "voluntary associations of consumers" organized along the lines of either the cooperative store established in Rochdale, England, in 1844, or contemporary Swedish co-ops. By reuniting production and consumption, separated since the early nineteenth century, thereby harmonizing economic interests, consumer

[75] Stuart Chase, *The Challenge of Waste*, rev. ed. (New York: League for Industrial Democracy, 1925), 6; George Soule, "Hard-Boiled Radicalism," *New Republic* 65 (21 January 1931): 261-65; ibid., *The Planned Society* (New York: Macmillan Co., 1932); Wesley C. Mitchell, "The Social Sciences and National Planning," in Mitchell, *The Backward Art of Spending Money and Other Essays*, 83-102. For Veblen's influence on the consumer movement, see Norman David Katz, "Consumers Union: The Movement and the Magazine, 1936-1957" (Ph.D. diss., Rutgers University, 1977), 14-50, 228-34. See also Robert B. Westbrook, "Tribune of the Technostructure: The Popular Economics of Stuart Chase," *American Quarterly* 32 (Fall 1980): 387-408.

[76] R. Lynd, "Foreword," 12; ibid., "The Consumer Becomes a 'Problem,' " 4-5; ibid., "Family Members as Consumers," 92; Robert S. Lynd, "Democracy's Third Estate: The Consumer," *Political Science Quarterly* 51 (December 1936): 504. On Robert Lynd as a consumer spokesman, see Smith, "Robert Lynd and Consumerism in the 1930's," 99-119; and Richard Wightman Fox, "Epitaph for Middletown: Robert S. Lynd and the Analysis of Consumer Culture," in *The Culture of Consumption*, ed. Fox and Lears, 101-141.

cooperatives would avert class conflict. They would also decentralize both the economy and government, a practical alternative to the bombast of Huey Long, Father Coughlin, and other critics of "modernization." The substitution of consumer co-ops for corporate capitalism, according to Sidney and Beatrice Webb, would mean production-for-use "carried on under democratic control without the incentive of profit making, or the stimulus of pecuniary gain." And though consumer cooperation embodied a program "quite as revolutionary as Bolshevism," Sonnichsen portrayed it as a peaceful "alternative to revolutionary and political socialism, not an antidote, or a compromise." The visit of Japanese evangelist Dr. Toyohiko Kagawa, who regarded consumer cooperation as "economic Christianity," to Providence in April 1936 stimulated interest in cooperatives. During the winter of 1936-37 a cooperative organizer, sponsored by the Inter-Church Commission for Social Action, a group of Protestant and Jewish activists, broadcast the philosophy of cooperation to Rhode Islanders.[77]

On the eve of the Second World War the consumer movement remained quite diffuse. It was also quite small, claiming fewer than a million members nationally. The great majority of its adherents appear to have been members of the new middle class. The 85,000 members of the Consumers Union in 1939, for example, were largely professionals—teachers, school administrators, and engineers—were better educated and earned more money than did the average American. Much as it had in the 1920s, the consumer movement continued to appeal to middle-class Americans who saw in

[77] Sidney Webb and Beatrice Webb, *The Consumers' Co-operative Movement* (London: Longmans, Green & Co., 1921), vi; Albert Sonnichsen, *Consumers' Cooperation* (New York: Macmillan Co., 1919), xi; Bertram B. Fowler, *Consumer Cooperation in America: Democracy's Way Out* (New York: Vanguard Press, 1936), 280; *Providence Journal*, 23 April, 7 November 1936; Records of the Inter-Church Commission for Social Action, 3 February, 7 October, 4 November 1936, 6 January 1937, in the Arthur E. Wilson Papers, RIHS. See also James Peter Warbasse, *Co-operative Democracy Through Voluntary Association of the People as Consumers*, 2nd ed. (New York: Macmillan Co., 1927); Emerson P. Harris, *Cooperation: The Hope of the Consumer* (New York: Macmillan Co., 1918); Horace M. Kallen, *The Decline and Rise of the Consumer: A Philosophy of Consumer Cooperation* (New York: D. Appleton-Century Co., 1936); Marquis Childs, *Sweden: The Middle Way*, rev. ed. (New Haven: Yale University Press, 1947); Samson, "The Emergence of a Consumer Interest," chap. 7. On Long and Coughlin, see Alan Brinkley, *Voices of Protest: Huey Long, Father Coughlin, and the Great Depression* (New York: Vintage Books, 1983).

consumer consciousness an antidote to the waste of an uncontrolled
or unplanned society in which the public interest was subordinated
to the narrower interests of organized producers. In spite of the fervent hopes of the staff of Consumers Union for a consumer-worker
alliance, organized labor held back from the consumer movement.
Few workers realized how they might increase their real income if
they too began to define themselves as consumers.[78]

Thus consumer spokesmen voiced the aspirations of middle-class
Americans who, for one reason or another, no longer thought of
themselves as producers in the conventional sense. In theory, the
consumer movement embodied an inclusive identity that would
transcend the petty jealousies and rivalries of producer groups. In
practice, however, its success, just like the success of antagonistic
producers, depended on how well it organized itself as another interest group in a pluralistic society. The consumer was "a sort of
myth," remarked a character in *The Consumer Seeks a Way*, Clark
Foreman and Michael Ross's plea for a planned society. "As the old
saying has it, everybody's business is nobody's business." Until they
organized, consumers would continue to be left out in the cold. Gardiner C. Means wrote in 1934, "the important thing is not to organize *individuals as consumers* but to organize the *consumer interest*." In so
doing, consumers underscored the irony of middle-class organization. In organizing themselves into yet one more interest group, the
middle classes called into question their claim that their class interests were identical with the public interest.[79]

[78] Robert S. Lynd, "Introduction," *Annals of the American Academy of Political and Social Science* 173 (May 1934): xiii; Means, "The Consumer and the New Deal," 16; Sorenson, *The Consumer Movement*, 50.

[79] Foreman and Ross, *The Consumer Seeks A Way*, 111; Means, "The Consumer and
the New Deal," 15.

9 THE MIDDLE CLASSES ON THE EVE
OF THE SECOND WORLD WAR

THE Great Depression, which threw millions of Americans out of work and threatened the material possessions and savings of millions more, raised fears about the survival of the middle classes. By 1935 observers as diverse as the native-born radical Alfred Bingham and the Italian-born Marxist Lewis Corey were warning of the dangers of fascism in the United States. Millions of Americans appeared to be rallying to the vague programs of demagogues like Huey Long and Father Charles Coughlin who promised a return to a society consisting of independent producers, broad ownership of property, and widely dispersed power. Though coming at the so-called crisis of the middle class from different angles, both Bingham and Corey envisioned a society in which the "new middle class" of salaried workers and professionals would make common cause with workingmen, reject a discredited capitalism, and adopt some form of democratic collectivism. This was precisely the kind of coalition that middle-class organizations like the Consumers Union and the League for Industrial Democracy were working to bring about.[1]

The Depression prompted still other observers to invoke the historic role of the middle classes as the broad and inclusive basis for a stable social order. Political scientist Harold D. Lasswell stressed the need for "the middle-income skill group," by which he meant farmers, small businessmen, intellectuals, and skilled workers, to become more conscious of its "moral vocation." Similarly, philosopher T. V.

[1] Alfred M. Bingham, *Insurgent America: Revolt of the Middle-Classes* (New York: Harper & Brothers, 1935); Lewis Corey, "The Crisis of the Middle Class," *Nation* 141 (14, 21, 28 August 1935): 176-78, 207-210, 238-41; ibid., *The Crisis of the Middle Class* (New York: Covici, Friede, 1935); Robert Morss Lovett, *The Middle Class and Organized Labor* (New York: League for Industrial Democracy, 1940). See also Donald L. Miller, *The New American Radicalism: Alfred M. Bingham and Non-Marxian Insurgency in the New Deal Era* (Port Washington, N.Y.: Kennikat Press, 1979), 88-111. On Long and Coughlin, see Alan Brinkley, *Voices of Protest: Huey Long, Father Coughlin, and the Great Depression* (New York: Vintage Books, 1983).

Smith argued that a "middle class of the skilled" had to "come self-consciously into its own to save itself and to save America." Arthur N. Holcombe, professor of government at Harvard, reminded his readers of "the true function of the middle class in the modern state," which was "to mitigate the violence of the struggle between the upper and lower classes and to assert the supremacy of community interests over class interests of any kind." For the middle class not to do so "would involve the abandonment of its best argument, namely, that its special class interests come nearer to coinciding with the general interests than those of any other class."[2]

These calls for middle-class solidarity revealed just how diffuse the middle classes had become. By 1940 the once unitary middle classes—producers subscribing to sobriety, strict Sabbath observance, domesticity, the purposive use of spare time, and other ascetic norms—had long since fragmented. The "old middle class" of independent producers was giving way to a new middle class of salaried workers and professionals, whose stake in society was based less on property than on occupational skill.[3] Although native-born Protestants still made up the great majority of the middle classes, the New Deal opened up new opportunities for upwardly mobile ethnic Americans like John Pastore, who in 1946 became Rhode Island's first Italian-American governor and in 1950 the first Italian-American to sit in the U.S. Senate; certainly, Rhode Island politics would never be the same after the "Bloodless Revolution" of 1935 when urban ethnics seized control of the state government from rural Yankees.[4] It was also possible to speak of the existence of upper and

[2] Harold D. Lasswell, "The Moral Vocation of the Middle-Income Skill Group," *International Journal of Ethics* 45 (January 1935): 127-37; T. V. Smith, *The Promise of American Politics*, 2nd ed. (Chicago: University of Chicago Press, 1936), 229-30; A. N. Holcombe, *The New Party Politics* (New York: W. W. Norton & Co., 1933), 116-17.

[3] Lewis Corey, "Problems of the Peace: IV. The Middle Class," *Antioch Review* 5 (Spring 1945): 68-87; C. Wright Mills, *White Collar: The American Middle Classes* (New York: Oxford University Press, 1951), 63-76.

[4] Samuel Lubell, *The Future of American Politics*, 3rd ed. (New York: Harper & Row, 1965), 77-88. Historians are just now turning their attention to the development of ethnic middle classes. See Daniel J. Walkowitz, *Worker City, Company Town: Iron and Cotton-Worker Protest in Troy and Cohoes, New York, 1855-84* (Urbana: University of Illinois Press, 1978); Roy Rosenzweig, *Eight Hours for What We Will: Workers and Leisure in an Industrial City, 1870-1920* (Cambridge: Cambridge University Press, 1983); and John J. Bukowczyk, "The Transformation of Working-Class Ethnicity: Corporate Control, Americanization, and the Polish Immigrant Middle Class in Bayonne, New Jersey, 1915-1925," *Labor History* 25 (Winter 1984): 53-82.

lower middle-class strata, distinguished by their occupations, leisure associations, and political outlooks.[5]

If the middle classes had once remade the antebellum North in their own image, those whom dramatist Charles Henry Meltzer called "the intermediate millions" were themselves the products of the social, economic, political, and cultural trends that shaped twentieth-century America. The gradual shift from a manufacturing to a service economy, the immigration of millions of non-Protestants, and the rapid growth of cities like Providence all dramatically altered the context in which middle-class consciousness and organization developed between 1820 and 1940.[6]

Between 1820 and 1860 shopkeepers, master craftsmen, and other middle-class northerners became conscious of themselves as a class. As deference declined in the wake of the American Revolution, churches and interdenominational moral reform societies took the place of the local notables who had previously set the tone for society. Middle-class consciousness crystallized in the cultural conflicts that ensued when advocates of abolition, prohibition, and other perfectionist reforms challenged traditional values defended by gentlemen, on the one hand, and workingmen, on the other. Antebellum middle-class consciousness presumed a harmony of interests among producers, celebrated the dignity of labor, condemned great wealth and luxury as solvents of virtue, and enjoined frugal-

[5] Although European historians have long been interested in the lower middle class, especially as the seedbed of fascist movements, the lower middle class remains a neglected topic in American history. The place to start is still C. Wright Mills, *White Collar*. Also useful are Jurgen Kocka, *White Collar Workers in America, 1890-1940: A Social-Political History in International Perspective*, trans. Maura Kealey (Beverly Hills: Sage Publications, 1980); Gregory H. Singleton, "Fundamentalism and Urbanization: A Quantitative Critique of Impressionistic Interpretations," in *The New Urban History: Quantitative Explorations by American Historians*, ed. Leo F. Schnore (Princeton: Princeton University Press, 1975), 205-227; and Samuel P. Hays, "Political Parties and the Community-Society Continuum," in *The American Party Systems: Stages of Political Development*, ed. William Nisbet Chambers and Walter Dean Burnham (New York: Oxford University Press, 1967), 152-81. See also Frederick M. Fiske, "The Elks: An American Ideology," *Journal of Voluntary Action Research* 2 (July 1973): 135-47; Roy Rosenzweig, "Boston Masons, 1900-1935: The Lower Middle Class in a Divided Society," ibid. 6 (July-October 1977): 119-26; and Lynn Dumenil, *Freemasonry and American Culture, 1880-1930* (Princeton: Princeton University Press, 1984), chaps. 4-6.

[6] Charles Henry Meltzer, "The Intermediate Millions," *North American Review* 209 (February 1919): 225-33.

View of Market Square looking east toward College Hill, 1938 (courtesy of the Rhode Island Historical Society)

ity, industry, sobriety, piety, domesticity, and the purposive use of spare time. Above all else, it identified the interests of the middle classes with the public interest.

Voluntary associations composed of shopkeepers and mechanics institutionalized total abstinence, strict Sabbath observance, domesticity, and self-improvement as cultural norms. Democratization and evangelization, which transformed the temperance movement from an attempt to revive paternalism into a program for middle-class respectability, also affected the Sabbatarian crusade and the drive for public schools. Adherents of each reform depended on voluntary organizations, frequently assisted by paid agents, propaganda, and political lobbying, to mold public opinion. Between the 1850s and the 1870s the constellation of values denoted by the term "rational recreation" came to inform the new civic culture of cities like Providence; voluntary associations like the Athenaeum, though limited to fee-paying members and governed by self-perpetuating boards of trustees, took the initiative in fashioning this new culture.

Yet this same organizational impulse soon undermined antebellum ideals. Following the Civil War, the producing classes splintered as first professionals, then businessmen and manufacturers, and finally workingmen organized. The broad antebellum producers' community, defended by advocates of the Social Gospel, Single Taxers, and the Knights of Labor, fell victim to segmentation. By the turn of the century, a few middle-class spokesmen were already beginning to define a new role for their class: no longer coextensive with the producers' community, the middle classes had become disinterested representatives of the public interest who mediated disputes between competing interest groups in a pluralistic society.

The inclusive civic culture also fragmented. Recreational activities, which had formerly bonded the heterogeneous population of an industrializing city, now sorted urban dwellers out along lines of neighborhood, ethnicity, sex, and above all class. New subcultures coalesced around exclusive leisure organizations and activities. One, consisting of upper middle-class businessmen and professionals, centered on the exclusive club. Another, in which vestiges of the undifferentiated producers' community survived, brought together small proprietors, white-collar workers, and workingmen in tens of thousands of fraternal lodges. Middle-class women created a national network of literary clubs. In the meantime total abstinence, the purposive use of spare time, domesticity, strict Sabbath observance, and other antebellum conventions attenuated.

In response to the perceived fragmentation of their society and their once unitary culture, middle-class Americans organized a host of new voluntary associations after 1880, only to call into question their claim that their class interests were identical with the public interest. Prohibitionists, Single Taxers, Christian socialists, and other middle-class moralists still intent on playing the mediator's role prescribed by antebellum ideals struck out at monopoly and partisanship as examples of unrestrained selfishness. Their campaigns of righteousness, whose highly charged rhetoric recalled the antebellum moral reform crusades, flourished as long as they made common cause with businessmen who wished to see government run as efficiently and as economically as a corporation. But social and economic differentiation overwhelmed the dream of moralists like Lucius F. C. Garvin of a middle way between monopolistic capitalism and bureaucratic socialism. Their failure to carry off political reform in the antebellum tradition, which foreshadowed the failure of the prohibition "experiment" in the 1920s, testified to the dissolution of the antebellum moral consensus.

Advocates of rational recreation recognized the need to counter segmentation with more specialized organizations of their own. Accordingly, they organized innumerable clubs differentiated by age, sex, and class. Civic associations like the Rhode Island Educational Union, which in the middle decades of the nineteenth century functioned as surrogates for government, gave way to lobbies like the Public Park Association that framed policies and trained bureaucrats for an administrative state. Instead of designating libraries, quasi-civic lyceums, and other "public" institutions that cut across class and ethnic lines and appealed to the whole family, rational recreation came to mean small parks, playgrounds, field houses, and other neighborhood centers around which a classless, homogeneous society could be preserved in an urban setting. Influenced by new theories that postulated the existence of an irrepressible social instinct, recreational reformers even acknowledged the value of the commercialized amusements they had so long resisted. Rejecting "destructive" reforms like prohibition as impracticable, they experimented with municipal dance halls, children's theater, and other "constructive" outlets for the social instinct.

Systematizers like Henry A. Barker, John Hutchins Cady, and Henry D. Sharpe forged translocal networks in which the long-standing American tradition of local autonomy could be perpetuated under new conditions. As corporate managers and university-trained professionals, they distanced themselves from the moralism that fired Single Taxers like Garvin. Where neighborhood workers hoped to arrest neighborhood deterioration by organizing neighbors into homogeneous peer groups, systematizers turned to institutional solutions like zoning. The "federative metropolis," similar to the London County Council, promised a middle way between haphazard development and annexation.

The success of businessmen and other producer groups in achieving the functional representation of their interests spurred the growth of the consumer movement after the First World War. Even before then, hundreds of thousands of middle-class women had joined consumers' organizations like the Consumers' League and the Housewives League in order to overcome the separation, prescribed by the cult of domesticity, between the home and the world and between production and consumption. They sought to annul this distinction in one of two ways: either by moralizing business practices, or by professionalizing the home. During the 1920s and 1930s the consumer movement incorporated members of the new middle class who no longer defined themselves as producers. Some, disciples of Thorstein Veblen, saw in the consumer movement and its emphasis on production-for-use the entering wedge for a planned society. Others attempted to realize the values once identified with a broad producers' community in consumer cooperatives. Proponents of the consumer movement argued that the consumer interest was more representative of the public interest than any of the more particularistic interests of rival producer groups.

In the 1930s, as they had a century earlier, middle-class Americans continued their search for a classless, harmonious society. What had changed since the antebellum temperance and antislavery crusades was their definition of what constituted a middle-class America, not their determination to make society over in their own image. Indeed, it was through this cultural imperialism, made possible by their organization into networks of voluntary association, that middle-class Americans defined themselves as a class.

BIBLIOGRAPHICAL ESSAY

THIS is a bibliography of sources on the middle classes. Those readers interested in sources on Providence should consult my footnotes and the bibliographical essay in Patrick T. Conley and Paul R. Campbell, *Providence: A Pictorial History* (Norfolk, Va.: Donning Co., 1982), 226-32.

There are no comprehensive histories of the American middle classes. Perhaps the closest thing is C. Wright Mills's *White Collar: The American Middle Classes* (New York: Oxford University Press, 1951), which concentrates on the lower middle class in the twentieth century. Two recent studies stress the importance of antebellum developments in middle-class formation, including the rise of a domestic economy, the creation of new social and economic relations, the privatization of the family, and the revivals of the Second Great Awakening. See Paul E. Johnson, *A Shopkeeper's Millennium: Society and Revivals in Rochester, New York, 1815-1837* (New York: Hill and Wang, 1978); and Mary P. Ryan, *Cradle of the Middle Class: The Family in Oneida County, New York, 1790-1865* (Cambridge: Cambridge University Press, 1981). Johnson's and Ryan's studies join older works by Samuel P. Hays and Robert H. Wiebe that posit the replacement of an "old middle class" of small businessmen by a "new middle class" of salaried office workers and professionals in the late nineteenth and early twentieth centuries. See Hays, *The Response to Industrialism, 1885-1914* (Chicago: University of Chicago Press, 1957) and Weibe, *The Search for Order, 1877-1920* (New York: Hill and Wang, 1967). For a review of these and other works on the making of the American middle classes, see Stuart M. Blumin, "The Hypothesis of Middle-Class Formation in Nineteenth-Century America: A Critique and Some Proposals," *American Historical Review* 90 (April 1985): 299-338.

Several other recent works also contribute to our understanding of antebellum middle-class culture. Karen Halttunen's *Confidence Men and Painted Women: A Study of Middle-Class Culture in America,*

1830-1870 (New Haven: Yale University Press, 1982) analyzes the cult of sincerity at the core of sentimental culture. Paul Boyer's *Urban Masses and Moral Order in America, 1820-1920* (Cambridge: Harvard University Press, 1978) emphasizes the role of moral reform societies in shaping the embryonic middle classes and propagating their values among often recalcitrant workingmen. See also Ronald G. Walters, *American Reformers, 1815-1860* (New York: Hill and Wang, 1978). Eric Foner's *Free Soil, Free Labor, Free Men: The Ideology of the Republican Party before the Civil War* (New York: Oxford University Press, 1970) delineates the free-labor ideology that pervaded the North on the eve of the Civil War.

Antebellum middle-class consciousness cannot be understood apart from the revivals of the Second Great Awakening. Sidney E. Mead argues that, in the wake of the revivals, churches became voluntary associations of explicit believers. "The Rise of the Evangelical Conception of the Ministry in America, 1607-1850," in *The Ministry in Historical Perspectives*, ed. H. Richard Niebuhr and Daniel D. Williams (New York: Harper & Brothers, 1956). Donald G. Mathews has shown how the Second Great Awakening reorganized American society by mobilizing hundreds of thousands of Americans into tightly disciplined peer groups or voluntary associations. "The Second Great Awakening as an Organizing Process, 1780-1830: An Hypothesis," *American Quarterly* 21 (Spring 1969): 23-43. Mathews develops his argument at greater length in *Religion in the Old South* (Chicago: University of Chicago Press, 1977). See also T. Scott Miyakawa, *Protestants and Pioneers: Individualism and Conformity on the American Frontier* (Chicago: University of Chicago Press, 1964), which emphasizes the role of the churches in organizing society in the trans-Allegheny West. Gordon S. Wood suggests that evangelical Protestantism, by encouraging its adherents to define themselves against classes at the social margins, promoted middle-class consciousness in "Evangelical America and Early Mormonism," *New York History* 61 (October 1980): 359-86. For accounts of the annus mirabilis of 1858, see Timothy L. Smith, *Revivalism and Social Reform: American Protestantism on the Eve of the Civil War* (1957; reprint, Baltimore: Johns Hopkins University Press, 1980); and Perry Miller, *The Life of the Mind in America, from the Revolution to the Civil War* (New York: Harcourt, Brace & World, 1965).

The temperance movement, the first reform to be evangelized

and democratized, played a critical role in the formation of the middle classes. Joseph R. Gusfield, *Symbolic Crusade: Status Politics and the American Temperance Movement* (Urbana: University of Illinois Press, 1963), shows how sobriety became a measure of respectability for middle-class northerners. Brian Harrison's *Drink and the Victorians: The Temperance Question in England, 1815-1872* (Pittsburgh: University of Pittsburgh Press, 1971) also emphasizes the appeal of respectability to temperance adherents. In *Deliver Us from Evil: An Interpretation of American Prohibition* (New York: W. W. Norton & Co., 1976), Norman H. Clark argues that Americans abstained from alcohol in order to strengthen the nuclear family. W. J. Rorabaugh depicts the temperance movement as a reaction against alarming levels of alcoholic consumption in *The Alcoholic Republic: An American Tradition* (New York: Oxford University Press, 1979). Rorabaugh identifies advocates of prohibition as the antebellum period's " 'go-ahead' men" in "Prohibition as Progress: New York State's License Elections, 1846," *Journal of Social History* 14 (Spring 1981): 425-43. The best account of the antebellum temperance crusade, however, is Ian R. Tyrrell's *Sobering Up: From Temperance to Prohibition in Antebellum America, 1800-1860* (Westport, Conn.: Greenwood Press, 1979).

One reason why the abolitionists were considered radicals by their contemporaries was that their agents, propaganda, and organizational networks allowed them to bypass local elites. See Leonard L. Richards, *"Gentlemen of Property and Standing": Anti-Abolition Mobs in Jacksonian America* (New York: Oxford University Press, 1970). The classic account by Gilbert Hobbs Barnes, *The Antislavery Impulse, 1830-1844* (1933; reprint, Gloucester, Mass.: Peter Smith, 1957), traces immediatism to the revivals. John L. Thomas examines the perfectionist impulse in "Romantic Reform in America, 1815-1860," *American Quarterly* 17 (Winter 1965): 656-81. Ronald G. Walters's *The Antislavery Appeal: American Abolitionism after 1830* (1978; reprint, New York: W. W. Norton & Co., 1984) delineates the abolitionist world-view. Robert H. Abzug portrays Theodore Dwight Weld, who trained Henry B. Stanton as an agent, in *Passionate Liberator: Theodore Dwight Weld and the Dilemma of Reform* (New York: Oxford University Press, 1980).

On the cult of domesticity, which remained a staple of middle-class culture well into the twentieth century, see Carroll Smith Rosenberg, *Religion and the Rise of the American City: The New York City*

Mission Movement, 1812-1870 (Ithaca: Cornell University Press, 1971); Kathryn Kish Sklar, *Catherine Beecher: A Study in American Domesticity* (New York: W. W. Norton & Co., 1973); Nancy F. Cott, *The Bonds of Womanhood: "Woman's Sphere" in New England, 1780-1835* (New Haven: Yale University Press, 1977); and Mary Ryan, *Cradle of the Middle Class*. Richard Sennett discusses privatization, the sharp distinction between the home and the outside world drawn by middle-class Americans, in *Families against the City: Middle Class Homes of Industrial Chicago, 1872-1890* (Cambridge: Harvard University Press, 1970). See also Sennett's *The Fall of Public Man* (New York: Random House, 1978).

Civic associations, as a number of studies suggest, were instrumental in the functional organization of antebellum communities. They certified middle-class status, provided opportunities for civic leadership, and enhanced local identifications. See Walter S. Glazer, "Participation and Power—Voluntary Associations and the Functional Organization of Cincinnati in 1840," *Historical Methods Newsletter* 5 (September 1972): 151-68; Don H. Doyle, "The Social Functions of Voluntary Associations in a Nineteenth-Century American Town," *Social Science History* 1 (Spring 1977): 333-35 (on Jacksonville, Illinois); Stuart M. Blumin, *The Urban Threshold: Growth and Change in a Nineteenth-Century American Community* (Chicago: University of Chicago Press, 1976) (on Kingston, New York); and Mary Ryan, *Cradle of the Middle Class* (on Utica, New York). Although it pays little attention to civic associations, Michael H. Frisch's *Town into City: Springfield, Massachusetts, and the Meaning of Community, 1840-1880* (Cambridge: Harvard University Press, 1972) is still the best account of the creation of the midcentury civic culture in medium-sized industrial cities like Providence.

On the new civic culture's embodiment in libraries, museums, and other didactic institutions, see Thomas Bender, *Toward an Urban Vision: Ideas and Institutions in Nineteenth-Century America* (1975; reprint, Baltimore: Johns Hopkins University Press, 1982); ibid., *Community and Social Change in America* (New Brunswick, N.J.: Rutgers University Press, 1978); Neil Harris, "The Gilded Age Revisited: Boston and the Museum Movement," *American Quarterly* 14 (Winter 1962): 545-66; and Robert Lewis, "Frontier and Civilization in the Thought of Frederick Law Olmsted," *American Quarterly* 29 (Fall 1977): 385-403. Helen E. Meller discusses the creation of a civic culture in Bristol, England, in *Leisure and the Changing City, 1870-1914* (London: Routledge & Kegan Paul, 1976). Donald M. Scott contends that lyceum lectures helped create a northern public in "The Popular Lecture and the Creation of a Public in Mid-Nineteenth-Century America," *Journal of American History* 66 (March 1980): 791-809.

In analyzing occupational segmentation after the Civil War, I have drawn on a number of different sources. For insight into professionalization, I consulted Kenneth S. Lynn, ed., *The Professions in America* (Boston: Houghton Mifflin Co., 1965); Monte A. Calvert, *The Mechanical Engineer in America, 1830-1910: Professional Cultures in Conflict* (Baltimore: Johns Hopkins University Press, 1967); Joseph F. Kett, *The Formation of the American Medical Profession: The Role of Institutions, 1780-1860* (New Haven: Yale University Press, 1968); Mary O. Furner, *Advocacy and Objectivity: A Crisis in the Professionalization of American Social Science, 1865-1905* (Lexington: University of Kentucky Press, 1975); Burton J. Bledstein, *The Culture of Professionalism: The Middle Class and the Development of Higher Education in America* (New York: W. W. Norton & Co., 1976); and Thomas L. Haskell, *The Emergence of Professional Social Science: The American Social Science Association and the Nineteenth-Century Crisis of Authority* (Urbana: University of Illinois Press, 1977). The development of trade associations has received far less attention. Useful are W. Lloyd Warner and Desmond D. Martin, "Big Trade and Business Associations," in Warner, ed., *The Emergent American Society*, vol. 1: *Large Scale Organizations* (New Haven: Yale University Press, 1967); Robert H. Wiebe, *Businessmen and Reform: A Study of the Progressive Movement* (Cambridge: Harvard University Press, 1962); and Louis Galambos, *Competition and Cooperation: The Emergence of a National Trade Association* (Baltimore: Johns Hopkins University Press, 1966).

Unions have of course been studied extensively. Nick Salvatore's *Eugene V. Debs: Citizen and Socialist* (Urbana: University of Illinois Press, 1982) and Leon Fink's *Workingmen's Democracy: The Knights of Labor and American Politics* (Urbana: University of Illinois Press, 1983) delineate the producerism that informed the nineteenth-century labor movement. Helpful in explaining the motivation of labor reformers are David Montgomery, *Beyond Equality: Labor and the Radical Republicans, 1862-1872* (1967; reprint, New York: Vintage

Books, 1972); and Ross E. Paulson, *Radicalism and Reform: The Vrooman Family and American Social Thought, 1837-1937* (Lexington: University of Kentucky Press, 1968). John L. Thomas, *Alternative America: Henry George, Edward Bellamy, Henry Demarest Lloyd and the Adversary Tradition* (Cambridge: Harvard University Press, 1983) is a superb portrait of three men who attempted to perpetuate the antebellum ideal of a homogeneous society in late nineteenth-century America. Stuart M. Blumin inquires into the decline of the artisan-manufacturer and the separation of brain work from manual labor in "Black Coats to White Collars: Economic Change, Nonmanual Work, and the Social Structure of Industrializing America," in *Small Business in American Life*, ed. Stuart W. Bruchey (New York: Columbia University Press, 1980).

My understanding of the Social Gospel, which impelled a number of middle-class reformers to establish ties to organized labor, derives from James Dombrowski, *The Early Days of Christian Socialism in America* (New York: Columbia University Press, 1936); Charles Howard Hopkins, *The Rise of the Social Gospel in American Protestantism, 1865-1915* (New Haven: Yale University Press, 1940); Aaron Ignatius Abell, *The Urban Impact on American Protestantism, 1865-1900* (Cambridge: Harvard University Press, 1943); Henry F. May, *Protestant Churches and Industrial America* (1949; reprint, New York: Harper & Row, 1967); and Robert T. Handy, *A Christian America: Protestant Hopes and Historical Realities* (New York: Oxford University Press, 1971). William R. Hutchison explores how liberal Protestant theologians coped with the dual assaults of Darwinian evolutionary theory and German higher criticism in *The Modernist Impulse in American Protestantism* (Cambridge: Harvard University Press, 1976). Clyde Griffen portrays liberal Episcopalians who banded together in the Church Association for the Advancement of the Interests of Labor in "Christian Socialism Instructed by Gompers," *Labor History* 12 (Spring 1971): 195-213. Herbert G. Gutman shows how labor leaders invoked millennial Protestant themes in "Protestantism and the American Labor Movement: The Christian Spirit in the Gilded Age," in his *Work, Culture, and Society in Industrializing America: Essays on American Working-Class and Social History* (New York: Vintage Books, 1977).

For insights into the segmentation of leisure, I have found a number of works particularly useful. Perhaps the best place to start is

Daniel T. Rodgers, *The Work Ethic in Industrial America, 1850-1920* (Chicago: University of Chicago Press, 1978), chap. 4. See also Arthur Meier Schlesinger, *The Rise of the City, 1878-1898* (New York: Macmillan Co., 1933), esp. chap. 9; Gunther Barth, *City People: The Rise of Modern City Culture in Nineteenth-Century America* (New York: Oxford University Press, 1980); Dale A. Somers, "The Leisure Revolution: Recreation in the American City, 1820-1920," *Journal of Popular Culture* 5 (Summer 1971): 125-47; and Neil Harris, "Four Stages of Cultural Growth: The American City," in Arthur Mann, Neil Harris, and Sam Bass Warner, Jr., *History and the Role of the City in American Life* (Indianapolis: Indiana Historical Society, 1972). See also Neil Harris, *Humbug: The Art of P. T. Barnum* (Boston: Little, Brown & Co., 1973).

On the role of clubs in the formation of a national upper class, see Max Weber, "The Protestant Sects and the Spirit of Capitalism," in *From Max Weber: Essays in Sociology*, trans., ed., and with an introduction by H. H. Gerth and C. Wright Mills (New York: Oxford University Press, 1946); E. Digby Baltzell, Jr., *Philadelphia Gentlemen: The Making of a National Upper Class* (Chicago: Quadrangle Books, 1971); and David C. Hammack, *Power and Society: Greater New York at the Turn of the Century* (New York: Russell Sage Foundation, 1982).

For analyses of the appeal and membership of late nineteenth- and early twentieth-century fraternal organizations, see Noel P. Gist, "Secret Societies: A Cultural Study of Fraternalism in the United States," *University of Missouri Studies* 15 (October 1940): 9-176; Roy Rosenzweig, "Boston Masons, 1900-1935: The Lower Middle Class in a Divided Society," *Journal of Voluntary Action Research* 6 (July-October 1977): 119-26; Brian Greenberg, "Worker and Community: Fraternal Orders in Albany, New York, 1845-1885," *Maryland Historian* 8 (Fall 1977): 38-53; and Lynn Dumenil, *Freemasonry and American Culture, 1880-1930* (Princeton: Princeton University Press, 1984). Benjamin G. Rader, *American Sports: From the Age of Folk Games to the Age of Spectators* (Englewood Cliffs, N.J.: Prentice-Hall, 1983), summarizes recent research into sports history. Stephen Hardy, *How Boston Played: Sport, Recreation, and Community, 1865-1915* (Boston: Northeastern University Press, 1982), is also useful. Karen J. Blair traces the history of the General Federation of Women's Clubs in *The Clubwoman as Feminist: True Woman-*

hood Redefined, 1868-1914 (New York: Holmes & Meier, 1980). On Sabbatarianism, see Roy Zebulon Chamlee, Jr., "The Sabbath Crusade, 1810-1920" (Ph.D. diss., George Washington University, 1968).

The best starting point for any discussion of progressivism is the review essay by Daniel T. Rodgers, "In Search of Progressivism," *Reviews in American History* 10 (December 1982): 113-32. In *The Age of Reform: From Bryan to F.D.R.* (New York: Vintage Books, 1955), Richard Hofstadter argues that progressive reform represented the attempt by upper middle-class businessmen and professionals to cope with their declining status. In several works, however, Richard L. McCormick emphasizes the genuine outrage many Americans felt about what they perceived as the collusion between greedy corporations and corrupt political machines. See "The Discovery that 'Business Corrupts Politics': A Reappraisal of the Origins of Progressivism," *American Historical Review* 86 (April 1981): 247-74; and *From Realignment to Reform: Political Change in New York State, 1893-1910* (Ithaca: Cornell University Press, 1981). Clyde Griffen highlights the importance of the Social Gospel in "The Progressive Ethos," in *The Development of an American Culture*, ed. Stanley Coben and Lorman Ratner, 2nd ed. (New York: St. Martin's Press, 1983). David P. Thelen interprets the Good Government crusades as revolts of taxpayers and consumers against corporate arrogance in *The New Citizenship: Origins of Progressivism in Wisconsin, 1885-1900* (Columbia: University of Missouri Press, 1972). Jon C. Teaford revises James Bryce's view of municipal government as America's "one conspicuous failure" in *The Unheralded Triumph: City Government in America, 1870-1900* (Baltimore: Johns Hopkins University Press, 1984).

On the commercialization of leisure, see Asa Briggs, *Mass Entertainment: The Origins of a Modern Industry* (Adelaide: Griffin Press, 1960); Robert Sklar, *Movie-Made America: A Cultural History of American Movies* (New York: Vintage Books, 1976); John F. Kasson, *Amusing the Million: Coney Island at the Turn of the Century* (New York: Hill and Wang, 1978); Lary May, *Screening Out the Past: The Birth of Mass Culture and the Motion Picture Industry* (New York: Oxford University Press, 1980); and Lewis A. Erenberg, *Steppin' Out: New York Nightlife and the Transformation of American Culture, 1890-1930* (1981; reprint, Chicago: University of Chicago Press, 1984). Alan Havig reviews twentieth-century recreational surveys in "The Commercial Amusement Audience in Early 20th-Century American Cities," *Journal of American Culture* 5 (Spring 1982): 1-19. Roy Rosenzweig, *Eight Hours for What We Will: Workers and Leisure in an Industrial City, 1870-1920* (Cambridge: Cambridge University Press, 1983), and Francis G. Couvares, *The Remaking of Pittsburgh: Class and Culture in an Industrializing City, 1877-1919* (Albany: State University of New York Press, 1984) argue that the commercialization of leisure undermined a plebeian culture organized around churches, mutual benefit societies, fraternal lodges, and unions. Stephen Yeo analyzes the threat posed by commercialization to middle-class organizations in late nineteenth-century Reading, England, in *Religion and Voluntary Organisations in Crisis* (London: Croom Helm, 1976).

A number of works discuss middle-class responses to commercialized amusements. On the working girls' clubs, see Kathy Lee Peiss, "Cheap Amusements: Gender Relations and the Use of Leisure Time in New York City, 1880 to 1920" (Ph.D. diss., Brown University, 1982). On boys' work, see David I. Macleod, *Building Character in the American Boy: The Boy Scouts, YMCA, and Their Forerunners, 1870-1920* (Madison: University of Wisconsin Press, 1983). Joseph F. Kett examines the play movement, which popularized G. Stanley Hall's views on developmental psychology, in *Rites of Passage: Adolescence in America, 1790 to the Present* (New York: Basic Books, 1977). The literature on the play movement is voluminous. Perhaps the best place to start is the review essay by Stephen Hardy and Alan G. Ingham, "Games, Structures, and Agency: Historians on the American Play Movement," *Journal of Social History* 17 (Winter 1983): 285-301. On settlements, see Allen F. Davis, *Spearheads for Reform: The Social Settlements and the Progressive Movement, 1890-1914* (New York: Oxford University Press, 1967); ibid., *American Heroine: The Life and Legend of Jane Addams* (New York: Oxford University Press, 1975); and, on the settlements as laboratories of urban sociology, Robert M. Crunden, *Ministers of Reform: The Progressives' Achievement in American Civilization, 1889-1920* (New York: Basic Books, 1982).

Aaron Abell's *The Urban Impact on American Protestantism* discusses the institutional church. Paul Boyer distinguishes between "coercive reforms" like prohibition and "positive environmentalism" in *Urban Masses and Moral Order in America*. Jon M. Kingsdale surveys "substitutes for the saloon" in "The 'Poor Man's Club': Social Functions of the Urban Working-Class Saloon," *American Quarterly* 25 (October 1973): 472-89. Both Jean B. Quandt, *From the Small Town to the Great Community: The Social Thought of Progressive Intellectuals* (New Brunswick, N.J.: Rutgers University Press, 1970), and David Stratton Locke, "The Village Vision: Goals and Limits in Urban Reform, 1890-1914" (Ph.D. diss., Brown University, 1972), explore the interest of progressive reformers like Jane Addams in re-creating the face-to-face community of small-town America in urban settings.

My interpretation of federation as a middle way between extreme centralization and anarchy has been influenced by Jon C. Teaford, *City and Suburb: The Political Fragmentation of Metropolitan America, 1850-1970* (Baltimore: Johns Hopkins University Press, 1979). Roy Lubove traces the bureaucratization of social work in *The Professional Altruist: The Emergence of Social Work as a Career, 1880-1930* (1965; reprint, New York: Atheneum, 1980). Kathleen D. McCarthy, *Noblesse Oblige: Charity and Cultural Philanthropy in Chicago, 1849-1929* (Chicago: University of Chicago Press, 1982), is also informative. Karen Blair examines the tension, among clubwomen, between self-culture and social reform in *The Clubwoman as Feminist*. On Protestant federations, see Charles Howard Hopkins, *The Rise of the Social Gospel in American Protestantism*. Peter H. Odegard, *Pressure Politics: The Story of the Anti-Saloon League* (New York: Columbia University Press, 1928) remains unsurpassed as an account of the first modern "pressure group." But see also K. Austin Kerr, "Organizing for Reform: The Anti-Saloon League and Innovation in Politics," *American Quarterly* 32 (Spring 1980): 37-53. On voluntary association as nurseries for future bureaucrats, see Robert L. Buroker, "From Voluntary Association to Welfare State: The Illinois Immigrants' Protective League, 1908-1926," *Journal of American History* 58 (December 1971): 643-60.

Samuel Haber, *Efficiency and Uplift: Scientific Management in the Progressive Era, 1890-1920* (Chicago: University of Chicago Press, 1964), remains the best introduction to the efficiency craze of the progressive period. Daniel Nelson discusses scientific management and welfare capitalism in *Managers and Workers: Origins of the New Factory System in the United States, 1880-1920* (Madison: University of Wisconsin Press, 1975). My discussion of city planning draws on Mel Scott's informative history, *American City Planning since 1890* (Berkeley: University of California Press, 1969); and Roy Lubove, "The

Roots of Urban Planning," in his *The Urban Community: Housing and Planning in the Progressive Era* (Englewood Cliffs, N.J.: Prentice-Hall, 1967). Jon A. Peterson analyzes the short-lived City Beautiful movement in "The City Beautiful Movement: Forgotten Origins and Lost Meanings," *Journal of Urban History* 2 (August 1976): 415-34. On haphazard urban growth, which lay behind attempts to federate cities and their suburbs, see Sam Bass Warner, Jr., *Streetcar Suburbs: The Process of Growth in Boston, 1870-1900* (1962; reprint, New York: Atheneum, 1976). For explanations of the eventual demise of the planning movement, see Barry D. Karl, *Executive Reorganization and Reform in the New Deal: The Genesis of Administrative Management, 1900-1939* (Cambridge: Harvard University Press, 1963); ibid., *The Uneasy State: The United States from 1915 to 1945* (Chicago: University of Chicago Press, 1983); and Otis L. Graham, Jr., *Toward a Planned Society: From Roosevelt to Nixon* (New York: Oxford University Press, 1976).

In his seminal book, *The Age of Reform*, Richard Hofstadter suggested that a consumer impulse fed into progressive reform movements. David P. Thelen has elaborated on this consumer impulse in *The New Citizenship* and, more recently, in "Patterns of Consumer Consciousness in the Progressive Movement: Robert M. La Follette, the Antitrust Persuasion, and Labor Legislation," in *The Quest for Social Justice*, ed. Ralph M. Aderman (Madison: University of Wisconsin Press, 1983). The best overview of the consumer movement is provided by Peter Edward Samson, "The Emergence of a Consumer Interest in America, 1870-1930" (Ph.D. diss., University of Chicago, 1980). For contemporary accounts, see Margaret G. Reid, *Consumers and the Market*, 3rd ed. (New York: F. S. Crofts & Co., 1942), and Helen Sorenson, *The Consumer Movement: What It Is and What It Means* (New York: Harper & Brothers, 1941). Louis Lee Athey traces the history of the Consumers' League in "The Consumers' Leagues and Social Reform, 1890-1923" (Ph.D. diss., University of Delaware, 1965). See also Maud Nathan's recollections in *The Story of an Epoch-Making Movement* (Garden City, N.Y.: Doubleday, Page & Co., 1926). Norman Isaac Silber traces the history of the Consumers Union in *Test and Protest: The Influence of Consumers Union* (New York: Holmes & Meier, 1983). Norman David Katz, "Consumers Union: The Movement and the Magazine, 1936-1957" (Ph.D. diss., Rutgers University, 1977), is particularly good on the

influence of Thorstein Veblen on early consumer advocates. Daniel
Horowitz compares the views of Veblen and two other men who
were instrumental in popularizing a consumer society in "Consumption and Its Discontents: Simon N. Patten, Thorstein Veblen,
and George Gunton," *Journal of American History* 67 (September
1980): 301-317. For portraits of some of the interwar period's best-
known consumer advocates, see Mark C. Smith, "Robert Lynd and
Consumerism in the 1930's," *Journal of the History of Sociology* 2 (Fall-
Winter, 1979-80): 99-119; Richard Wightman Fox, "Epitaph for
Middletown: Robert S. Lynd and the Analysis of Consumer Culture," in *The Culture of Consumption: Critical Essays in American History,
1880-1980,* ed. Richard Wightman Fox and T. J. Jackson Lears
(New York: Pantheon Books, 1983); and Robert B. Westbrook,
"Tribune of the Technostructure: The Popular Economics of
Stuart Chase," *American Quarterly* 32 (Fall 1980): 387-408.

On the home economics movement, see Emma Seifrit Weigley, "It
Might Have Been Euthenics: The Lake Placid Conferences and the
Home Economics Movement," *American Quarterly* 26 (March 1974):
79-96; Barbara Ehrenreich and Deirdre English, *For Her Own Good:
150 Years of the Experts' Advice to Women* (Garden City, N.Y.: Anchor
Books, 1979); and Dolores Hayden, *The Grand Domestic Revolution:
A History of Feminist Designs for American Homes, Neighborhoods, and
Cities* (Cambridge: M.I.T. Press, 1981). On the concern about the
adulteration of food, which led to the passage of the Pure Food and
Drug Act of 1906, see Robert Crunden, *Ministers of Reform.* For the
contemporary fear that inflation undermined frugality and other
ingrained values, see Daniel Pope, "American Economists and the
High Cost of Living," *Journal of the History of the Behavioral Sciences*
17 (January 1981): 75-87.

On the rise of the department store, see Daniel J. Boorstin, *The
Americans: The Democratic Experience* (New York: Vintage Books,
1974); Gunther Barth, *City People*; Susan Porter Benson, "Palace of
Consumption and Machine for Selling: The American Department
Store, 1880-1940," *Radical History Review* 21 (Fall 1979): 199-221;
and William R. Leach, "Transformations in a Culture of Consumption: Women and Department Stores, 1890-1925," *Journal of American History* 71 (September 1984): 319-42.

In discussing advertising, I have drawn on Otis Pease, *The Responsibilities of American Advertising: Private Control and Public Influence,*

1920-1940 (New Haven: Yale University Press, 1958); Daniel Pope, *The Making of Modern Advertising* (New York: Basic Books, 1983); and Stephen Fox, *The Mirror Makers: A History of American Advertising and Its Creators* (New York: William Morrow & Co., 1984).

Works that shed light on the development of a consumer culture in the first half of the twentieth century include Lary May, *Screening Out the Past*; Lewis A. Erenberg, *Steppin' Out*; Stuart Ewen, *Captains of Consciousness: Advertising and the Social Roots of the Consumer Culture* (New York: McGraw-Hill, 1976); Elaine Tyler May, *Great Expectations: Marriage and Divorce in Post-Victorian America* (Chicago: University of Chicago Press, 1980); T. J. Jackson Lears, *No Place of Grace: Antimodernism and the Transformation of American Culture, 1880-1920* (New York: Pantheon Books, 1981); Richard Wightman Fox and T. J. Jackson Lears, eds., *The Culture of Consumption*; and Warren I. Susman, *Culture as History: The Transformation of American Society in the Twentieth Century* (New York: Pantheon Books, 1984).

INDEX

abolitionists, *see* antislavery movement

Ackerman, Frederick L., 335

Adams, John Quincy, 14

Addams, Jane, 257

advertising, 305-306, 335-36; Town Criers, 305-306

Aldrich, Nelson W., 155-56, 181, 183, 203

Algeo, Sara M., 209

Allen, Zachariah, 89-91, 95

Allyn, Robert, 74

Almy, William, 18

American Association of University Women, 331, 344

Ames, Wyllys, 45, 67

amusement(s): attendance at, in 1912, 254; customary, 21, 35, 62-65; motion pictures as, 220-21, 257-60; shore resorts and, 221-23; theaters as, 67-68, 219-20

Andrews, E. Benjamin, 117, 186, 193-94, 271

Anthony, Henry B., 144-45, 181

anti-abolitionists: social characteristics of, 39-41, 48; and town meetings, 12, 39, 41-43

antislavery movement: and anti-abolitionists, 12, 43, 51; membership in, 36, 38, 43-48; and middle-class consciousness, 12-13, 49-50, 52-53; and public opinion, 37-38, 49-51; and temperance movement, 37, 48, 49-50; and voluntary associations, 38, 49, 51-52. *See also* antislavery societies

antislavery societies: American Anti-Slavery Society, 37, 38; Providence Anti-Slavery Society, 36; Providence Ladies' Anti-Slavery Society, 38; Providence Society for Abolishing the Slave Trade, 36; Rhode Island Anti-Slavery Society, 43; Union Congrega-

tional Anti-Slavery Society, 46

Arnold, Matthew, 85

Aronovici, Carol, 250-51, 268, 270

artisans, 14-18, 25-26, 59-60, 79, 95-96, 105-106. *See also* Providence Association of Mechanics and Manufacturers

Ashley, Samuel S., 48

Baker, William C., 194, 233

Banigan, Joseph, 179

Baptist church(es), 26, 46-47, 66-67, 68, 73, 168, 171; Calvary, 254; First, 254; Pine Street, 26-27, 46-47, 68

Barker, Henry A., 171, 288, 290

Barker, Joseph A., 47-48, 90, 229

Barnard, Henry, 80

Barstow, Amos C., 34, 44, 45, 48, 60, 71, 74, 90, 103, 182, 186, 229, 230

Barstow, Amos C., Jr., 192

Barton, Bruce, 306

Barus, Annie (Mrs. Carl), 237, 314-15, 319

Bassett, Edward D., 191

Beacon Hill Improvement Association, 190

Beckwith, Henry T., 230

Beecher, Henry Ward, 169

Bellamy, Edward, 190

Benson, George, 36

Benson, Helen, 36

Bicknell, Thomas W., 193

Bingham, Alfred, 348

Birney, James, 37

blacks, 19-20, 41, 47, 141, 155, 161, 163, 330

Blackstone Improvement Society, 189, 192

Blain, John, 46-47

Bogman, Joseph, 43-44, 45

Bosworth, Smith, 40

Bowditch, Josiah, 126

LIBRARY OF CONGRESS CATALOGING-IN-PUBLICATION DATA

Gilkeson, John S., 1948-
  Middle-class Providence, 1820-1940.
  Bibliography: p.
  Includes index.
  1. Providence (R.I.)—History. 2. Middle classes—
Rhode Island—Providence—History. 3. Providence
(R.I.)—Social conditions. I. Title.
F89.P957G55 1986 974.5′2   85-43284
ISBN 0-691-04734-0 (alk. paper)

John S. Gilkeson, Jr., is Assistant Professor of American Literature and Civilization at Middlebury College in Middlebury, Vermont.

DATE DUE